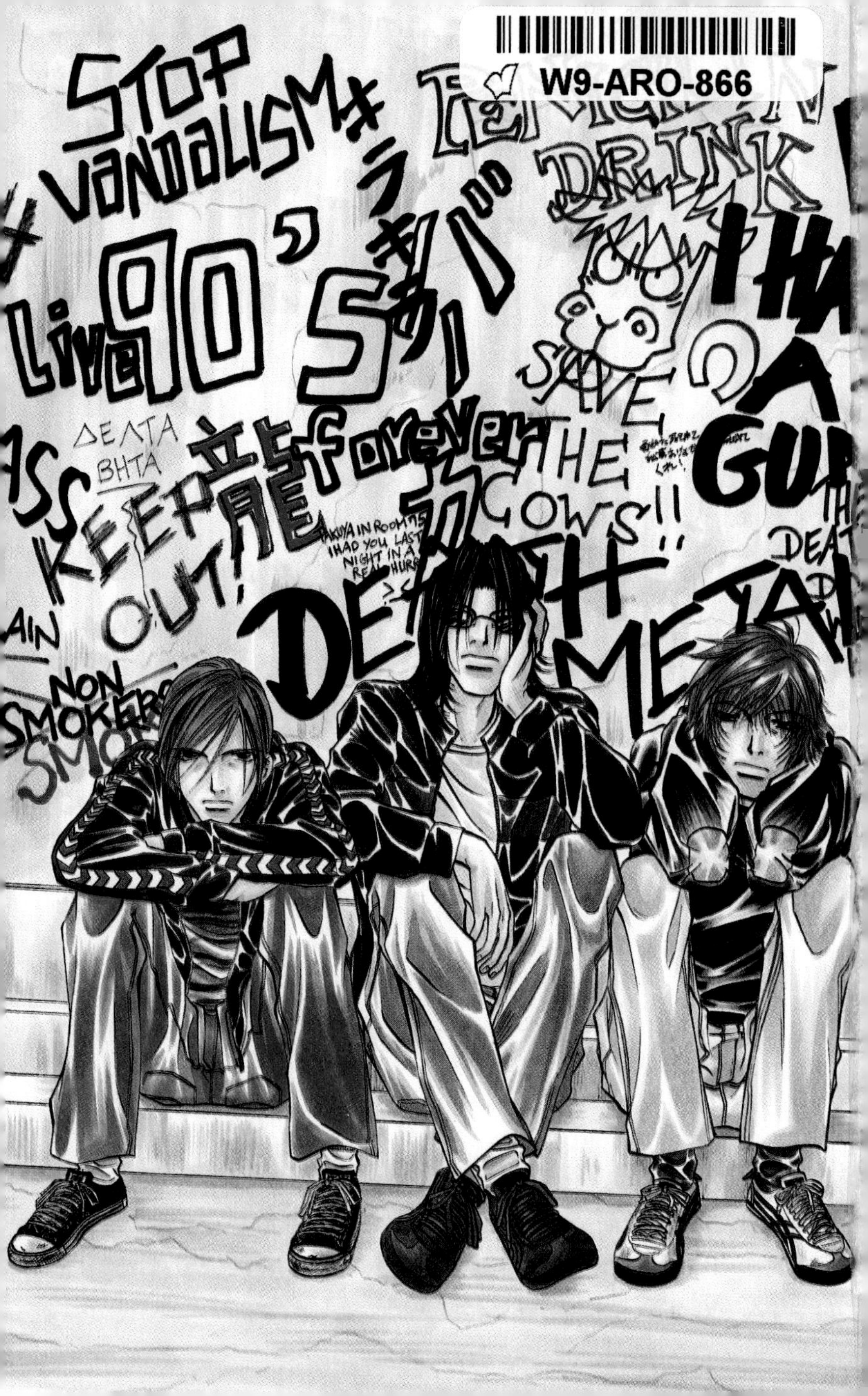
STOP
VANDALISM
Live 90's
DRINK
ΔΕΛΤΑ
ΒΗΤΑ
KEEP OUT!
forever
SAVE THE COWS!!
NON
SMOKERS

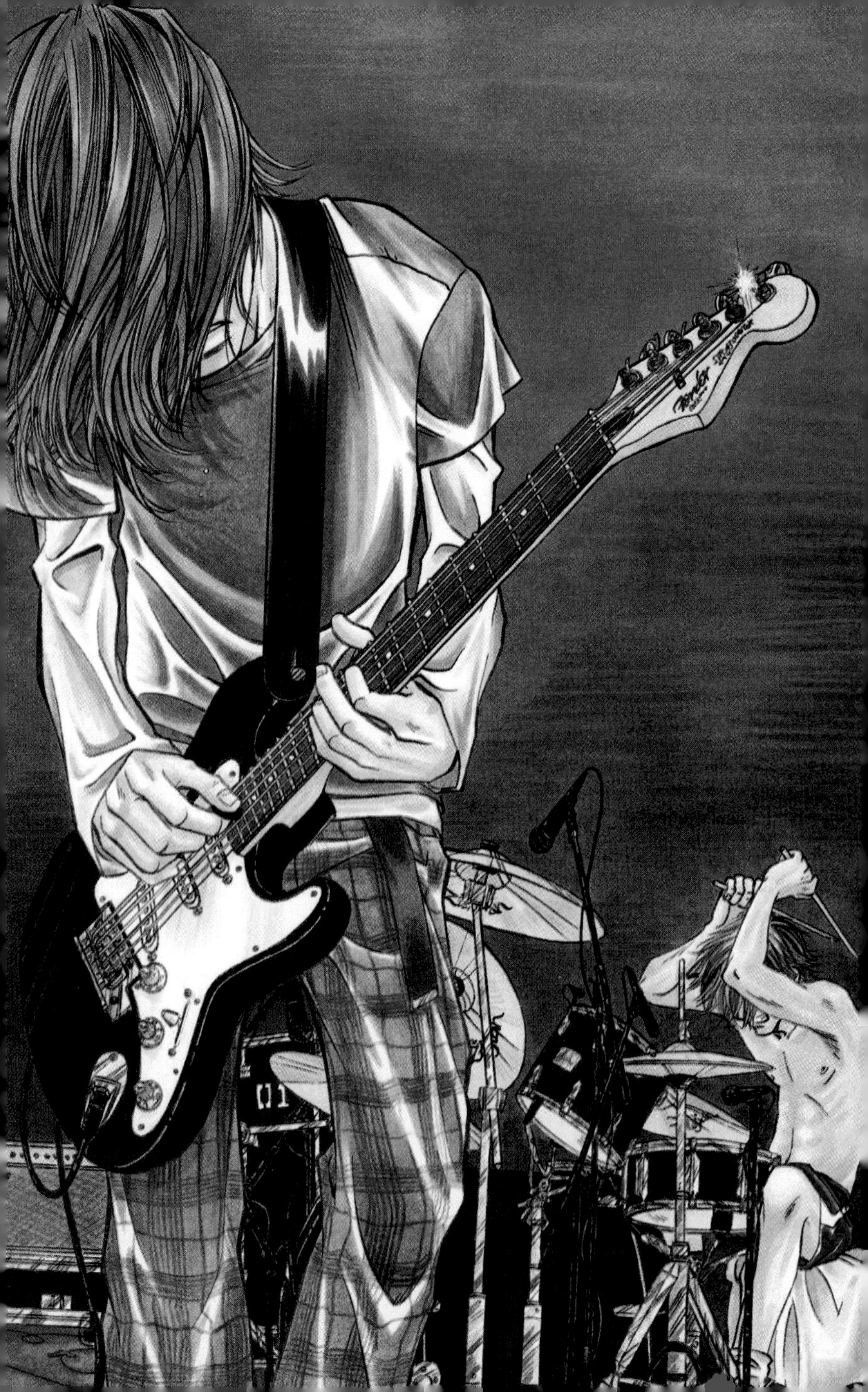

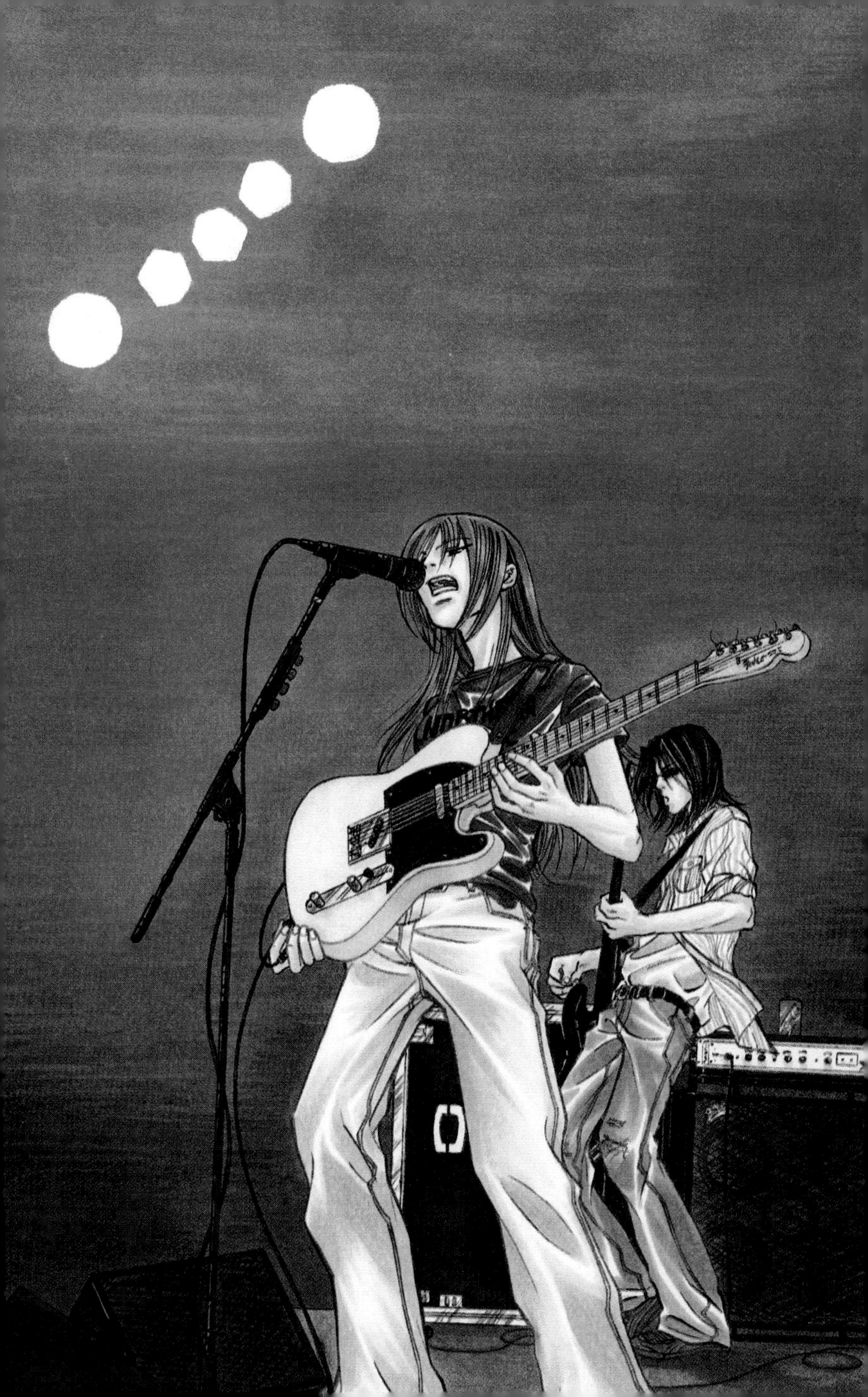

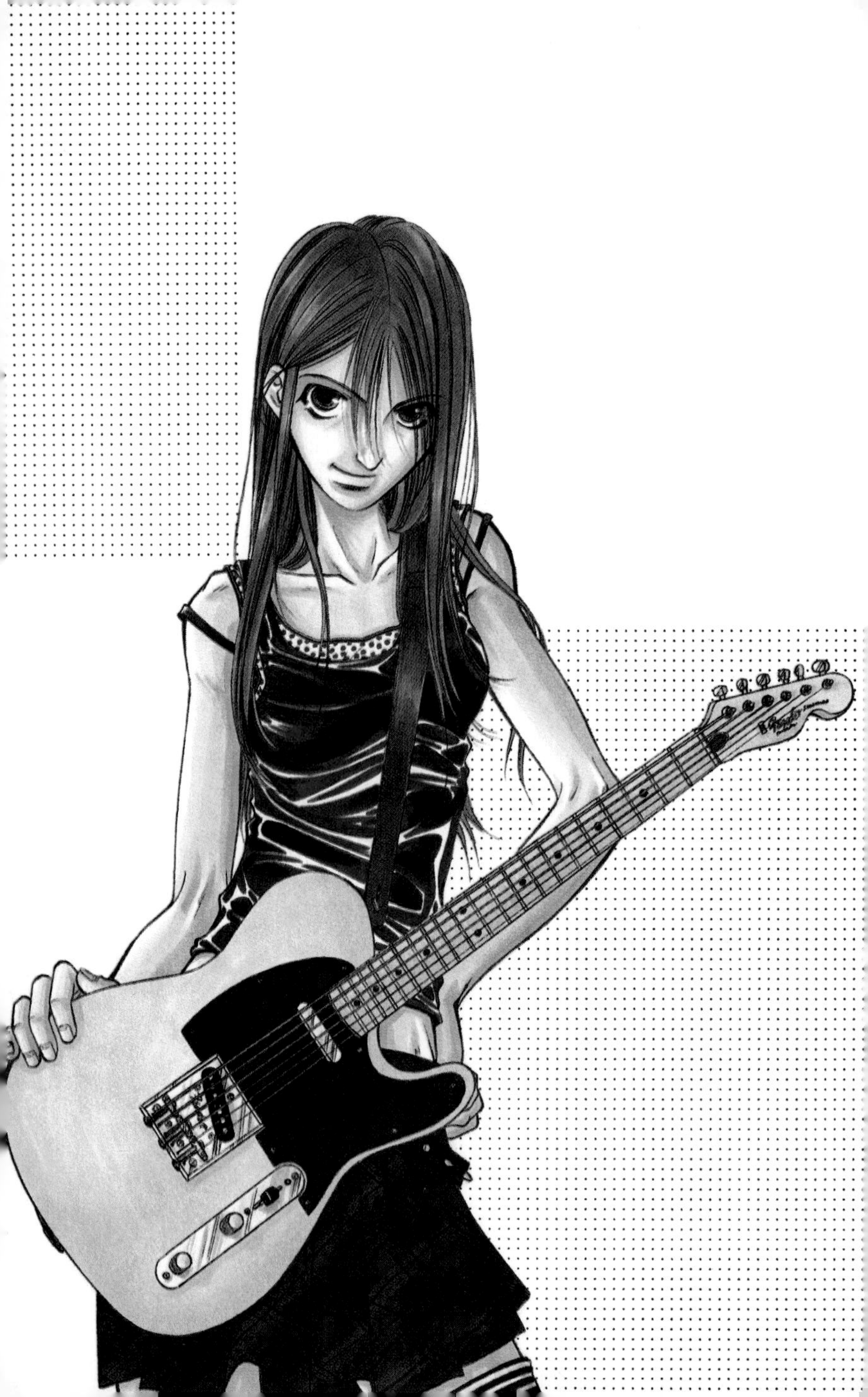

YONEN BUZZ

CHRISTINA PLAKA

HAMBURG // LONDON // LOS ANGELES // TOKYO

Yonen Buzz Vol. 1
created by Christina Plaka

Translation - Annika Romero
Associate Editor - Peter Ahlstrom
Retouch and Lettering - Lucas Rivera
Production Artist - Fawn Lau
Cover Layout - Christian Lownds

Editor - Julie Taylor
German Editor - Joachim Kaps
Digital Imaging Manager - Chris Buford
Production Managers - Jennifer Miller and Mutsumi Miyazaki
Managing Editor - Lindsey Johnston
VP of Production - Ron Klamert
Publisher and E.I.C. - Mike Kiley
President and C.O.O. - John Parker
C.E.O. - Stuart Levy

A  Manga

TOKYOPOP Inc.
5900 Wilshire Blvd. Suite 2000
Los Angeles, CA 90036

E-mail: info@TOKYOPOP.com
Come visit us online at www.TOKYOPOP.com

ISBN: 1-59816-403-1

First TOKYOPOP printing: January 2006
10 9 8 7 6 5 4 3 2 1
Printed in Canada

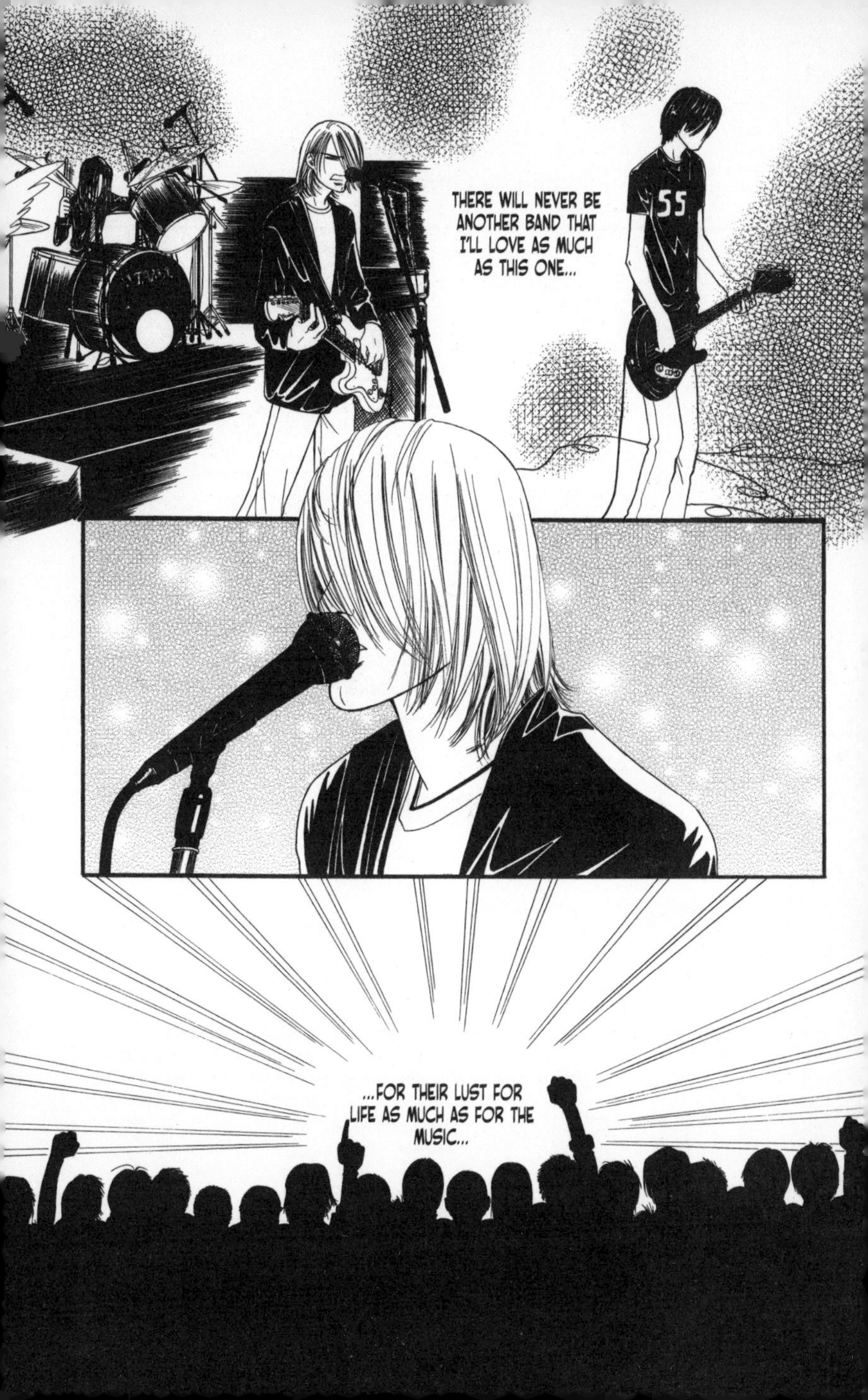
THERE WILL NEVER BE ANOTHER BAND THAT I'LL LOVE AS MUCH AS THIS ONE...
55
...FOR THEIR LUST FOR LIFE AS MUCH AS FOR THE MUSIC...

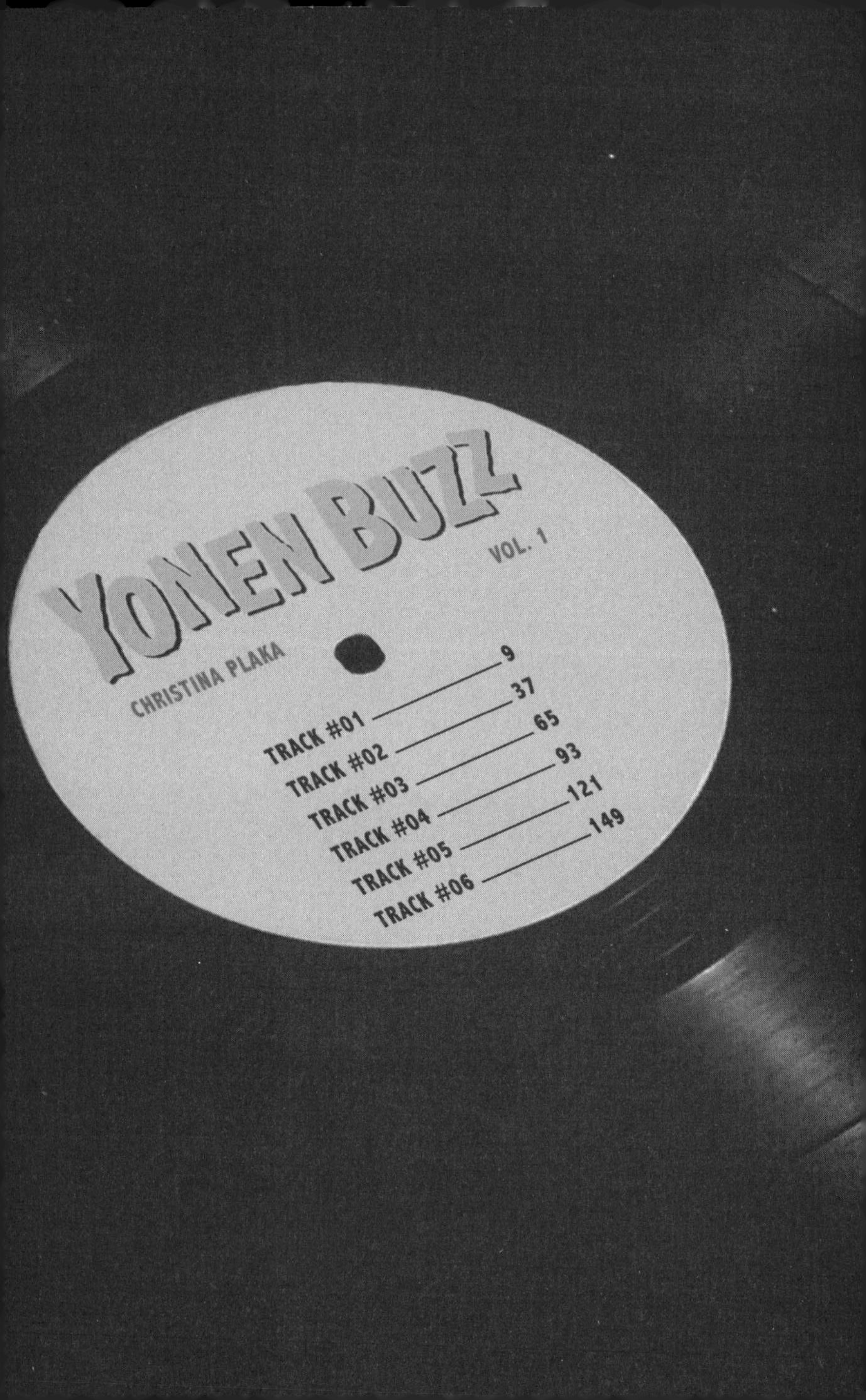
YONEN BUZZ
VOL. 1
CHRISTINA PLAKA
TRACK #01 9
TRACK #02 37
TRACK #03 65
TRACK #04 93
TRACK #05 121
TRACK #06 149

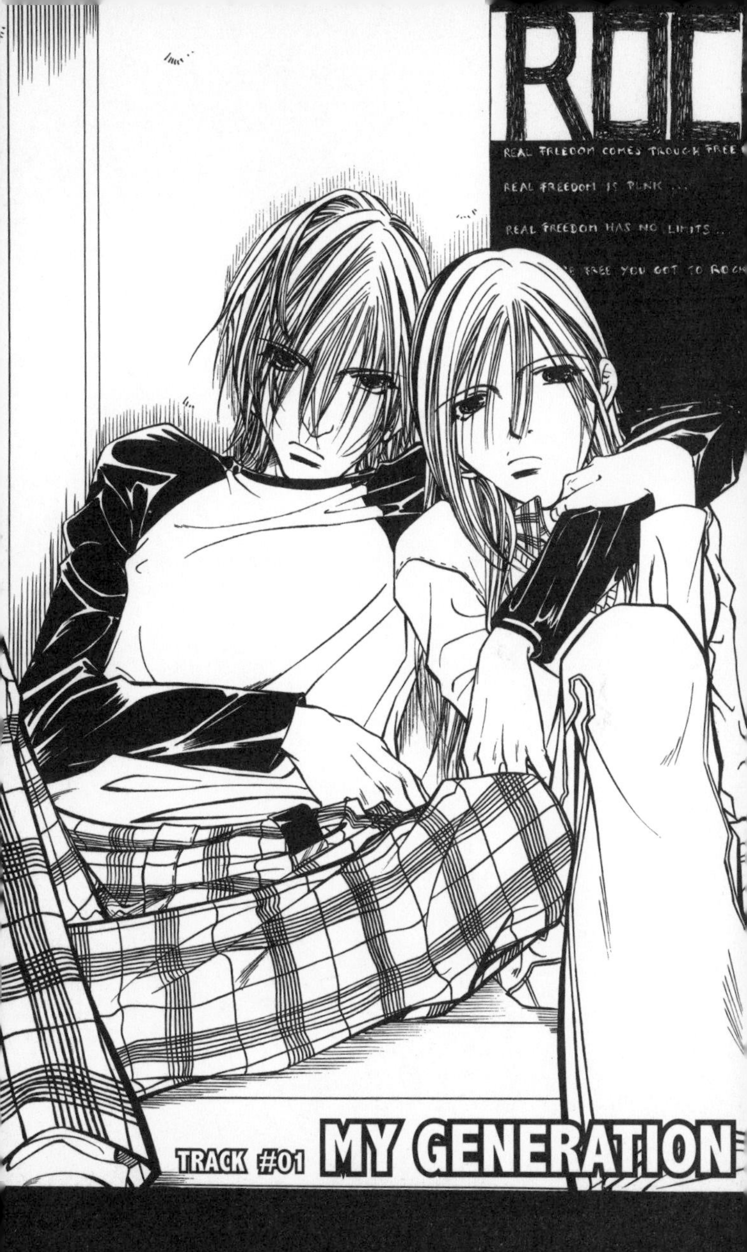

ROC
REAL FREEDOM COMES TROUGH FREE
REAL FREEDOM IS PUNK ...
REAL FREEDOM HAS NO LIMITS ...
FREE YOU GOT TO ROCK
TRACK #01 MY GENERATION

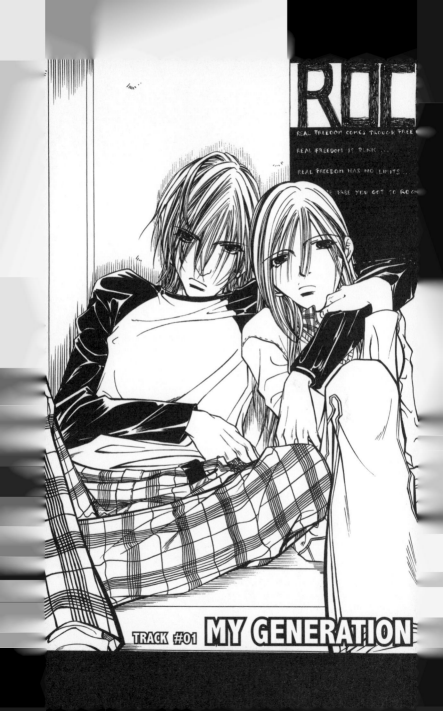

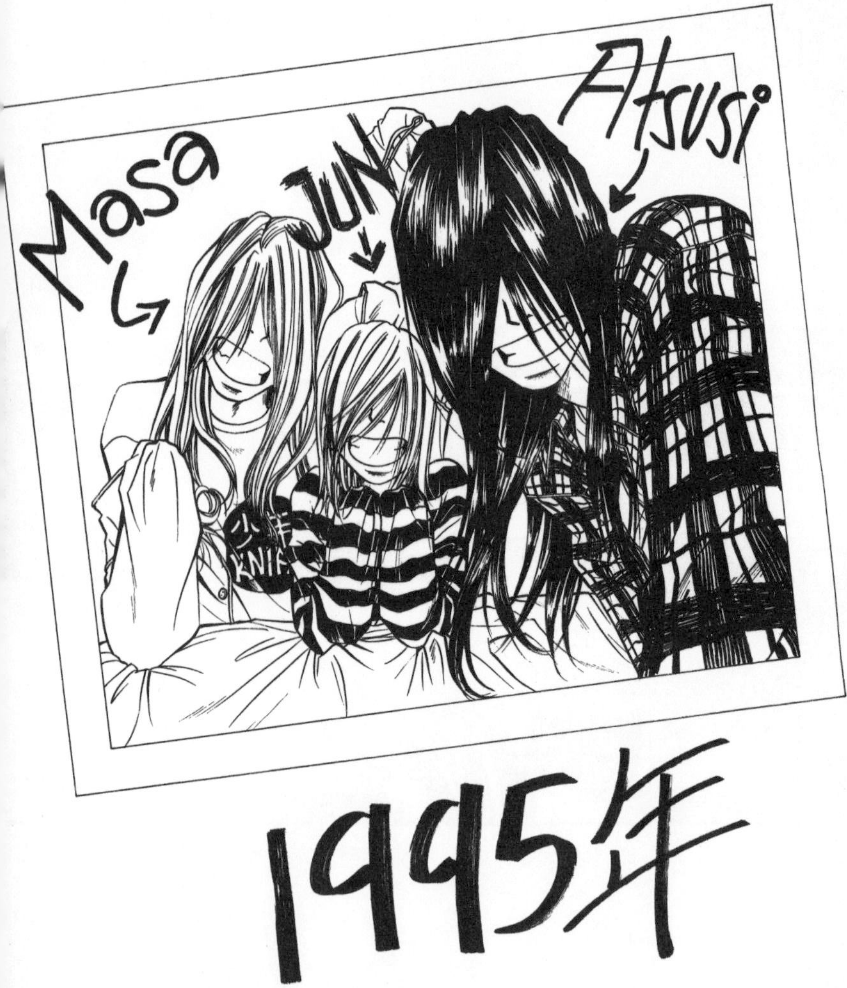
Masa
JUN
Atsusi

1995年

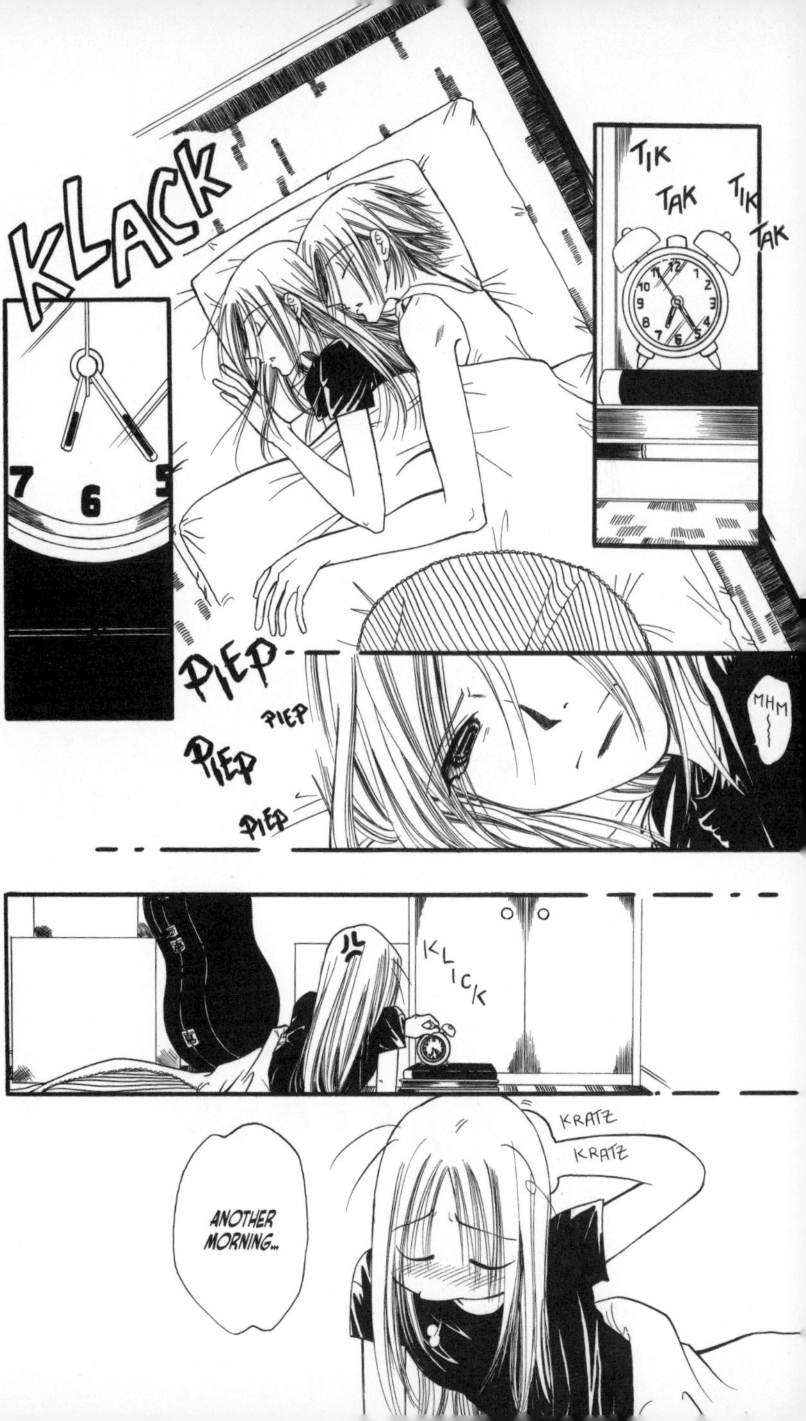
TIK
TAK
TIK
TAK
KLACK
MHM
PIEP
PIEP
PIEP
PIEP
KLICK
KRATZ
KRATZ
ANOTHER MORNING...

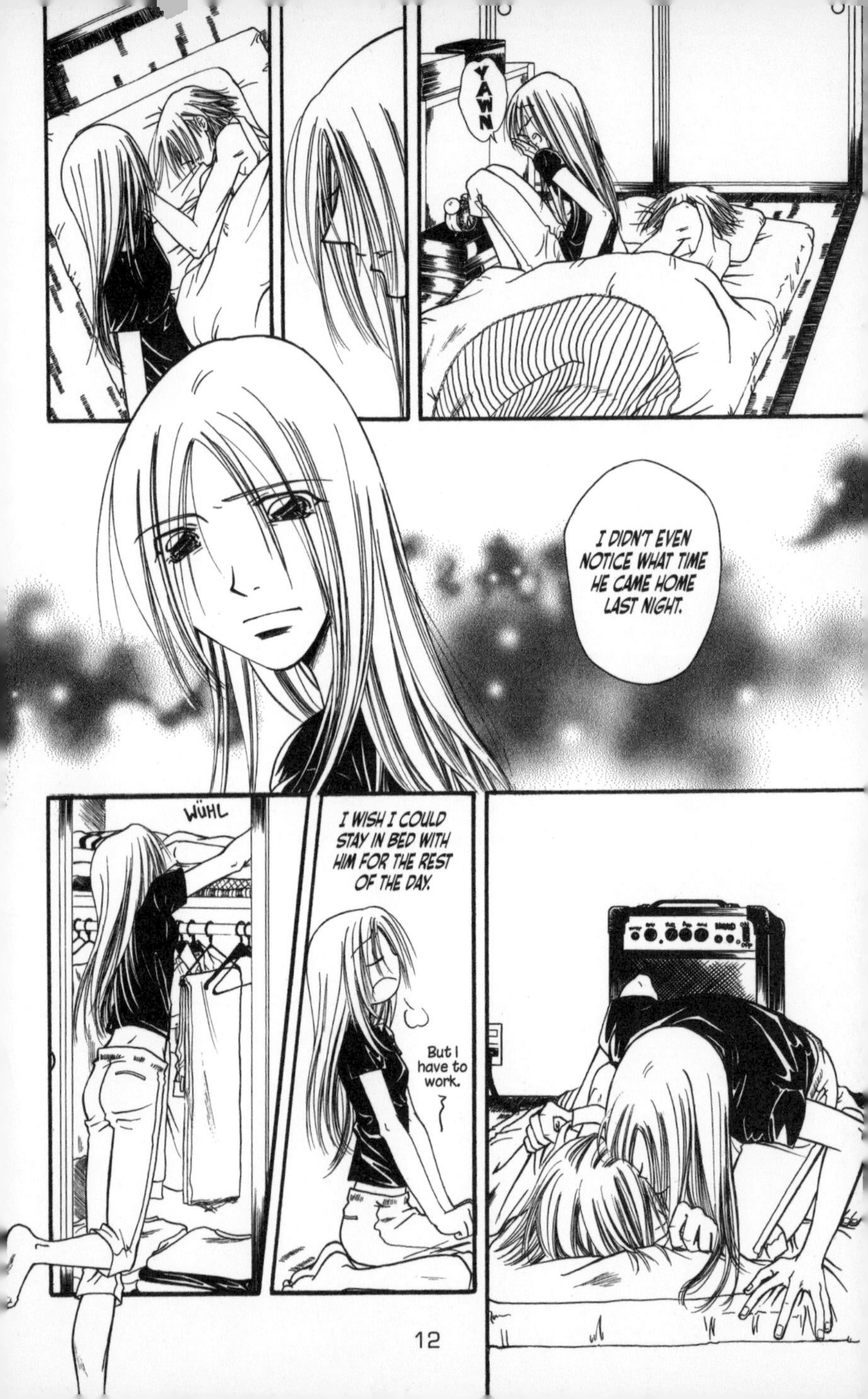
YAWN
I DIDN'T EVEN NOTICE WHAT TIME HE CAME HOME LAST NIGHT.
I WISH I COULD STAY IN BED WITH HIM FOR THE REST OF THE DAY.
But I have to work.
WÜHL

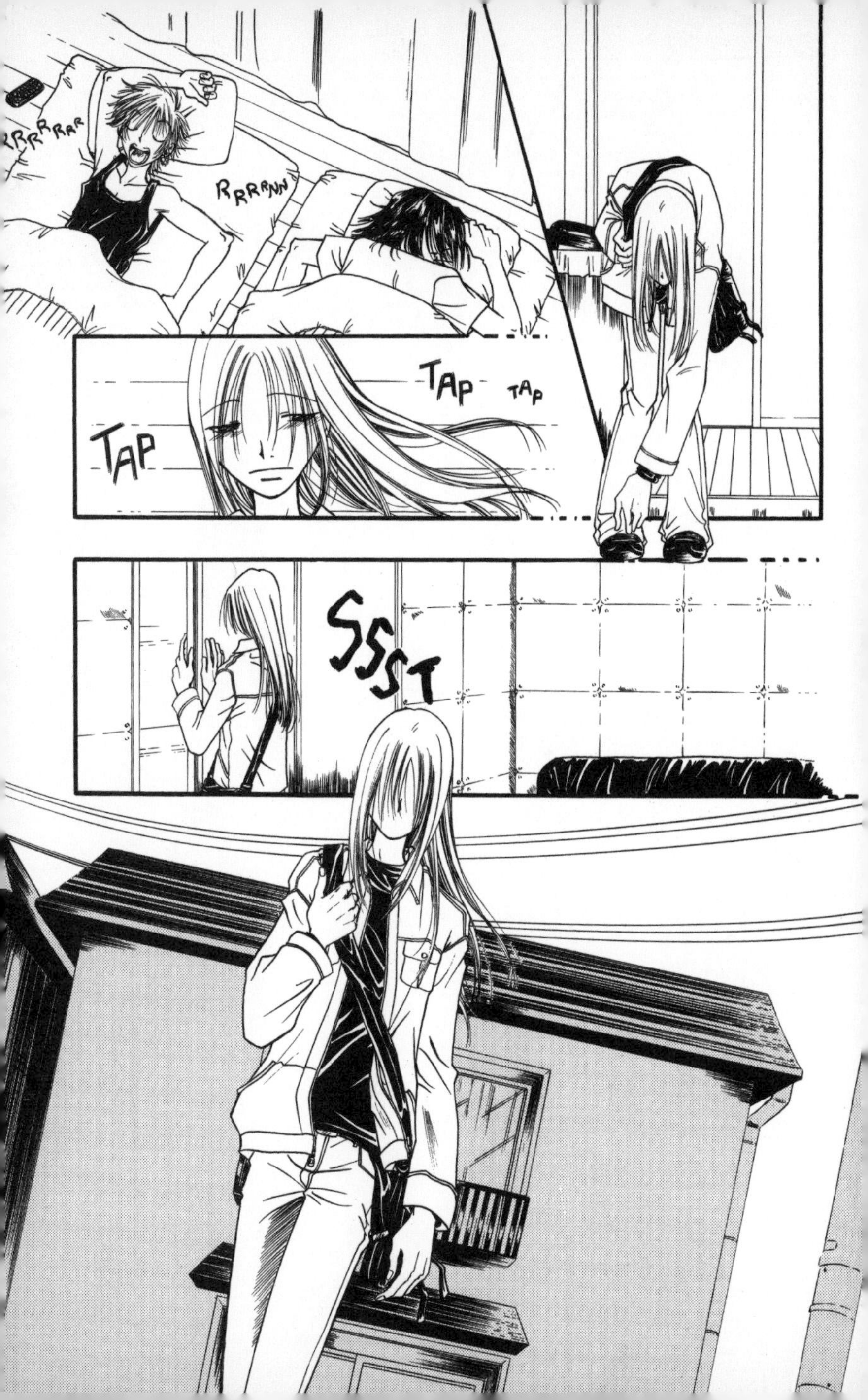
RRRRRAR
RRRRNN
TAP
TAP
TAP
SSST

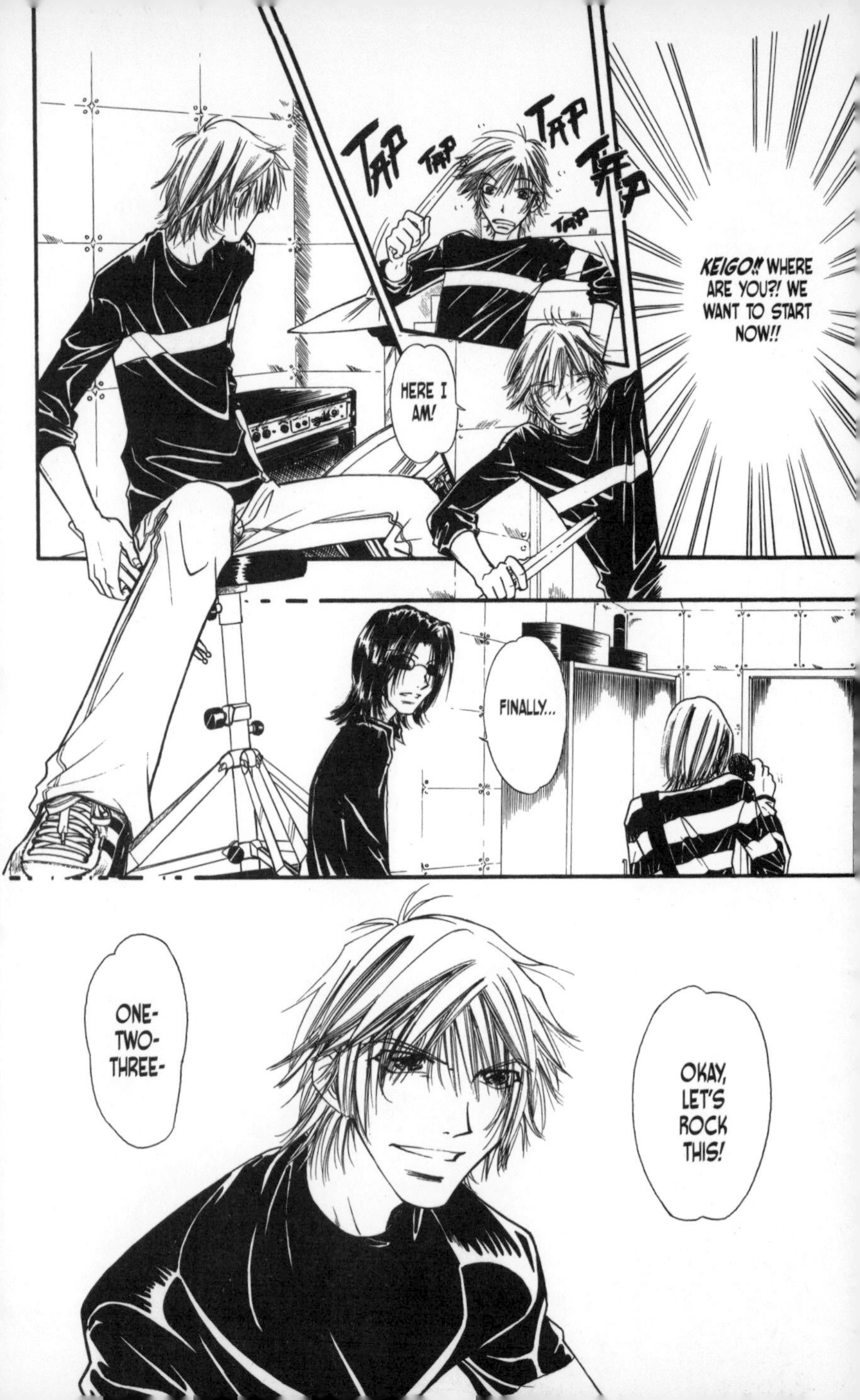
KEIGO!! WHERE ARE YOU?! WE WANT TO START NOW!!
TAP
TAP
TAP
TAP
HERE I AM!
FINALLY...
OKAY, LET'S ROCK THIS!
ONE-TWO-THREE-

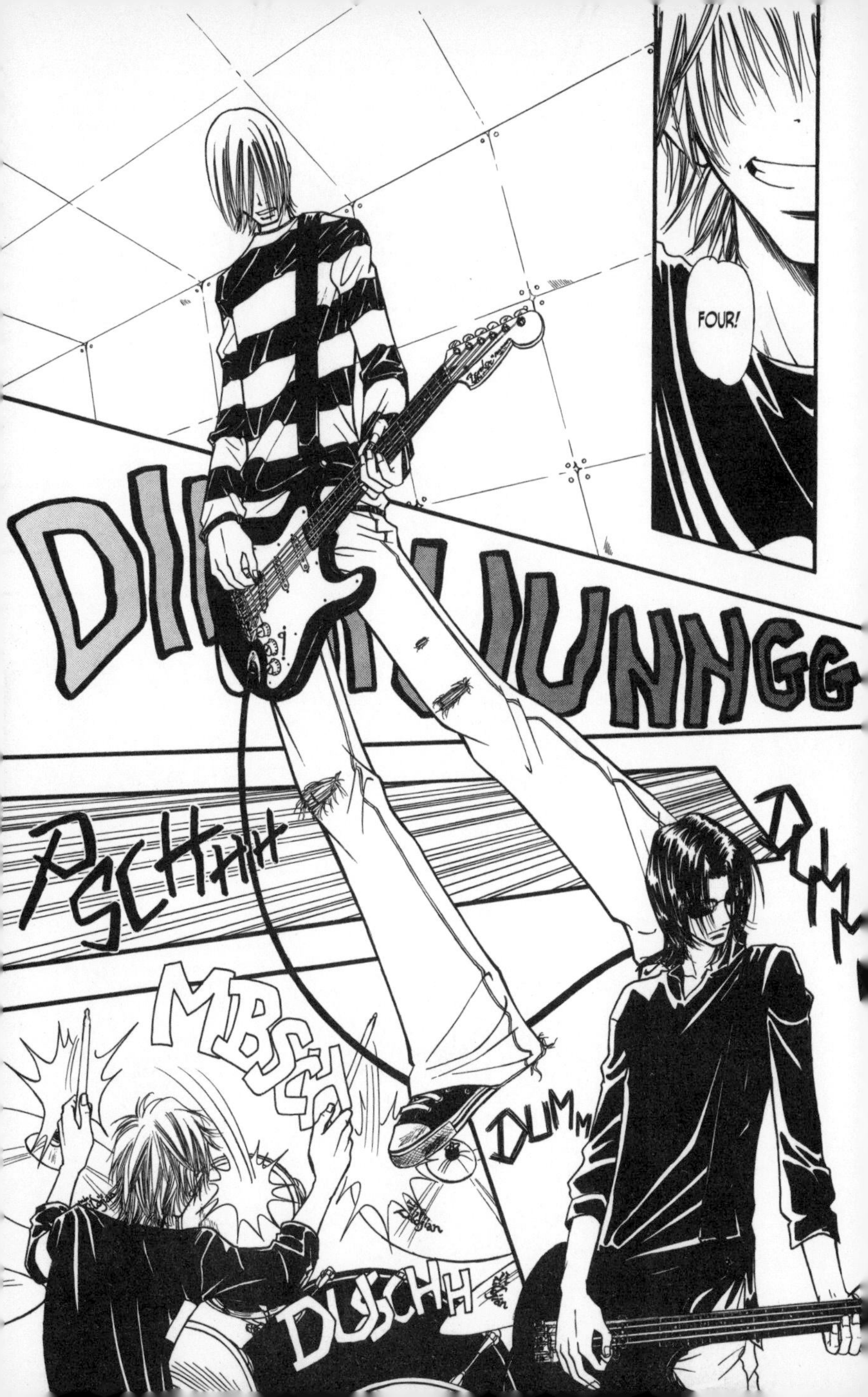
FOUR!
DI
UNNGG
PSCHHHH
DUMM
MBSCH
DUMM
DUSCHH

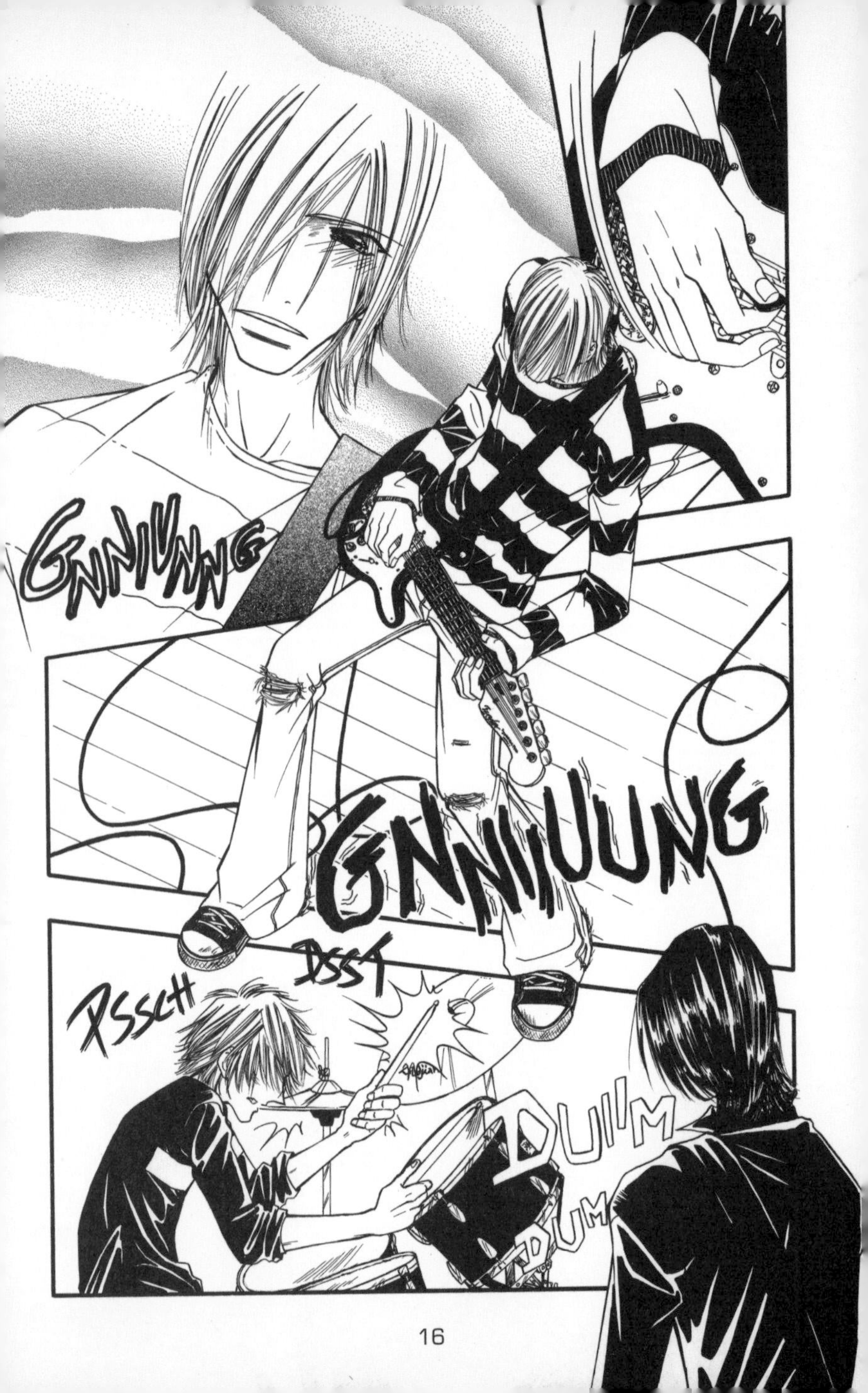
GNNIUNNG
GNNIUUNG
DUM
DUM
DSST
PSSCH

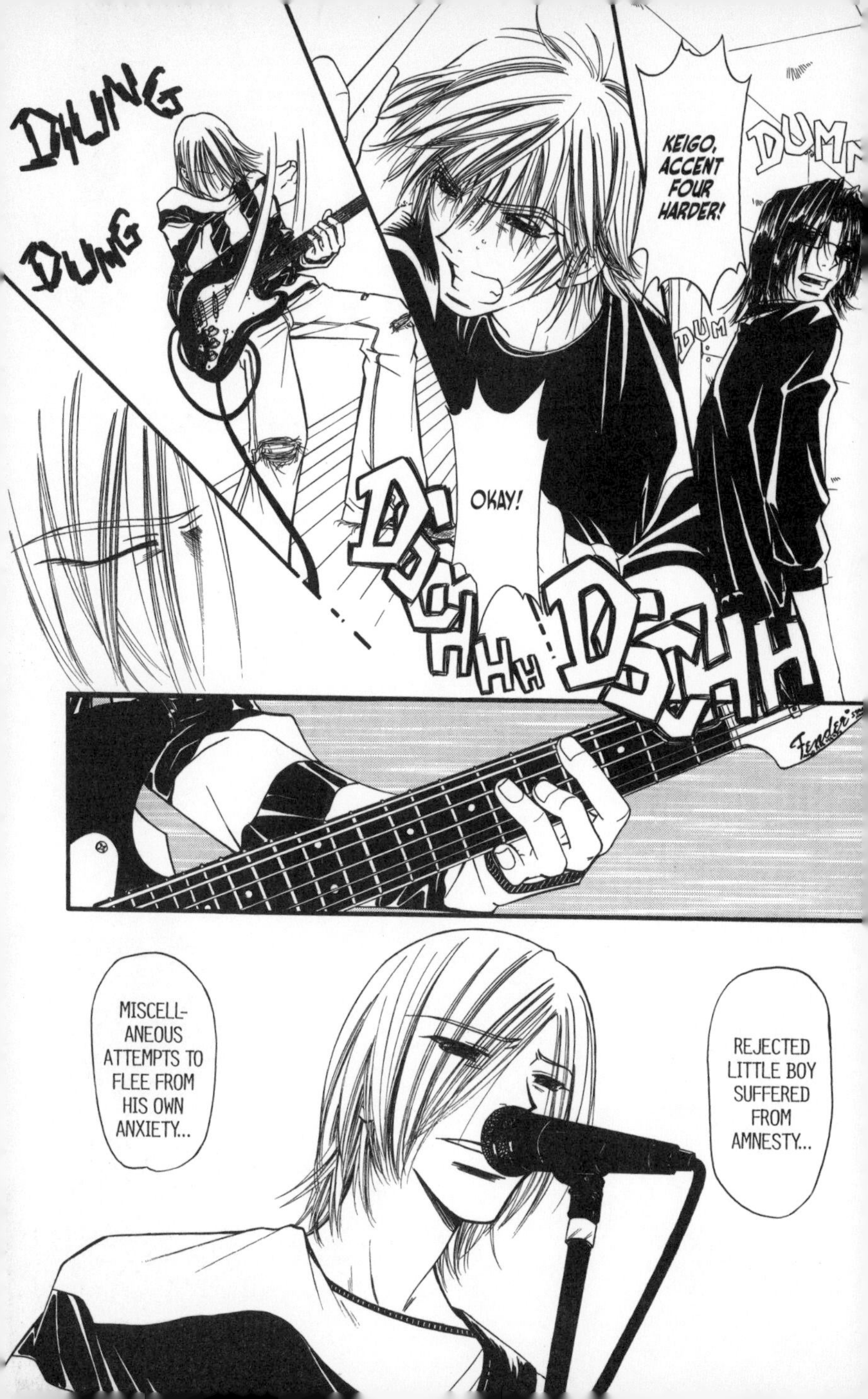
DUM
KEIGO, ACCENT FOUR HARDER!
DUM
OKAY!
DSCHHH
DSCHH
DHUNG
DUNG
Fender
REJECTED LITTLE BOY SUFFERED FROM AMNESTY...
MISCELL-ANEOUS ATTEMPTS TO FLEE FROM HIS OWN ANXIETY...

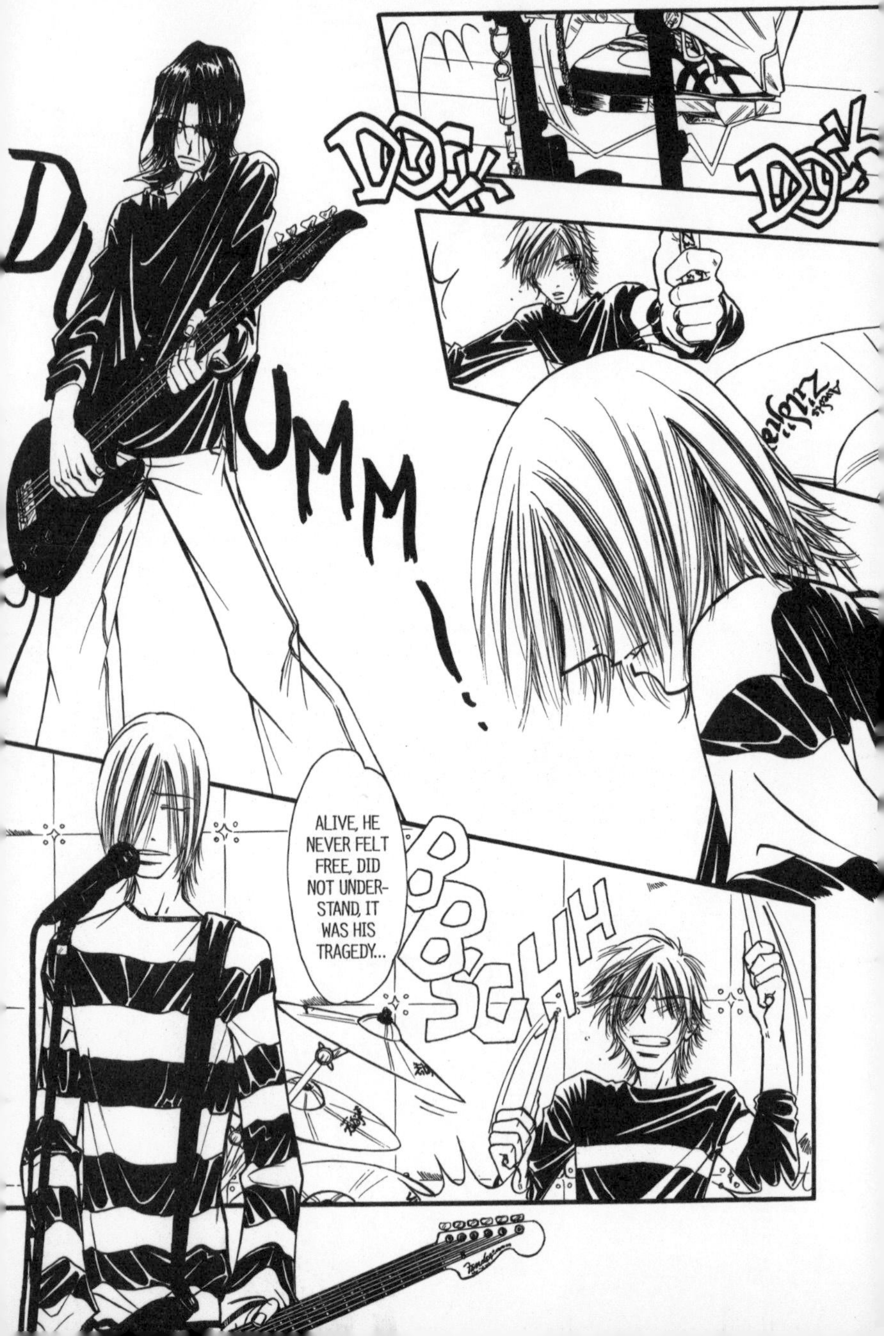
DOK
DOK
DUMM!
BSCHH
ALIVE, HE NEVER FELT FREE, DID NOT UNDER-STAND, IT WAS HIS TRAGEDY...

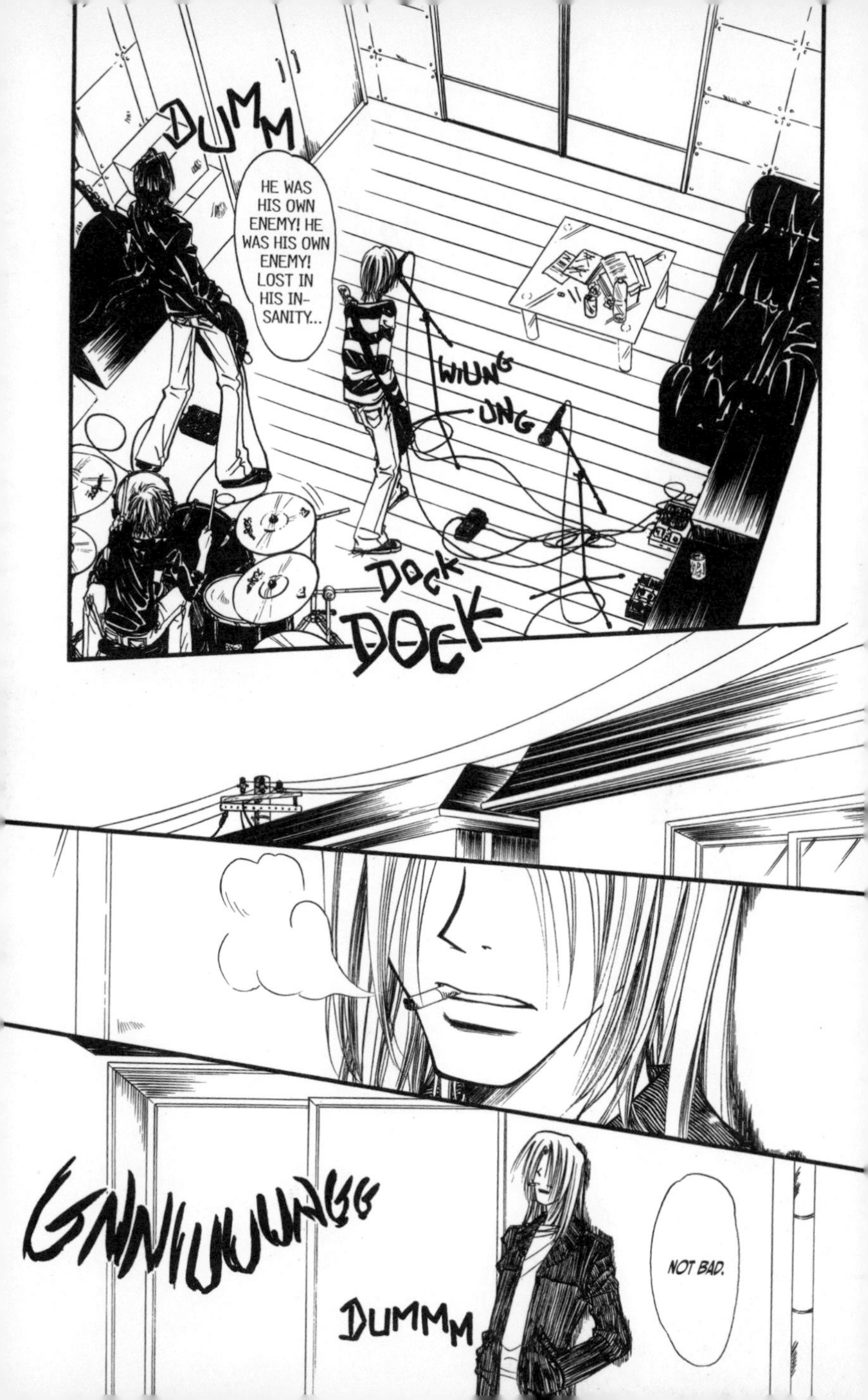
DUMMM
HE WAS HIS OWN ENEMY! HE WAS HIS OWN ENEMY! LOST IN HIS IN-SANITY...
WIUNG
UNG
DOCK
DOCK
NOT BAD.
GNNIUUUNGG
DUMMM

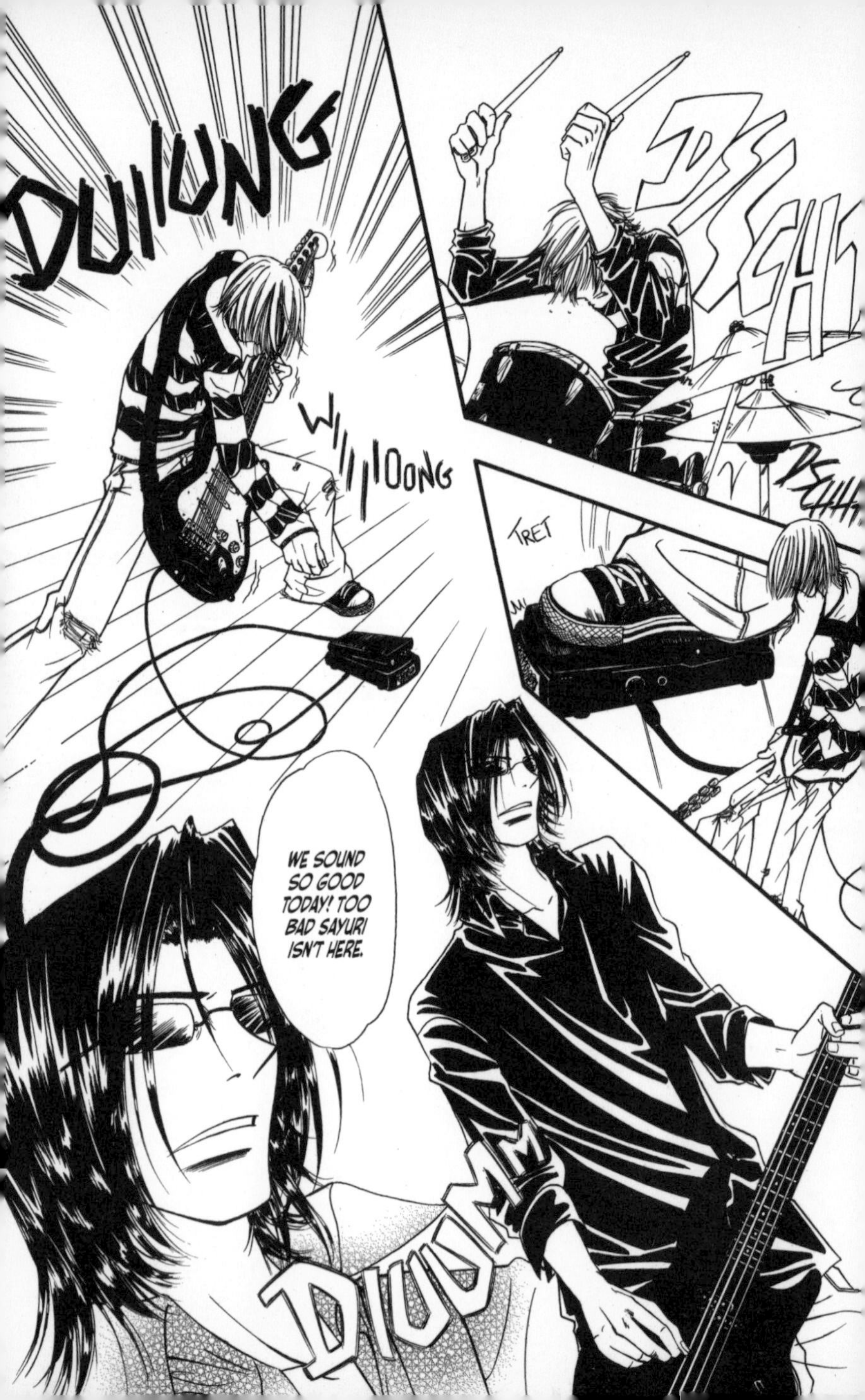
DUIIUNG
WIIIIOONG
TRET
WE SOUND SO GOOD TODAY! TOO BAD SAYURI ISN'T HERE.
DIUUM

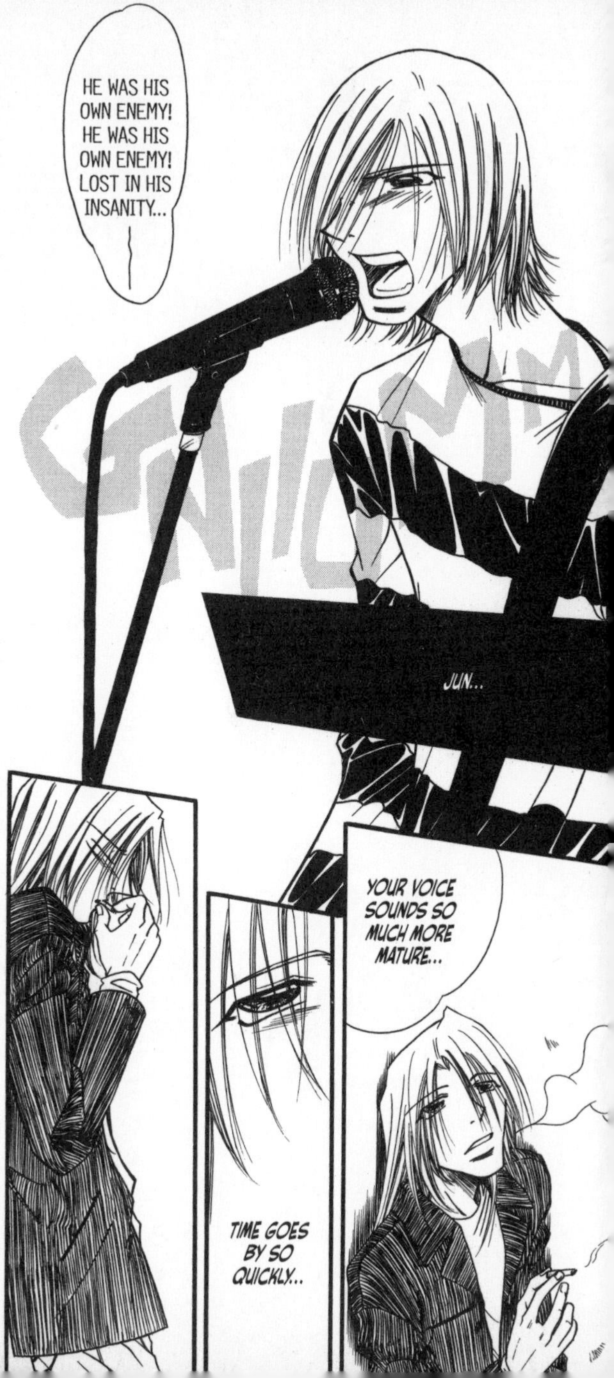
HE WAS HIS OWN ENEMY! HE WAS HIS OWN ENEMY! LOST IN HIS INSANITY...
JUN...
YOUR VOICE SOUNDS SO MUCH MORE MATURE...
TIME GOES BY SO QUICKLY...

Well, here I am again. I know, I know--it's been a long time since you were able to find some of my new work at the bookstore. It's been one and a half years, in fact--but don't worry, it's worth the wait!

If you like this book, I hope you'll also enjoy the prequel, *Plastic Chew*.

I'll be revealing loads of secrets in this story, so keep on reading.

Thank you so much for reading my manga. Check it out!!

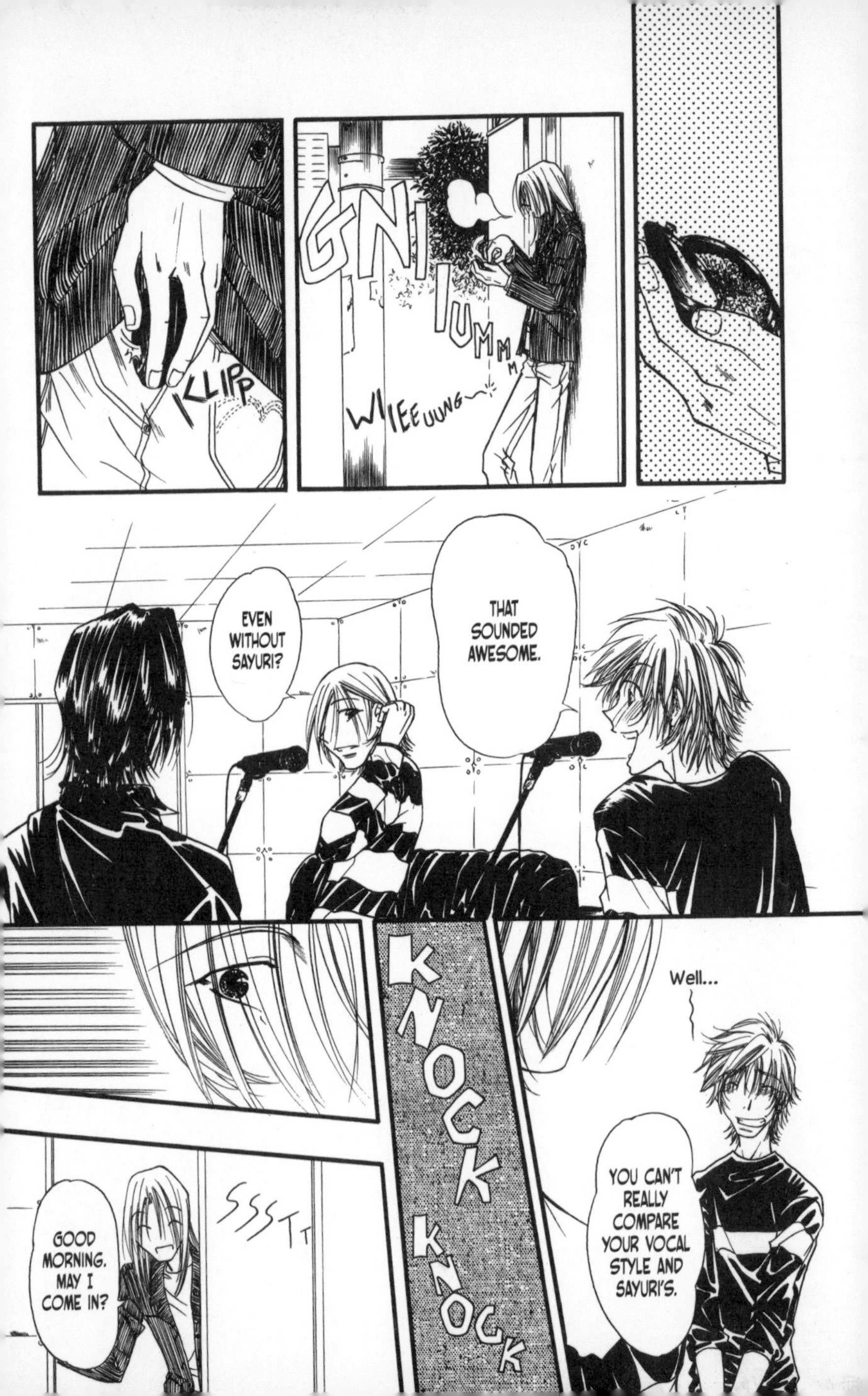
GNIIUMMM
WIIEEUUNG~
KLIPP
THAT SOUNDED AWESOME.
EVEN WITHOUT SAYURI?
Well...
YOU CAN'T REALLY COMPARE YOUR VOCAL STYLE AND SAYURI'S.
KNOCK KNOCK
SSSTT
GOOD MORNING. MAY I COME IN?

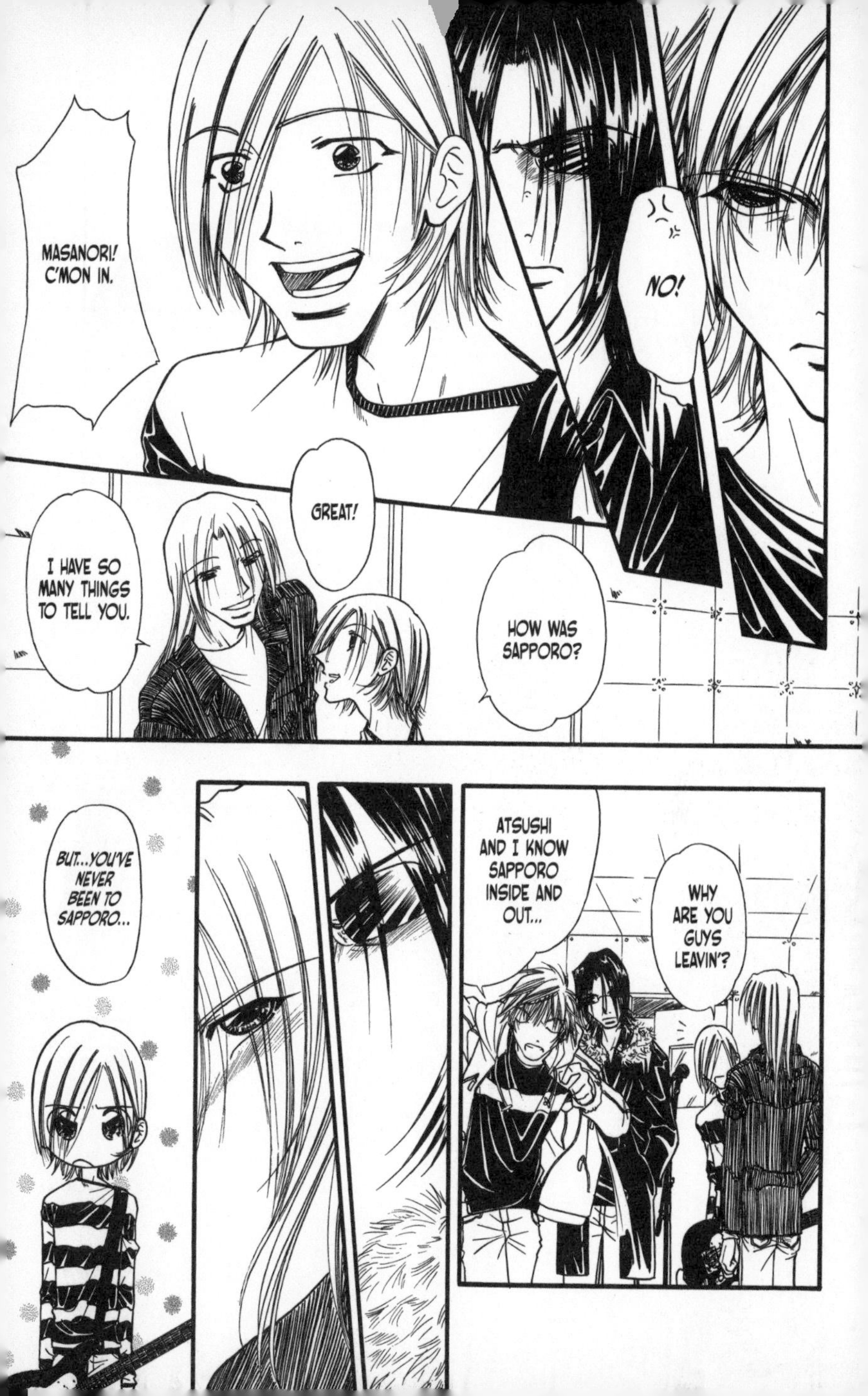
NO!
MASANORI! C'MON IN.
HOW WAS SAPPORO?
GREAT!
I HAVE SO MANY THINGS TO TELL YOU.
WHY ARE YOU GUYS LEAVIN'?
ATSUSHI AND I KNOW SAPPORO INSIDE AND OUT...
BUT...YOU'VE NEVER BEEN TO SAPPORO...

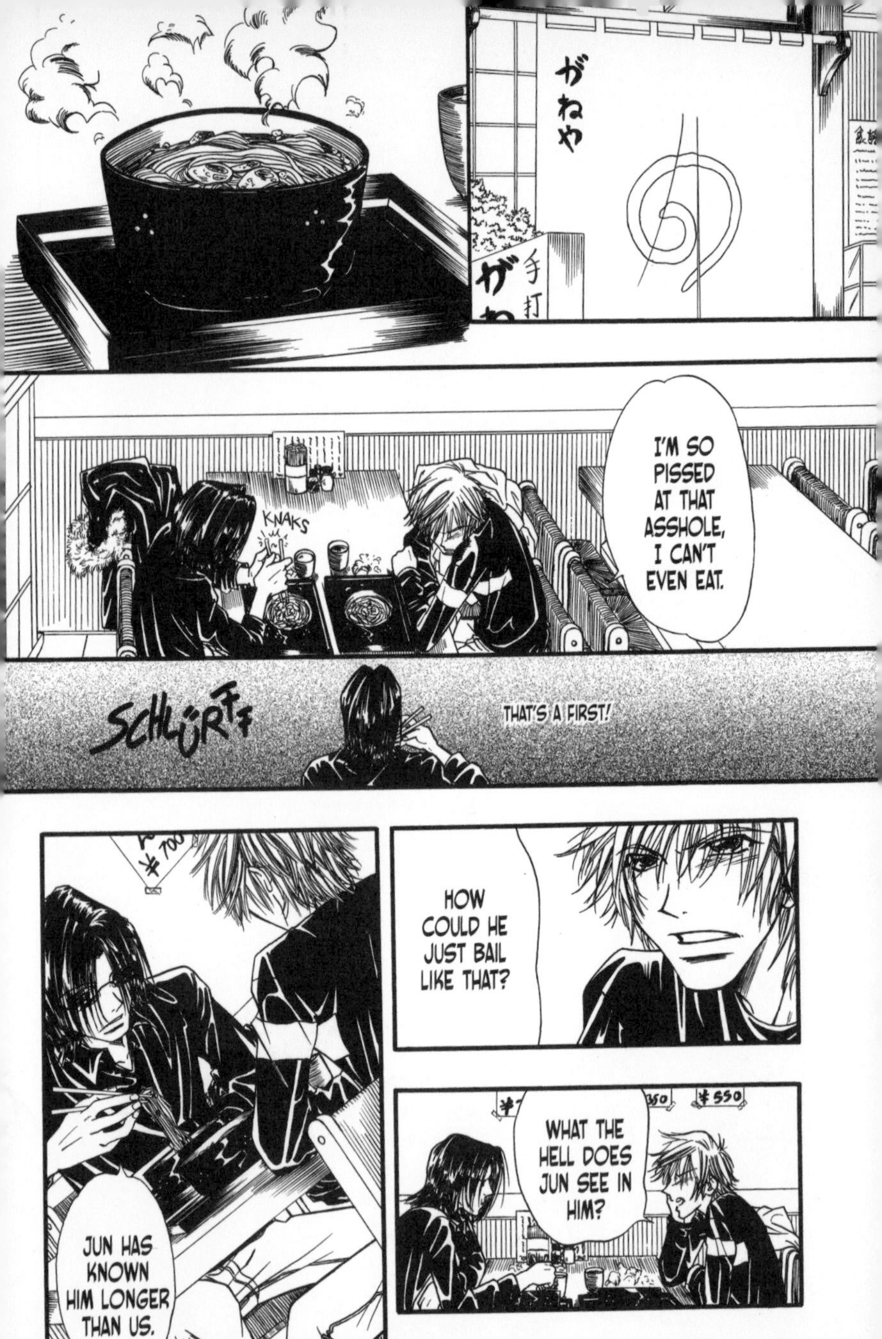
がねや
手打
がね
I'M SO PISSED AT THAT ASSHOLE, I CAN'T EVEN EAT.
KNAKS
THAT'S A FIRST!
SCHLÜRFF
HOW COULD HE JUST BAIL LIKE THAT?
¥550
WHAT THE HELL DOES JUN SEE IN HIM?
¥700
JUN HAS KNOWN HIM LONGER THAN US.

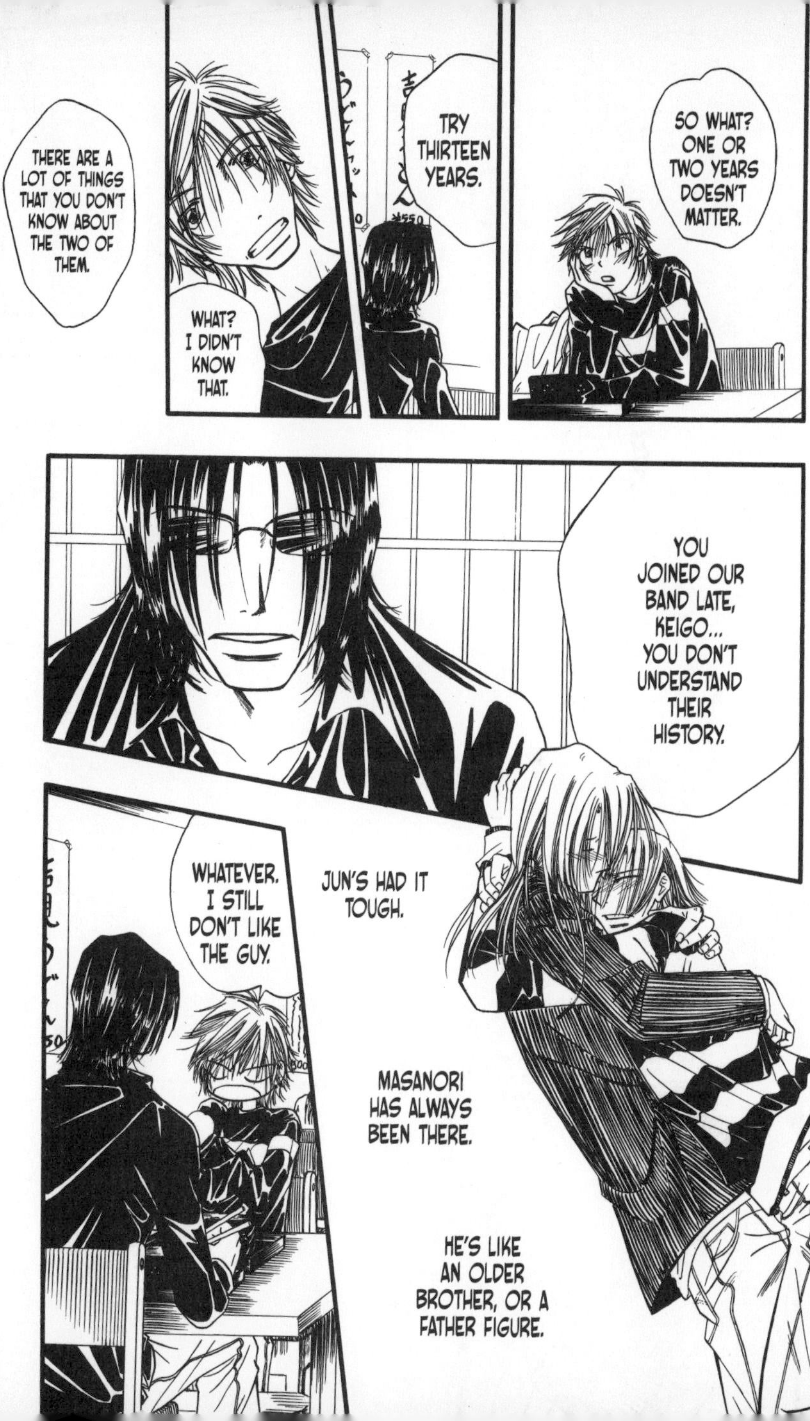
SO WHAT? ONE OR TWO YEARS DOESN'T MATTER.
TRY THIRTEEN YEARS.
WHAT? I DIDN'T KNOW THAT.
THERE ARE A LOT OF THINGS THAT YOU DON'T KNOW ABOUT THE TWO OF THEM.
YOU JOINED OUR BAND LATE, KEIGO... YOU DON'T UNDERSTAND THEIR HISTORY.
JUN'S HAD IT TOUGH.
MASANORI HAS ALWAYS BEEN THERE.
HE'S LIKE AN OLDER BROTHER, OR A FATHER FIGURE.
WHATEVER. I STILL DON'T LIKE THE GUY.

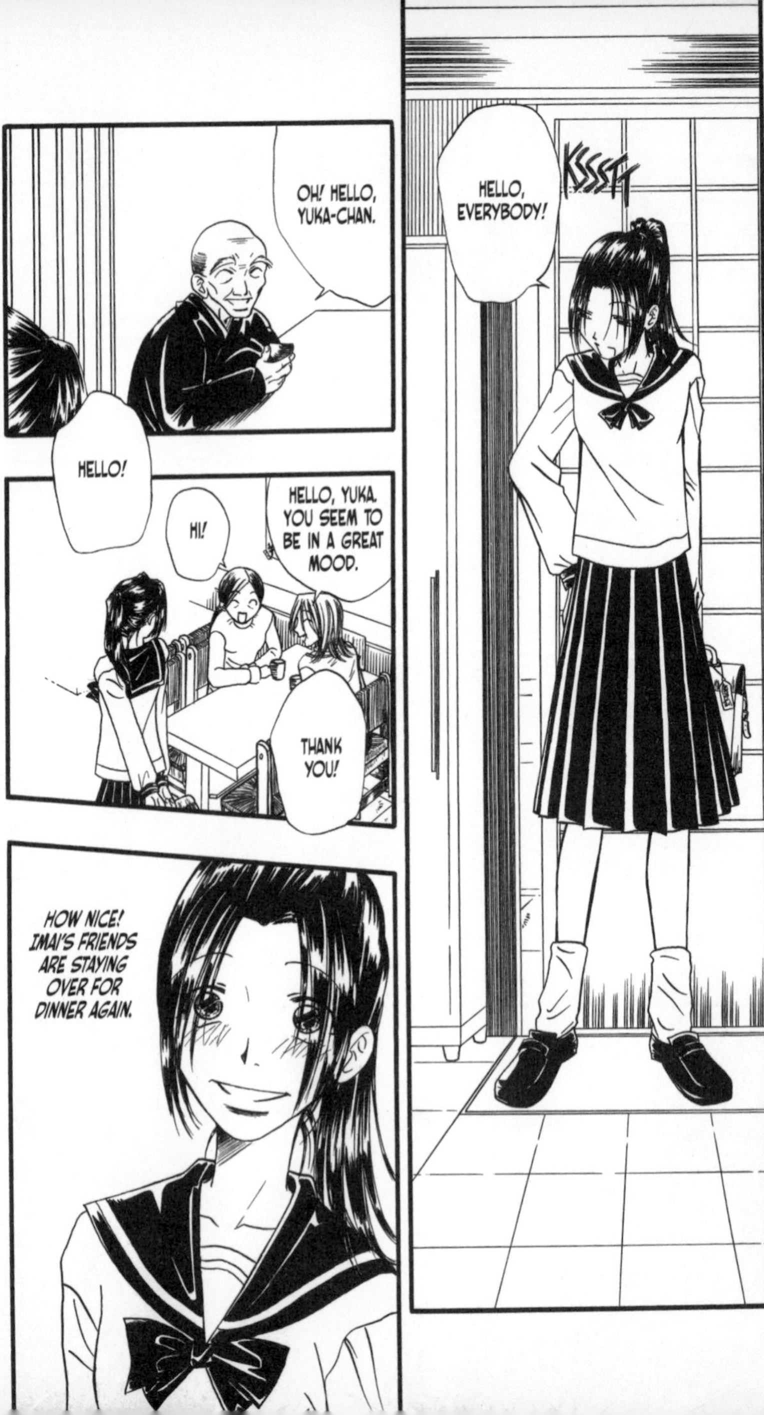
HELLO, EVERYBODY!
KSSSTT
OH! HELLO, YUKA-CHAN.
HELLO, YUKA. YOU SEEM TO BE IN A GREAT MOOD.
HI!
HELLO!
THANK YOU!
HOW NICE! IMAI'S FRIENDS ARE STAYING OVER FOR DINNER AGAIN.

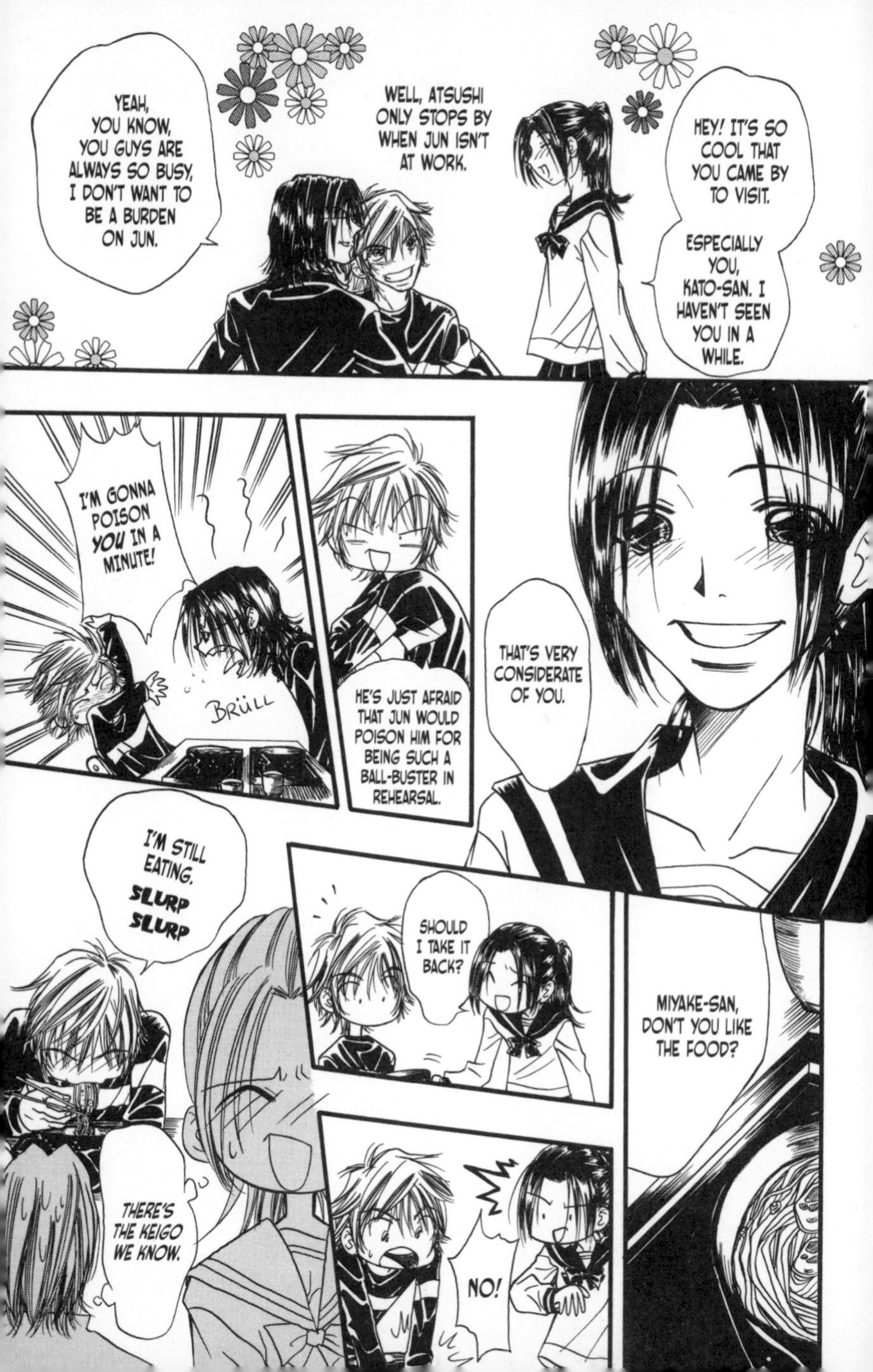
HEY! IT'S SO COOL THAT YOU CAME BY TO VISIT.
ESPECIALLY YOU, KATO-SAN. I HAVEN'T SEEN YOU IN A WHILE.
WELL, ATSUSHI ONLY STOPS BY WHEN JUN ISN'T AT WORK.
YEAH, YOU KNOW, YOU GUYS ARE ALWAYS SO BUSY, I DON'T WANT TO BE A BURDEN ON JUN.
THAT'S VERY CONSIDERATE OF YOU.
HE'S JUST AFRAID THAT JUN WOULD POISON HIM FOR BEING SUCH A BALL-BUSTER IN REHEARSAL.
I'M GONNA POISON YOU IN A MINUTE!
BRÜLL
MIYAKE-SAN, DON'T YOU LIKE THE FOOD?
SHOULD I TAKE IT BACK?
NO!
I'M STILL EATING.
SLURP SLURP
THERE'S THE KEIGO WE KNOW.

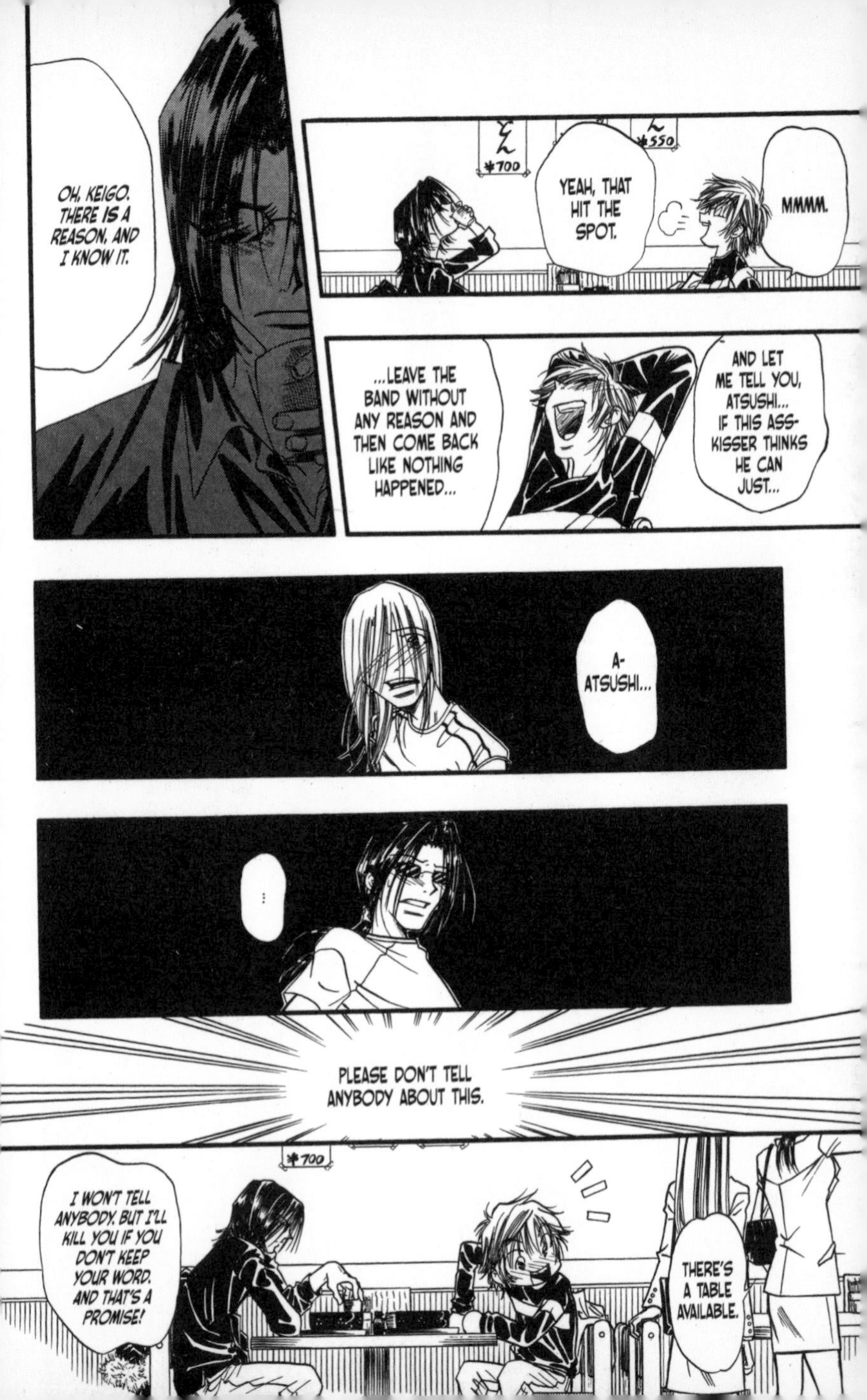
MMMM.
YEAH, THAT HIT THE SPOT.
AND LET ME TELL YOU, ATSUSHI... IF THIS ASS-KISSER THINKS HE CAN JUST...
...LEAVE THE BAND WITHOUT ANY REASON AND THEN COME BACK LIKE NOTHING HAPPENED...
OH, KEIGO. THERE IS A REASON, AND I KNOW IT.
A-ATSUSHI...
...
PLEASE DON'T TELL ANYBODY ABOUT THIS.
THERE'S A TABLE AVAILABLE.
I WON'T TELL ANYBODY. BUT I'LL KILL YOU IF YOU DON'T KEEP YOUR WORD. AND THAT'S A PROMISE!

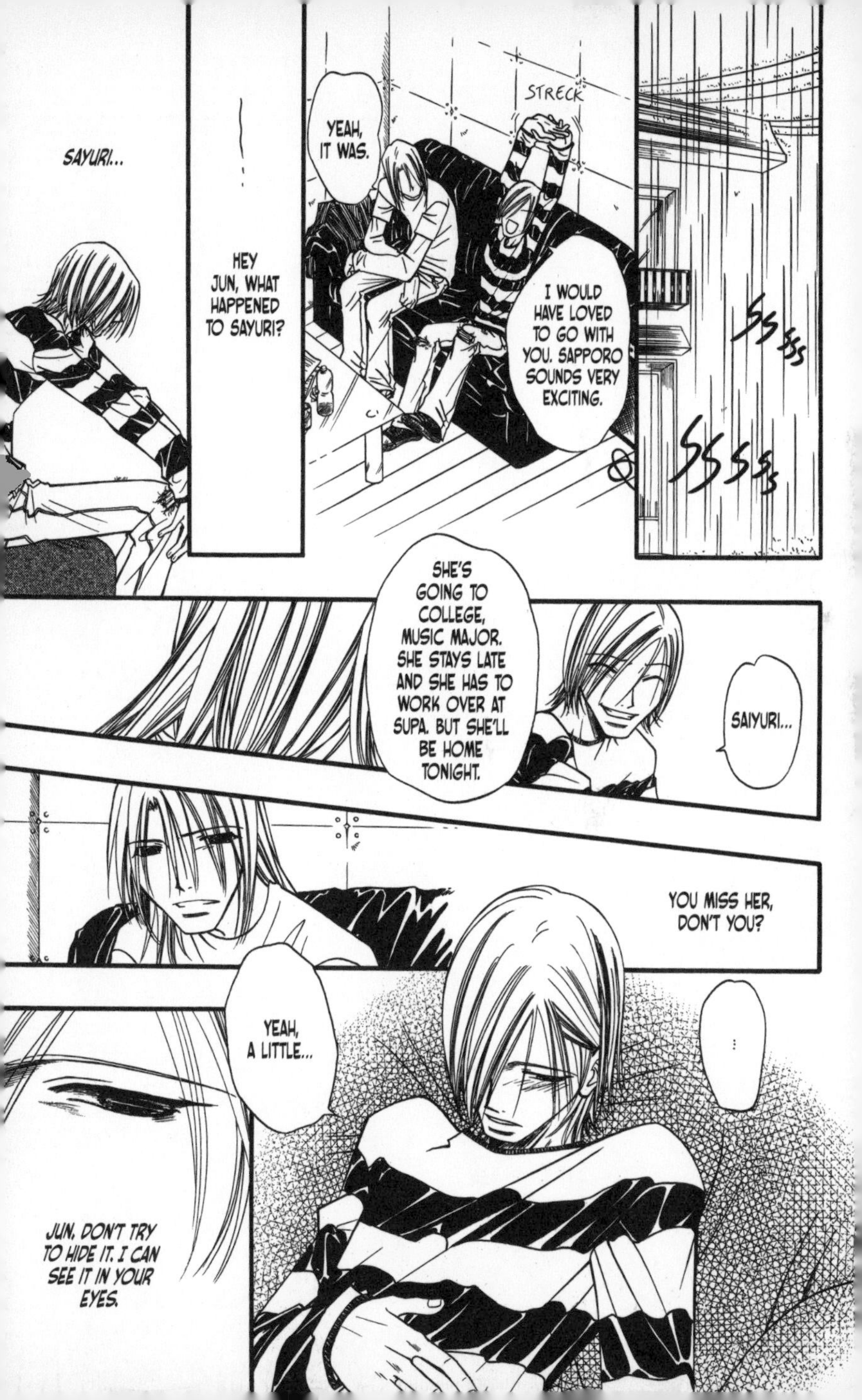
SSSS
SSSS
STRECK
YEAH, IT WAS.
I WOULD HAVE LOVED TO GO WITH YOU. SAPPORO SOUNDS VERY EXCITING.
HEY JUN, WHAT HAPPENED TO SAYURI?
SAYURI...
SAIYURI...
SHE'S GOING TO COLLEGE, MUSIC MAJOR. SHE STAYS LATE AND SHE HAS TO WORK OVER AT SUPA. BUT SHE'LL BE HOME TONIGHT.
YOU MISS HER, DON'T YOU?
...
YEAH, A LITTLE...
JUN, DON'T TRY TO HIDE IT. I CAN SEE IT IN YOUR EYES.

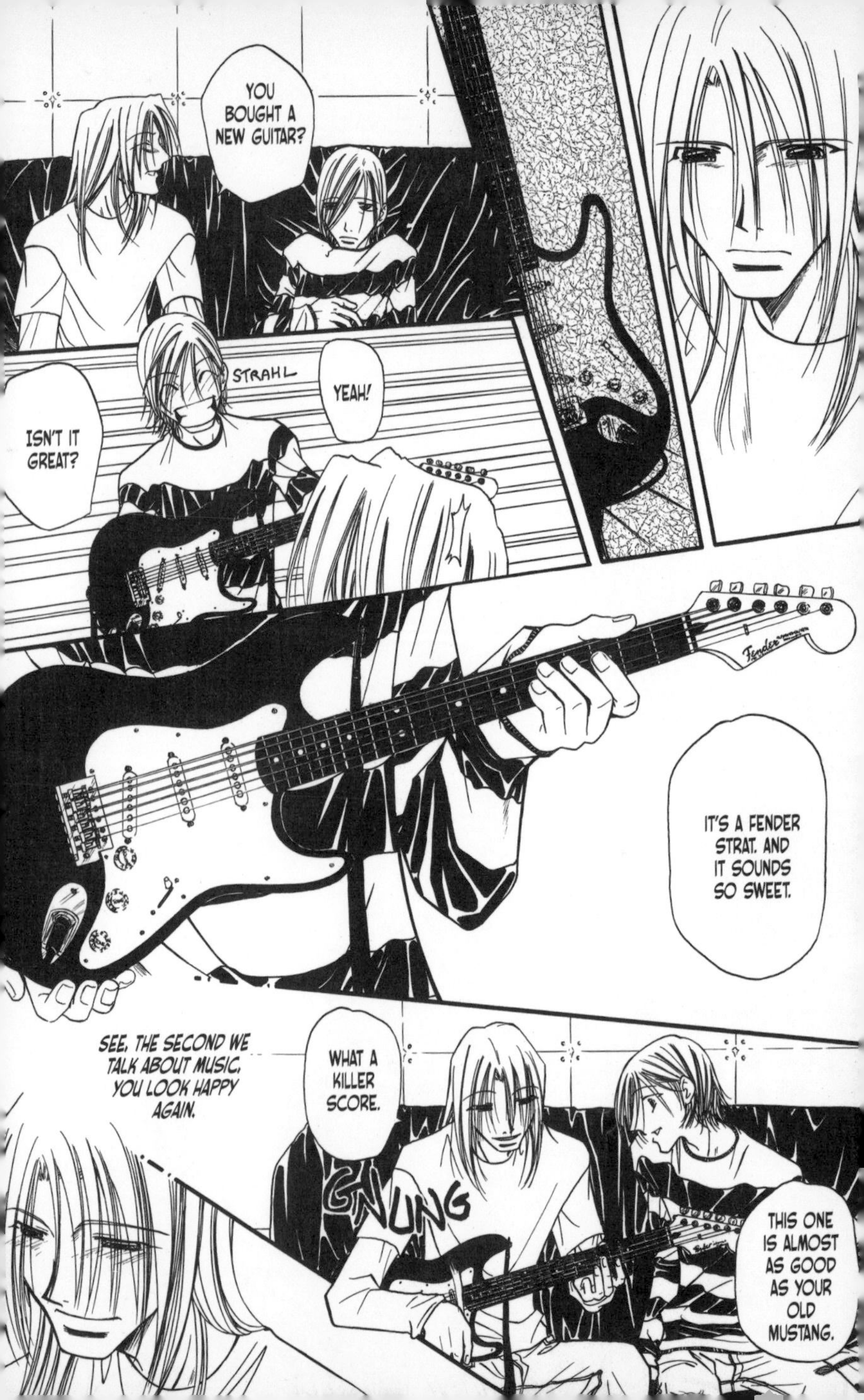
YOU BOUGHT A NEW GUITAR?
STRAHL
YEAH!
ISN'T IT GREAT?
IT'S A FENDER STRAT. AND IT SOUNDS SO SWEET.
THIS ONE IS ALMOST AS GOOD AS YOUR OLD MUSTANG.
WHAT A KILLER SCORE.
GNUNG
SEE, THE SECOND WE TALK ABOUT MUSIC, YOU LOOK HAPPY AGAIN.

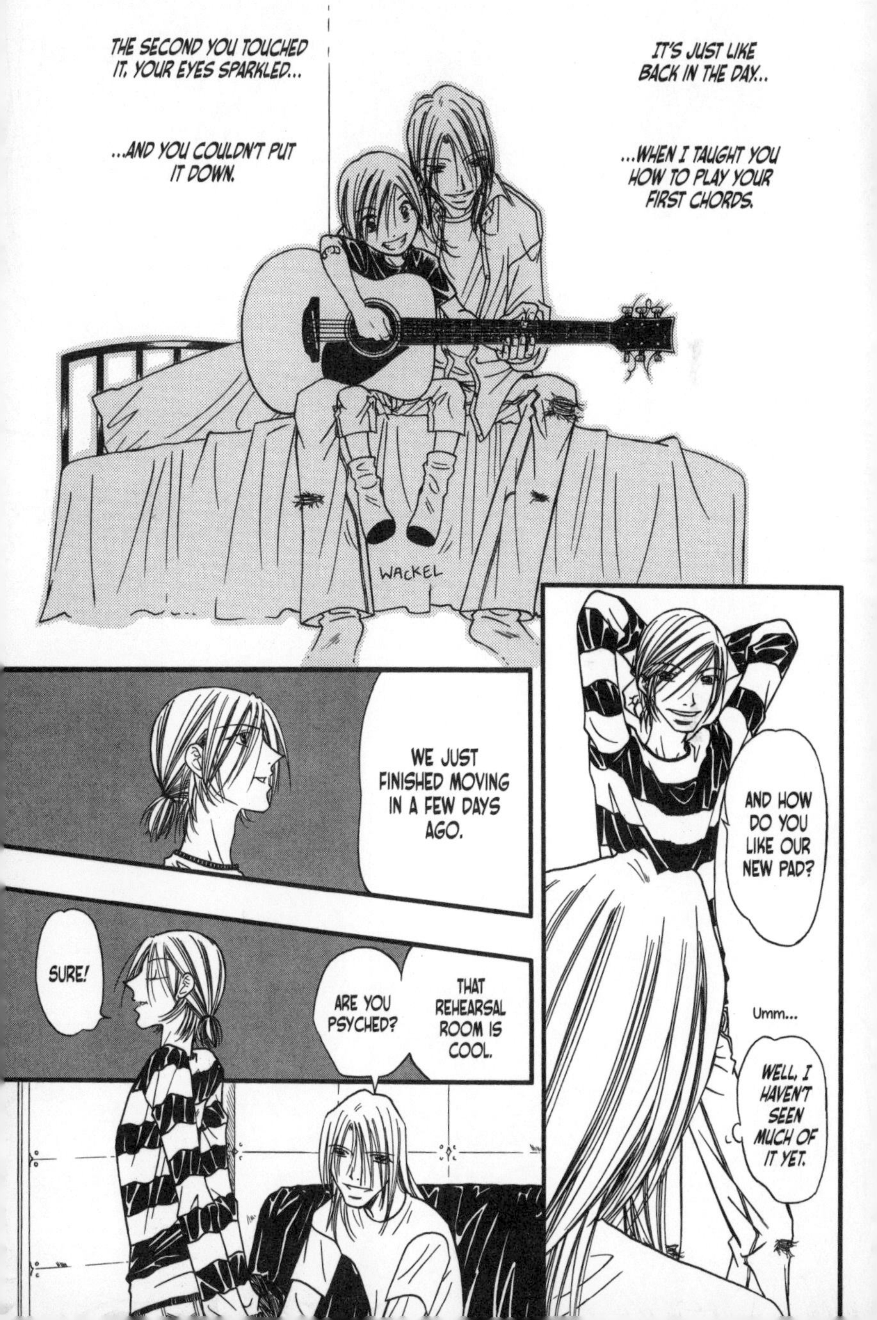
IT'S JUST LIKE BACK IN THE DAY...
...WHEN I TAUGHT YOU HOW TO PLAY YOUR FIRST CHORDS.
THE SECOND YOU TOUCHED IT, YOUR EYES SPARKLED...
...AND YOU COULDN'T PUT IT DOWN.
WACKEL
AND HOW DO YOU LIKE OUR NEW PAD?
Umm...
WELL, I HAVEN'T SEEN MUCH OF IT YET.
WE JUST FINISHED MOVING IN A FEW DAYS AGO.
THAT REHEARSAL ROOM IS COOL.
ARE YOU PSYCHED?
SURE!

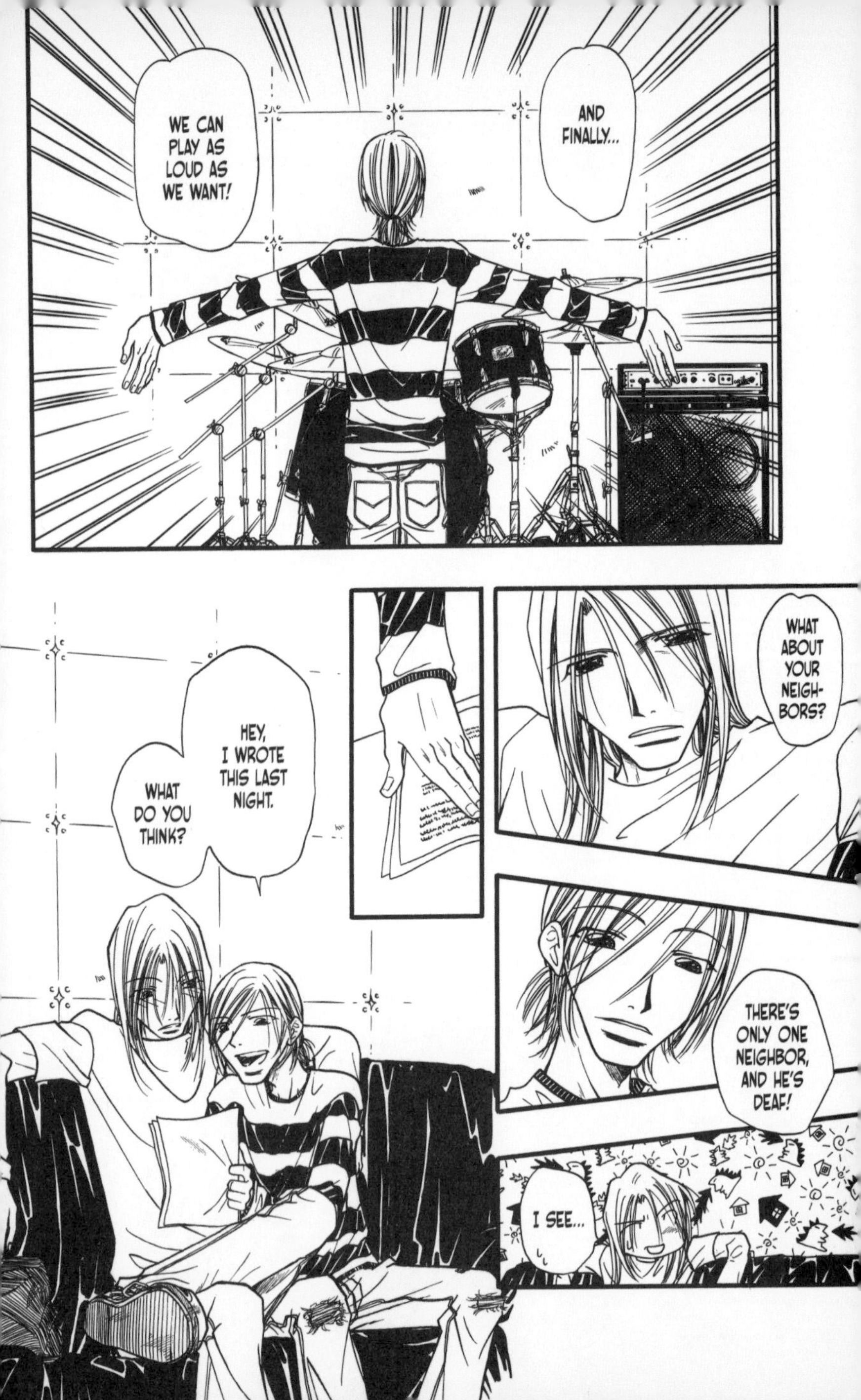
AND FINALLY...
WE CAN PLAY AS LOUD AS WE WANT!
WHAT ABOUT YOUR NEIGH-BORS?
THERE'S ONLY ONE NEIGHBOR, AND HE'S DEAF!
I SEE...
HEY, I WROTE THIS LAST NIGHT.
WHAT DO YOU THINK?

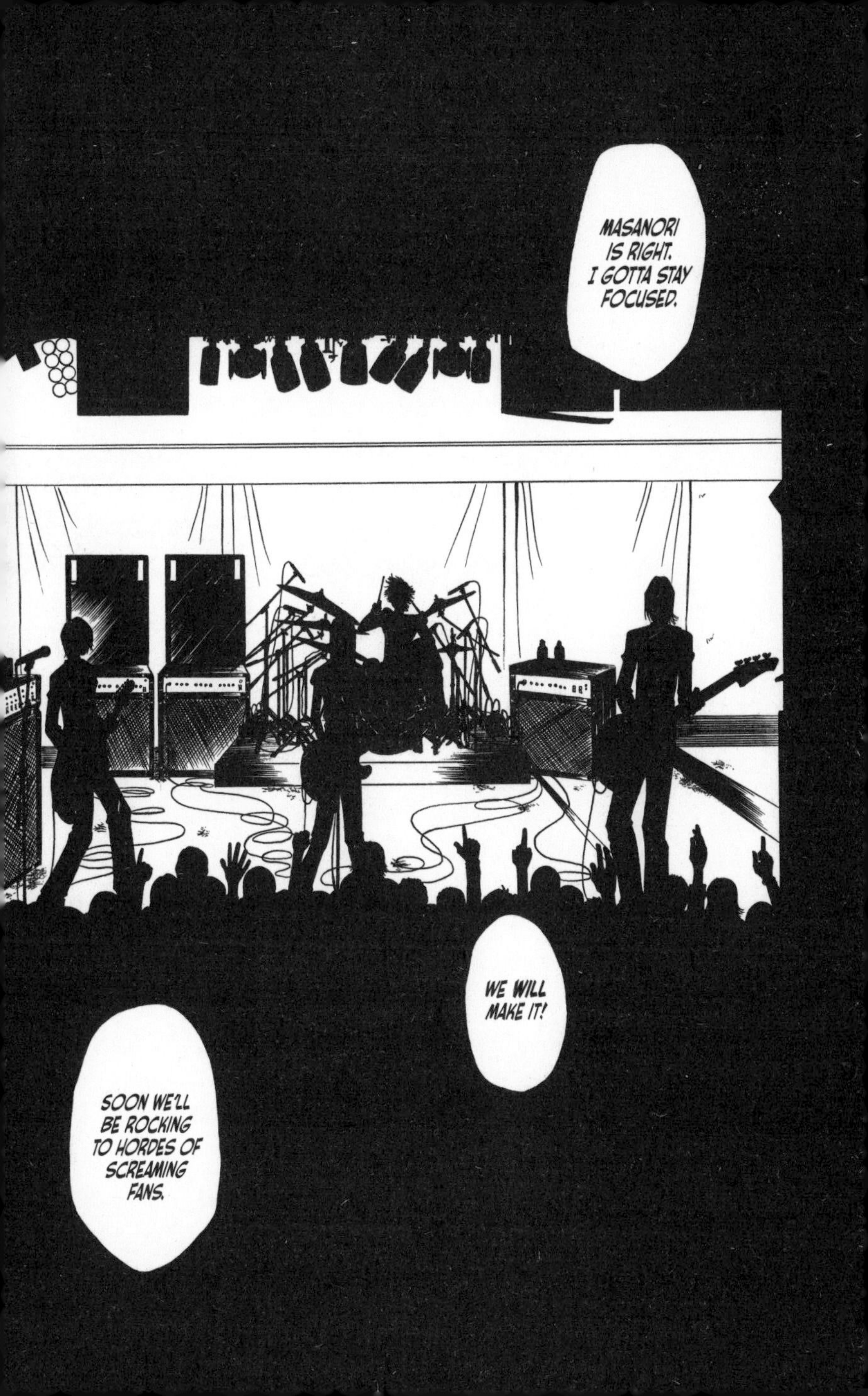
MASANORI IS RIGHT. I GOTTA STAY FOCUSED.
WE WILL MAKE IT!
SOON WE'LL BE ROCKING TO HORDES OF SCREAMING FANS.

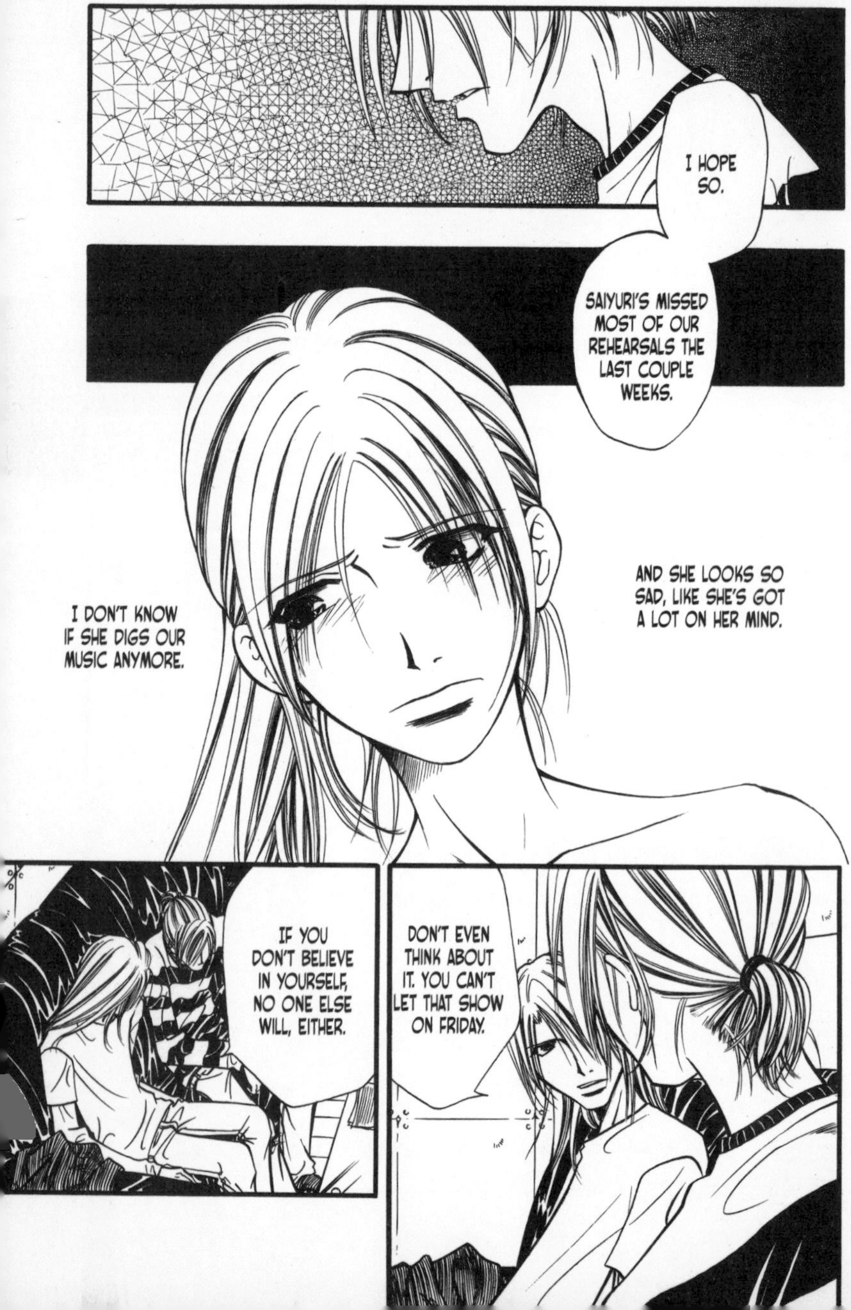
I HOPE SO.
SAIYURI'S MISSED MOST OF OUR REHEARSALS THE LAST COUPLE WEEKS.
AND SHE LOOKS SO SAD, LIKE SHE'S GOT A LOT ON HER MIND.
I DON'T KNOW IF SHE DIGS OUR MUSIC ANYMORE.
DON'T EVEN THINK ABOUT IT. YOU CAN'T LET THAT SHOW ON FRIDAY.
IF YOU DON'T BELIEVE IN YOURSELF, NO ONE ELSE WILL, EITHER.

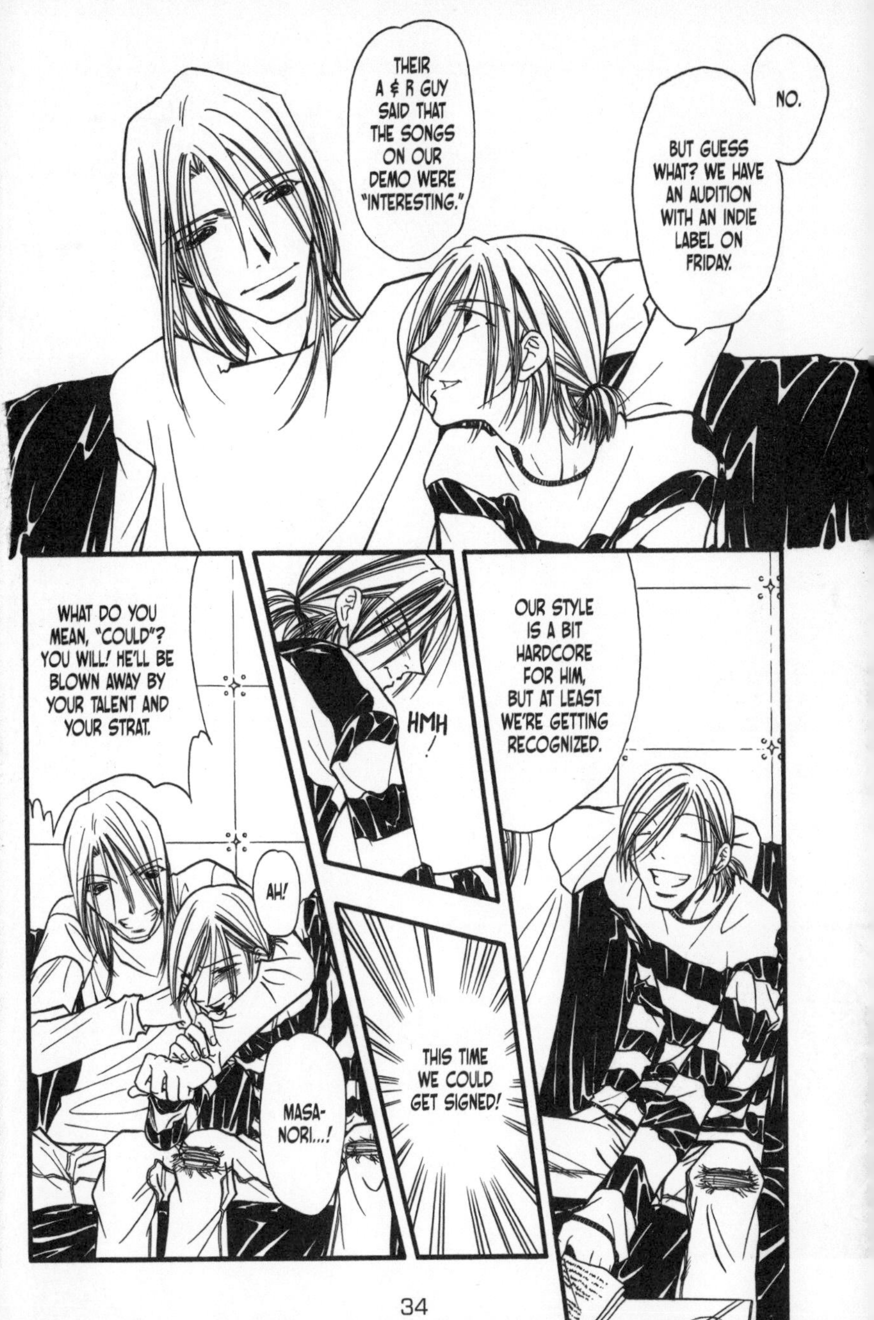
NO.
BUT GUESS WHAT? WE HAVE AN AUDITION WITH AN INDIE LABEL ON FRIDAY.
THEIR A & R GUY SAID THAT THE SONGS ON OUR DEMO WERE "INTERESTING."
OUR STYLE IS A BIT HARDCORE FOR HIM, BUT AT LEAST WE'RE GETTING RECOGNIZED.
HMH!
THIS TIME WE COULD GET SIGNED!
MASA-NORI...!
AH!
WHAT DO YOU MEAN, "COULD"? YOU WILL! HE'LL BE BLOWN AWAY BY YOUR TALENT AND YOUR STRAT.

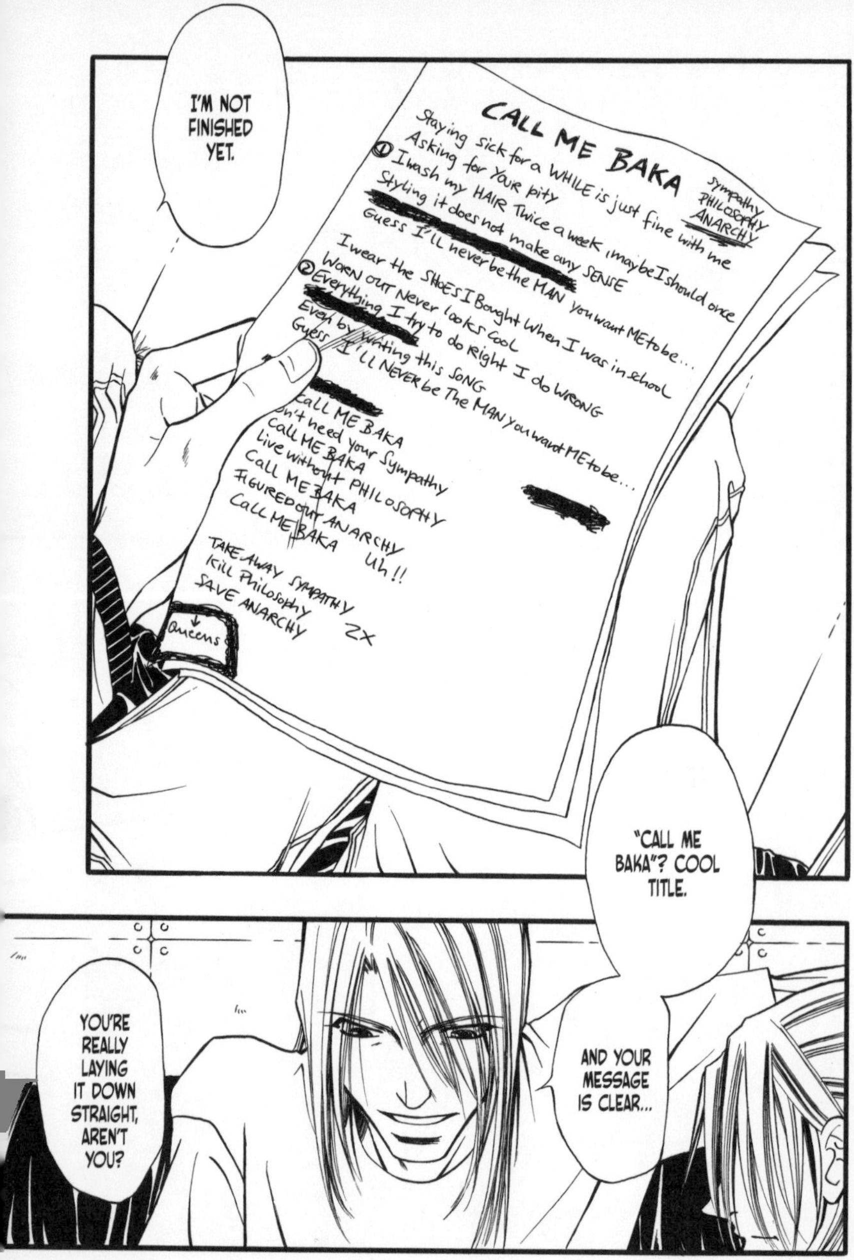
I'M NOT FINISHED YET.
CALL ME BAKA
Sympathy PHILOSOPHY ANARCHY
Staying sick for a WHILE is just fine with me
Asking for Your pity
① I wash my HAIR Twice a week, maybe I should once
Styling it does not make any SENSE
[redacted]
Guess I'll never be the MAN you want ME to be...
I wear the SHOES I Bought When I was in school
② WORN OUT Never looks Cool
[redacted]
Everything I try to do Right I do WRONG
Even by writing this SONG
Guess I'll NEVER be The MAN you want ME to be...
[redacted]
Call ME BAKA
on't need your Sympathy
Call ME BAKA
Live without PHILOSOPHY
Call ME BAKA
FIGURED OUT ANARCHY
Call ME BAKA Uh!!
TAKE AWAY SYMPATHY
Kill Philosophy 2X
SAVE ANARCHY
Queens
"CALL ME BAKA"? COOL TITLE.
AND YOUR MESSAGE IS CLEAR...
YOU'RE REALLY LAYING IT DOWN STRAIGHT, AREN'T YOU?

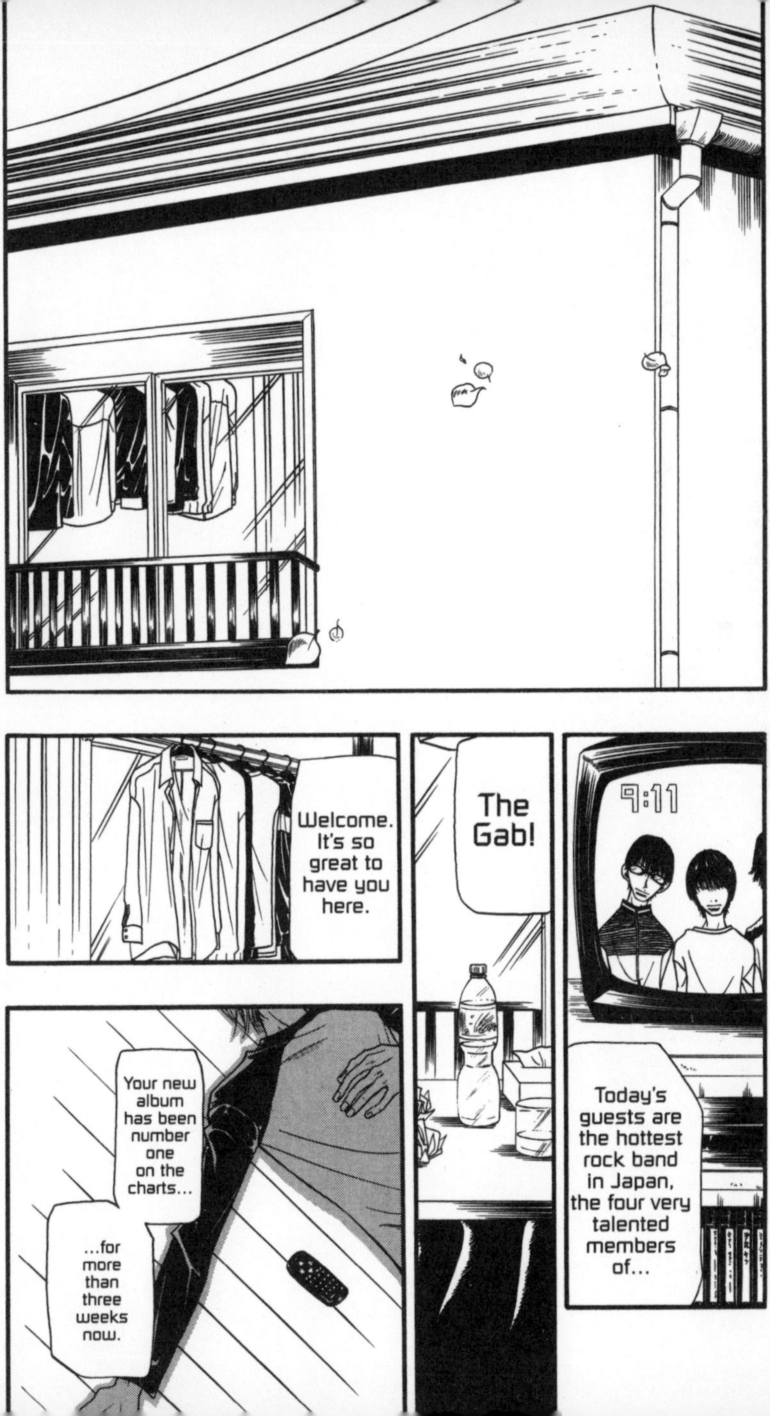
9:11
Today's guests are the hottest rock band in Japan, the four very talented members of...
The Gab!
Welcome. It's so great to have you here.
Your new album has been number one on the charts...
...for more than three weeks now.

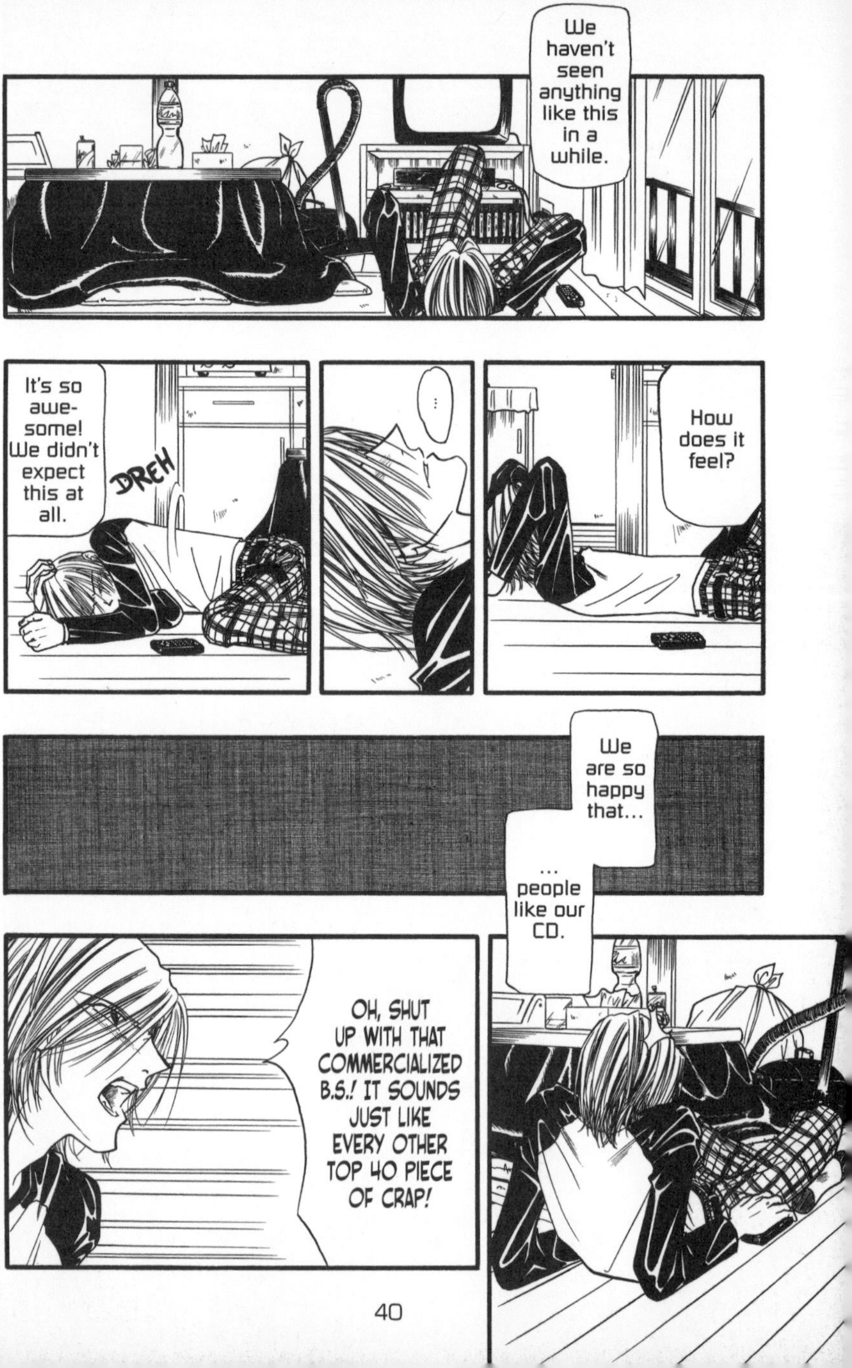
We haven't seen anything like this in a while.
How does it feel?
...
It's so awe-some! We didn't expect this at all.
DREH
We are so happy that...
... people like our CD.
OH, SHUT UP WITH THAT COMMERCIALIZED B.S.! IT SOUNDS JUST LIKE EVERY OTHER TOP 40 PIECE OF CRAP!

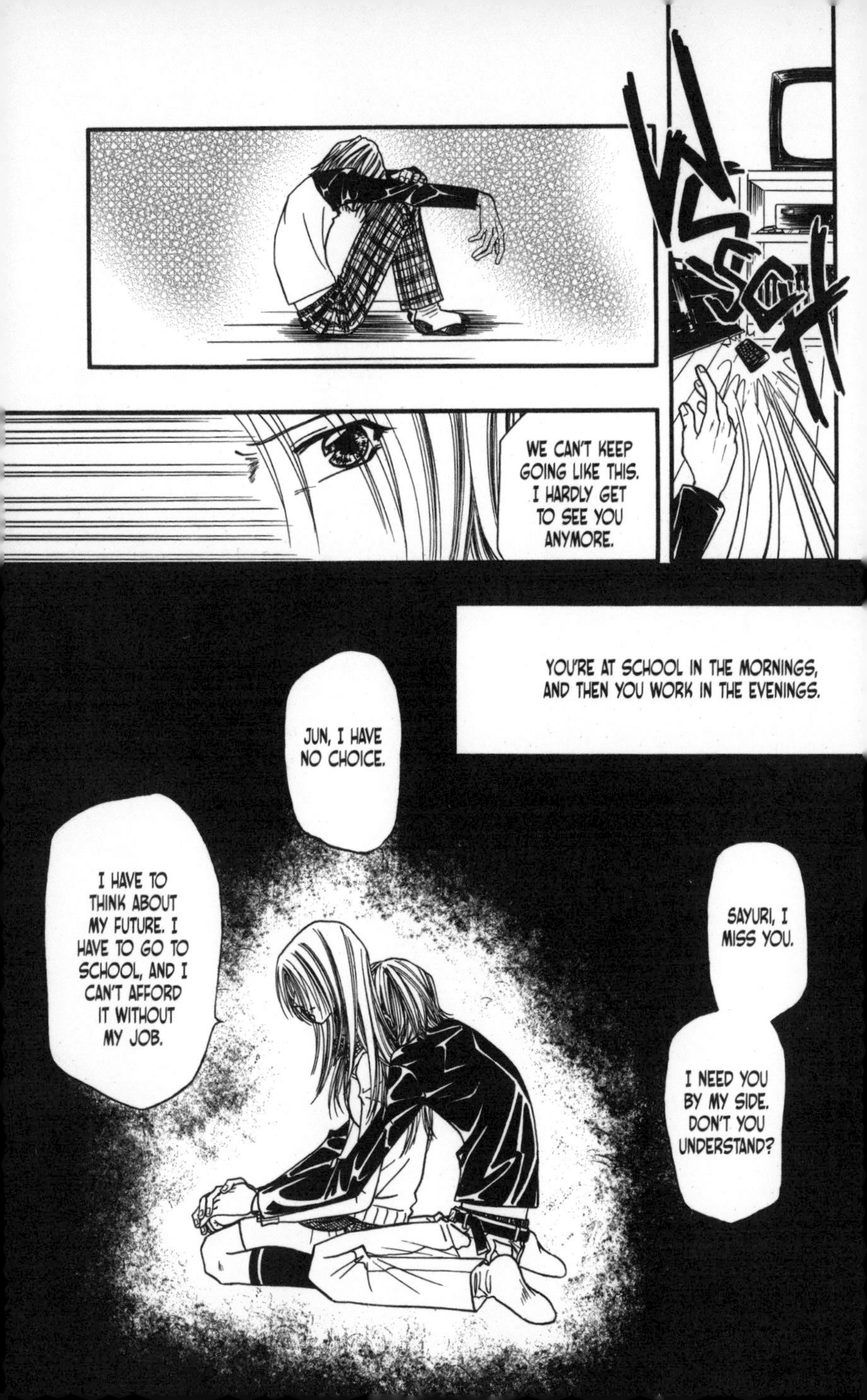
WE CAN'T KEEP GOING LIKE THIS. I HARDLY GET TO SEE YOU ANYMORE.
YOU'RE AT SCHOOL IN THE MORNINGS, AND THEN YOU WORK IN THE EVENINGS.
JUN, I HAVE NO CHOICE.
I HAVE TO THINK ABOUT MY FUTURE. I HAVE TO GO TO SCHOOL, AND I CAN'T AFFORD IT WITHOUT MY JOB.
SAYURI, I MISS YOU.
I NEED YOU BY MY SIDE. DON'T YOU UNDERSTAND?

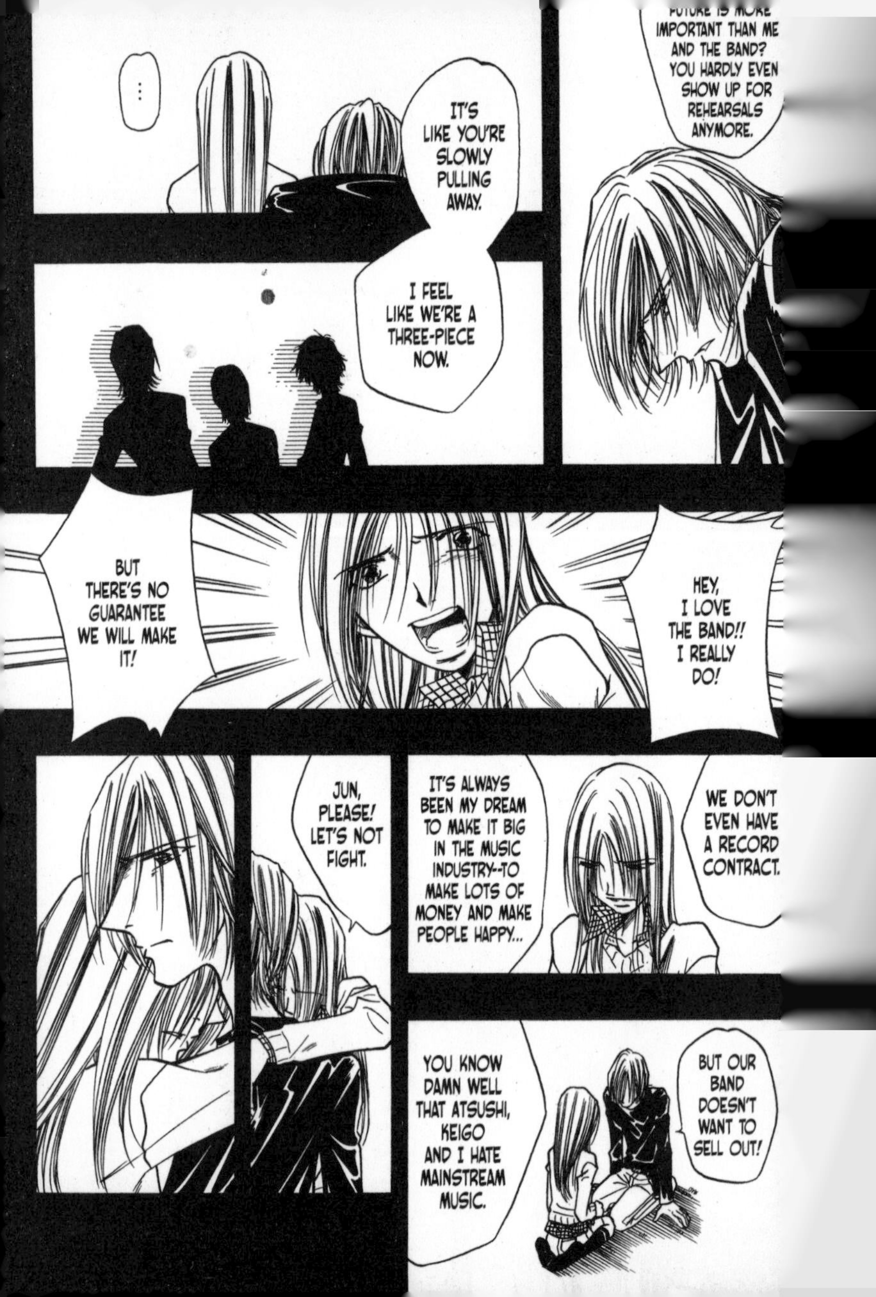
FUTURE IS MORE IMPORTANT THAN ME AND THE BAND? YOU HARDLY EVEN SHOW UP FOR REHEARSALS ANYMORE.
...
IT'S LIKE YOU'RE SLOWLY PULLING AWAY.
I FEEL LIKE WE'RE A THREE-PIECE NOW.
HEY, I LOVE THE BAND!! I REALLY DO!
BUT THERE'S NO GUARANTEE WE WILL MAKE IT!
WE DON'T EVEN HAVE A RECORD CONTRACT.
IT'S ALWAYS BEEN MY DREAM TO MAKE IT BIG IN THE MUSIC INDUSTRY--TO MAKE LOTS OF MONEY AND MAKE PEOPLE HAPPY...
BUT OUR BAND DOESN'T WANT TO SELL OUT!
YOU KNOW DAMN WELL THAT ATSUSHI, KEIGO AND I HATE MAINSTREAM MUSIC.
JUN, PLEASE! LET'S NOT FIGHT.

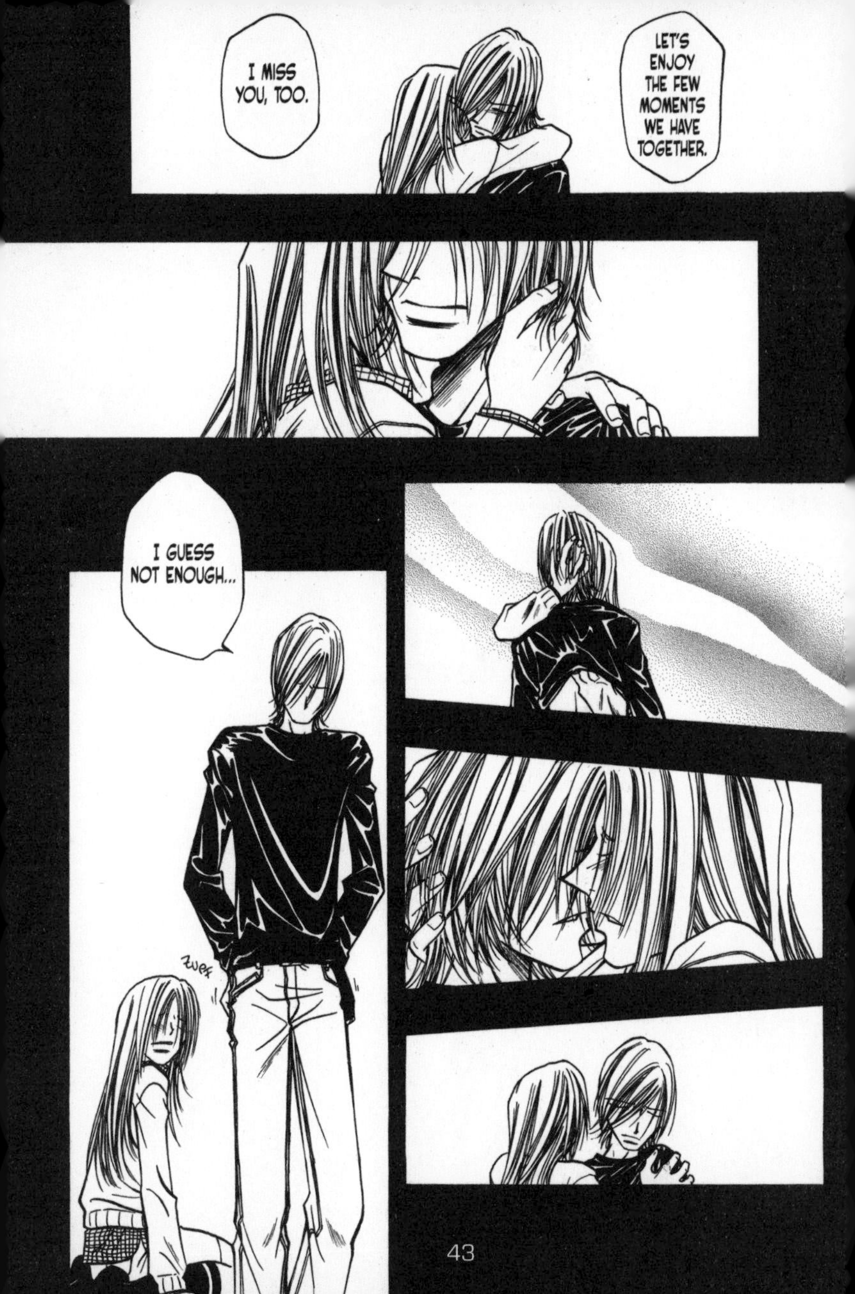
LET'S ENJOY THE FEW MOMENTS WE HAVE TOGETHER.
I MISS YOU, TOO.
I GUESS NOT ENOUGH...
zwef

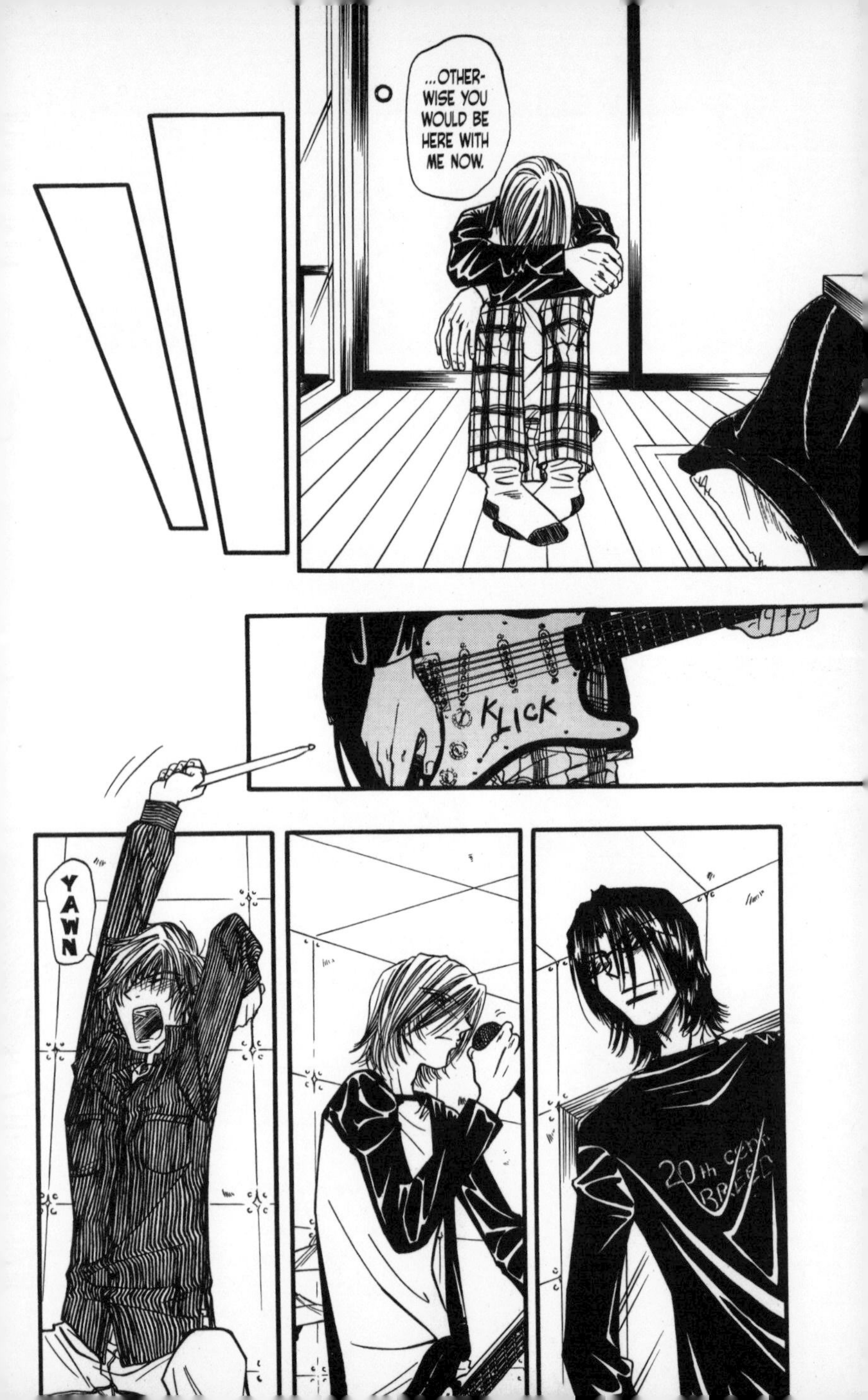
...OTHER-WISE YOU WOULD BE HERE WITH ME NOW.
KLICK
YAWN
20th cent. BREED

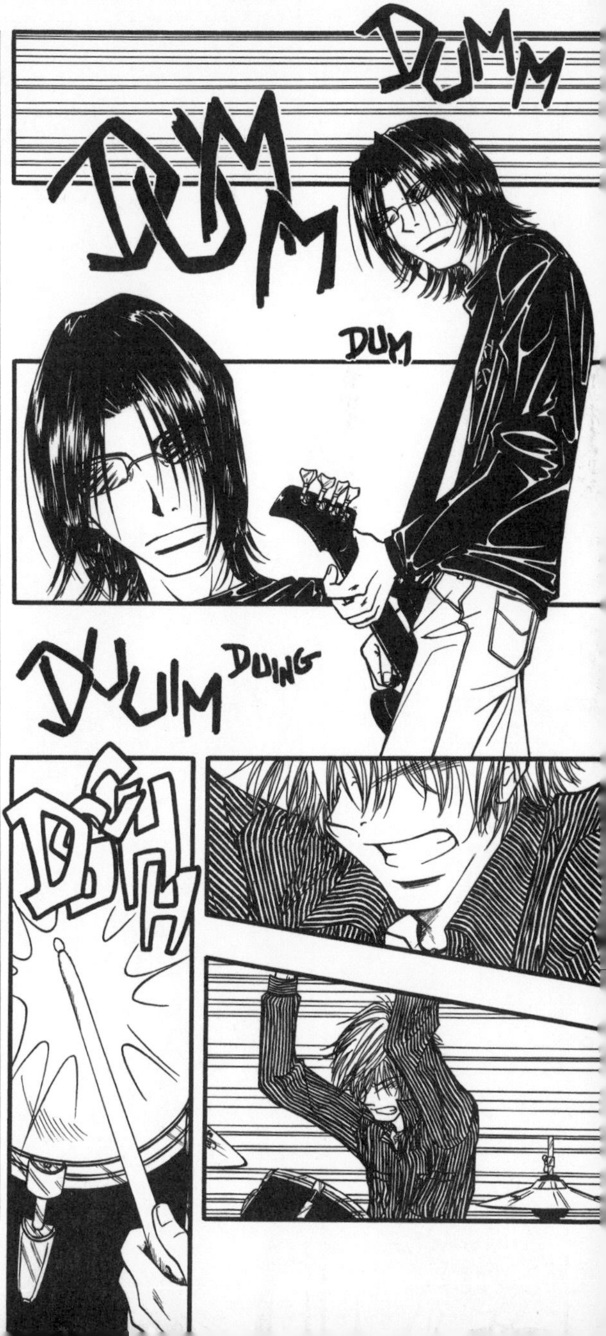
DUMM
DUMM
DUM
DUUM
DUING

At this point, I would like to apologize for mutilating the faces of the band members. I know... I am no caricaturist.

I absolutely wanted an image in the profile. Please look at it with a sense of humor and please do not feel offended if you are fans of the band.

If you are wondering why I mentioned Nirvana as the first band, check out Jun's thoughts in *Plastic Chew* (coming soon).

I will try to deliver some of the most important info about a variety of bands. I use the Internet, radio, TV, etc. as a source for information.

Please write me in case you notice any mistakes!

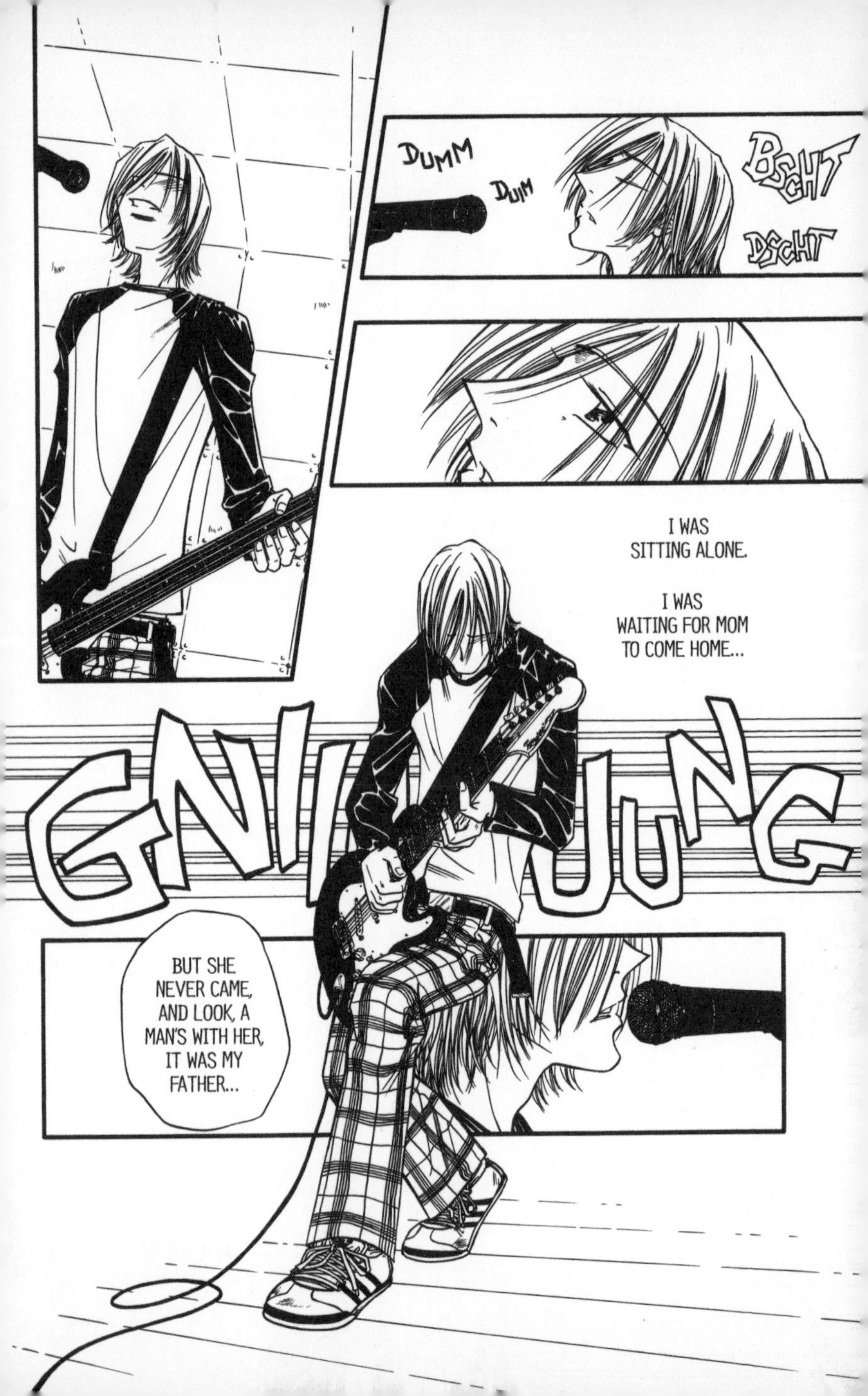
BSCHT
DUMM
DUIM
DSCHT
I WAS SITTING ALONE.
I WAS WAITING FOR MOM TO COME HOME...
GNIIUUNG
BUT SHE NEVER CAME, AND LOOK, A MAN'S WITH HER, IT WAS MY FATHER...

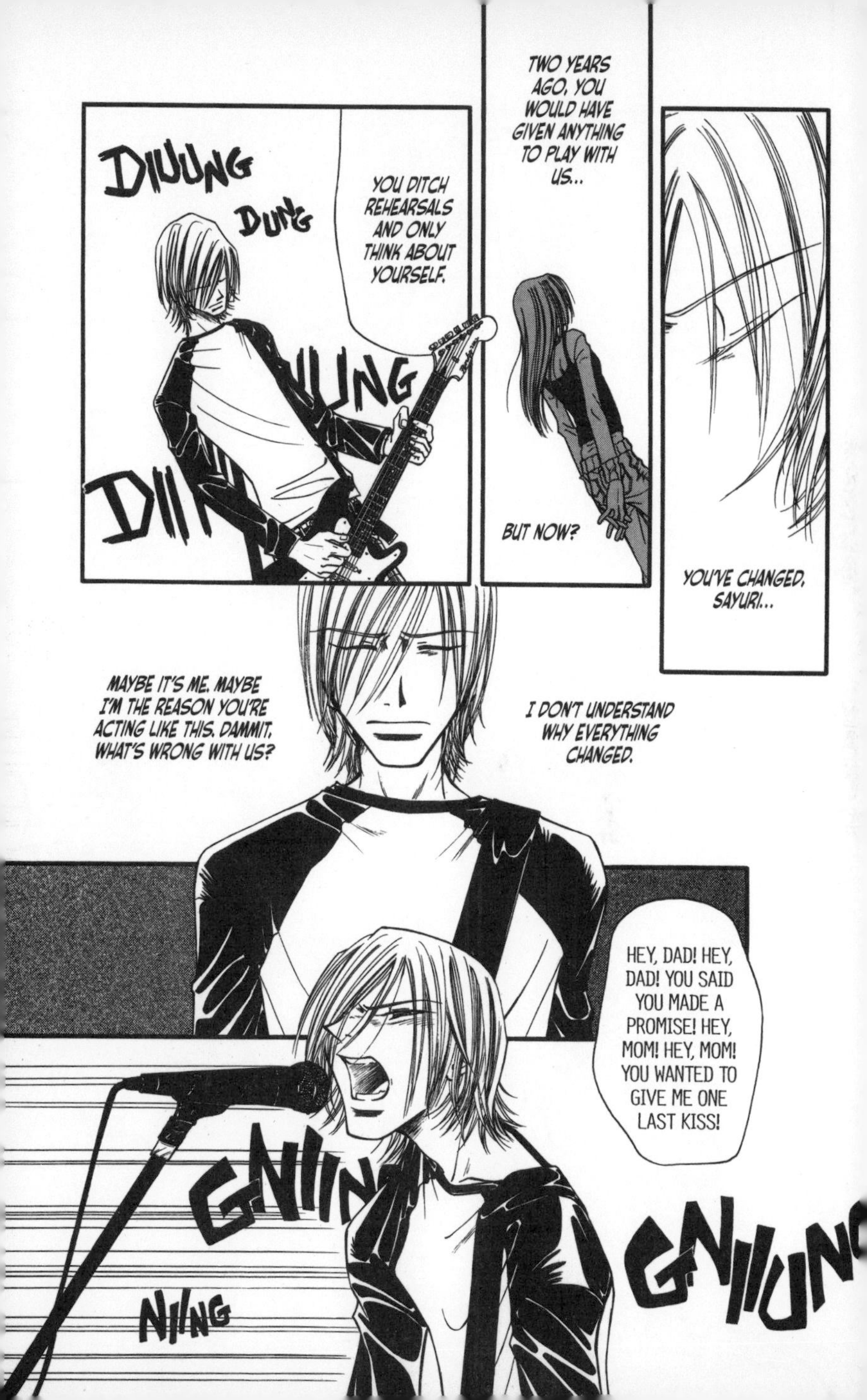

YOU'VE CHANGED, SAYURI...
TWO YEARS AGO, YOU WOULD HAVE GIVEN ANYTHING TO PLAY WITH US...
BUT NOW?
DIUUNG
DUNG
YOU DITCH REHEARSALS AND ONLY THINK ABOUT YOURSELF.
UNG
DII
I DON'T UNDERSTAND WHY EVERYTHING CHANGED.
MAYBE IT'S ME. MAYBE I'M THE REASON YOU'RE ACTING LIKE THIS. DAMMIT. WHAT'S WRONG WITH US?
HEY, DAD! HEY, DAD! YOU SAID YOU MADE A PROMISE! HEY, MOM! HEY, MOM! YOU WANTED TO GIVE ME ONE LAST KISS!
GNIIUN
GNIIN
NIING

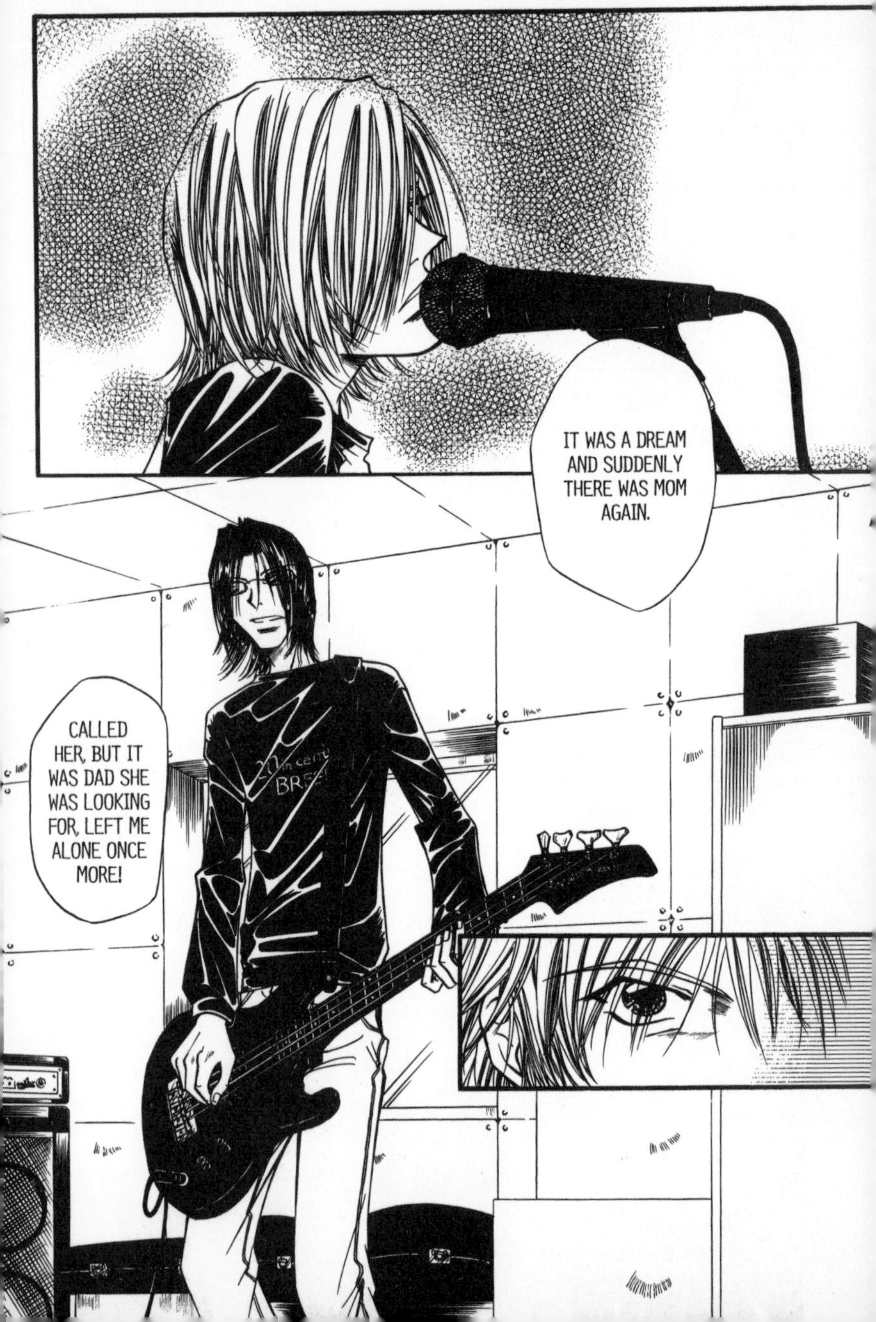
IT WAS A DREAM AND SUDDENLY THERE WAS MOM AGAIN.
CALLED HER, BUT IT WAS DAD SHE WAS LOOKING FOR, LEFT ME ALONE ONCE MORE!

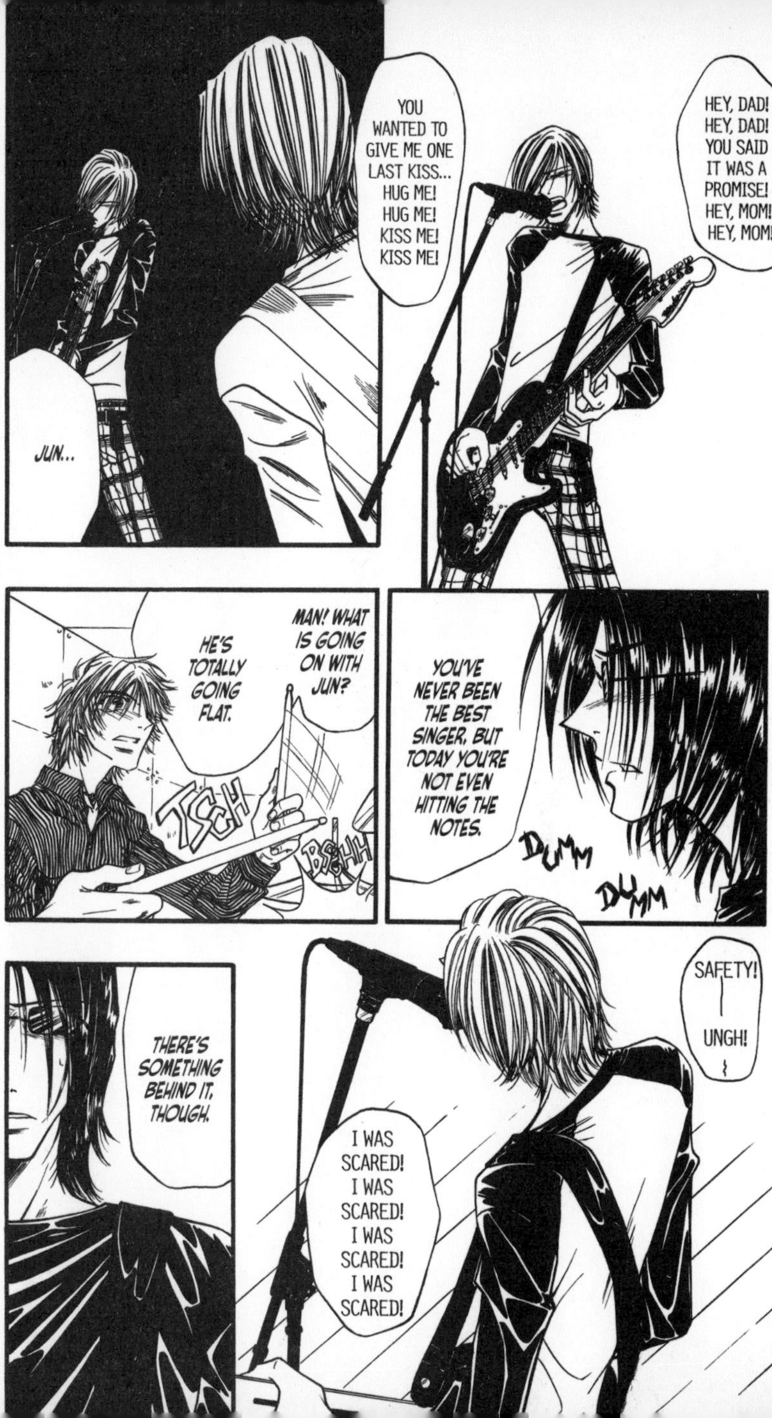
HEY, DAD! HEY, DAD! YOU SAID IT WAS A PROMISE! HEY, MOM! HEY, MOM!
YOU WANTED TO GIVE ME ONE LAST KISS... HUG ME! HUG ME! KISS ME! KISS ME!
JUN...
YOU'VE NEVER BEEN THE BEST SINGER. BUT TODAY YOU'RE NOT EVEN HITTING THE NOTES.
DUMM
DUMM
MAN! WHAT IS GOING ON WITH JUN?
HE'S TOTALLY GOING FLAT.
TSCH
BSHH
SAFETY! UNGH!
I WAS SCARED! I WAS SCARED! I WAS SCARED! I WAS SCARED!
THERE'S SOMETHING BEHIND IT, THOUGH.

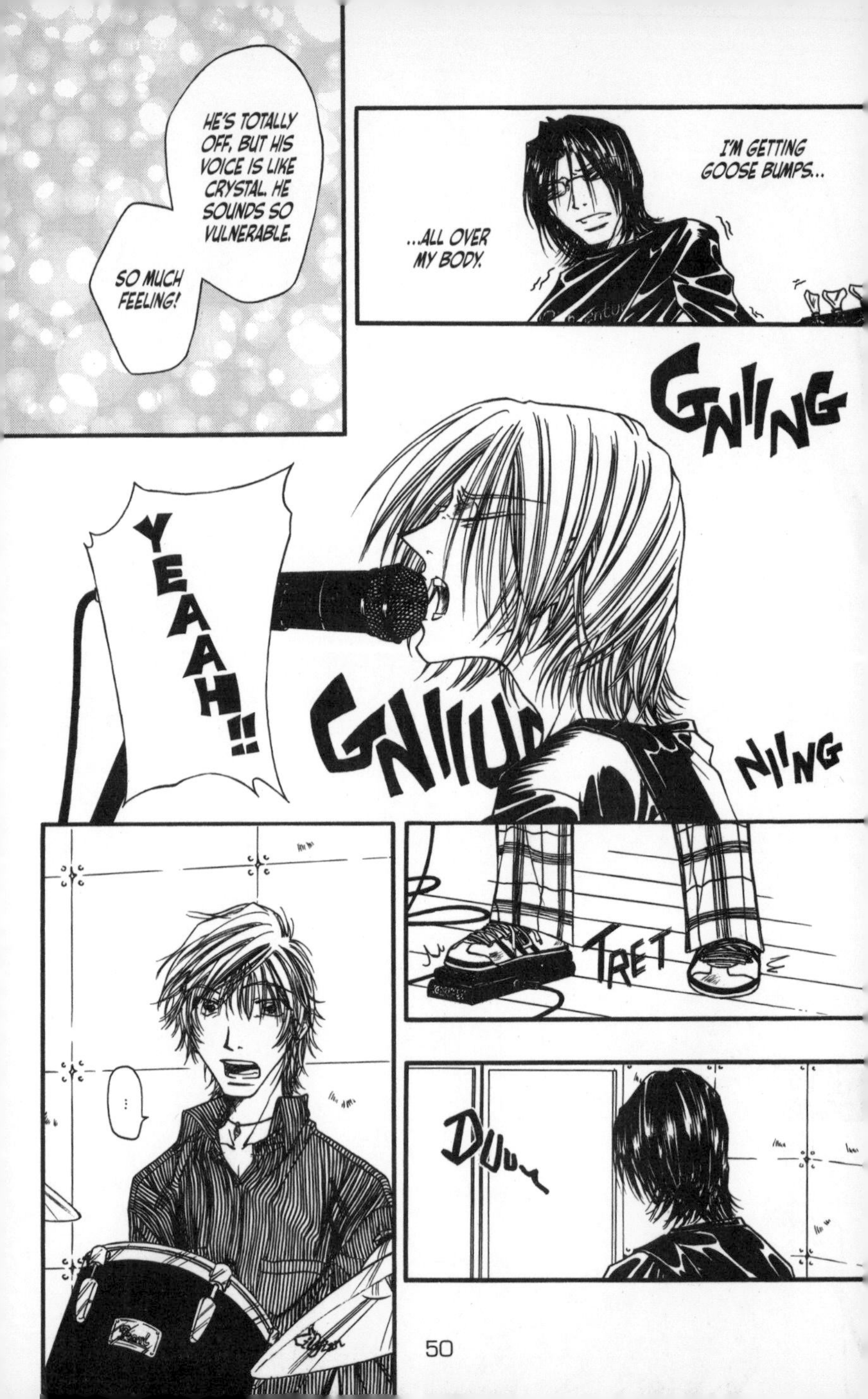
I'M GETTING GOOSE BUMPS...
...ALL OVER MY BODY.
HE'S TOTALLY OFF, BUT HIS VOICE IS LIKE CRYSTAL. HE SOUNDS SO VULNERABLE.
SO MUCH FEELING!
GNIING
YEAAAH!!
GNIIU
NIING
TRET
DUU
...

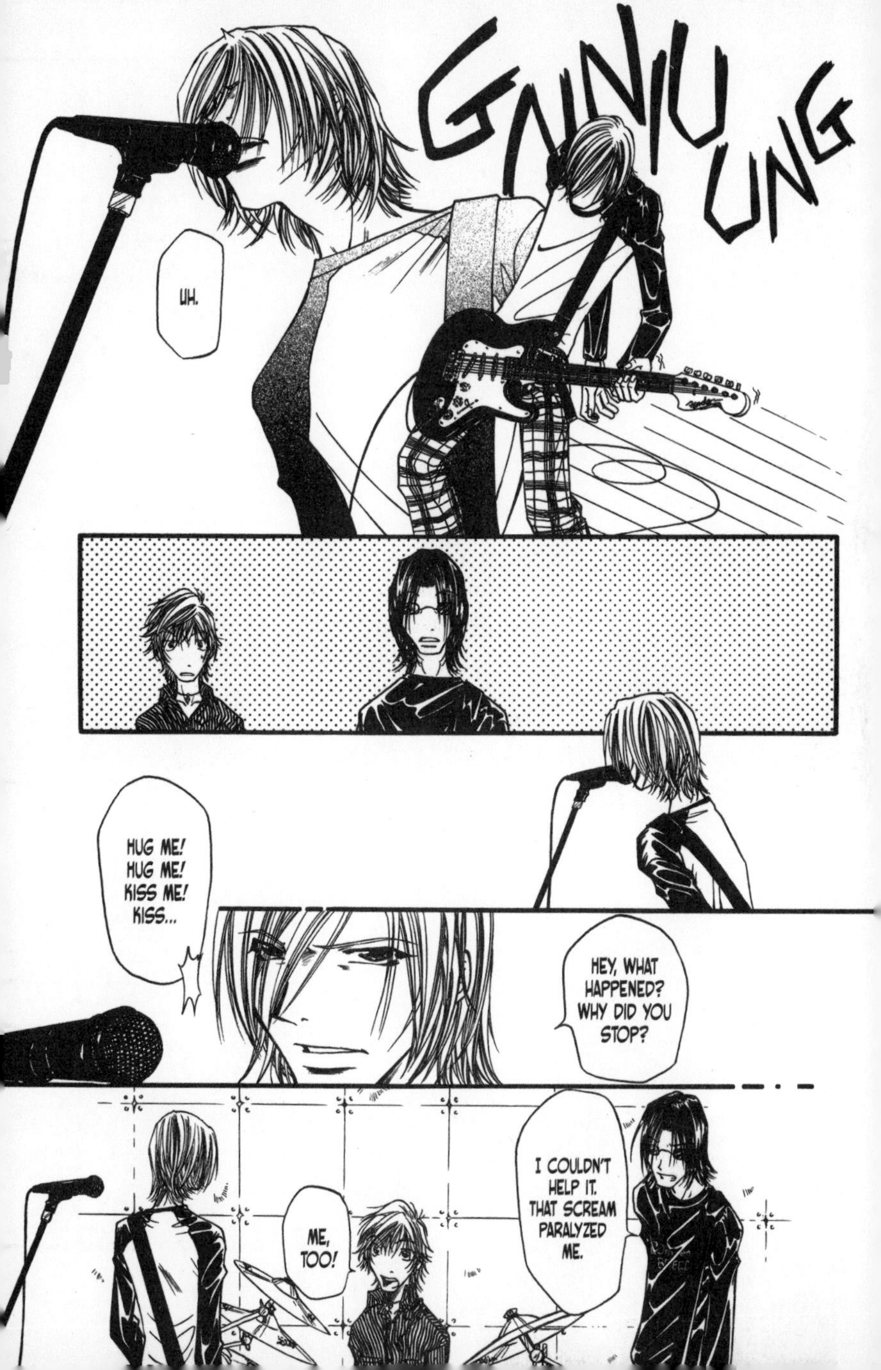
GAWU
UNG
UH.
HUG ME! HUG ME! KISS ME! KISS...
HEY, WHAT HAPPENED? WHY DID YOU STOP?
I COULDN'T HELP IT. THAT SCREAM PARALYZED ME.
ME, TOO!

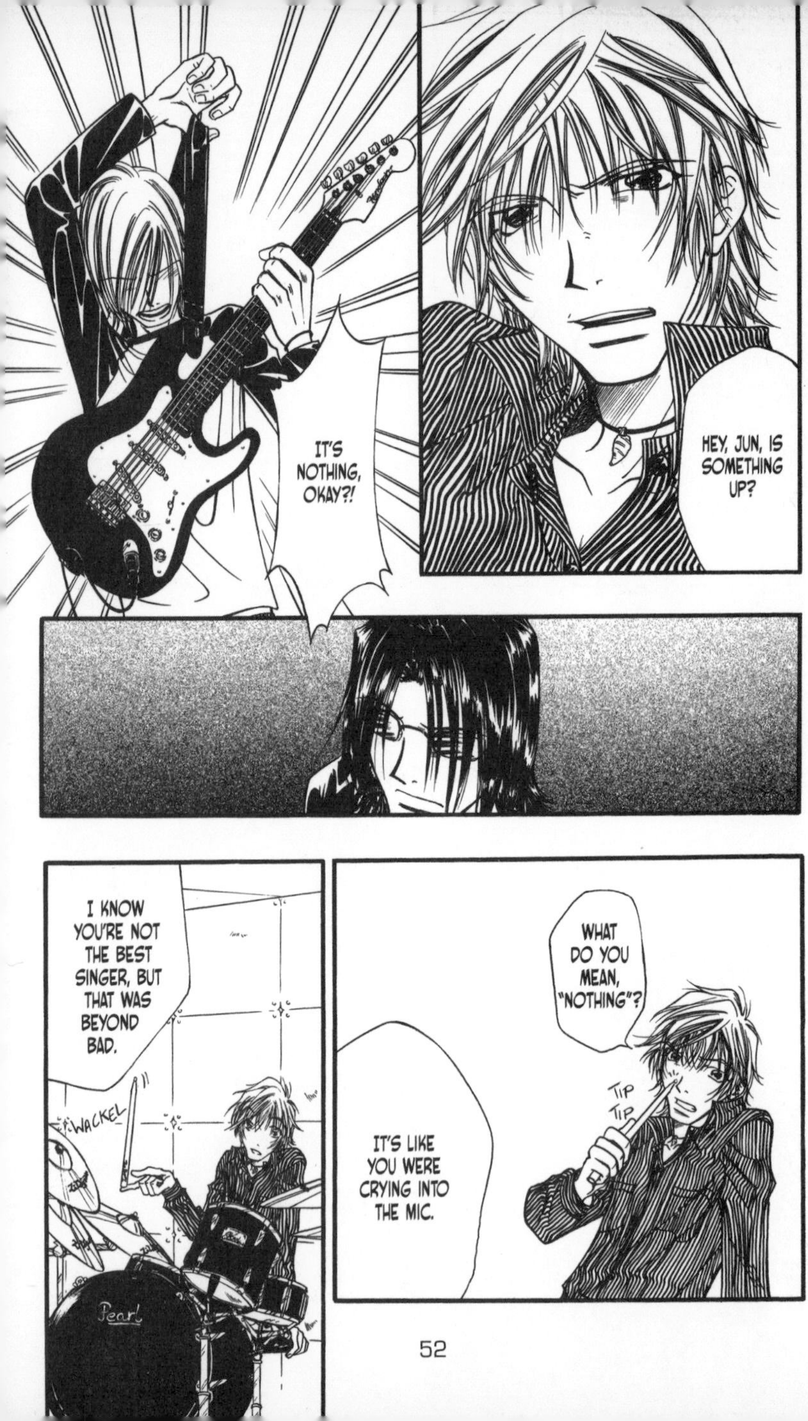
HEY, JUN, IS SOMETHING UP?
IT'S NOTHING, OKAY?!
WHAT DO YOU MEAN, "NOTHING"?
TIP TIP
IT'S LIKE YOU WERE CRYING INTO THE MIC.
I KNOW YOU'RE NOT THE BEST SINGER, BUT THAT WAS BEYOND BAD.
WACKEL

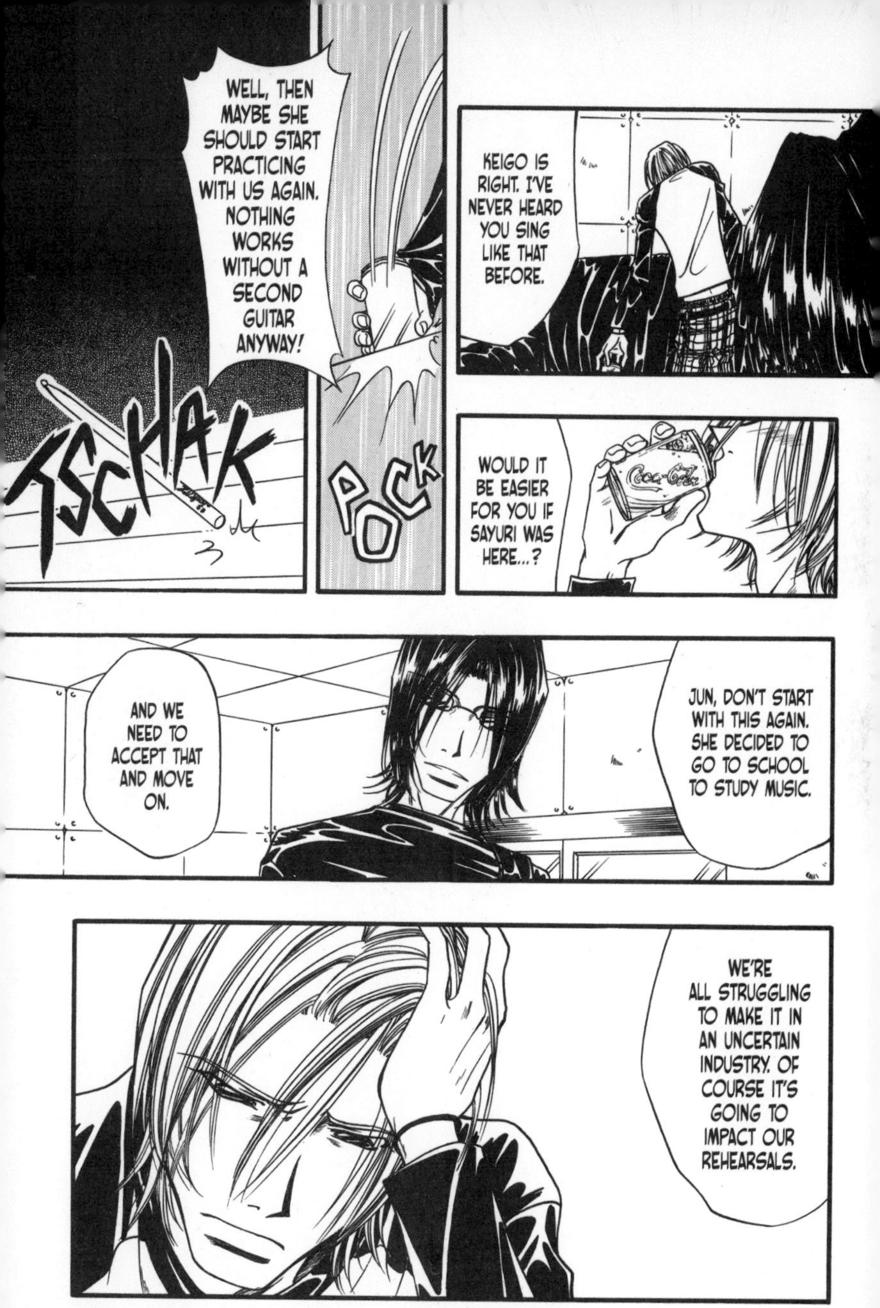
KEIGO IS RIGHT. I'VE NEVER HEARD YOU SING LIKE THAT BEFORE.
WOULD IT BE EASIER FOR YOU IF SAYURI WAS HERE...?
POCK
WELL, THEN MAYBE SHE SHOULD START PRACTICING WITH US AGAIN. NOTHING WORKS WITHOUT A SECOND GUITAR ANYWAY!
TSCHAK
JUN, DON'T START WITH THIS AGAIN. SHE DECIDED TO GO TO SCHOOL TO STUDY MUSIC.
AND WE NEED TO ACCEPT THAT AND MOVE ON.
WE'RE ALL STRUGGLING TO MAKE IT IN AN UNCERTAIN INDUSTRY. OF COURSE IT'S GOING TO IMPACT OUR REHEARSALS.

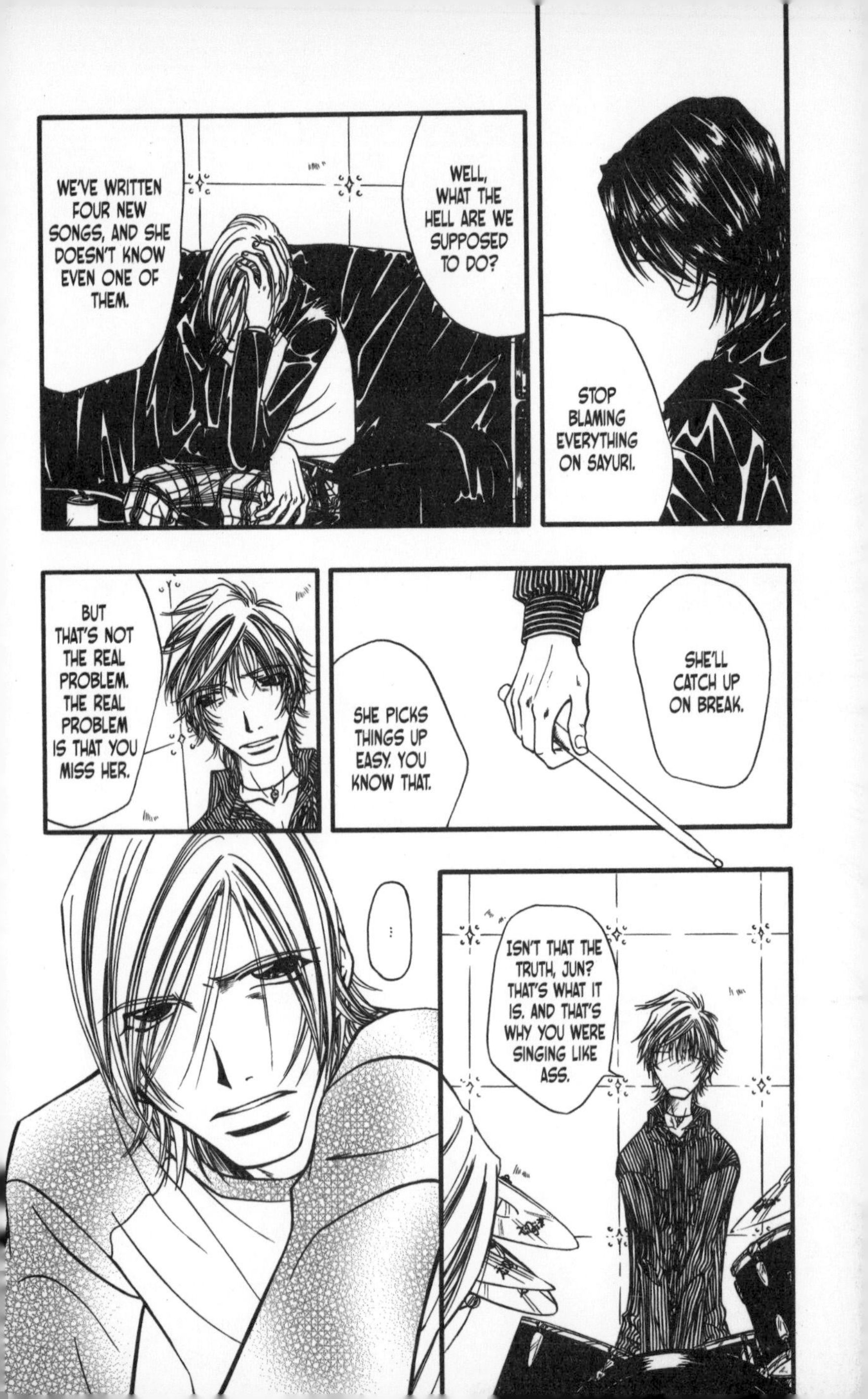
STOP BLAMING EVERYTHING ON SAYURI.
WELL, WHAT THE HELL ARE WE SUPPOSED TO DO?
WE'VE WRITTEN FOUR NEW SONGS, AND SHE DOESN'T KNOW EVEN ONE OF THEM.
SHE'LL CATCH UP ON BREAK.
SHE PICKS THINGS UP EASY. YOU KNOW THAT.
BUT THAT'S NOT THE REAL PROBLEM. THE REAL PROBLEM IS THAT YOU MISS HER.
ISN'T THAT THE TRUTH, JUN? THAT'S WHAT IT IS. AND THAT'S WHY YOU WERE SINGING LIKE ASS.
...

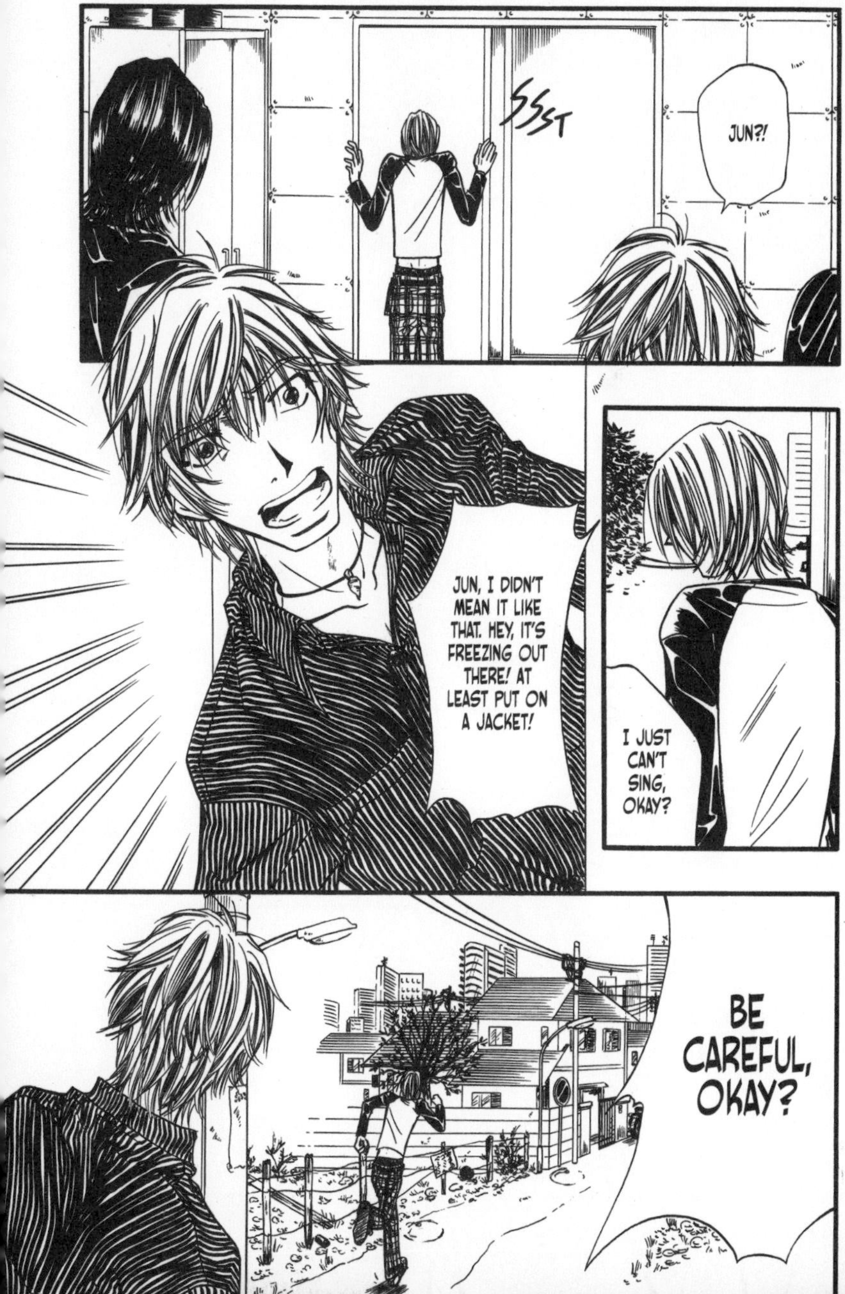
JUN?!
SSST
I JUST CAN'T SING, OKAY?
JUN, I DIDN'T MEAN IT LIKE THAT. HEY, IT'S FREEZING OUT THERE! AT LEAST PUT ON A JACKET!
BE CAREFUL, OKAY?

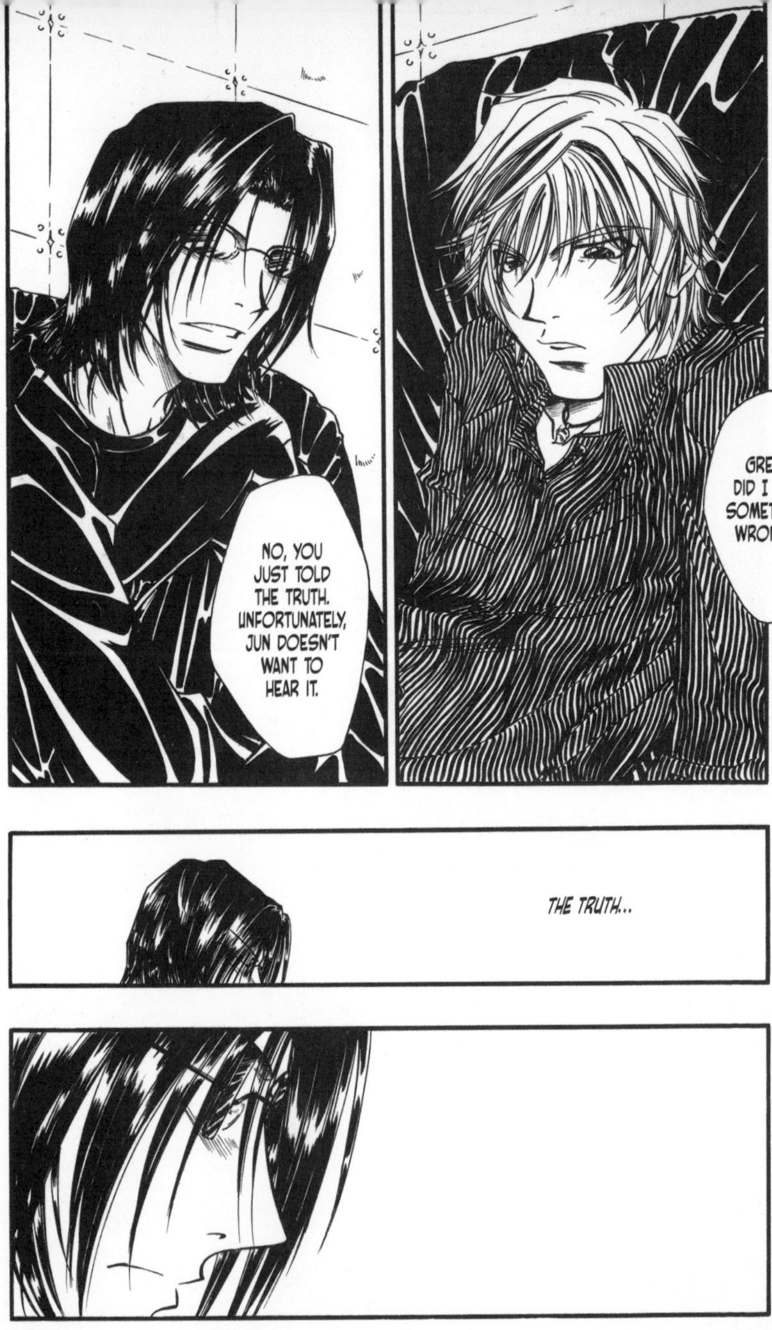
GREAT. DID I SAY SOMETHING WRONG?
NO, YOU JUST TOLD THE TRUTH. UNFORTUNATELY, JUN DOESN'T WANT TO HEAR IT.
THE TRUTH...

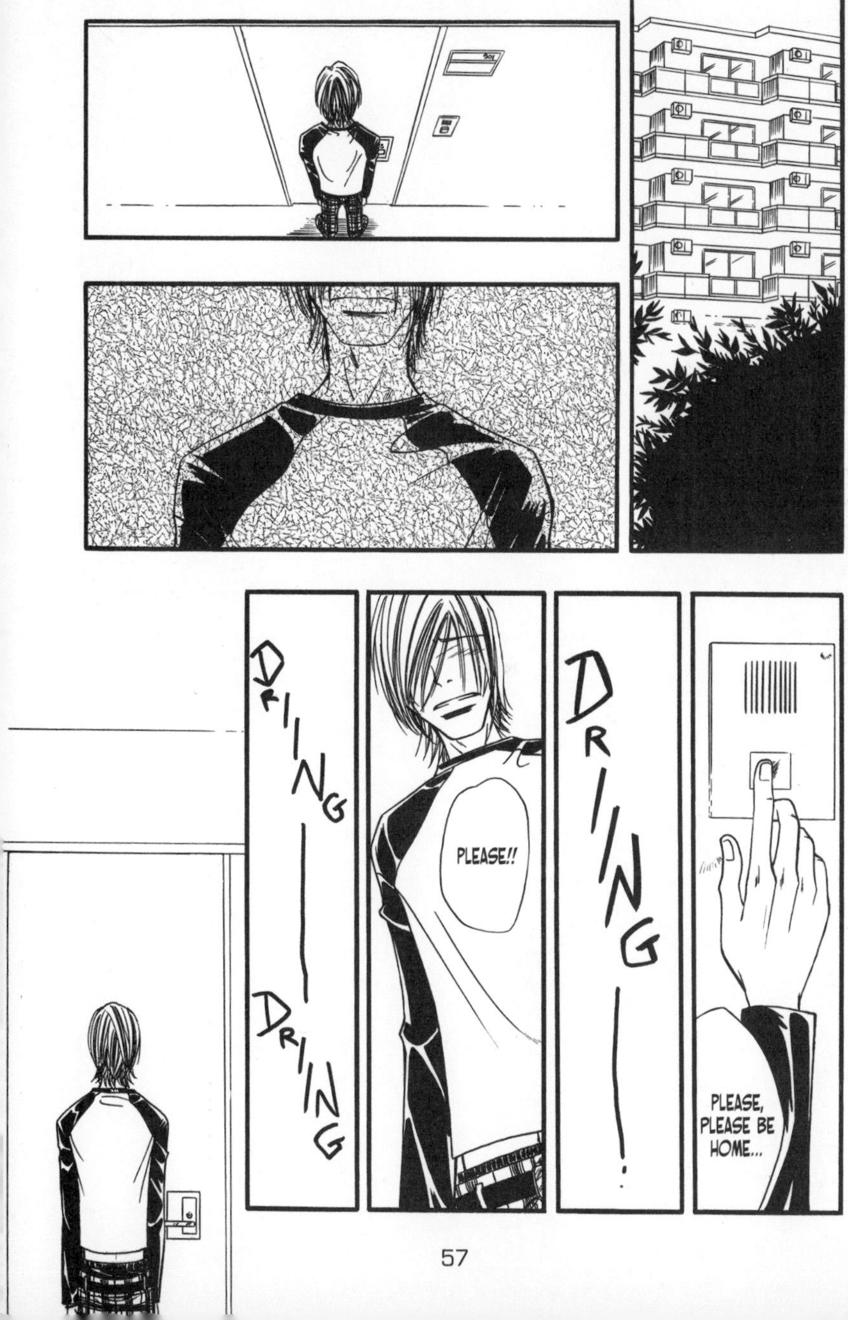
PLEASE, PLEASE BE HOME...
DRIIING—!
PLEASE!!
DRIIING—DRIIING

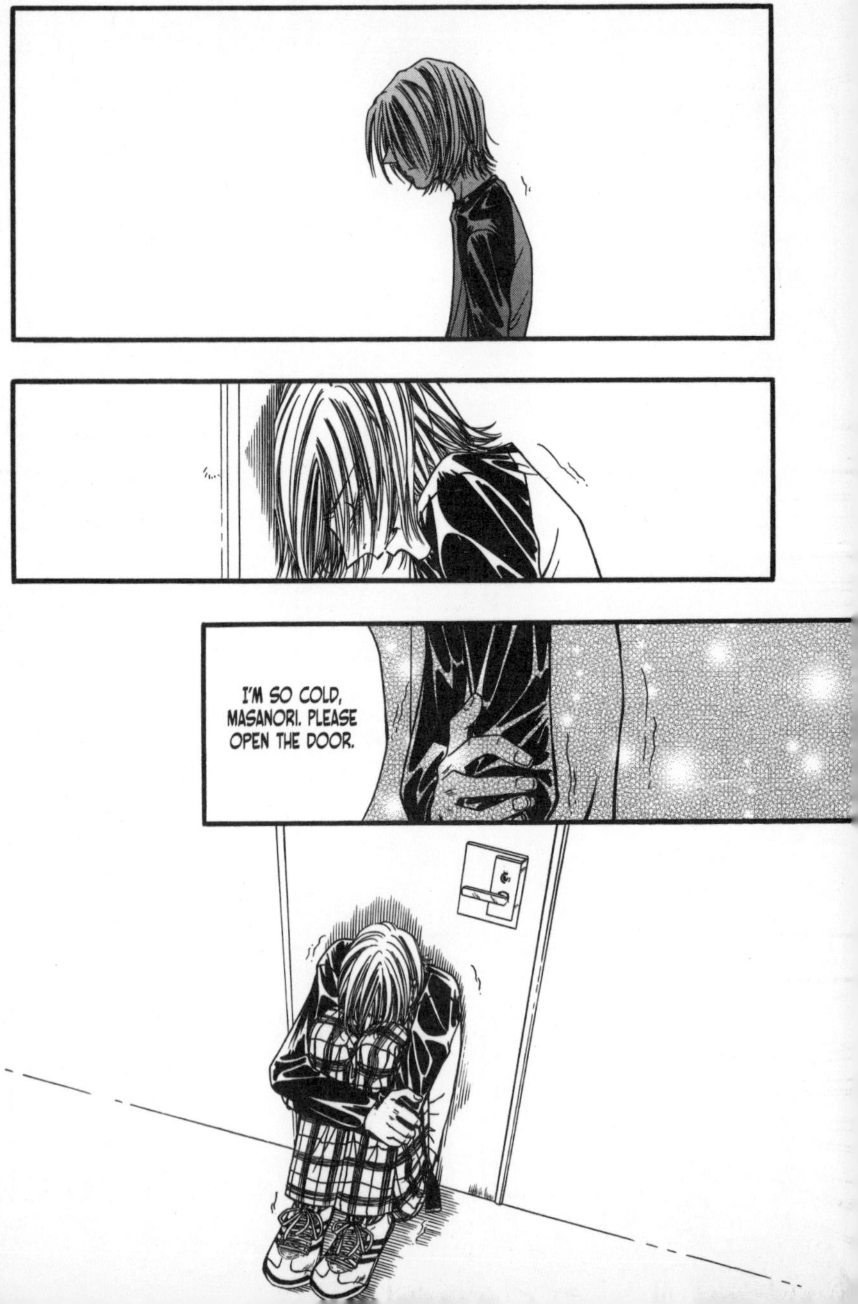
I'M SO COLD, MASANORI. PLEASE OPEN THE DOOR.

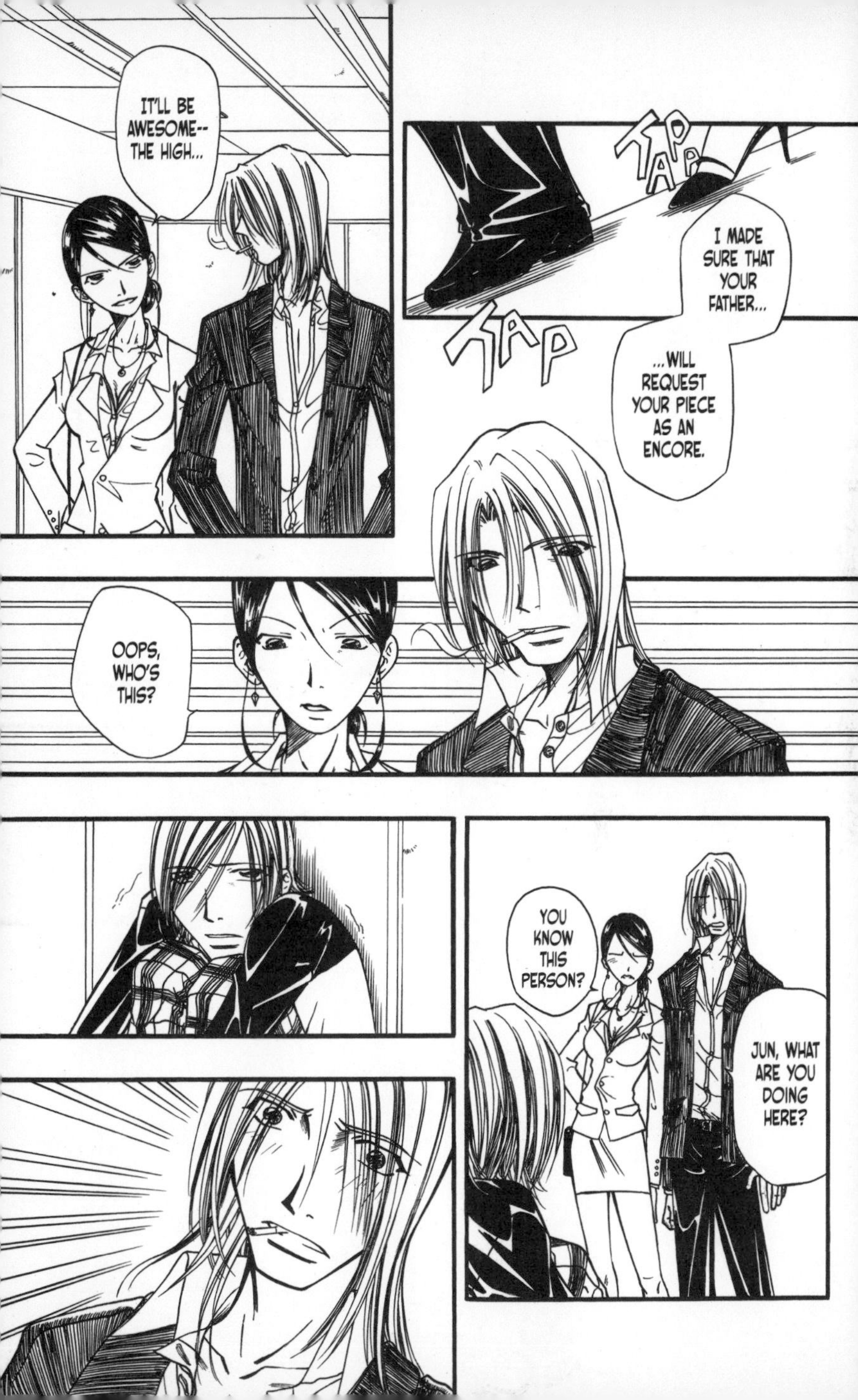
KAPP
KAP
IT'LL BE AWESOME-- THE HIGH...
I MADE SURE THAT YOUR FATHER...
...WILL REQUEST YOUR PIECE AS AN ENCORE.
OOPS, WHO'S THIS?
JUN, WHAT ARE YOU DOING HERE?
YOU KNOW THIS PERSON?

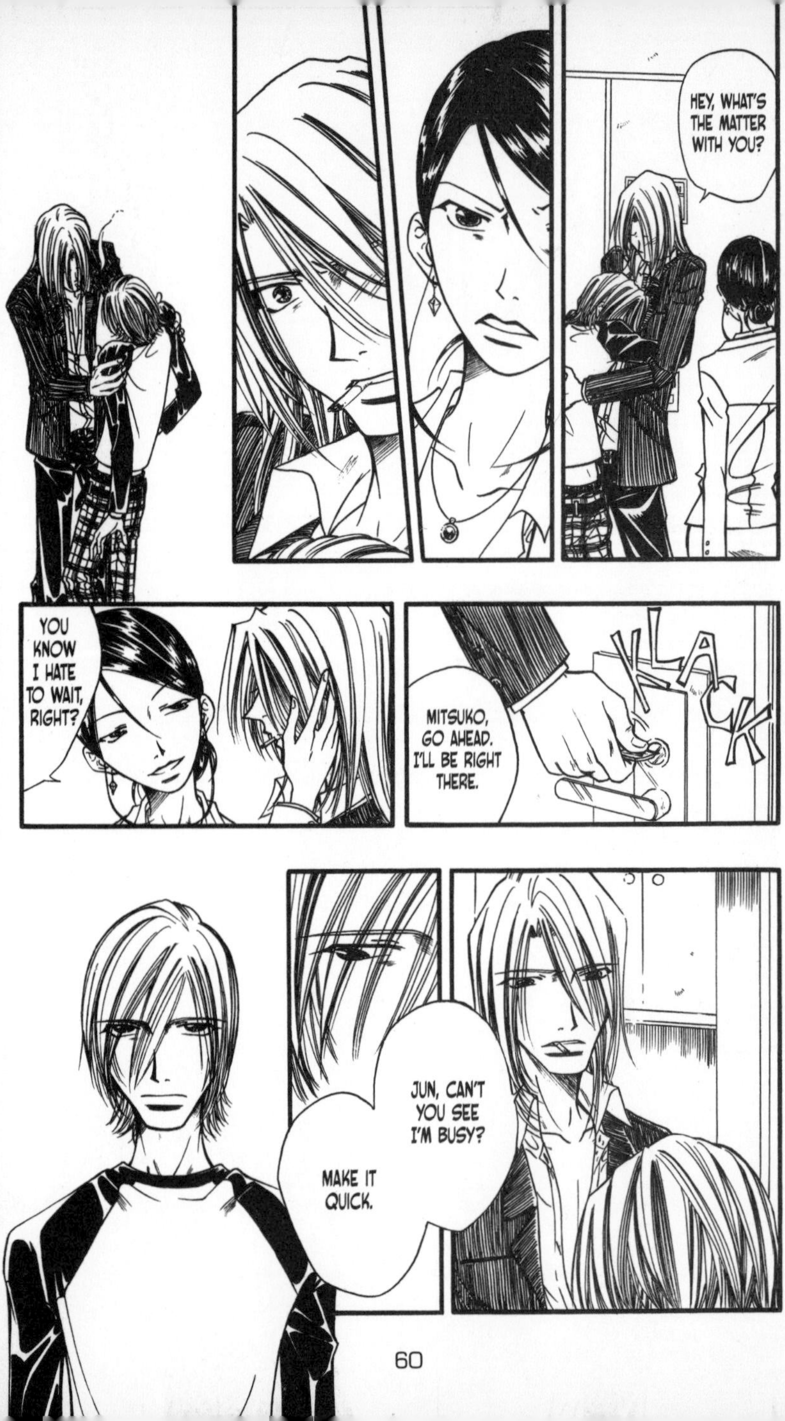
HEY, WHAT'S THE MATTER WITH YOU?
MITSUKO, GO AHEAD. I'LL BE RIGHT THERE.
KLACK
YOU KNOW I HATE TO WAIT, RIGHT?
JUN, CAN'T YOU SEE I'M BUSY?
MAKE IT QUICK.

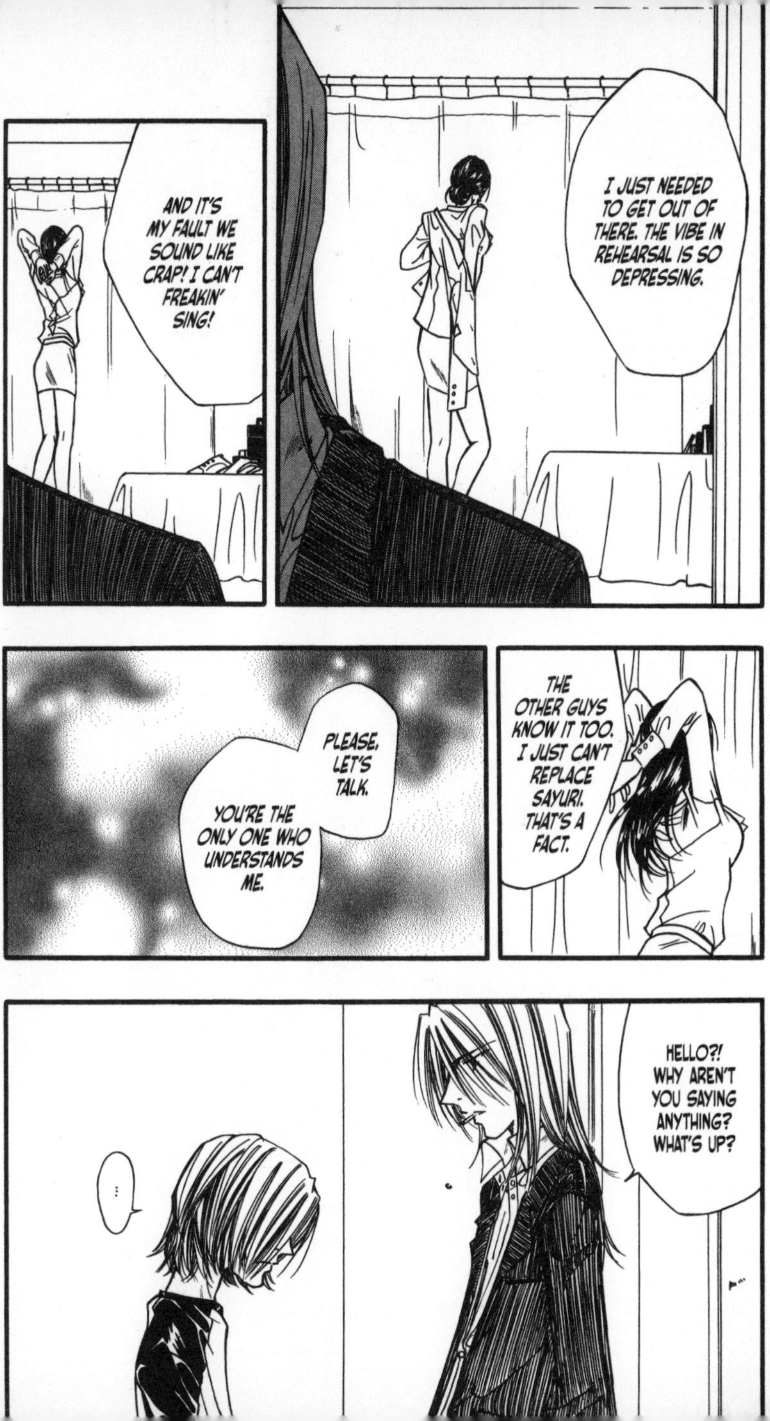
I JUST NEEDED TO GET OUT OF THERE. THE VIBE IN REHEARSAL IS SO DEPRESSING.
AND IT'S MY FAULT WE SOUND LIKE CRAP! I CAN'T FREAKIN' SING!
THE OTHER GUYS KNOW IT TOO. I JUST CAN'T REPLACE SAYURI. THAT'S A FACT.
PLEASE, LET'S TALK.
YOU'RE THE ONLY ONE WHO UNDERSTANDS ME.
HELLO?! WHY AREN'T YOU SAYING ANYTHING? WHAT'S UP?
...

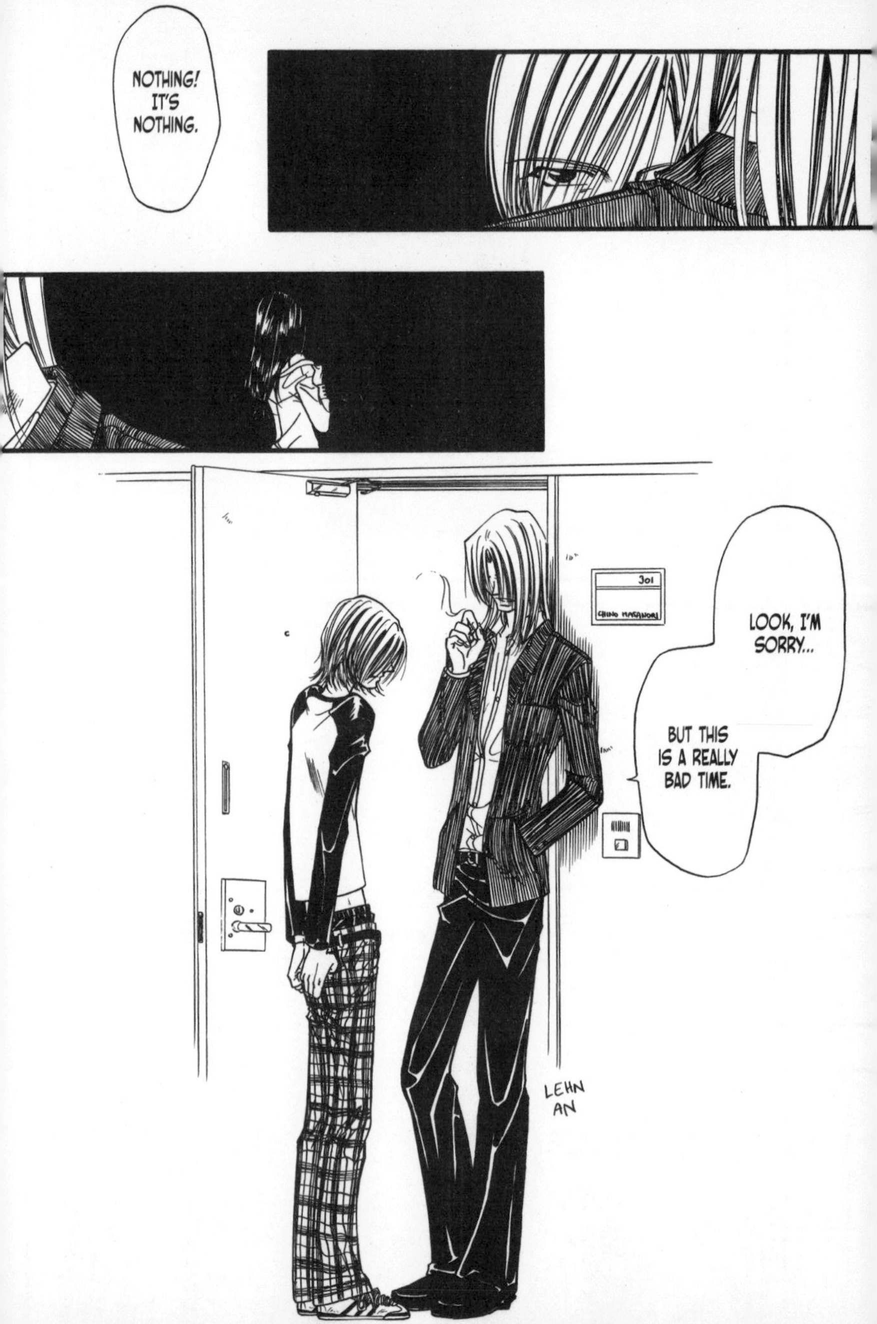
NOTHING! IT'S NOTHING.
LOOK, I'M SORRY...
BUT THIS IS A REALLY BAD TIME.
301
CHINO MASANORI
LEHN AN

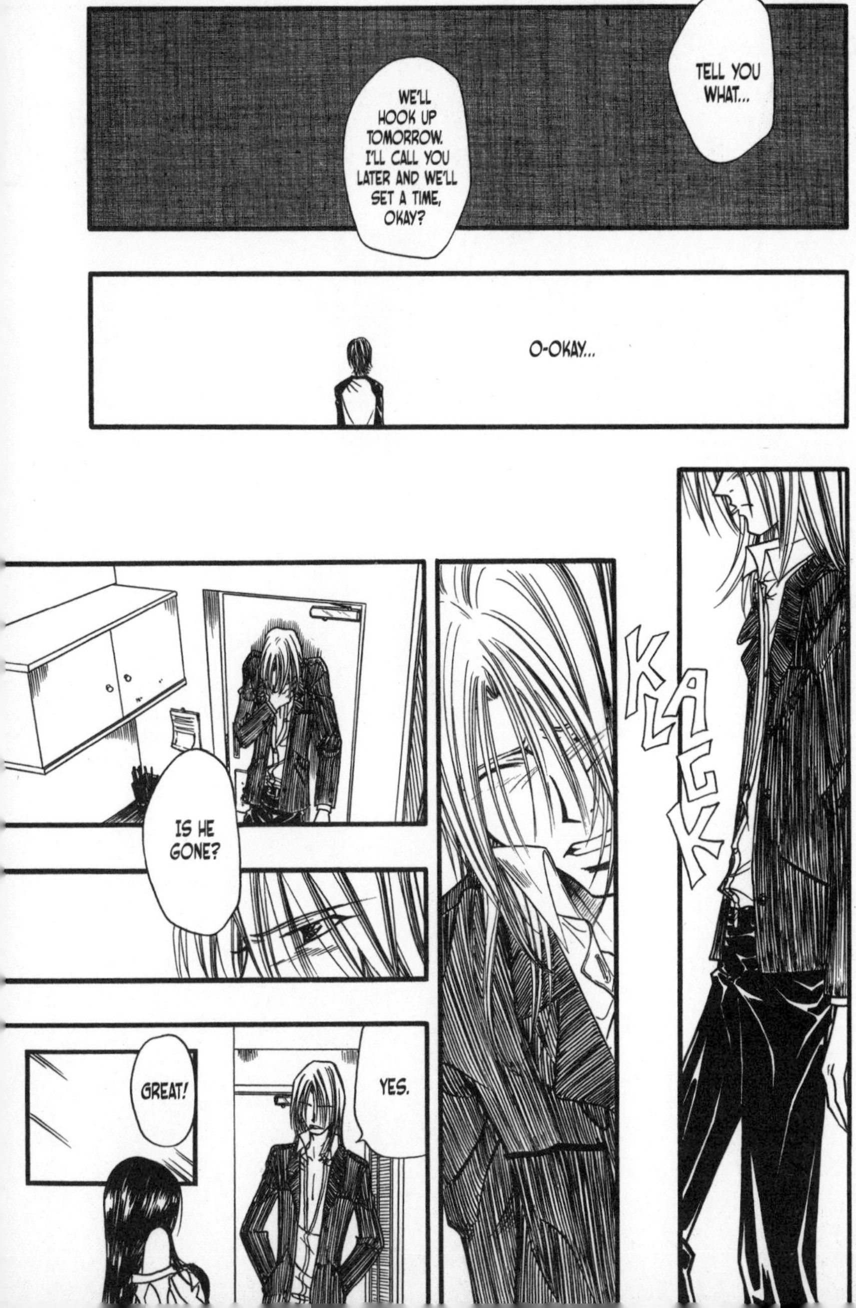
TELL YOU WHAT...
WE'LL HOOK UP TOMORROW. I'LL CALL YOU LATER AND WE'LL SET A TIME, OKAY?
O-OKAY...
KLACK
IS HE GONE?
YES.
GREAT!

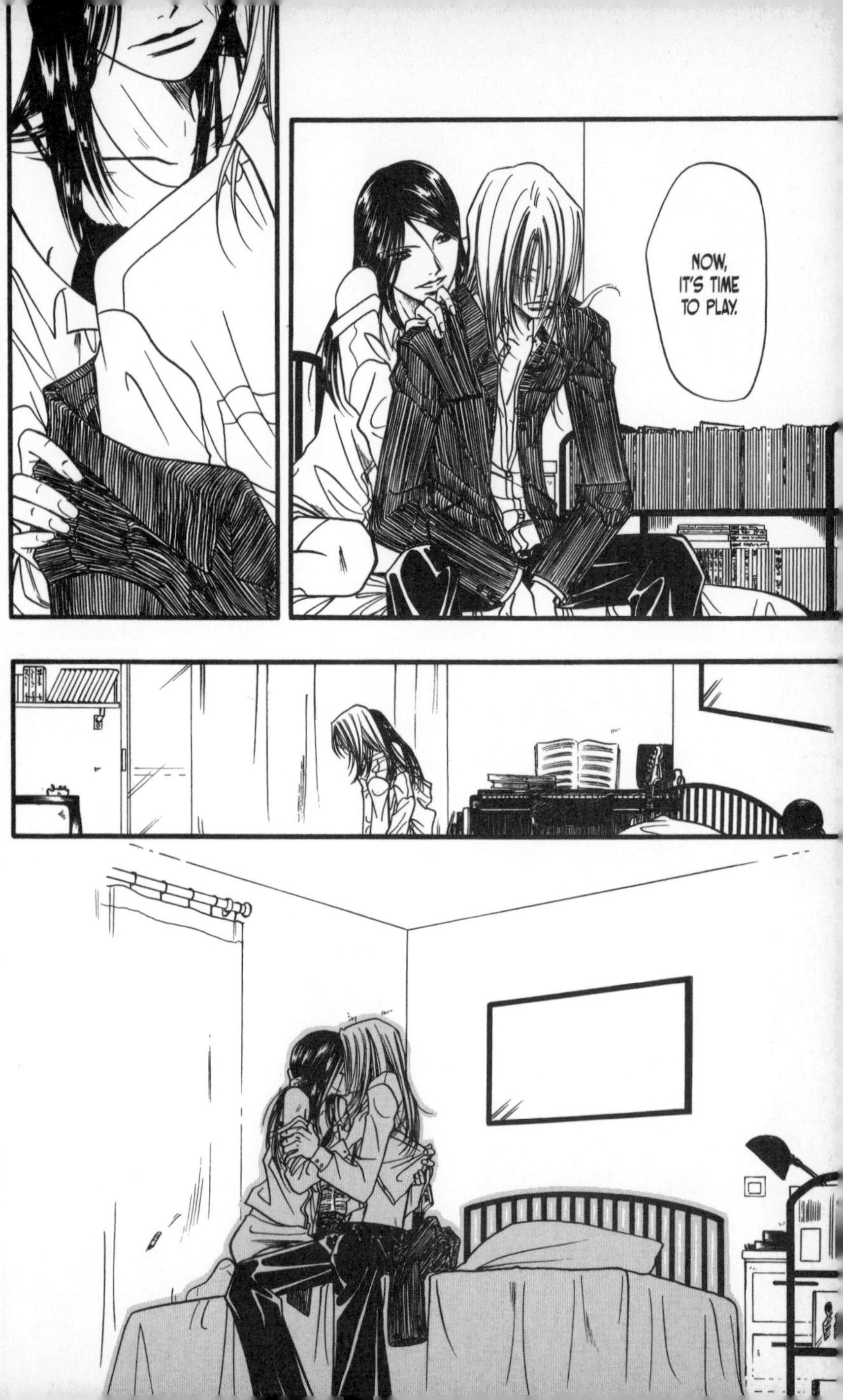
NOW, IT'S TIME TO PLAY.

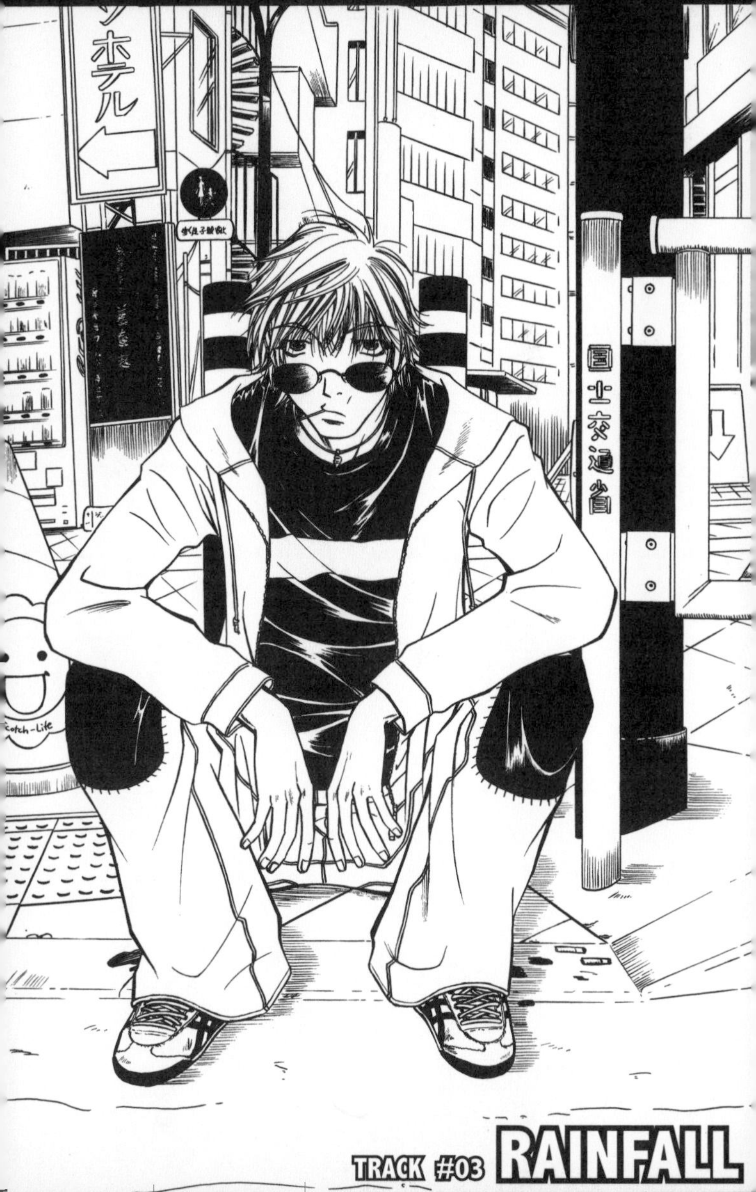
ホテル
国土交通省
TRACK #03 RAINFALL

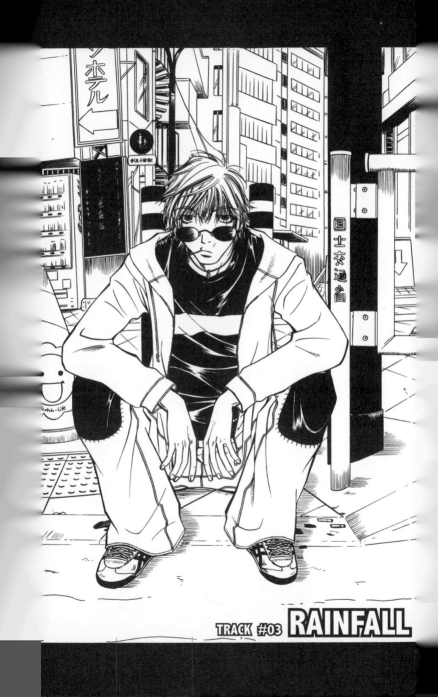

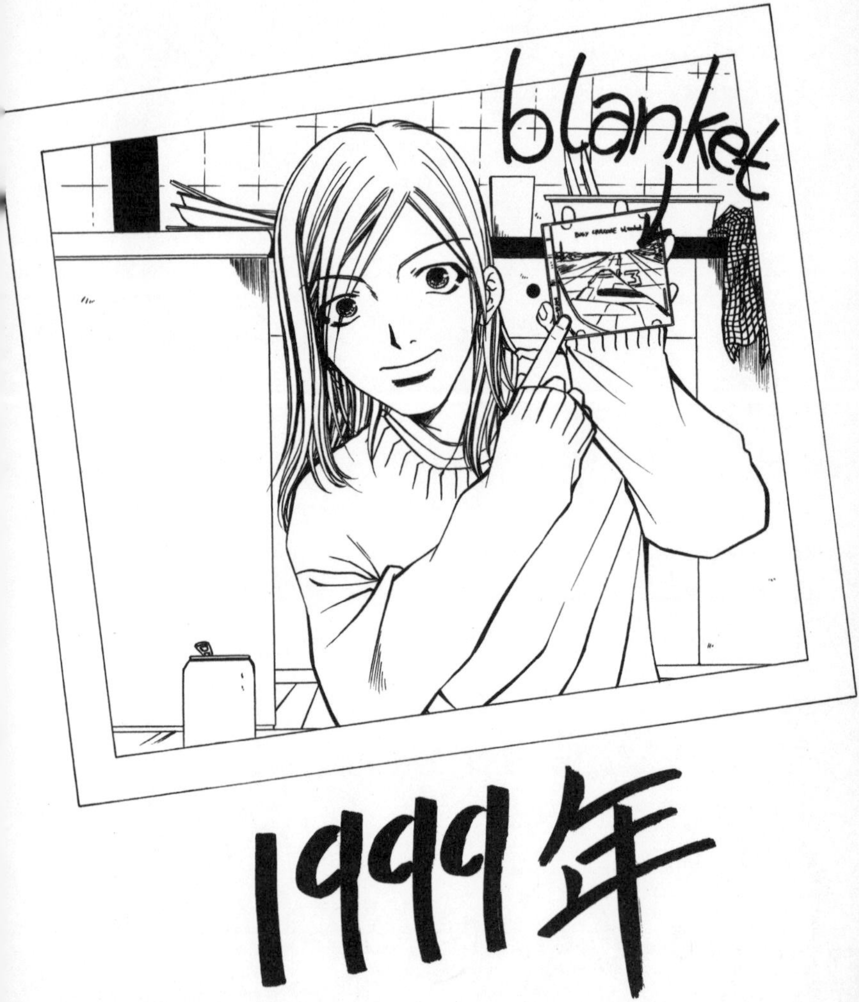
blanket

1999年

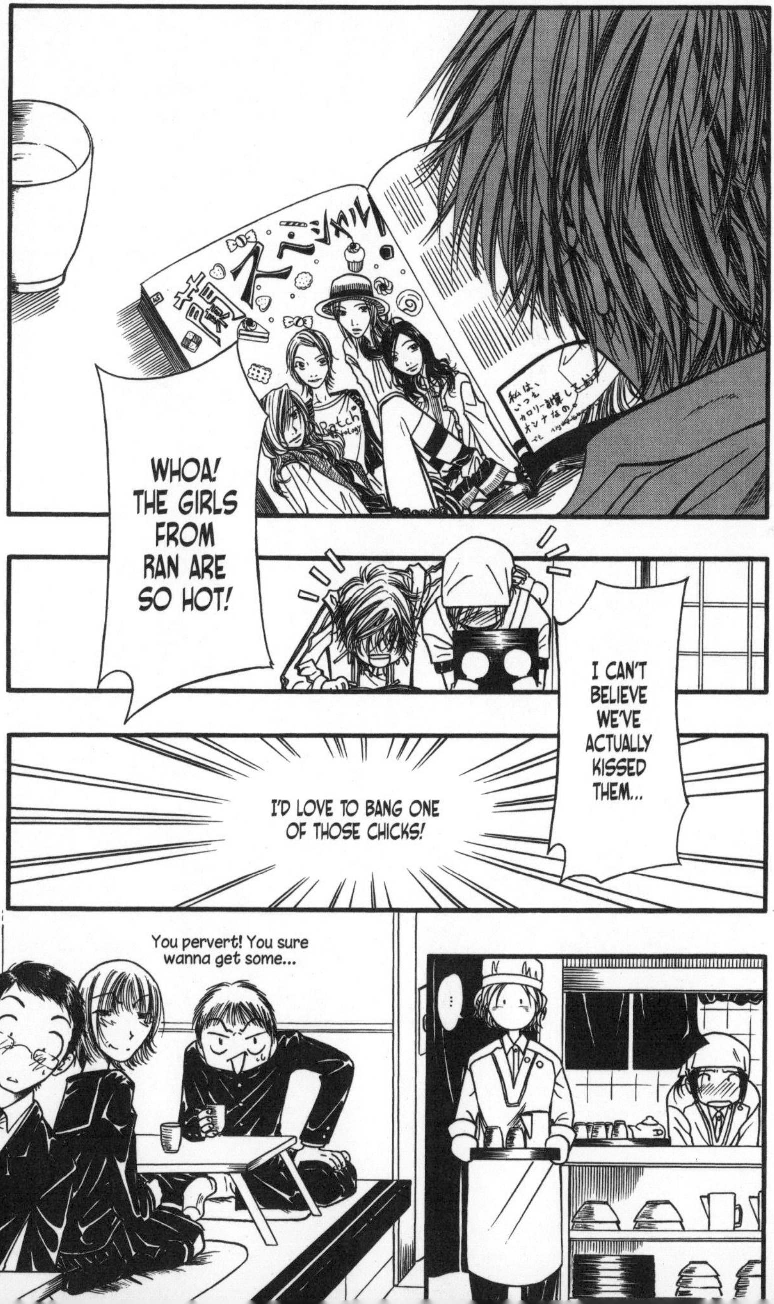
WHOA! THE GIRLS FROM RAN ARE SO HOT!
I CAN'T BELIEVE WE'VE ACTUALLY KISSED THEM...
I'D LOVE TO BANG ONE OF THOSE CHICKS!
...
You pervert! You sure wanna get some...

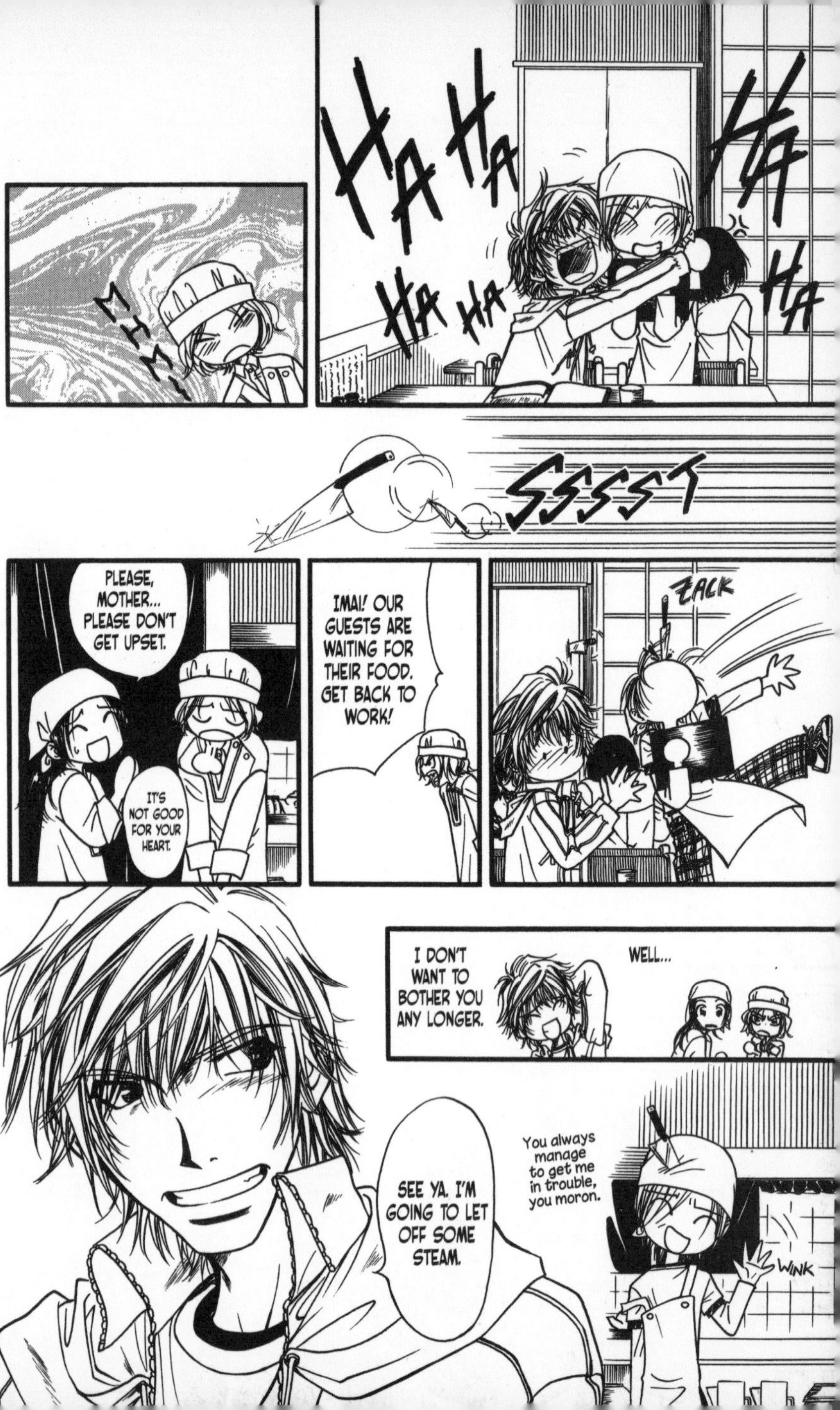
HA HA HA HA HA HA HA
MHM
SSSST
ZACK
IMAI! OUR GUESTS ARE WAITING FOR THEIR FOOD. GET BACK TO WORK!
PLEASE, MOTHER... PLEASE DON'T GET UPSET.
IT'S NOT GOOD FOR YOUR HEART.
I DON'T WANT TO BOTHER YOU ANY LONGER.
WELL...
You always manage to get me in trouble, you moron.
WINK
SEE YA. I'M GOING TO LET OFF SOME STEAM.

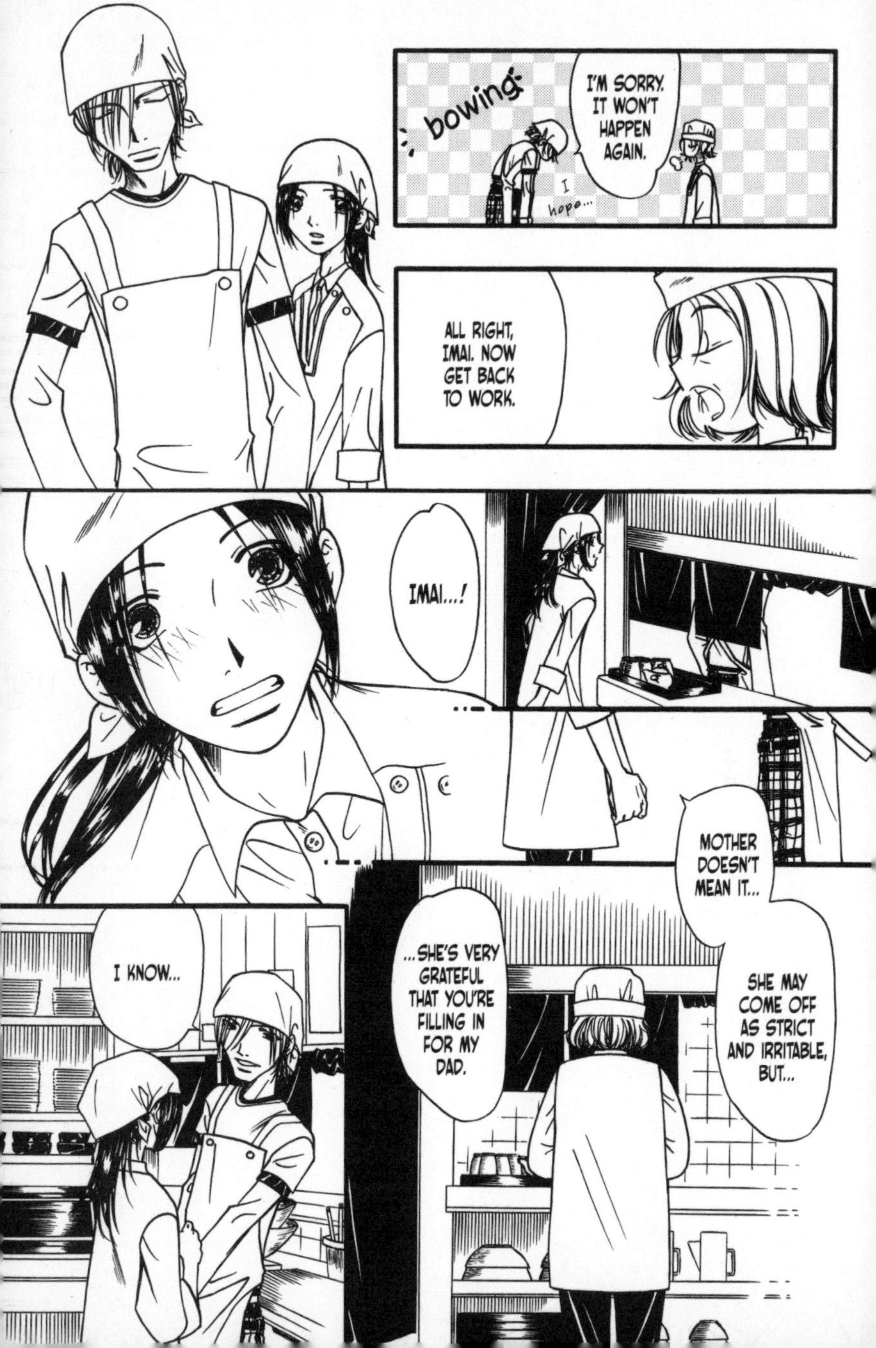
bowing
I'M SORRY. IT WON'T HAPPEN AGAIN.
I hope...
ALL RIGHT, IMAI. NOW GET BACK TO WORK.
IMAI...!
MOTHER DOESN'T MEAN IT...
SHE MAY COME OFF AS STRICT AND IRRITABLE, BUT...
...SHE'S VERY GRATEFUL THAT YOU'RE FILLING IN FOR MY DAD.
I KNOW...

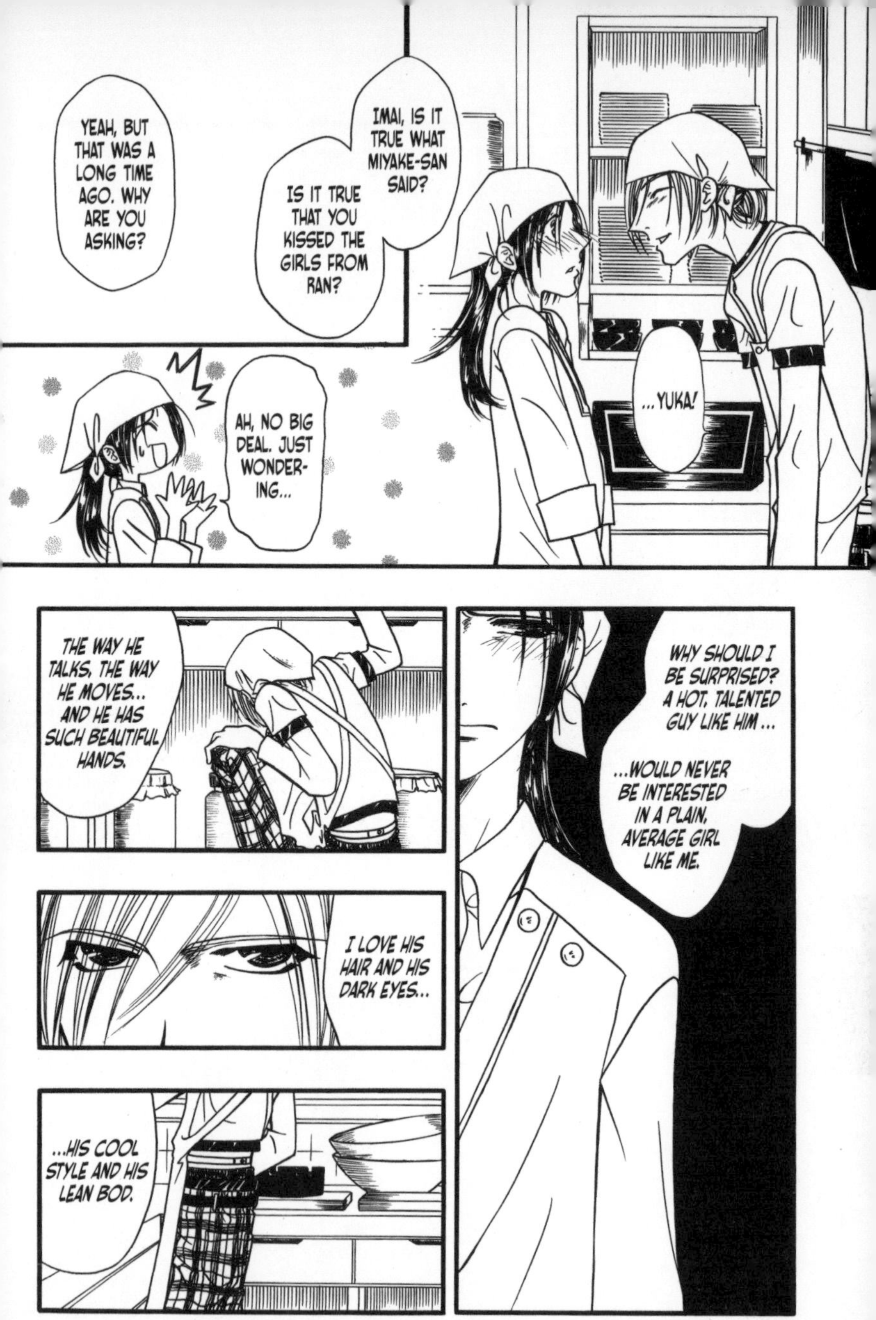
...YUKA!
IMAI, IS IT TRUE WHAT MIYAKE-SAN SAID?
IS IT TRUE THAT YOU KISSED THE GIRLS FROM RAN?
YEAH, BUT THAT WAS A LONG TIME AGO. WHY ARE YOU ASKING?
AH, NO BIG DEAL. JUST WONDER-ING...
WHY SHOULD I BE SURPRISED? A HOT, TALENTED GUY LIKE HIM ...
...WOULD NEVER BE INTERESTED IN A PLAIN, AVERAGE GIRL LIKE ME.
THE WAY HE TALKS, THE WAY HE MOVES... AND HE HAS SUCH BEAUTIFUL HANDS.
I LOVE HIS HAIR AND HIS DARK EYES...
...HIS COOL STYLE AND HIS LEAN BOD.

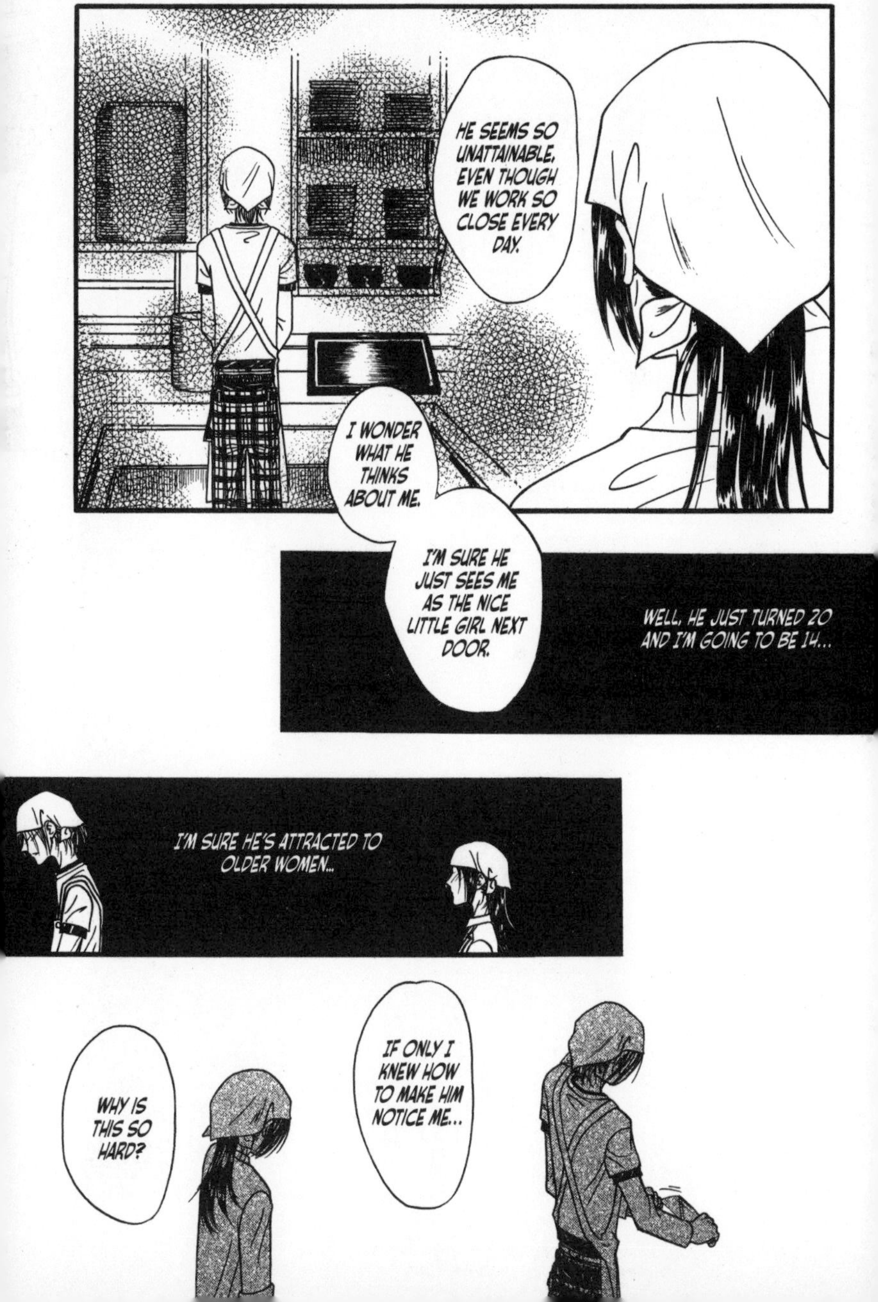
HE SEEMS SO UNATTAINABLE. EVEN THOUGH WE WORK SO CLOSE EVERY DAY.
I WONDER WHAT HE THINKS ABOUT ME.
I'M SURE HE JUST SEES ME AS THE NICE LITTLE GIRL NEXT DOOR.
WELL, HE JUST TURNED 20 AND I'M GOING TO BE 14...
I'M SURE HE'S ATTRACTED TO OLDER WOMEN...
IF ONLY I KNEW HOW TO MAKE HIM NOTICE ME...
WHY IS THIS SO HARD?

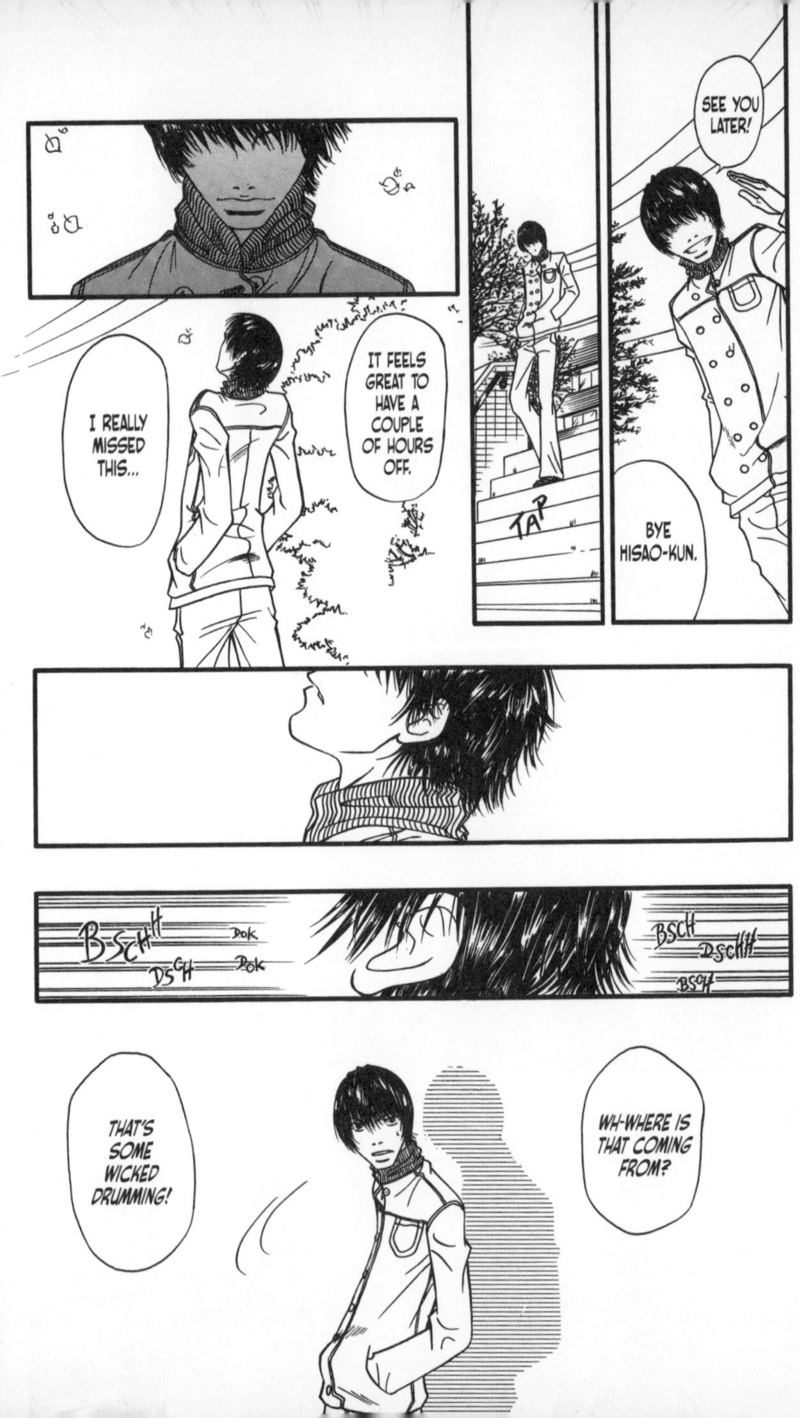
SEE YOU LATER!
BYE HISAO-KUN.
TAP
IT FEELS GREAT TO HAVE A COUPLE OF HOURS OFF.
I REALLY MISSED THIS...
BSCH
DSCHH
BSCH
DOK
DOK
B-SCHH
DSCH
WH-WHERE IS THAT COMING FROM?
THAT'S SOME WICKED DRUMMING!

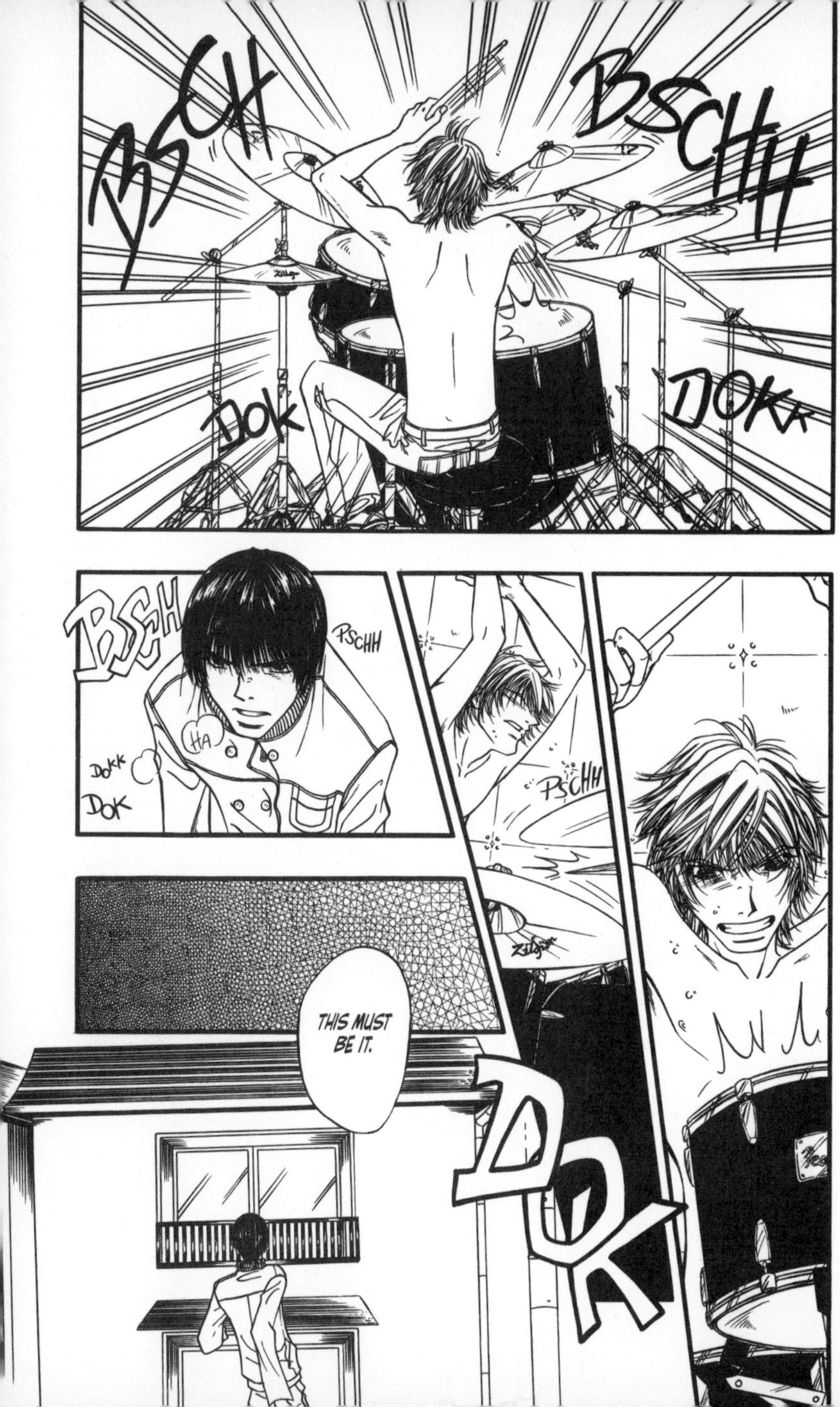
BSCHH
BSCH
DOKKK
DOK
DOK
PSCHH
BSCH
PSCHH
HA
DOKK
DOK
THIS MUST BE IT.

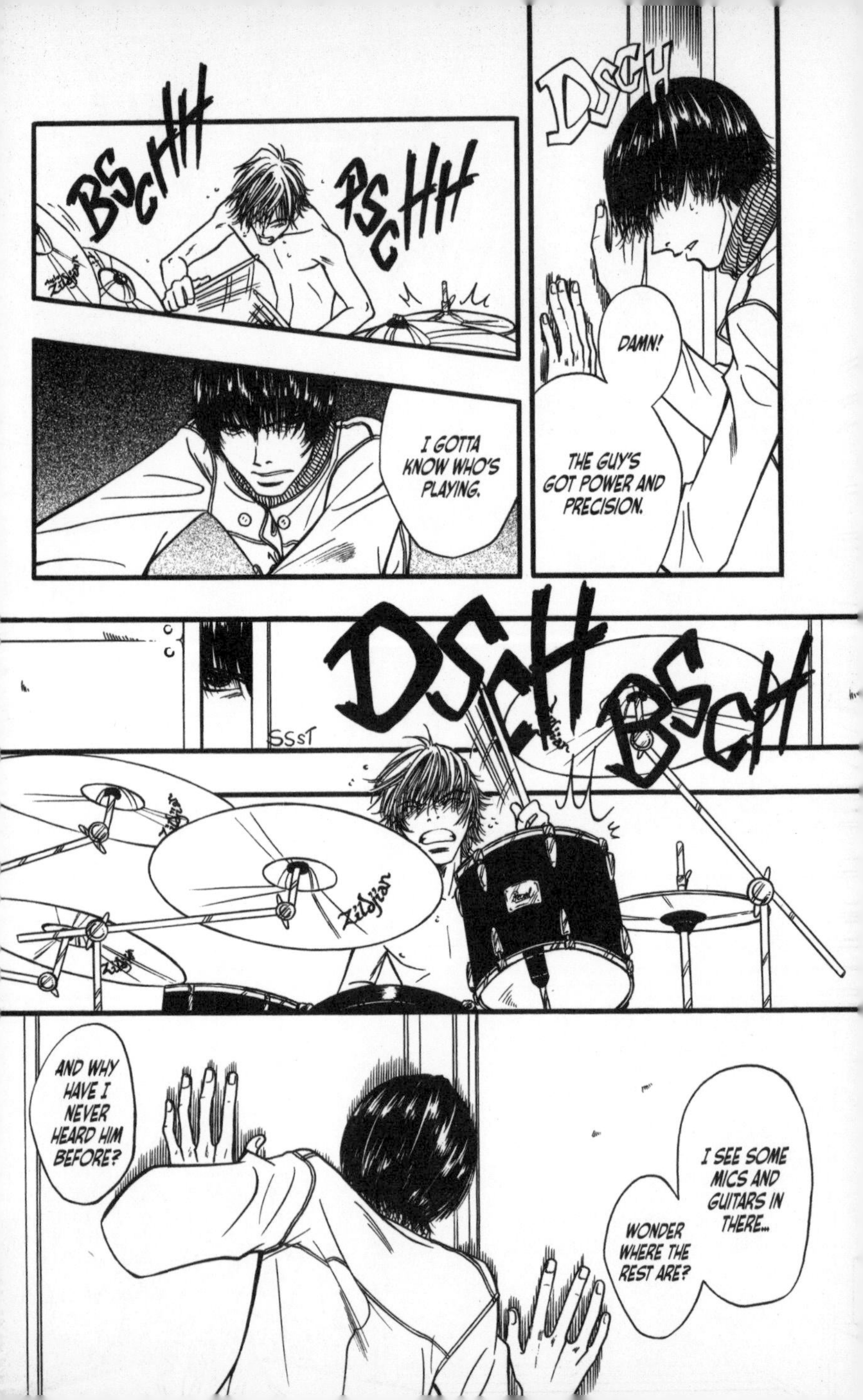
DSCH
DAMN!
THE GUY'S GOT POWER AND PRECISION.
BSCHH
PSCHH
I GOTTA KNOW WHO'S PLAYING.
DSCH
BSCH
SSST
I SEE SOME MICS AND GUITARS IN THERE...
WONDER WHERE THE REST ARE?
AND WHY HAVE I NEVER HEARD HIM BEFORE?

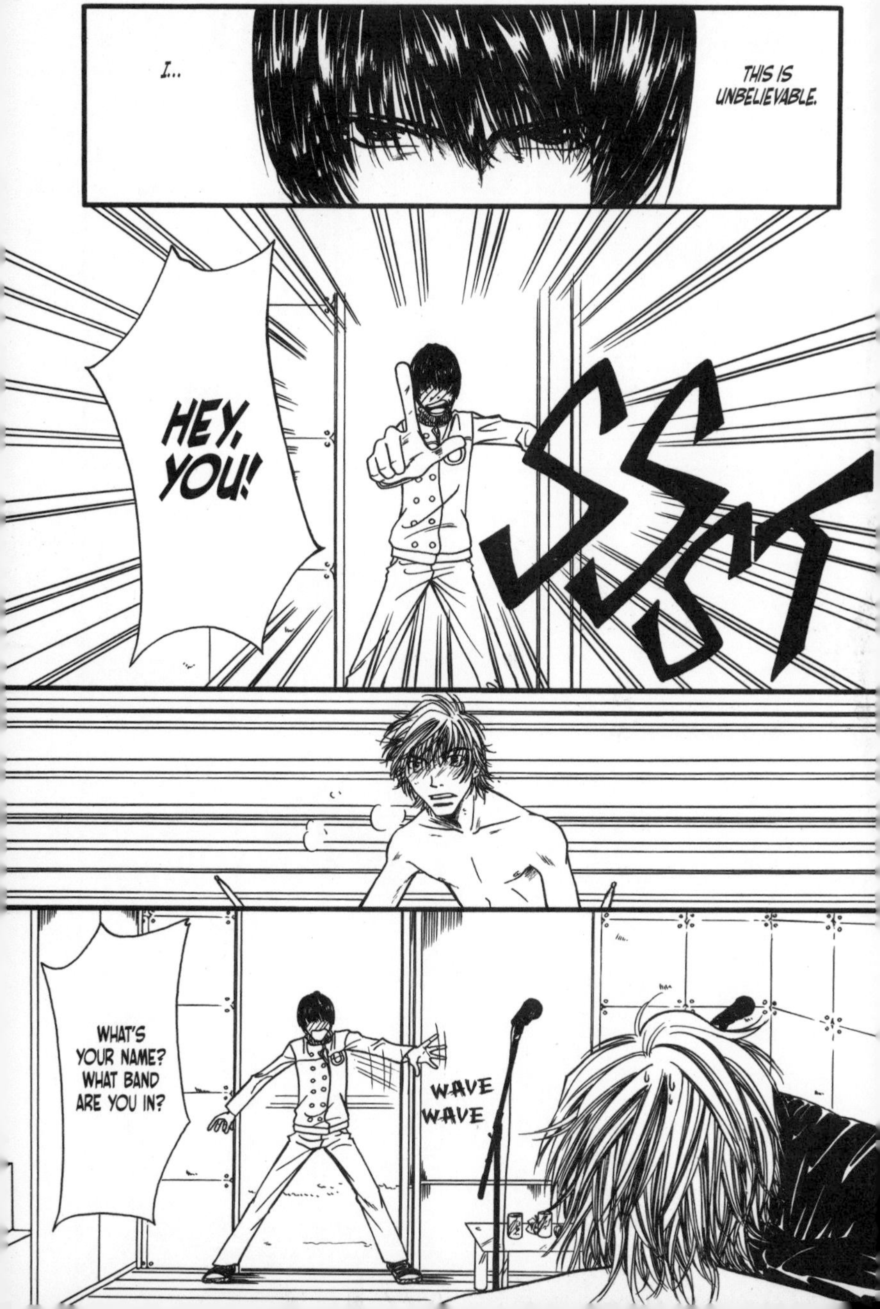
THIS IS UNBELIEVABLE.
I...
SSST
HEY, YOU!
WAVE WAVE
WHAT'S YOUR NAME? WHAT BAND ARE YOU IN?

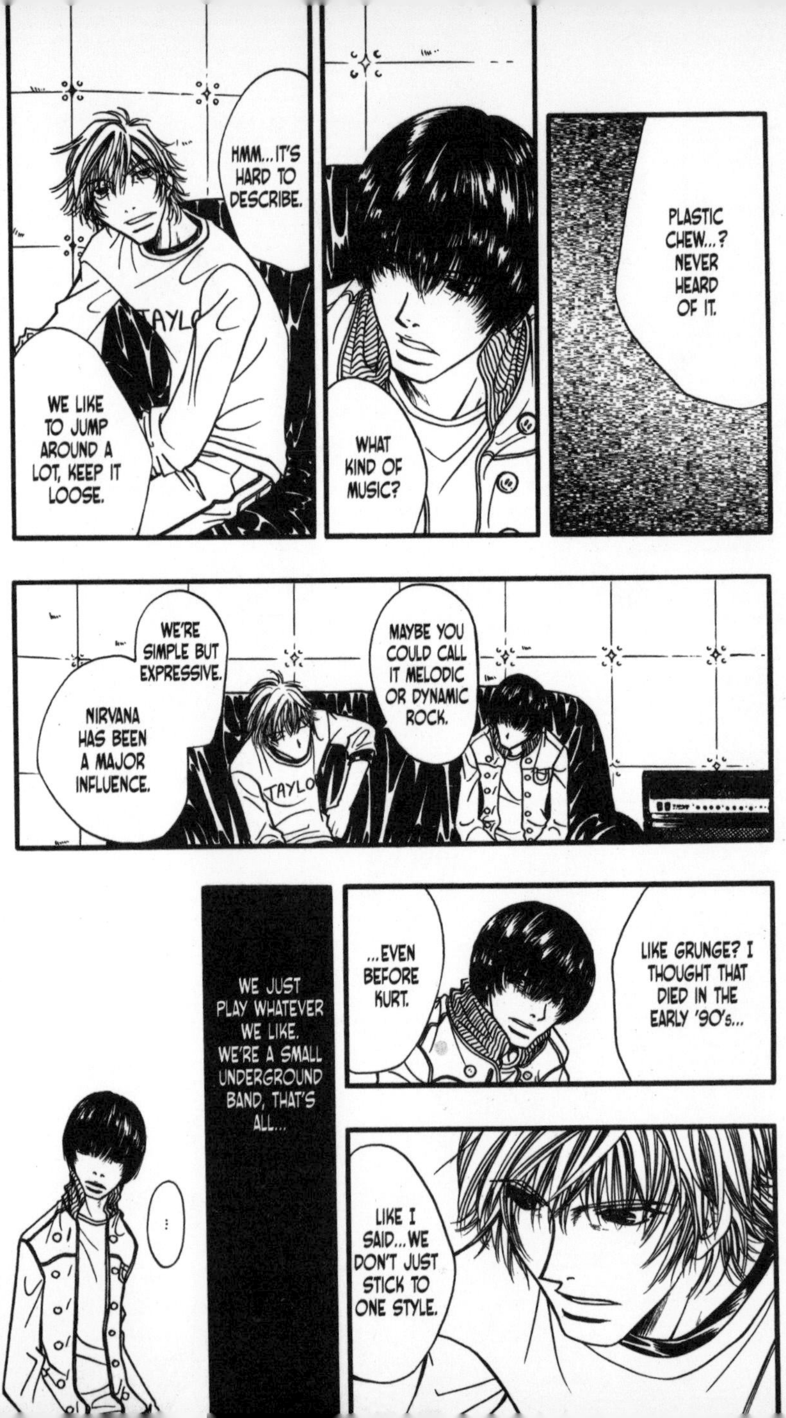
PLASTIC CHEW...? NEVER HEARD OF IT.
WHAT KIND OF MUSIC?
HMM...IT'S HARD TO DESCRIBE.
WE LIKE TO JUMP AROUND A LOT, KEEP IT LOOSE.
MAYBE YOU COULD CALL IT MELODIC OR DYNAMIC ROCK.
WE'RE SIMPLE BUT EXPRESSIVE.
NIRVANA HAS BEEN A MAJOR INFLUENCE.
LIKE GRUNGE? I THOUGHT THAT DIED IN THE EARLY '90's...
...EVEN BEFORE KURT.
LIKE I SAID...WE DON'T JUST STICK TO ONE STYLE.
WE JUST PLAY WHATEVER WE LIKE. WE'RE A SMALL UNDERGROUND BAND, THAT'S ALL...
...

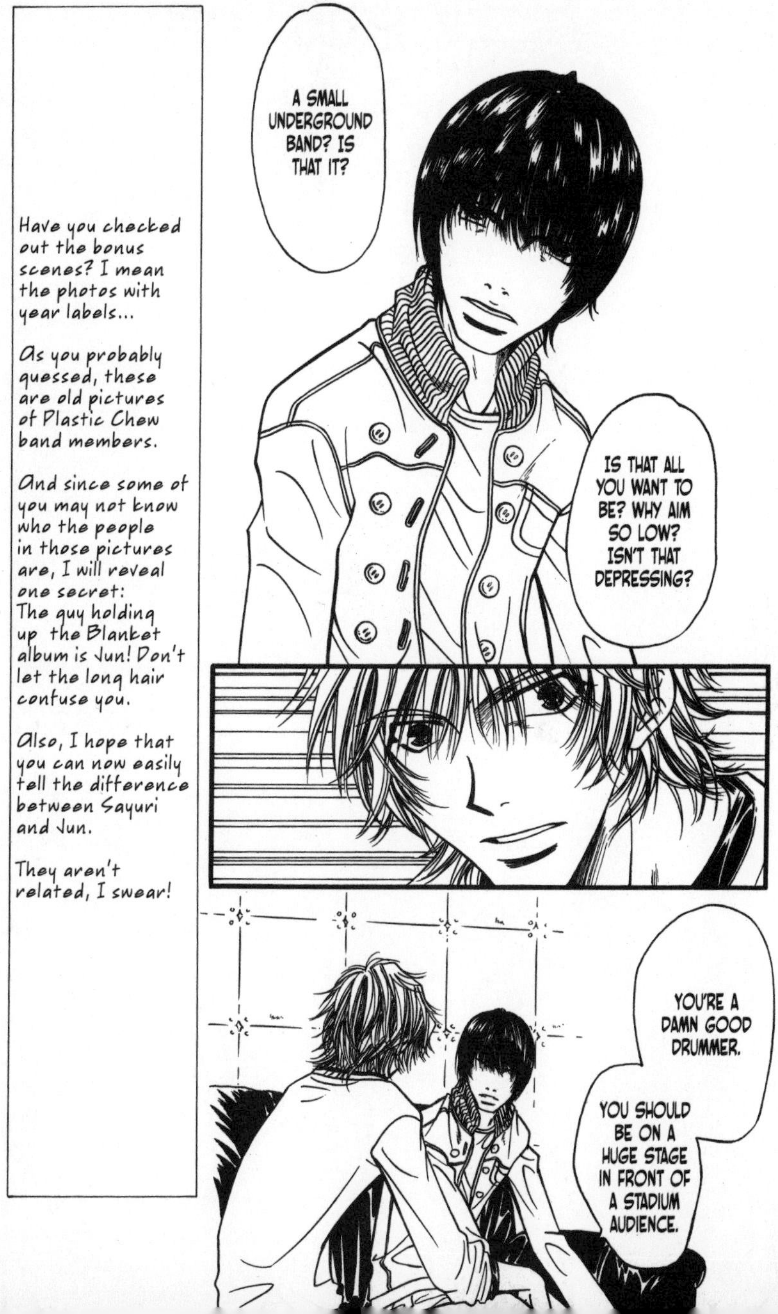
A SMALL UNDERGROUND BAND? IS THAT IT?
IS THAT ALL YOU WANT TO BE? WHY AIM SO LOW? ISN'T THAT DEPRESSING?
YOU'RE A DAMN GOOD DRUMMER.
YOU SHOULD BE ON A HUGE STAGE IN FRONT OF A STADIUM AUDIENCE.

Have you checked out the bonus scenes? I mean the photos with year labels...

As you probably guessed, these are old pictures of Plastic Chew band members.

And since some of you may not know who the people in those pictures are, I will reveal one secret: The guy holding up the Blanket album is Jun! Don't let the long hair confuse you.

Also, I hope that you can now easily tell the difference between Sayuri and Jun.

They aren't related, I swear!

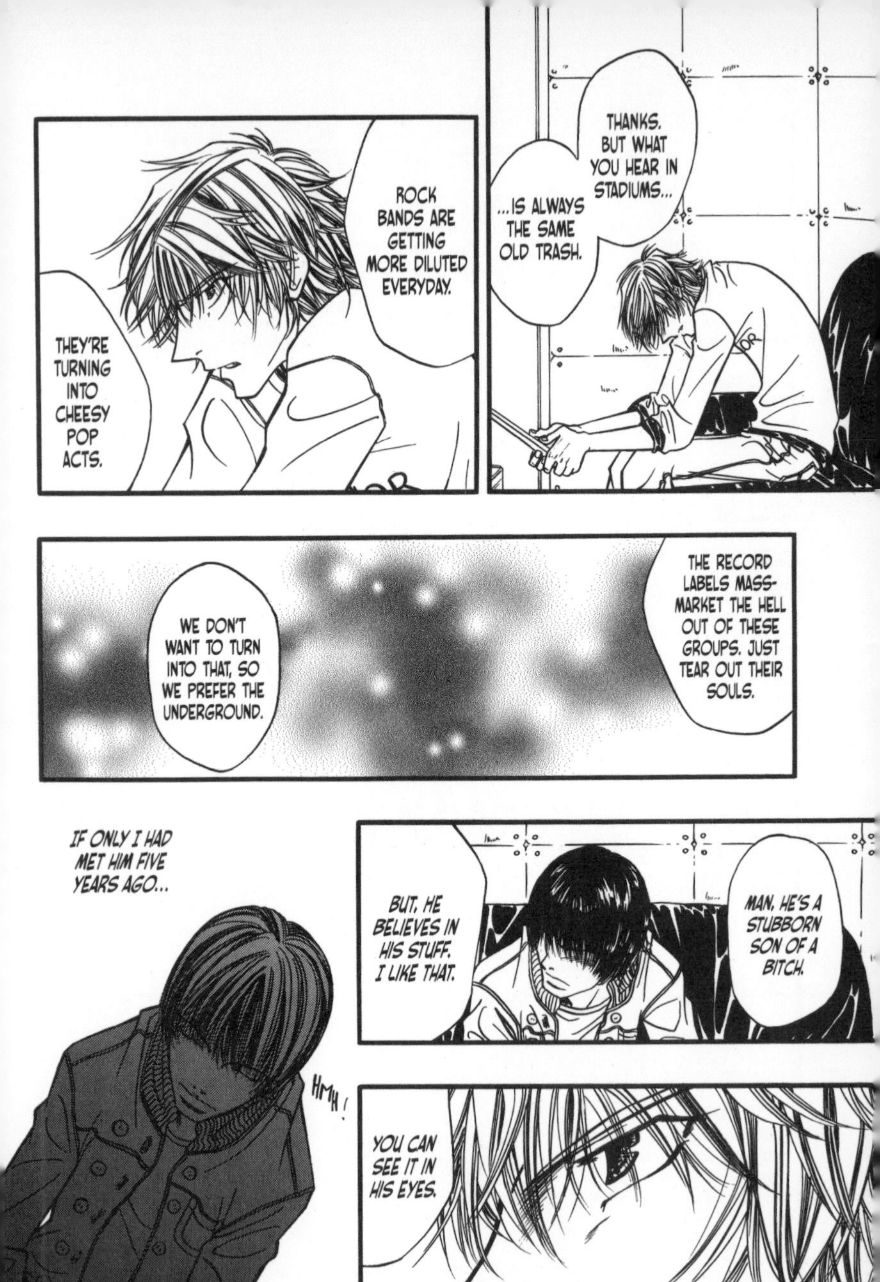
THANKS. BUT WHAT YOU HEAR IN STADIUMS...
...IS ALWAYS THE SAME OLD TRASH.
ROCK BANDS ARE GETTING MORE DILUTED EVERYDAY.
THEY'RE TURNING INTO CHEESY POP ACTS.
THE RECORD LABELS MASS-MARKET THE HELL OUT OF THESE GROUPS. JUST TEAR OUT THEIR SOULS.
WE DON'T WANT TO TURN INTO THAT, SO WE PREFER THE UNDERGROUND.
MAN, HE'S A STUBBORN SON OF A BITCH.
BUT, HE BELIEVES IN HIS STUFF. I LIKE THAT.
YOU CAN SEE IT IN HIS EYES.
IF ONLY I HAD MET HIM FIVE YEARS AGO...
HMH!

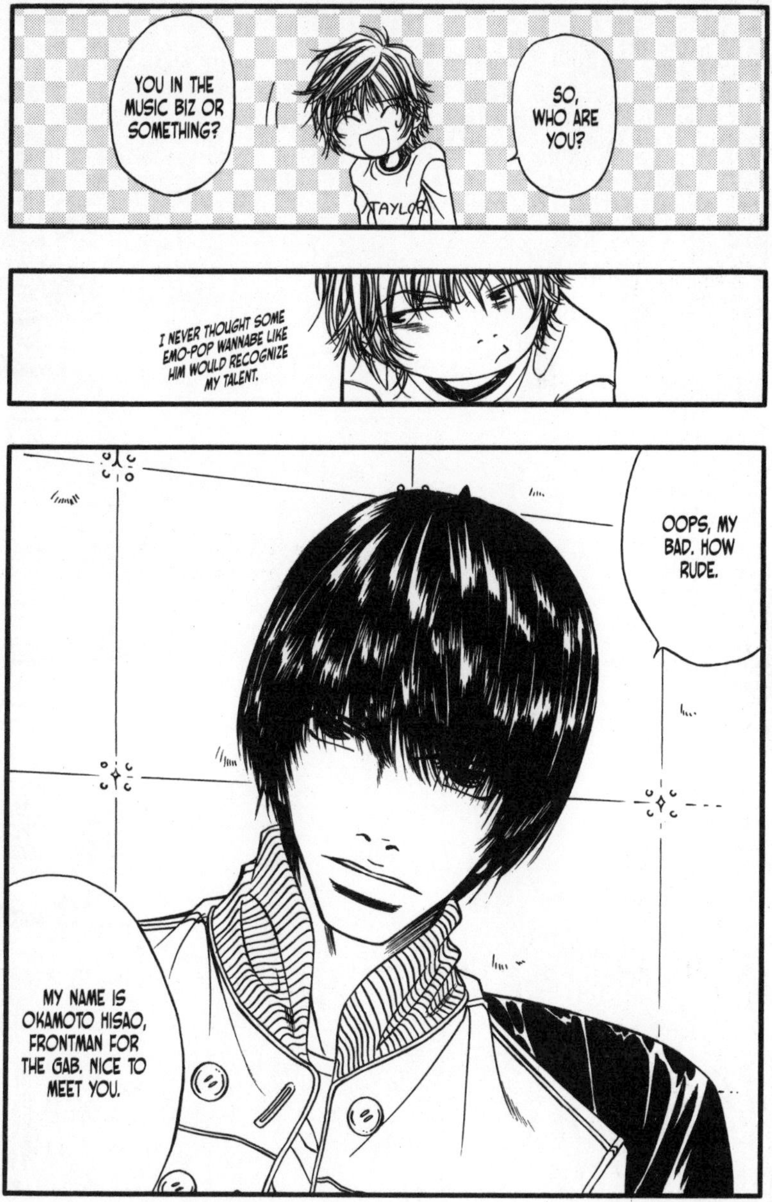
SO, WHO ARE YOU?
YOU IN THE MUSIC BIZ OR SOMETHING?
TAYLOR
I NEVER THOUGHT SOME EMO-POP WANNABE LIKE HIM WOULD RECOGNIZE MY TALENT.
OOPS, MY BAD. HOW RUDE.
MY NAME IS OKAMOTO HISAO, FRONTMAN FOR THE GAB. NICE TO MEET YOU.

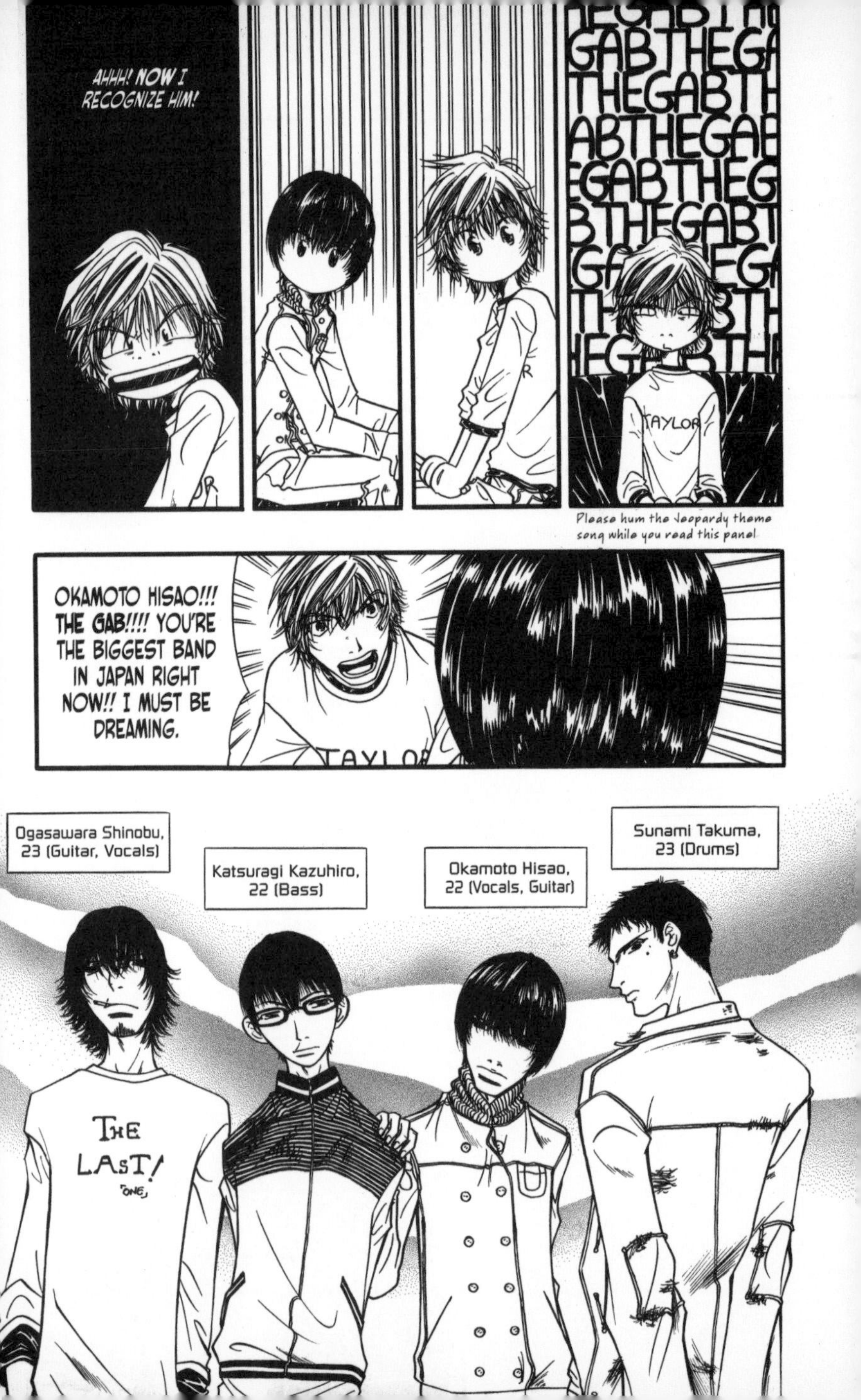
TAYLOR
Please hum the Jeopardy theme song while you read this panel
AHHH! NOW I RECOGNIZE HIM!
OKAMOTO HISAO!!! THE GAB!!!! YOU'RE THE BIGGEST BAND IN JAPAN RIGHT NOW!! I MUST BE DREAMING.
TAYLOR
Sunami Takuma, 23 (Drums)
Okamoto Hisao, 22 (Vocals, Guitar)
Katsuragi Kazuhiro, 22 (Bass)
Ogasawara Shinobu, 23 (Guitar, Vocals)
THE LAST! 「ONE」

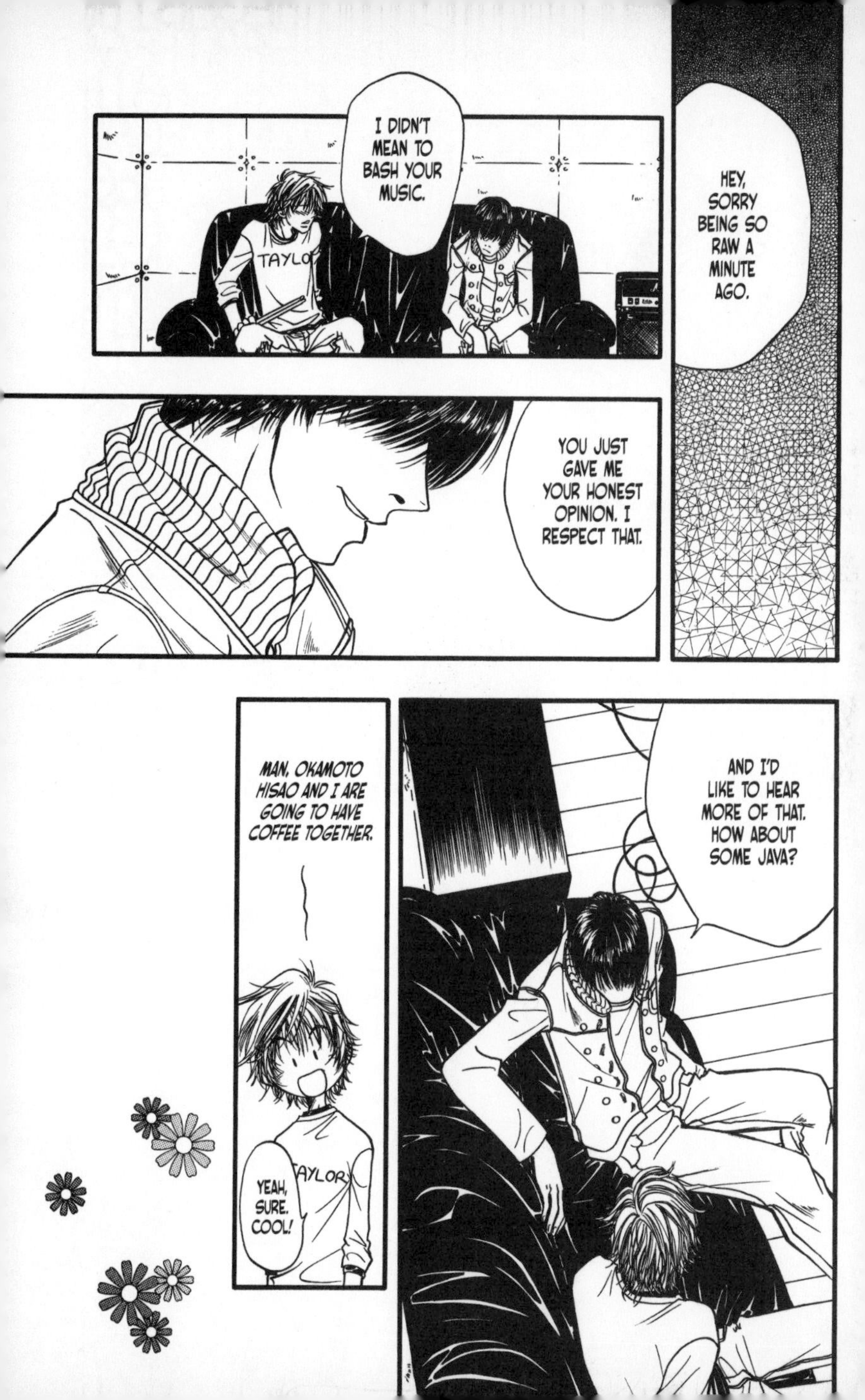

HEY, SORRY BEING SO RAW A MINUTE AGO.
I DIDN'T MEAN TO BASH YOUR MUSIC.
YOU JUST GAVE ME YOUR HONEST OPINION. I RESPECT THAT.
AND I'D LIKE TO HEAR MORE OF THAT. HOW ABOUT SOME JAVA?
MAN, OKAMOTO HISAO AND I ARE GOING TO HAVE COFFEE TOGETHER.
YEAH, SURE. COOL!

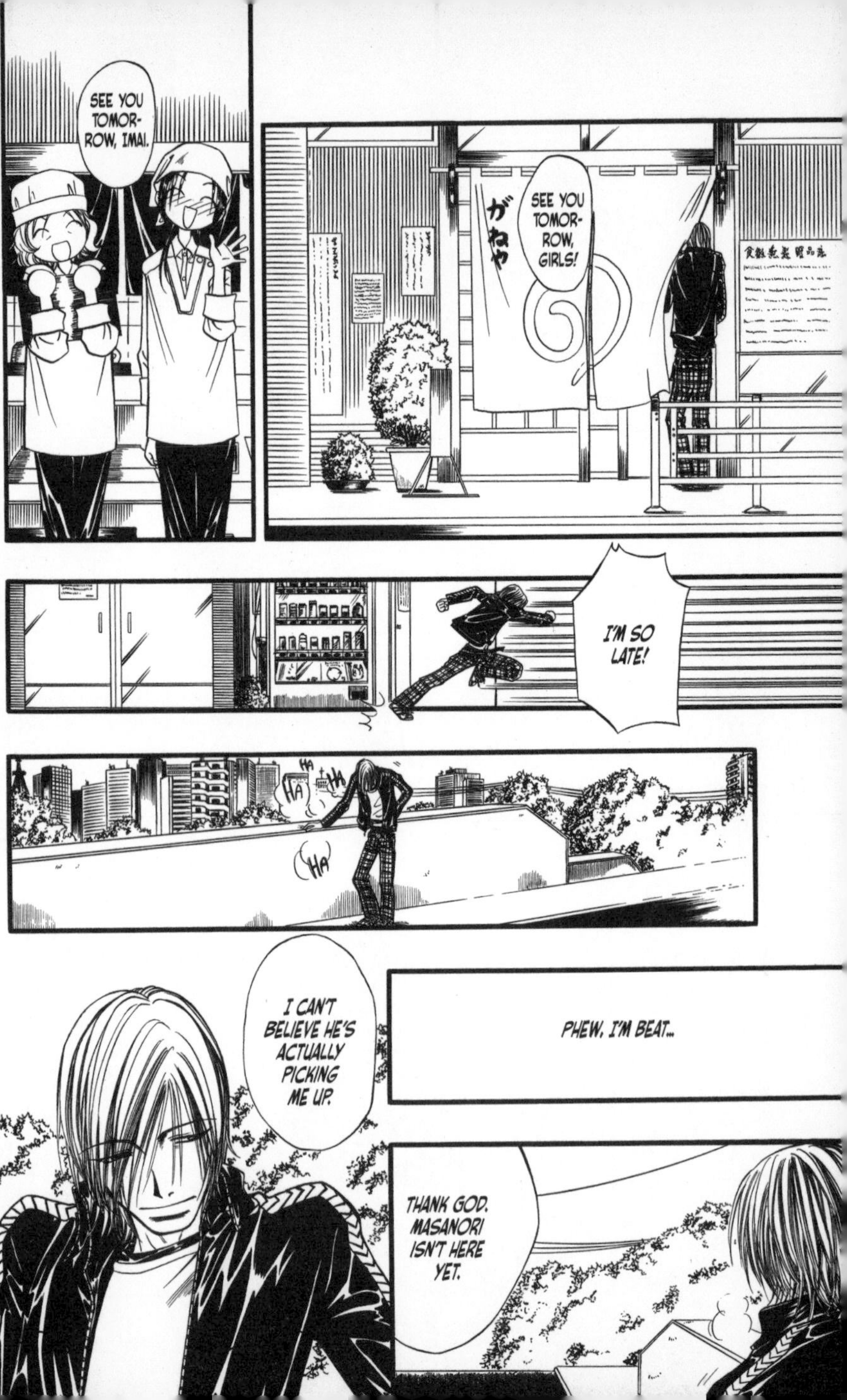
がねや
SEE YOU TOMORROW, GIRLS!
SEE YOU TOMORROW, IMAI.
I'M SO LATE!
HA
HA
HA
HA
PHEW, I'M BEAT...
THANK GOD. MASANORI ISN'T HERE YET.
I CAN'T BELIEVE HE'S ACTUALLY PICKING ME UP.

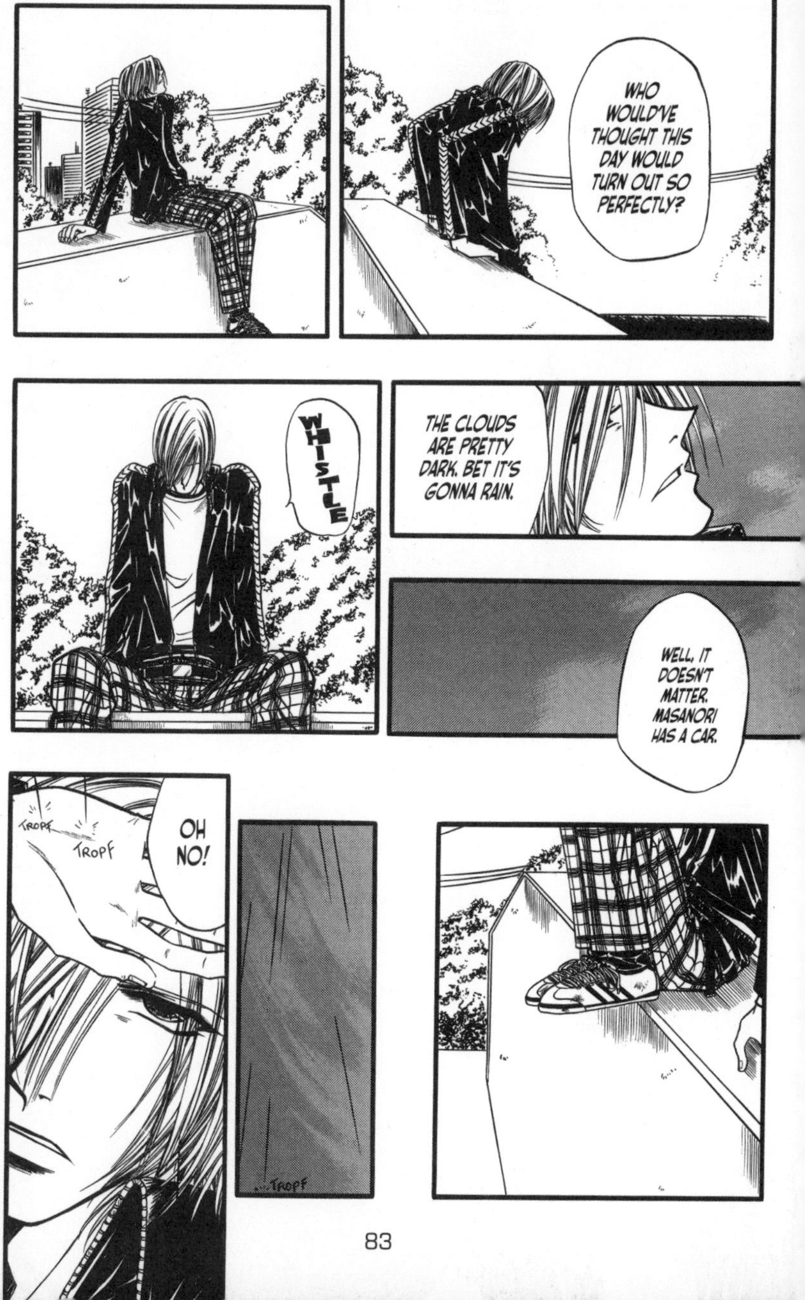
WHO WOULD'VE THOUGHT THIS DAY WOULD TURN OUT SO PERFECTLY?
THE CLOUDS ARE PRETTY DARK. BET IT'S GONNA RAIN.
WELL, IT DOESN'T MATTER. MASANORI HAS A CAR.
WHISTLE
...TROPF
TROPF
TROPF
OH NO!

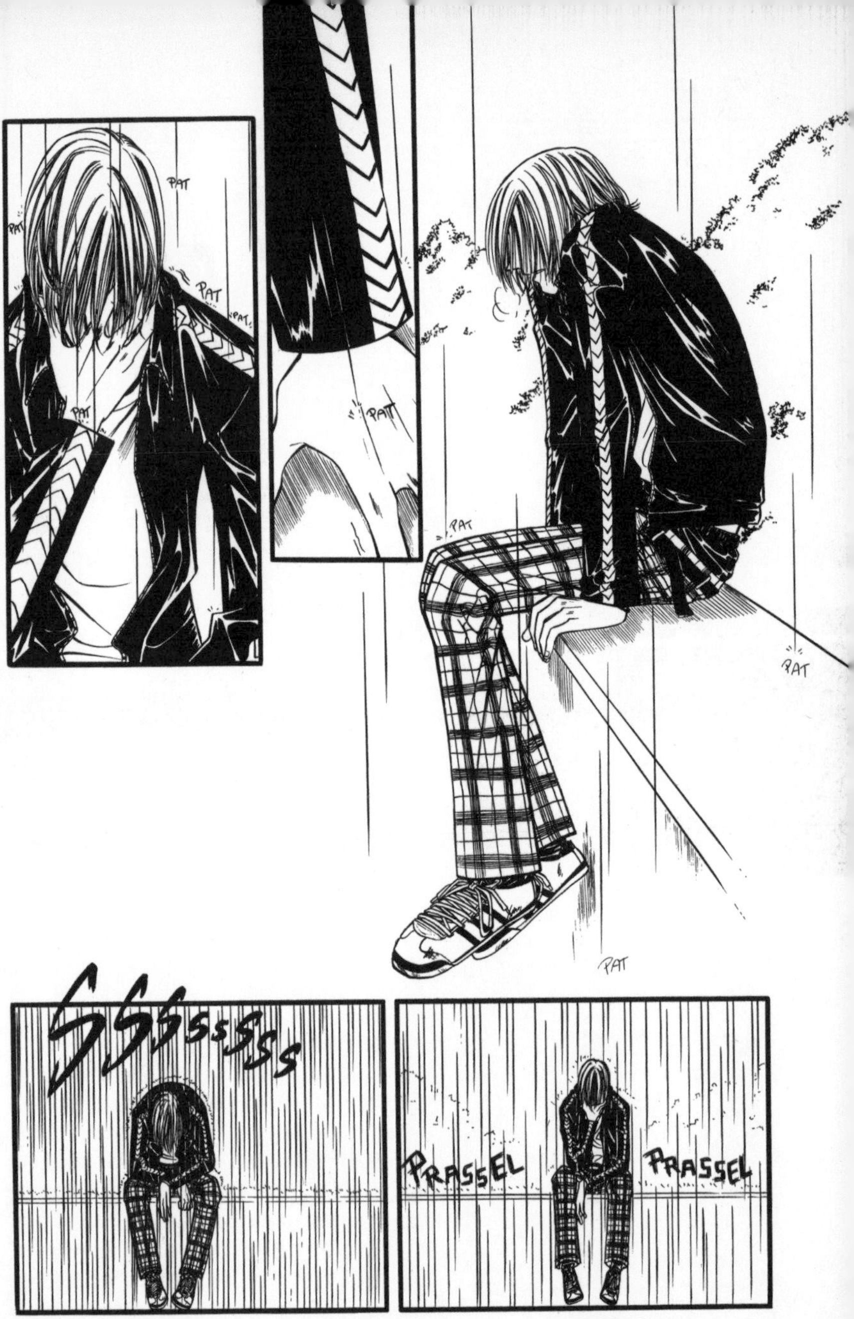
PAT
PAT
PAT
PAT
PAT
PAT
PAT
PAT
PAT
PAT
PRASSEL
PRASSEL
SSSSSSSS

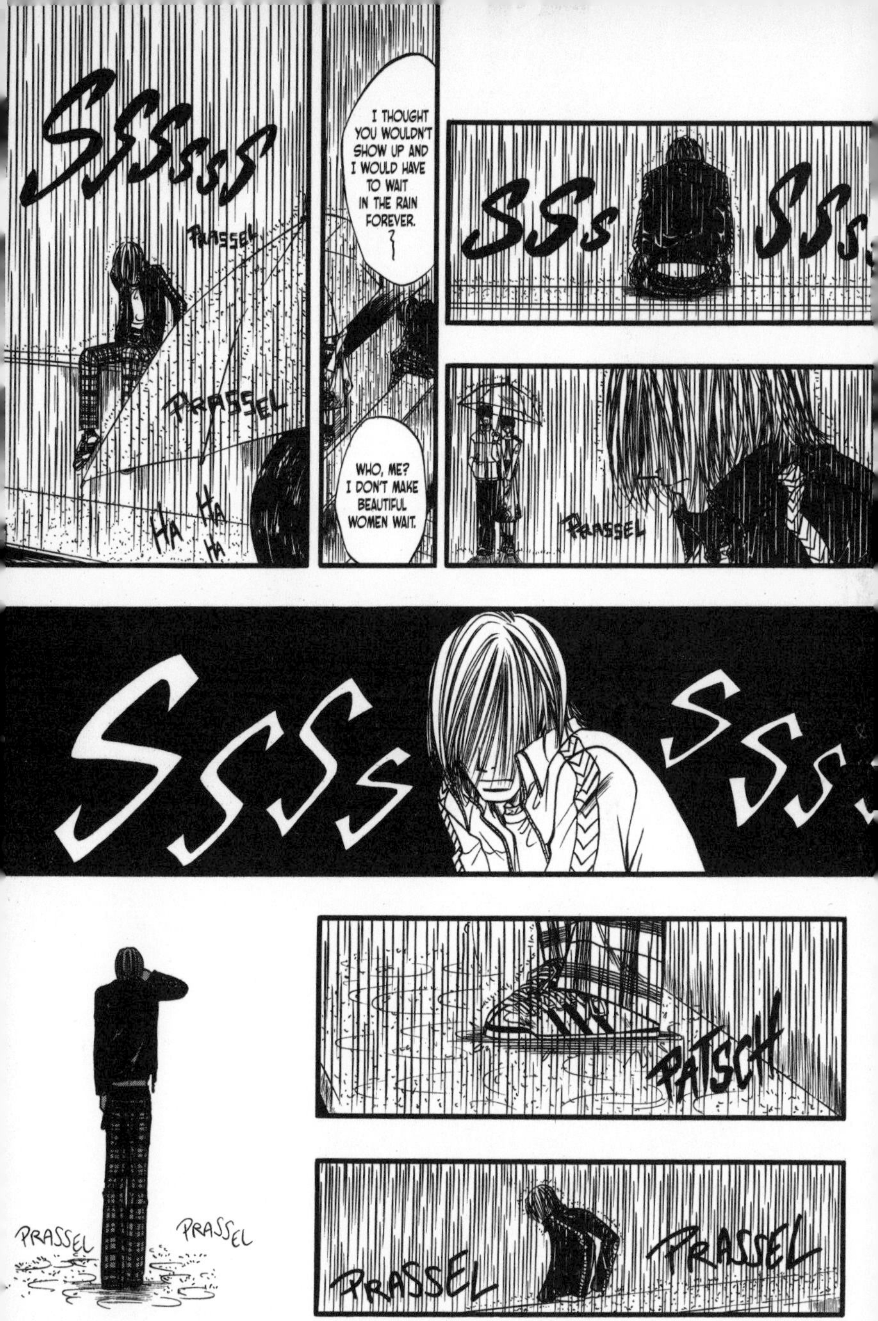
SSs SSs
PRASSEL
I THOUGHT YOU WOULDN'T SHOW UP AND I WOULD HAVE TO WAIT IN THE RAIN FOREVER.
WHO, ME? I DON'T MAKE BEAUTIFUL WOMEN WAIT.
SSSsss
PRASSEL
PRASSEL
HA HA HA
SSSs SSS
PATSCH
PRASSEL
PRASSEL
PRASSEL
PRASSEL

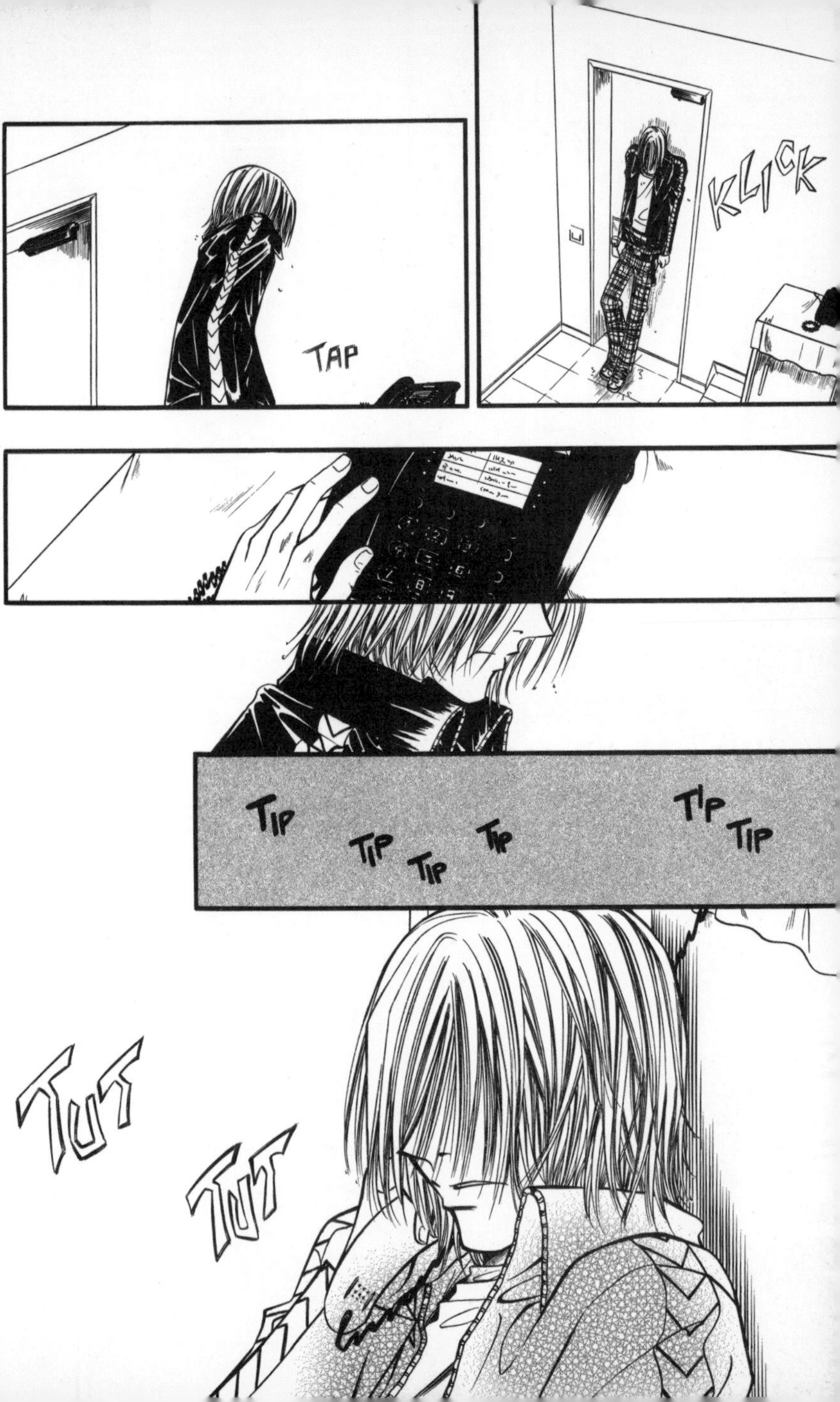
KLICK
TAP
TIP
TIP
TIP
TIP
TIP
TIP
TUT
TUT

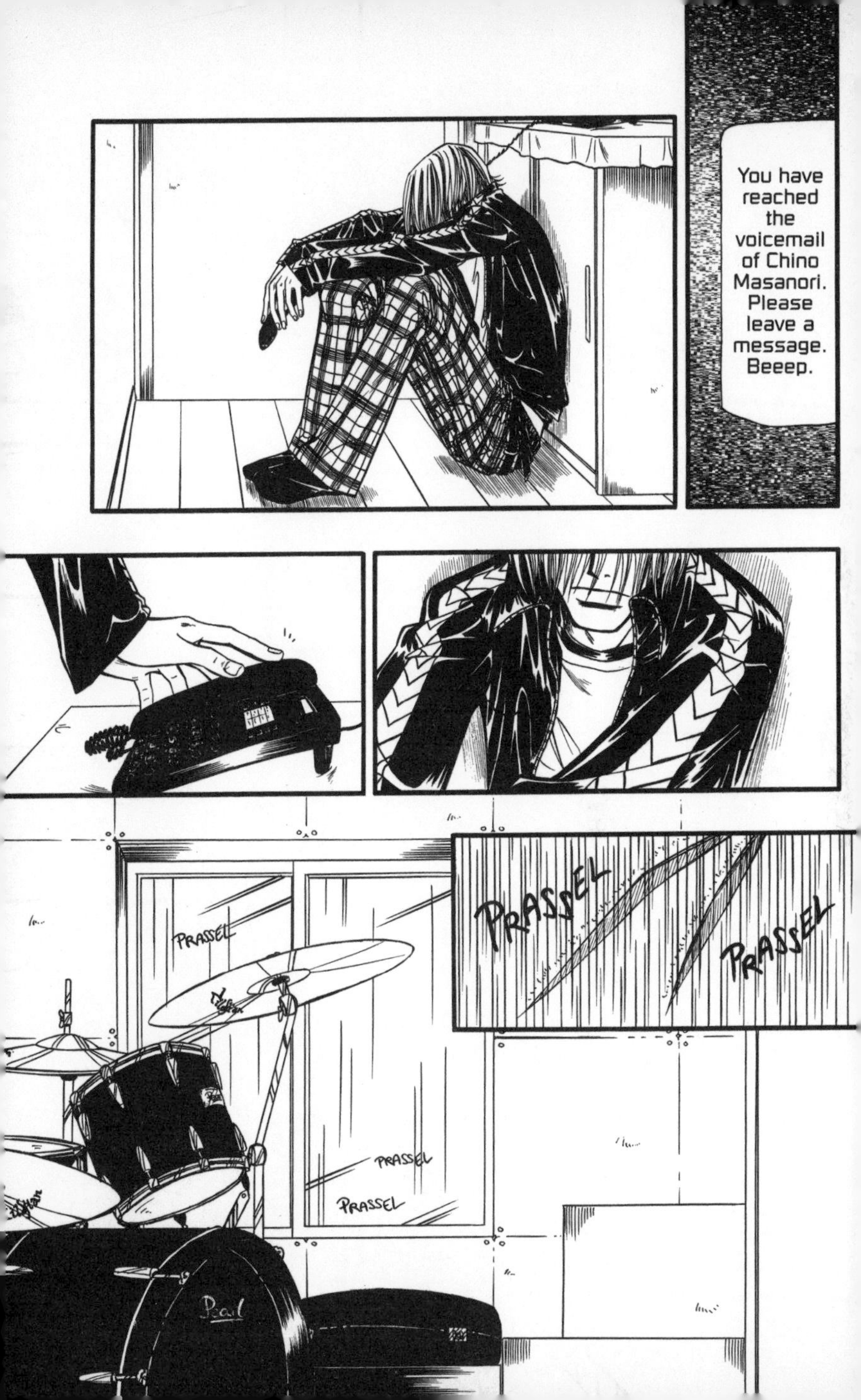
You have reached the voicemail of Chino Masanori. Please leave a message. Beeep.
PRASSEL
PRASSEL
PRASSEL
PRASSEL
PRASSEL

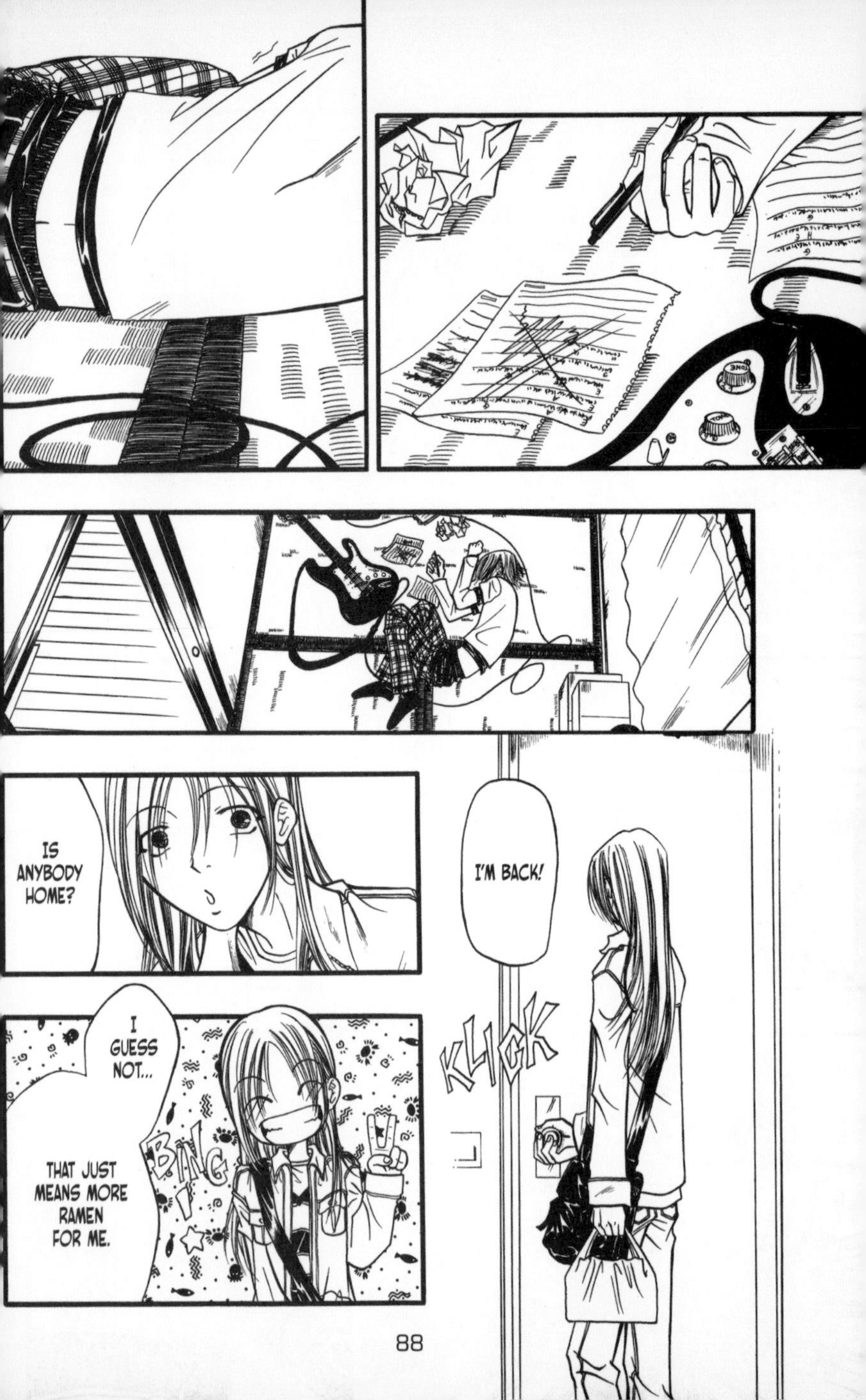
I'M BACK!
KLICK
IS ANYBODY HOME?
I GUESS NOT...
BING
THAT JUST MEANS MORE RAMEN FOR ME.

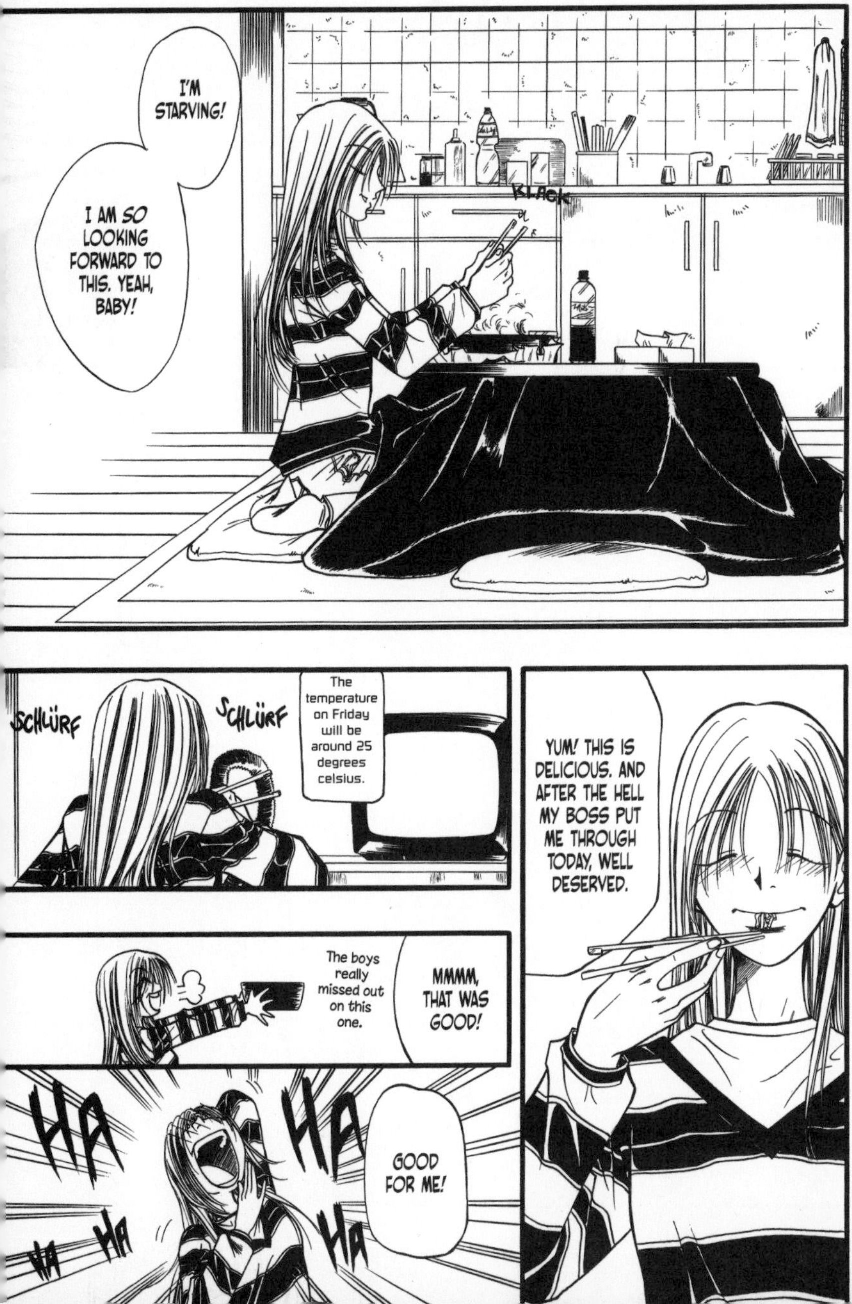
I'M STARVING!
I AM SO LOOKING FORWARD TO THIS. YEAH, BABY!
KLACK
YUM! THIS IS DELICIOUS. AND AFTER THE HELL MY BOSS PUT ME THROUGH TODAY, WELL DESERVED.
The temperature on Friday will be around 25 degrees celsius.
SCHLÜRF
SCHLÜRF
MMMM, THAT WAS GOOD!
The boys really missed out on this one.
HA HA
GOOD FOR ME!
HA
HA HA HA

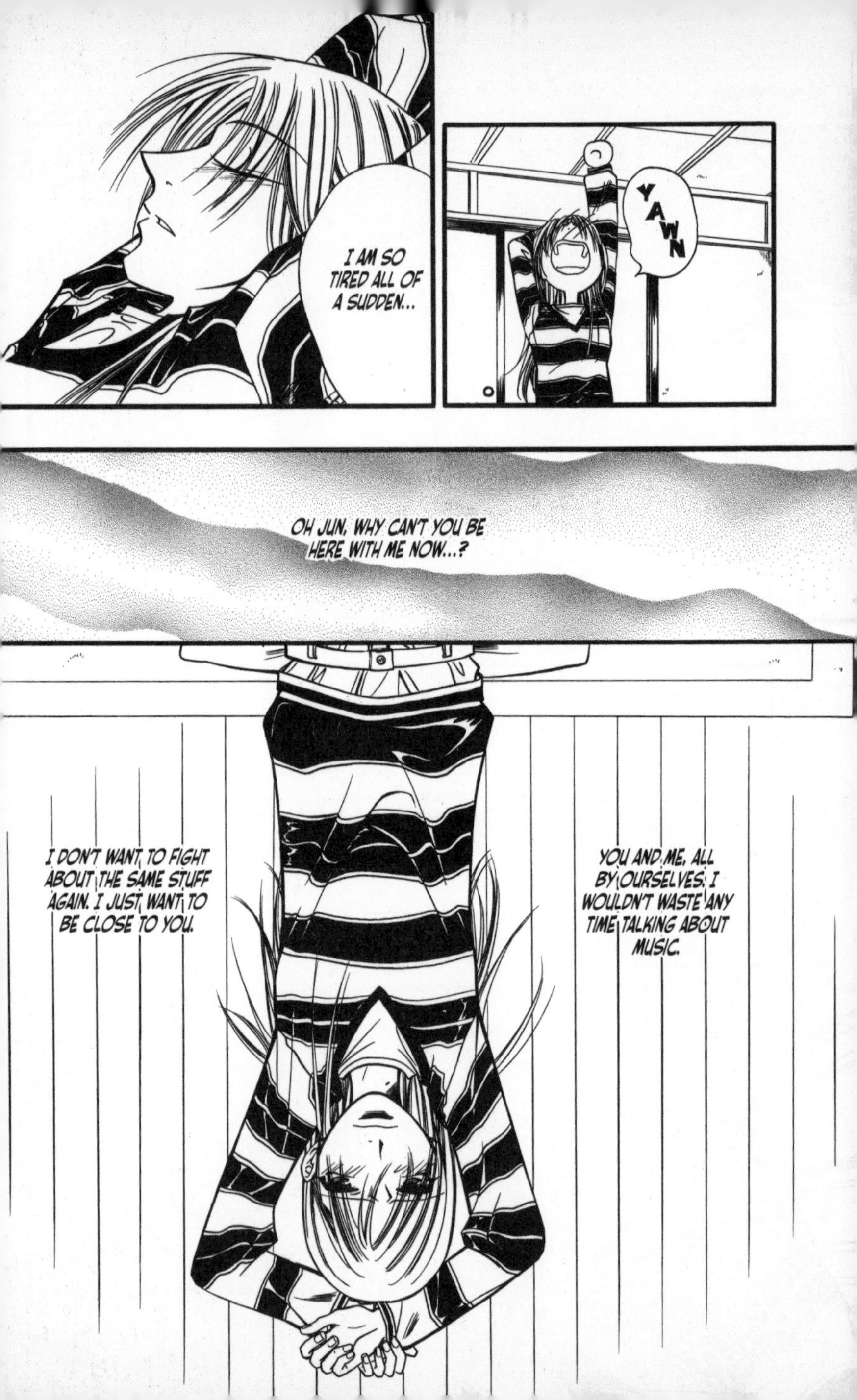
YAWN
I AM SO TIRED ALL OF A SUDDEN...
OH JUN, WHY CAN'T YOU BE HERE WITH ME NOW...?
YOU AND ME, ALL BY OURSELVES. I WOULDN'T WASTE ANY TIME TALKING ABOUT MUSIC.
I DON'T WANT TO FIGHT ABOUT THE SAME STUFF AGAIN. I JUST WANT TO BE CLOSE TO YOU.

BAD FRIEND

You hate me for things I haven't done
But I never dared deny
And all your feelings for me are gone
Never thought I wish I could cry

You said it wasn't my fault in fact
But I never dared smile
Cause you're the one with the right to act
I'm afraid you'll stay for a while

Beat me up
Take away the pain
Do not stop
Soothe me again
Knock me down
Take away the pain
Heal my wounds
Soothe me again

Lyrics - CHINO Masanori

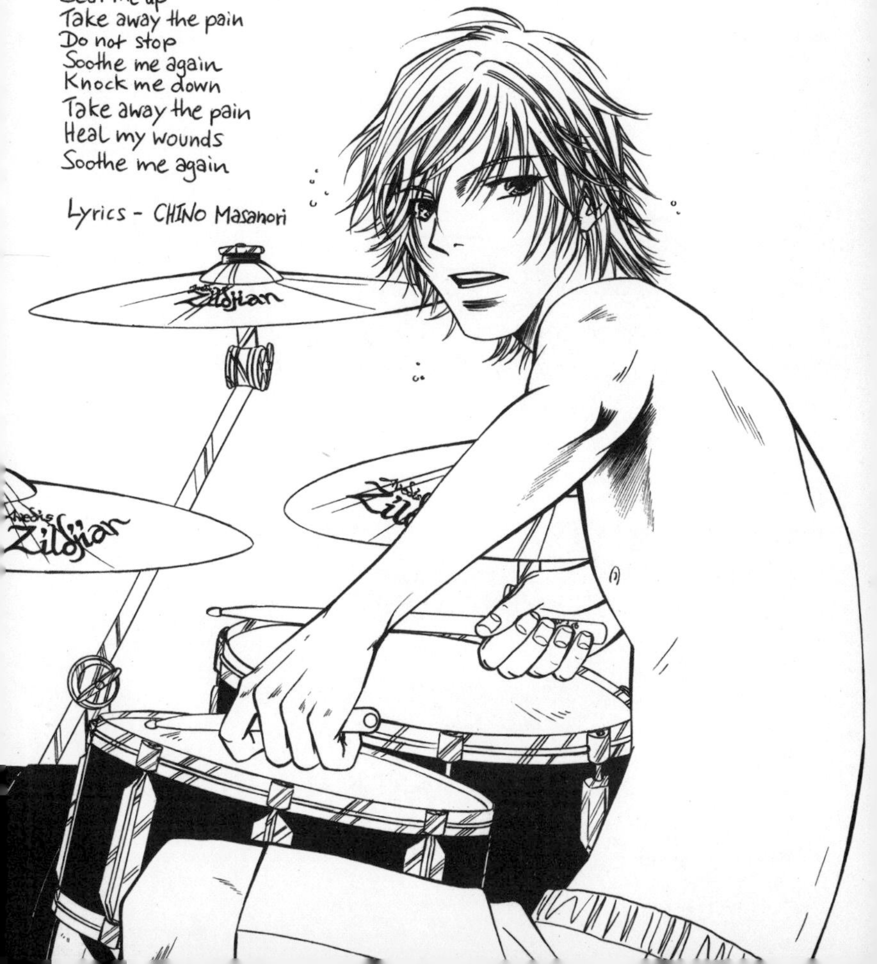
Zildjian
Avedis Zildjian

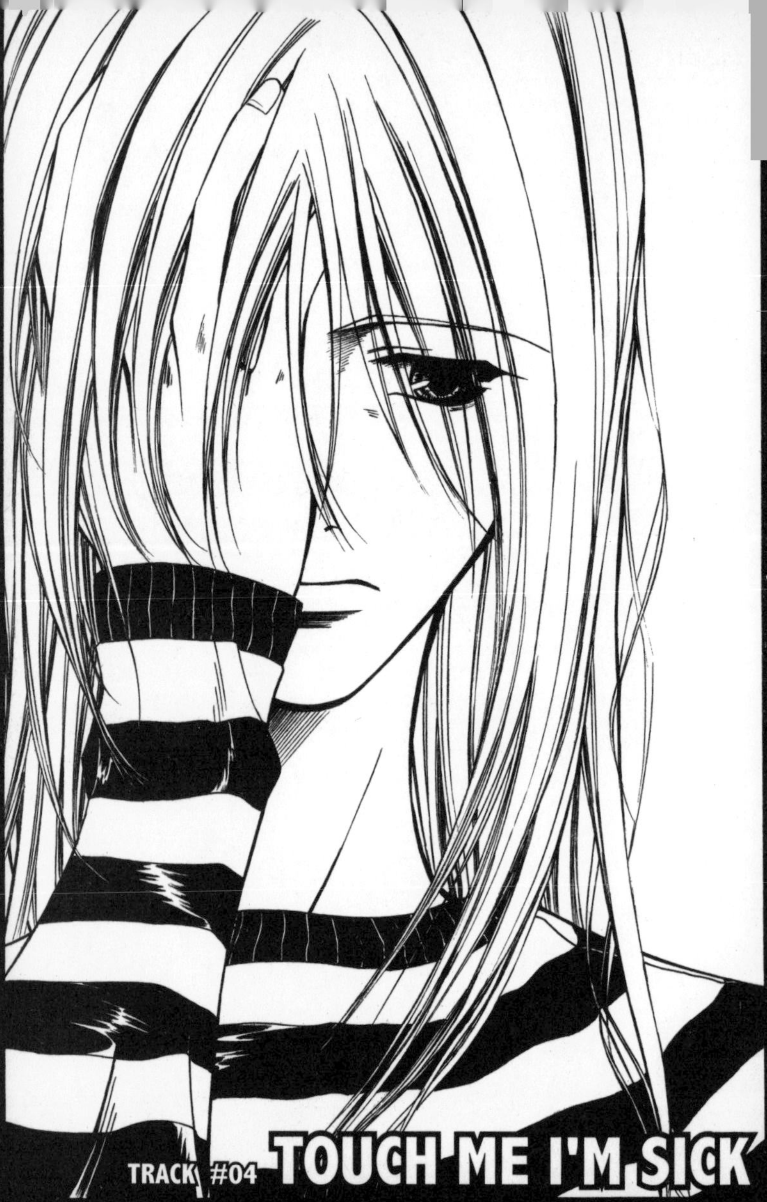
TRACK #04
TOUCH ME I'M SICK

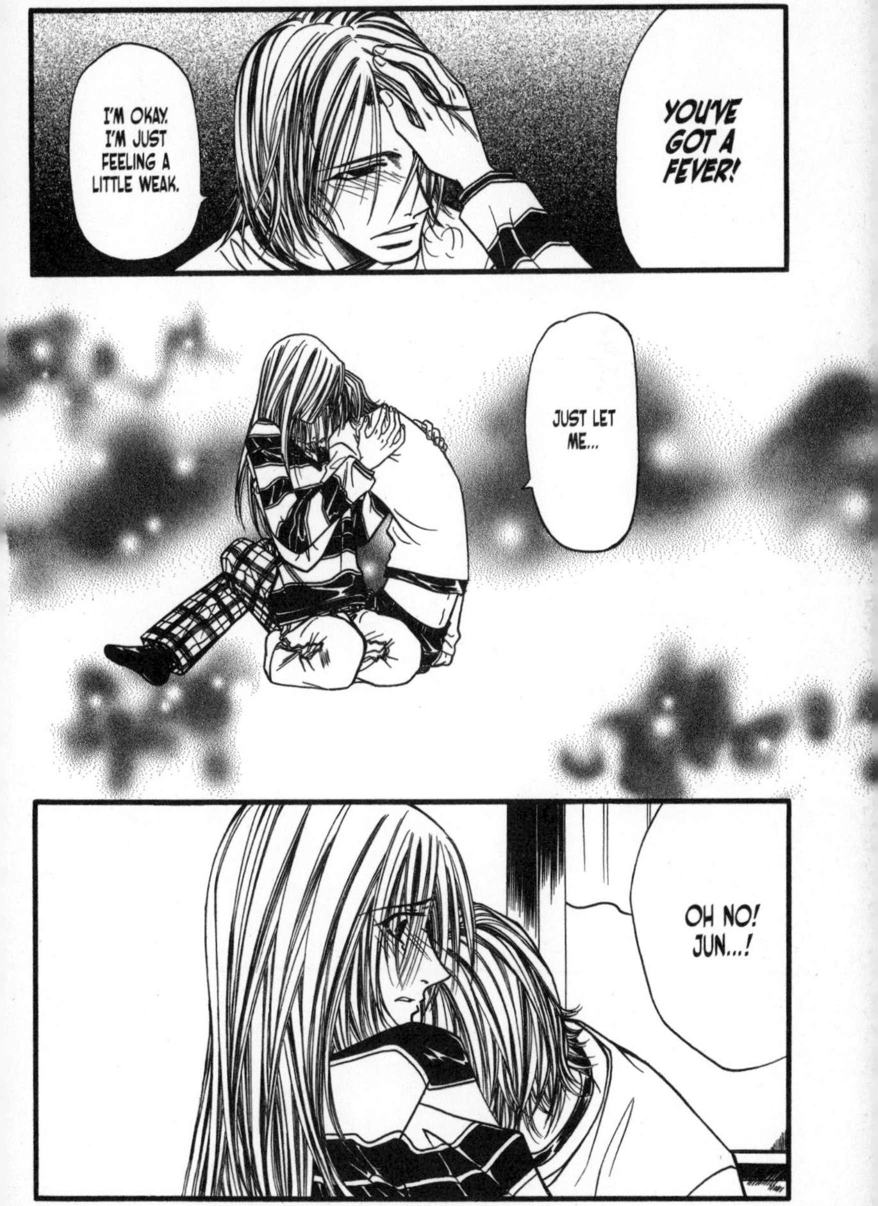
YOU'VE GOT A FEVER!
I'M OKAY. I'M JUST FEELING A LITTLE WEAK.
JUST LET ME...
OH NO! JUN...!

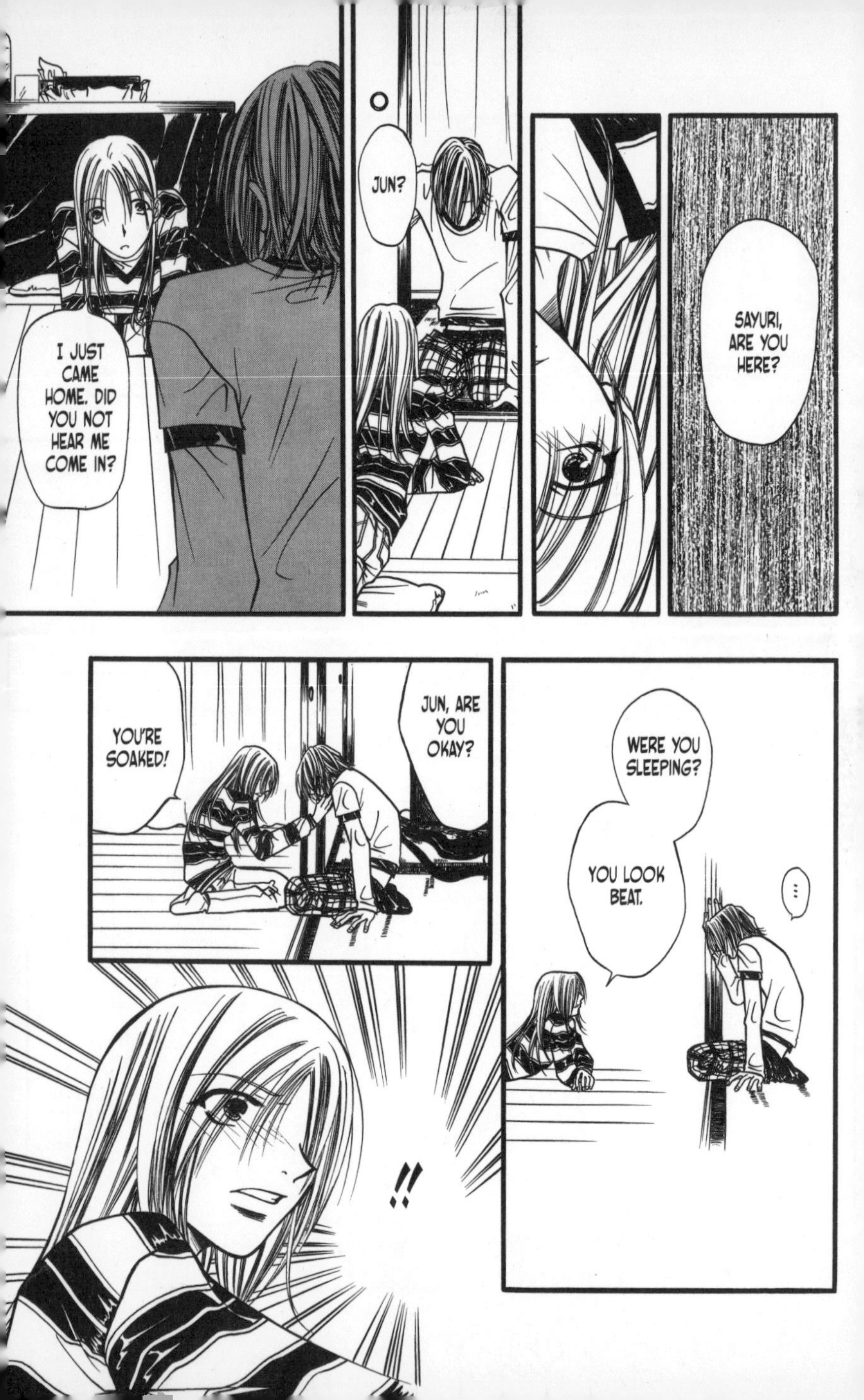
SAYURI, ARE YOU HERE?
JUN?
I JUST CAME HOME. DID YOU NOT HEAR ME COME IN?
WERE YOU SLEEPING?
YOU LOOK BEAT.
...
JUN, ARE YOU OKAY?
YOU'RE SOAKED!
!!

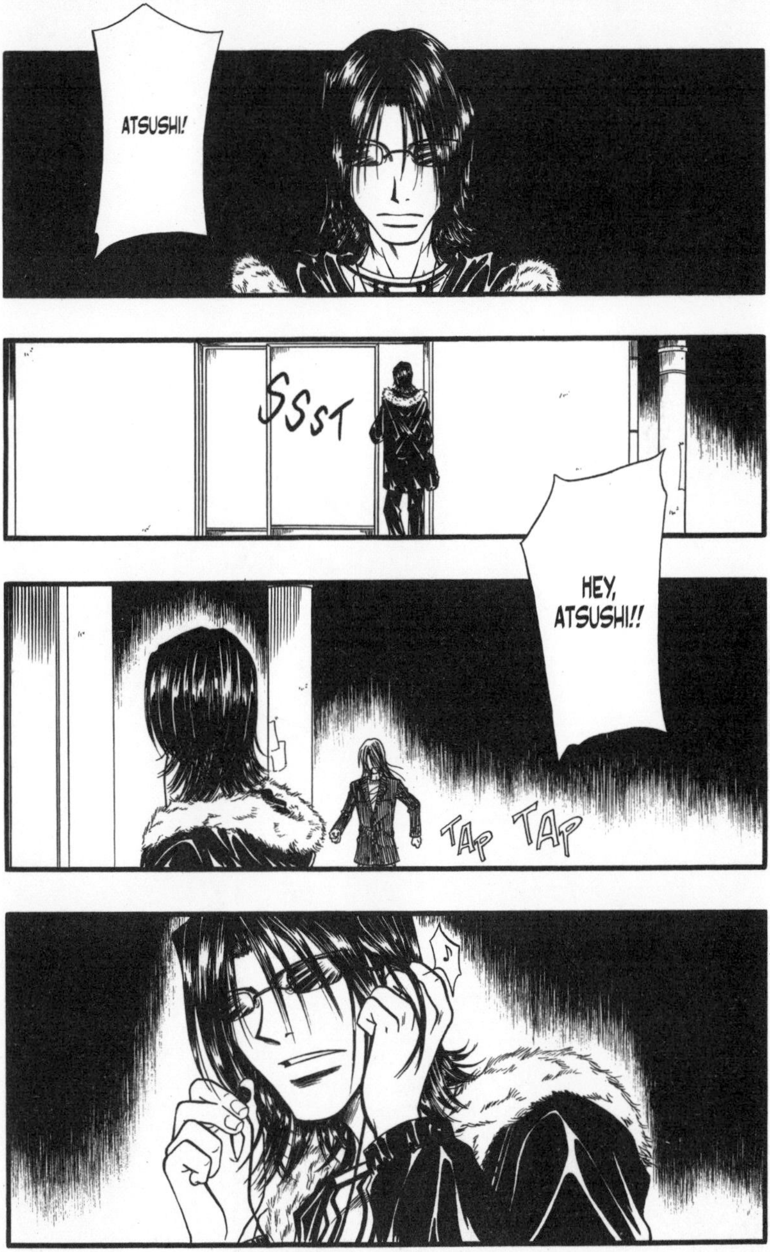
ATSUSHI!
SSST
HEY, ATSUSHI!!
TAP TAP

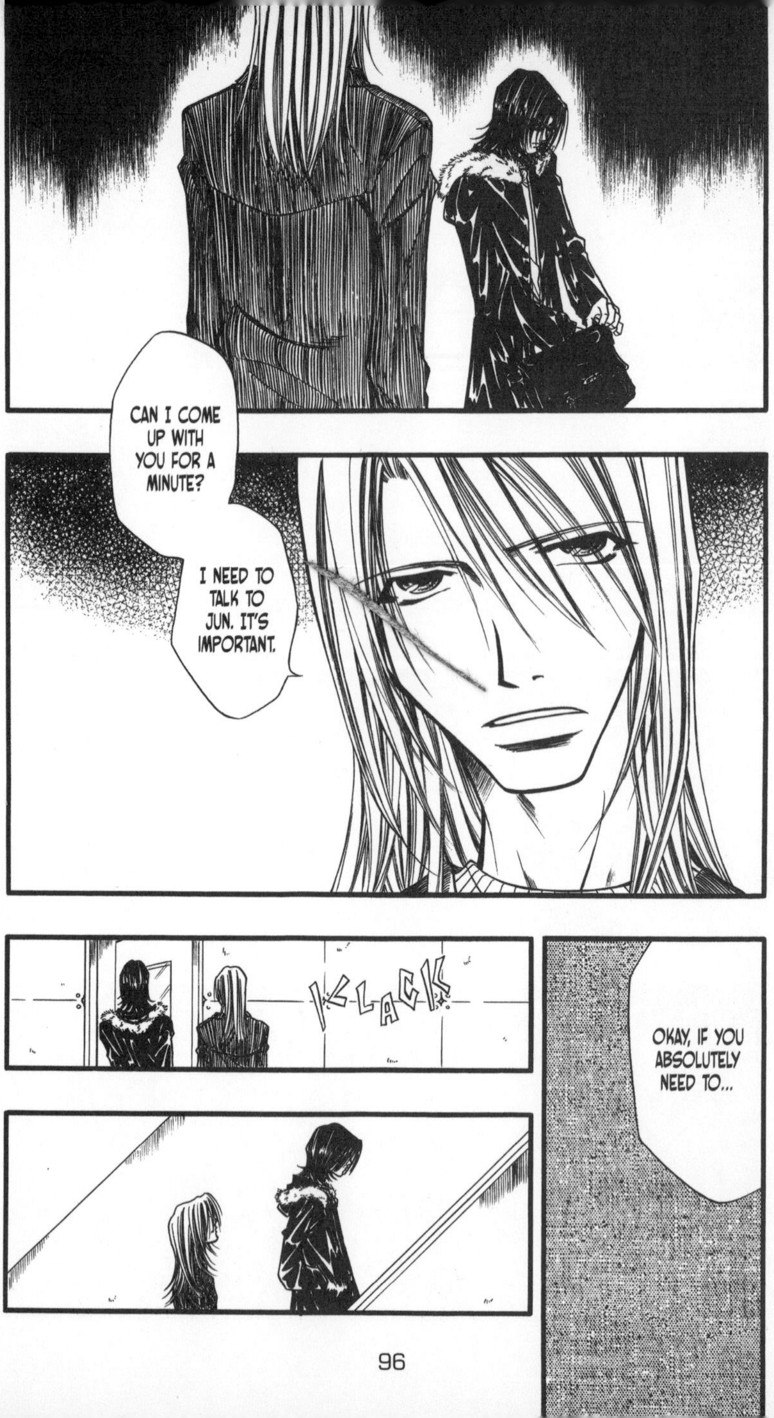
CAN I COME UP WITH YOU FOR A MINUTE?
I NEED TO TALK TO JUN. IT'S IMPORTANT.
OKAY, IF YOU ABSOLUTELY NEED TO...
KLACK

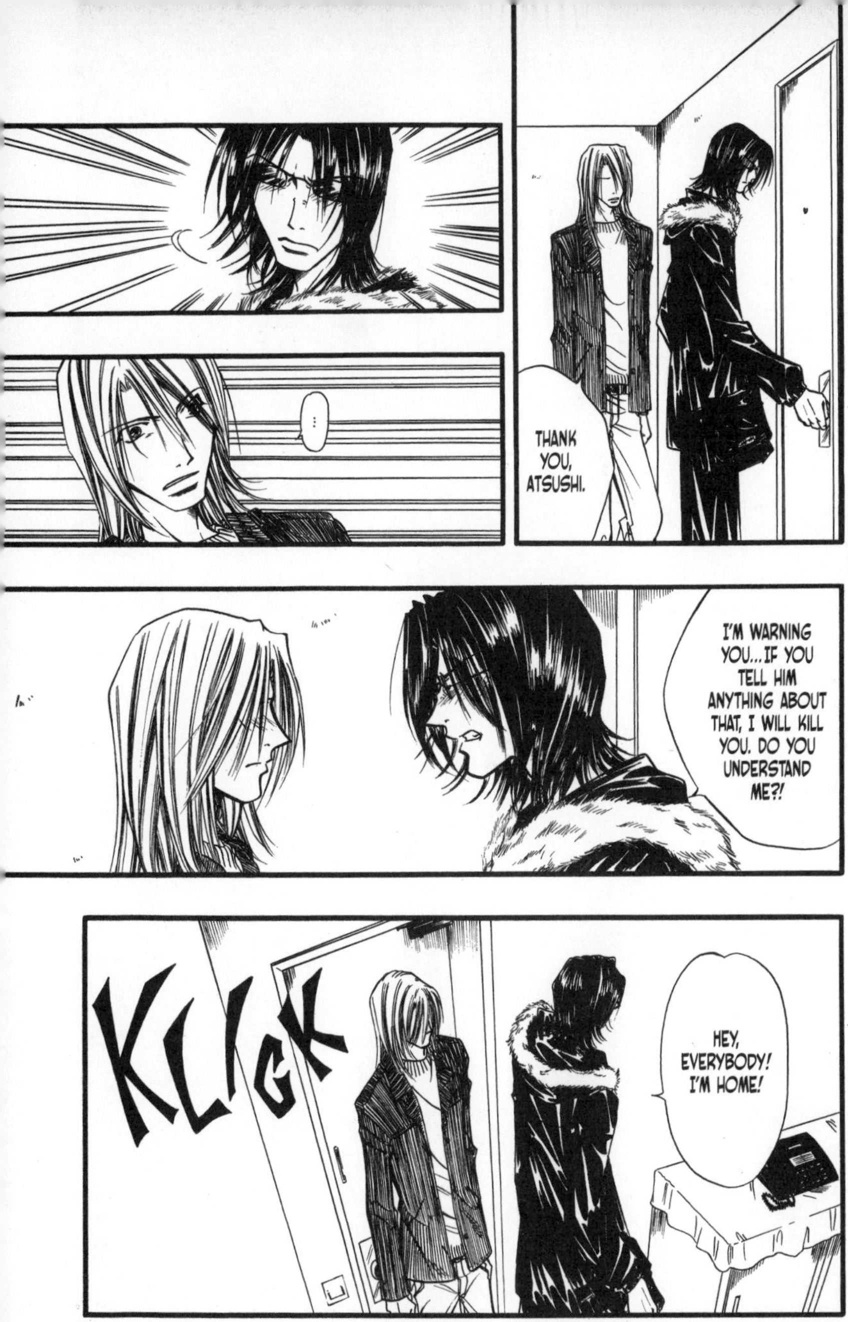
THANK YOU, ATSUSHI.
...
I'M WARNING YOU...IF YOU TELL HIM ANYTHING ABOUT THAT, I WILL KILL YOU. DO YOU UNDERSTAND ME?!
HEY, EVERYBODY! I'M HOME!
KLICK

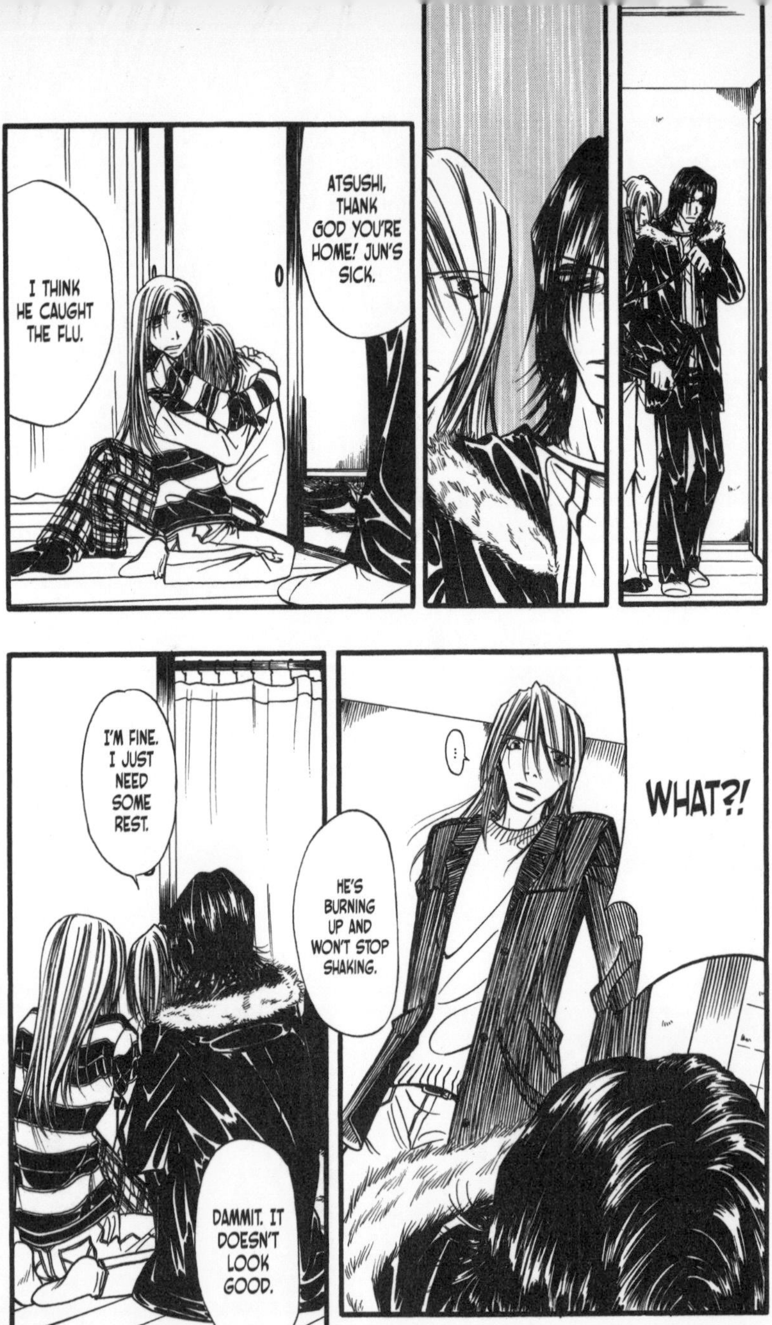
ATSUSHI, THANK GOD YOU'RE HOME! JUN'S SICK.
I THINK HE CAUGHT THE FLU.
WHAT?!
…
HE'S BURNING UP AND WON'T STOP SHAKING.
I'M FINE. I JUST NEED SOME REST.
DAMMIT. IT DOESN'T LOOK GOOD.

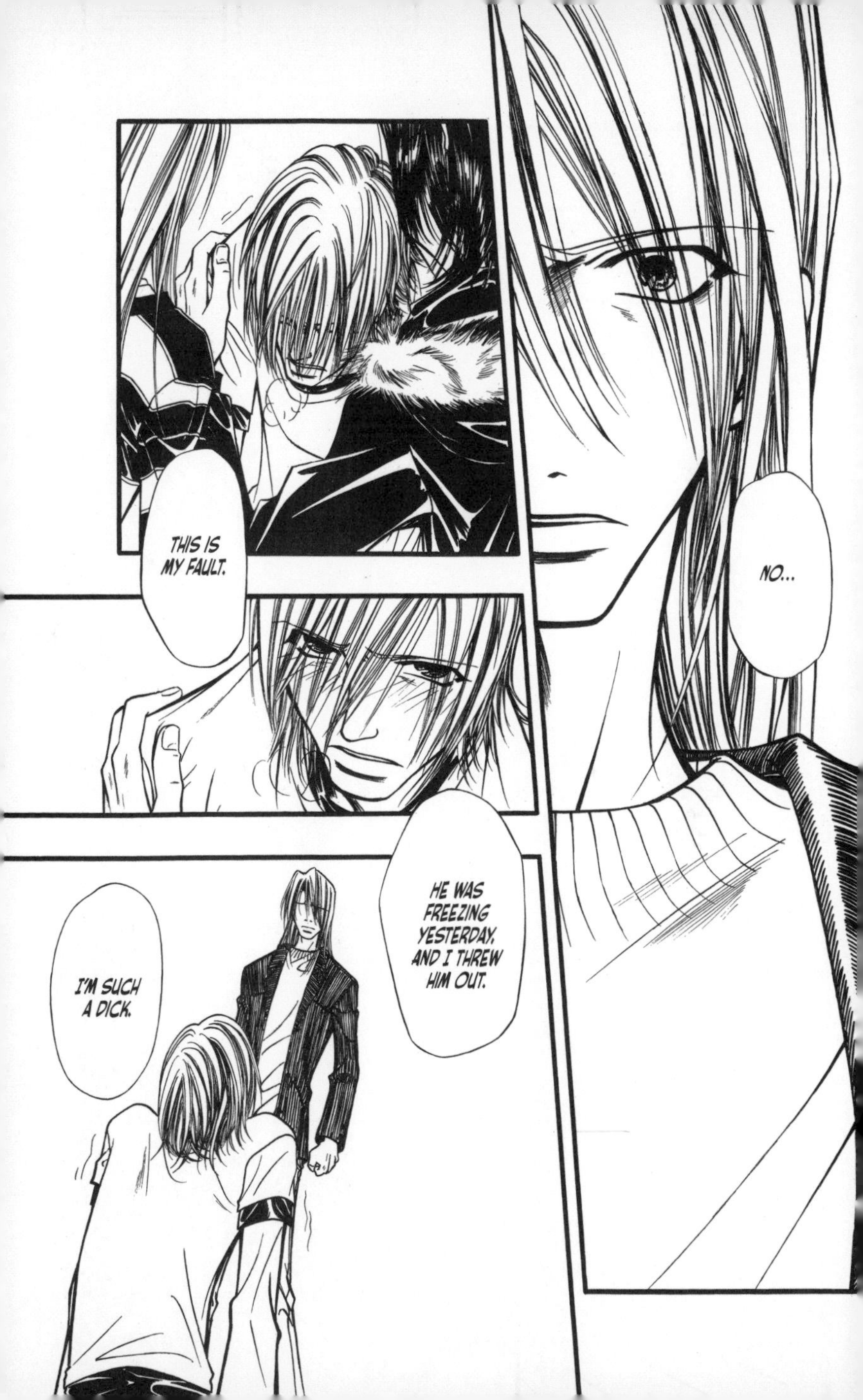
NO...
THIS IS MY FAULT.
HE WAS FREEZING YESTERDAY. AND I THREW HIM OUT.
I'M SUCH A DICK.

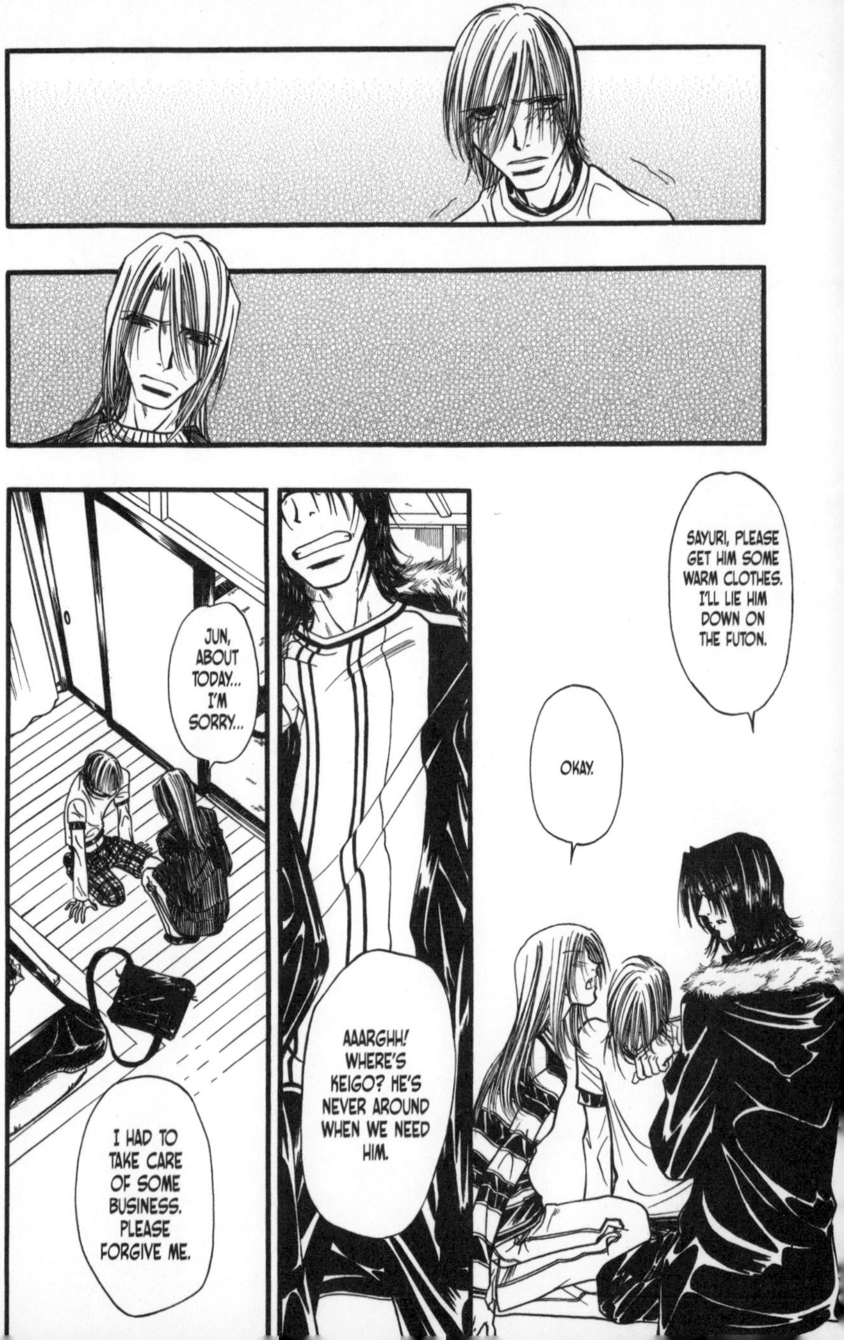
SAYURI, PLEASE GET HIM SOME WARM CLOTHES. I'LL LIE HIM DOWN ON THE FUTON.
OKAY.
AAARGHH! WHERE'S KEIGO? HE'S NEVER AROUND WHEN WE NEED HIM.
JUN, ABOUT TODAY... I'M SORRY...
I HAD TO TAKE CARE OF SOME BUSINESS. PLEASE FORGIVE ME.

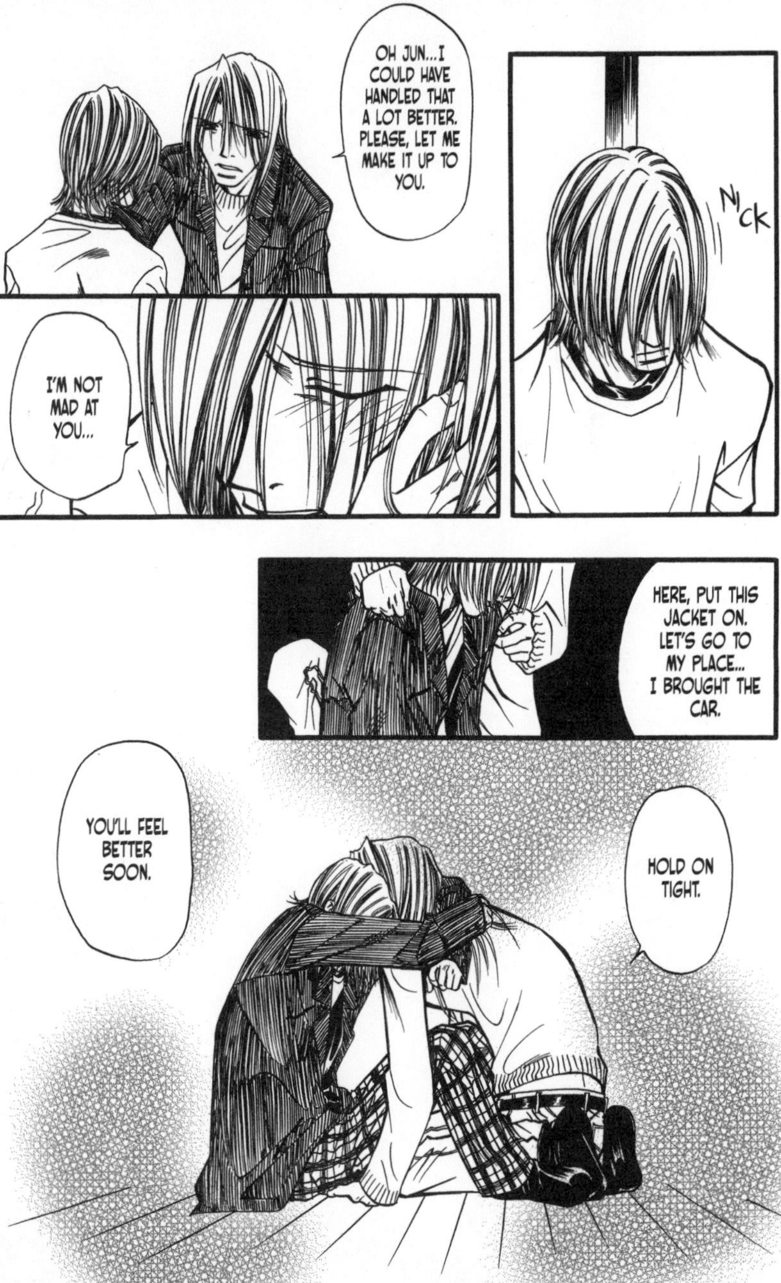
NICK
OH JUN...I COULD HAVE HANDLED THAT A LOT BETTER. PLEASE, LET ME MAKE IT UP TO YOU.
I'M NOT MAD AT YOU...
HERE, PUT THIS JACKET ON. LET'S GO TO MY PLACE... I BROUGHT THE CAR.
HOLD ON TIGHT.
YOU'LL FEEL BETTER SOON.

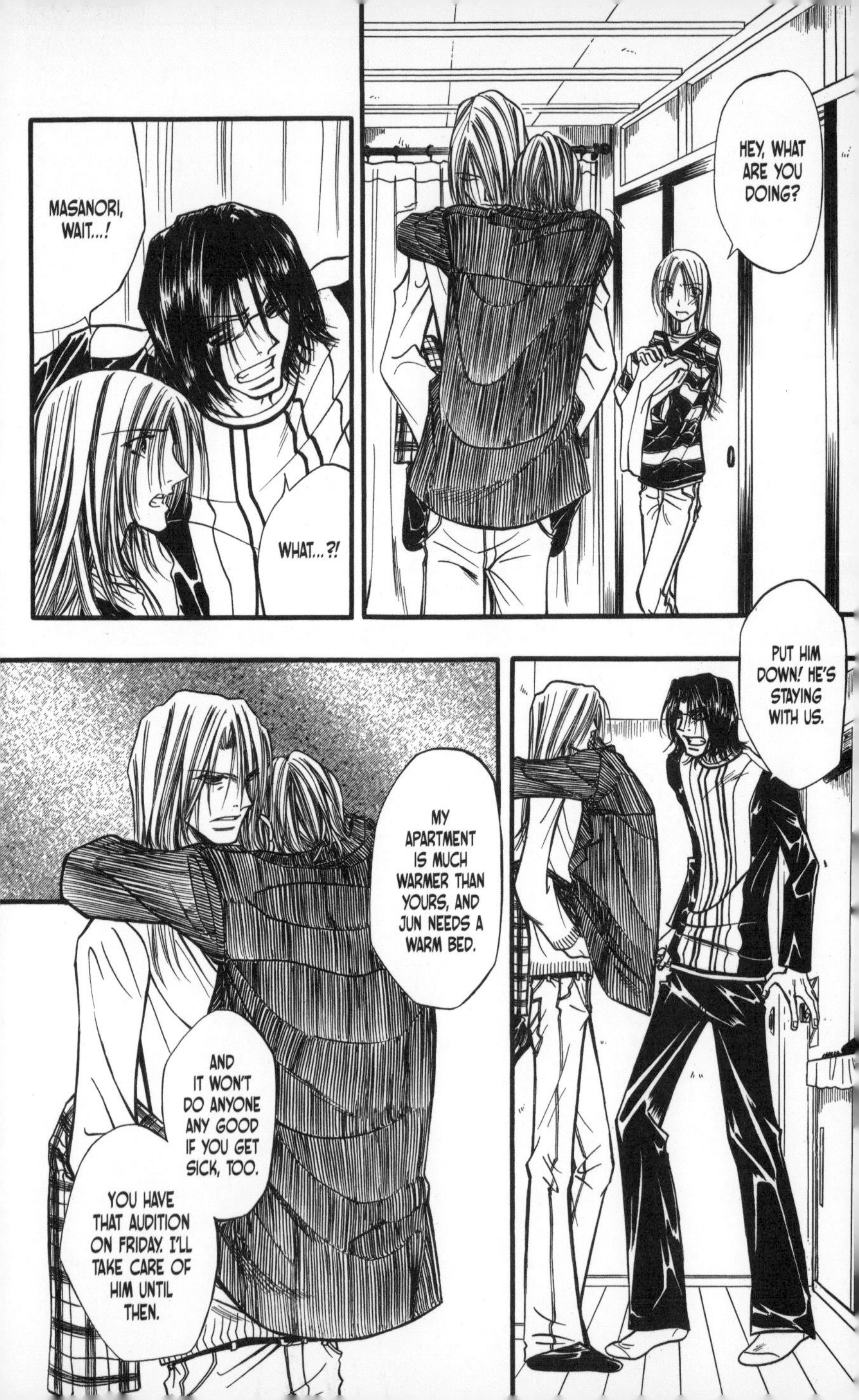
HEY, WHAT ARE YOU DOING?
MASANORI, WAIT...!
WHAT...?!
PUT HIM DOWN! HE'S STAYING WITH US.
MY APARTMENT IS MUCH WARMER THAN YOURS, AND JUN NEEDS A WARM BED.
AND IT WON'T DO ANYONE ANY GOOD IF YOU GET SICK, TOO.
YOU HAVE THAT AUDITION ON FRIDAY. I'LL TAKE CARE OF HIM UNTIL THEN.

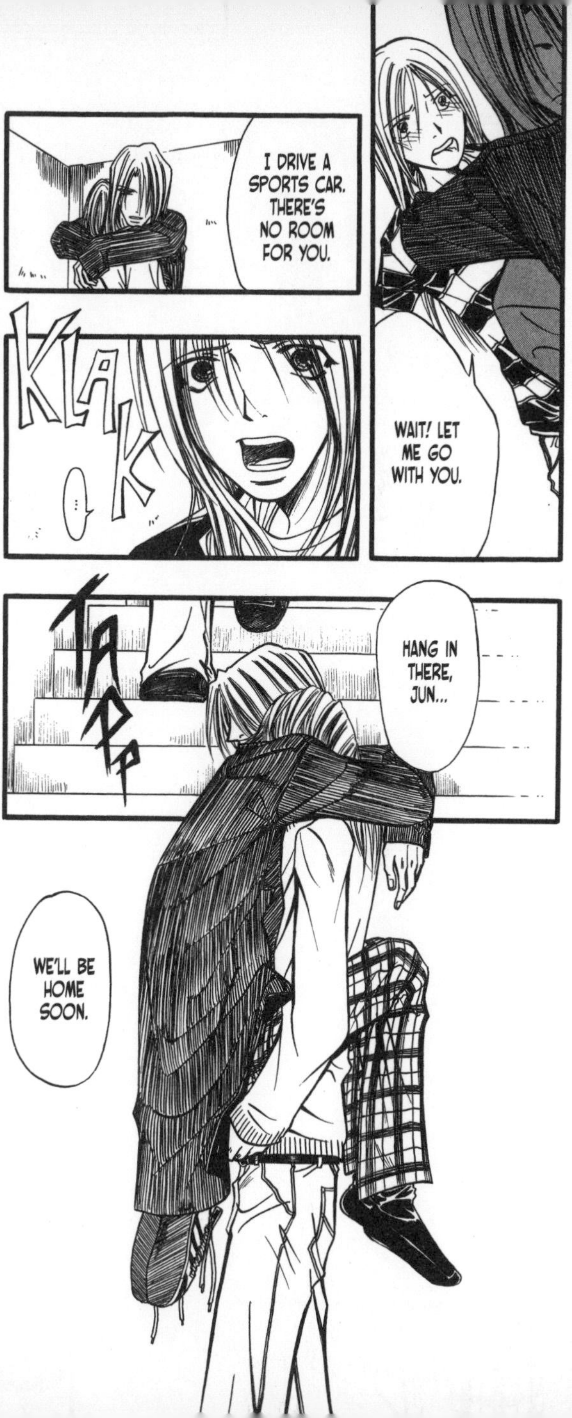
WAIT! LET ME GO WITH YOU.
I DRIVE A SPORTS CAR. THERE'S NO ROOM FOR YOU.
KLAK
...
TAPP
HANG IN THERE, JUN...
WE'LL BE HOME SOON.

I'd like to use this opportunity to thank all of those people who helped me with my work, who inspired me, and who opened my eyes. First, I would like to thank my dad, my family, my boss, Jo, and everyone at TOKYOPOP for their valuable criticism, cooperation, and support.

Thank you very much, Stuart Levy, for your harsh criticism and for your advice as well as your never-ending knowledge about music, film, and implementation, which you kindly shared with me.

A very big thank you goes out to Yuya from Kodansha. Because of him and his books, I was able to gather more information about original Japanese backgrounds and history.

Many thanks again to Benjamin, the greatest inspiration alive. He inspired me especially when it came to Jun's new look.

And last but not least, thanks to all my friends who support me and who make the long days at the university go by faster.

Thanks to all the people I forgot to mention and to all of the people who write me.

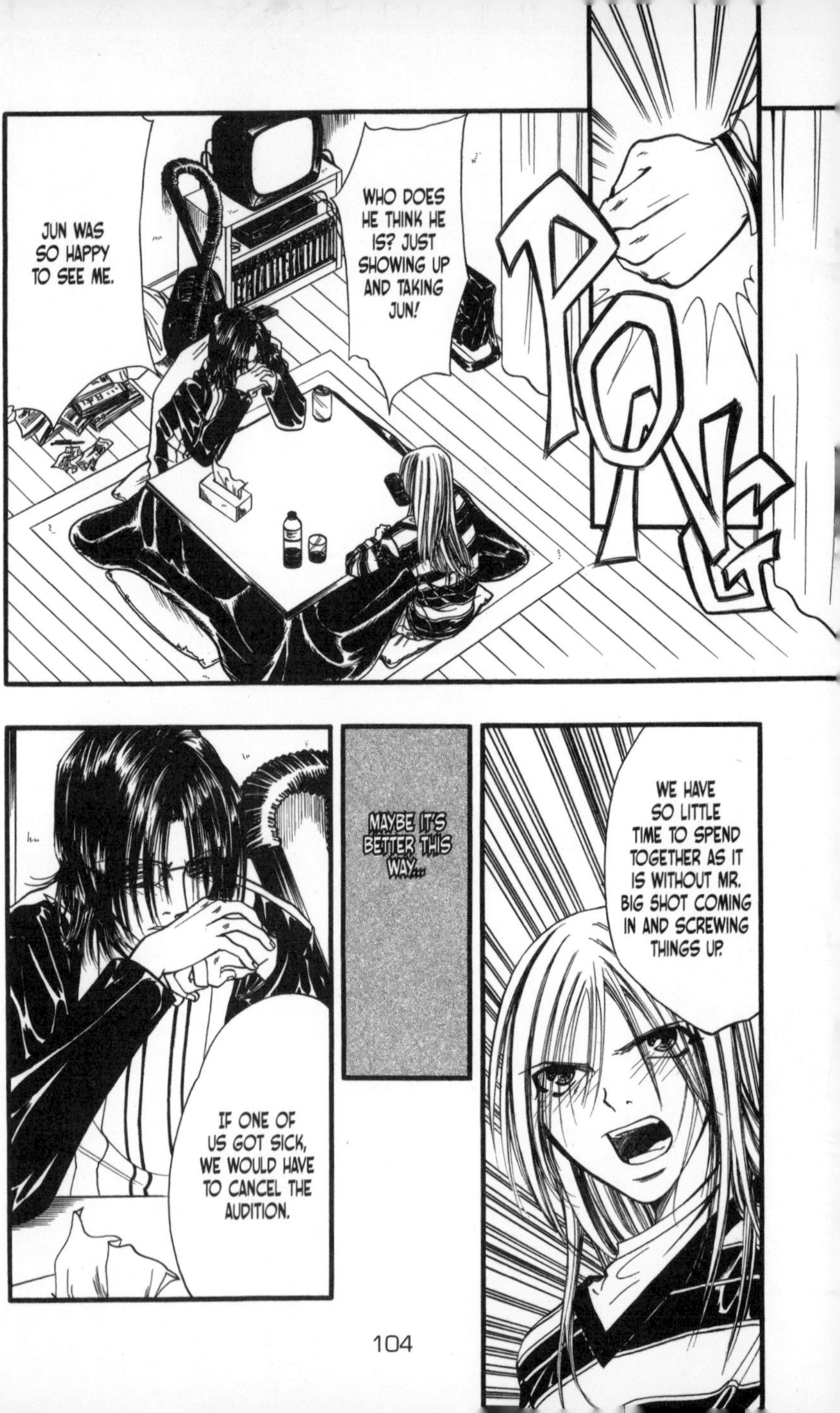
WHO DOES HE THINK HE IS? JUST SHOWING UP AND TAKING JUN!
JUN WAS SO HAPPY TO SEE ME.
WE HAVE SO LITTLE TIME TO SPEND TOGETHER AS IT IS WITHOUT MR. BIG SHOT COMING IN AND SCREWING THINGS UP.
MAYBE IT'S BETTER THIS WAY...
IF ONE OF US GOT SICK, WE WOULD HAVE TO CANCEL THE AUDITION.

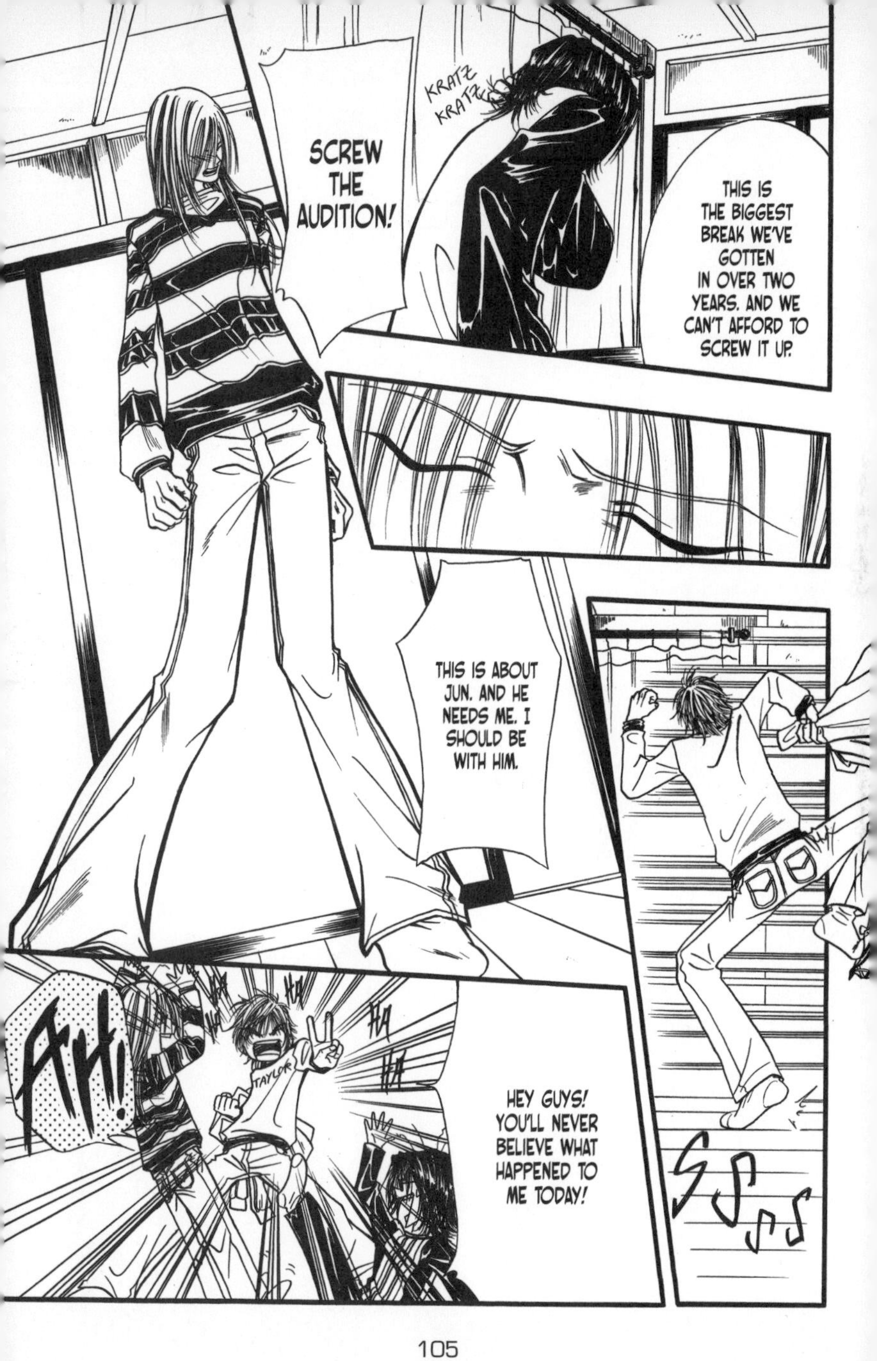
KRATZ KRATZ
THIS IS THE BIGGEST BREAK WE'VE GOTTEN IN OVER TWO YEARS. AND WE CAN'T AFFORD TO SCREW IT UP.
SCREW THE AUDITION!
THIS IS ABOUT JUN. AND HE NEEDS ME. I SHOULD BE WITH HIM.
HEY GUYS! YOU'LL NEVER BELIEVE WHAT HAPPENED TO ME TODAY!
AH!
TAYLOR

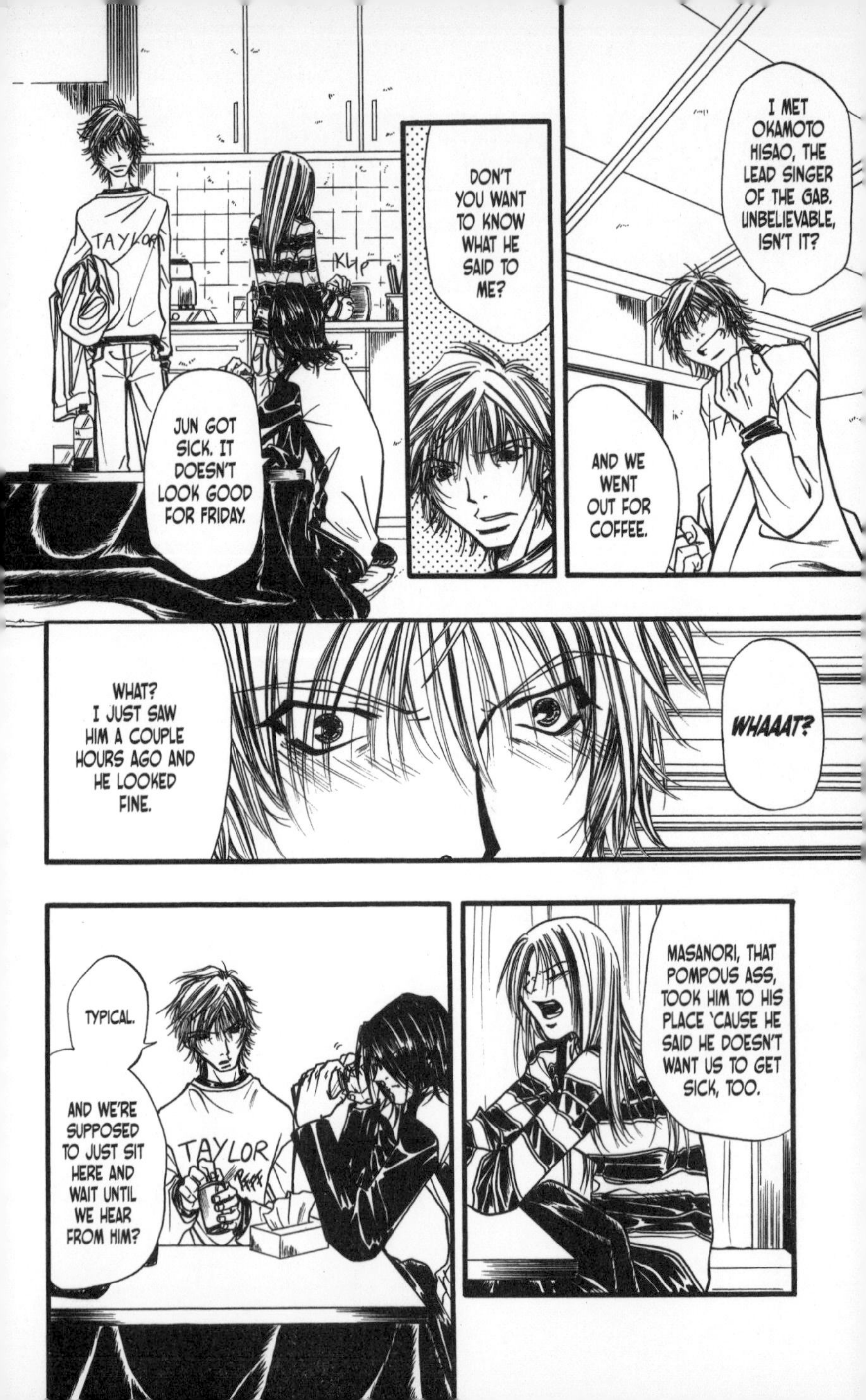
I MET OKAMOTO HISAO, THE LEAD SINGER OF THE GAB. UNBELIEVABLE, ISN'T IT?
AND WE WENT OUT FOR COFFEE.
DON'T YOU WANT TO KNOW WHAT HE SAID TO ME?
JUN GOT SICK. IT DOESN'T LOOK GOOD FOR FRIDAY.
WHAAAT?
WHAT? I JUST SAW HIM A COUPLE HOURS AGO AND HE LOOKED FINE.
MASANORI, THAT POMPOUS ASS, TOOK HIM TO HIS PLACE 'CAUSE HE SAID HE DOESN'T WANT US TO GET SICK, TOO.
TYPICAL.
AND WE'RE SUPPOSED TO JUST SIT HERE AND WAIT UNTIL WE HEAR FROM HIM?

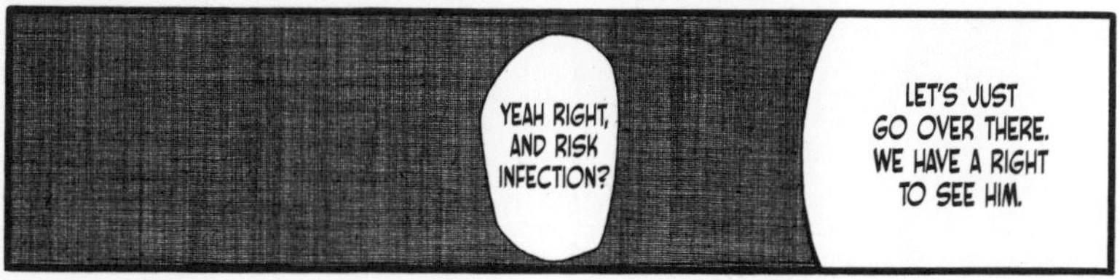
LET'S JUST GO OVER THERE. WE HAVE A RIGHT TO SEE HIM.
YEAH RIGHT, AND RISK INFECTION?

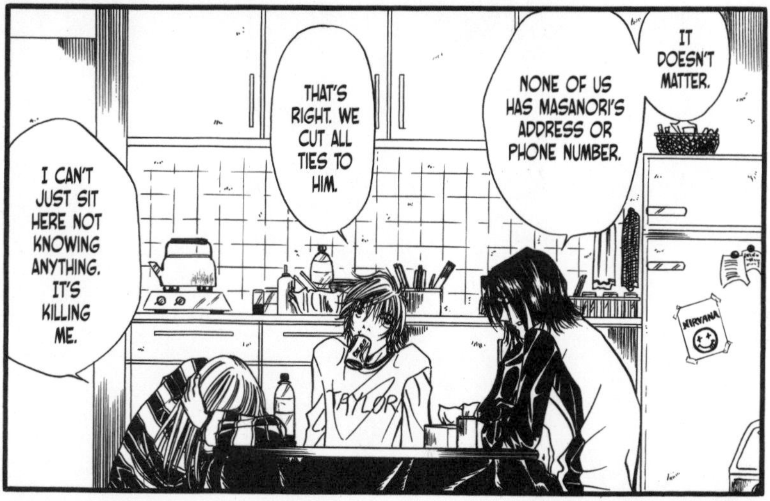
IT DOESN'T MATTER.
NONE OF US HAS MASANORI'S ADDRESS OR PHONE NUMBER.
THAT'S RIGHT. WE CUT ALL TIES TO HIM.
I CAN'T JUST SIT HERE NOT KNOWING ANYTHING. IT'S KILLING ME.
TAYLOR

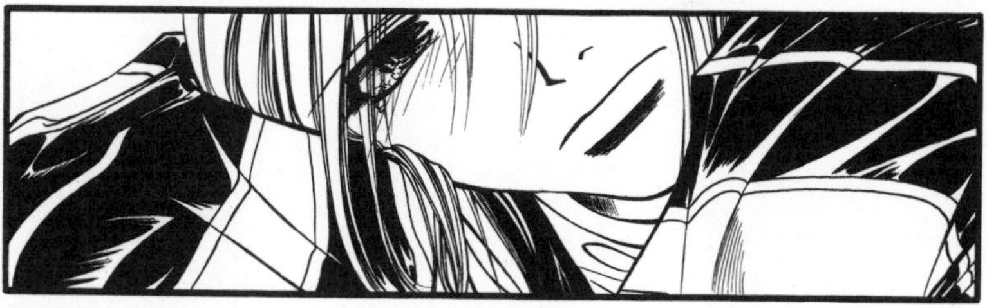

WHY DIDN'T YOU INSIST ON STAYING WITH US, JUN?

WERE YOU NOT ABLE TO...OR DID YOU NOT WANT TO STAY...?

DO YOU PREFER TO BE WITH HIM INSTEAD OF BEING WITH US...OR BEING WITH ME...?

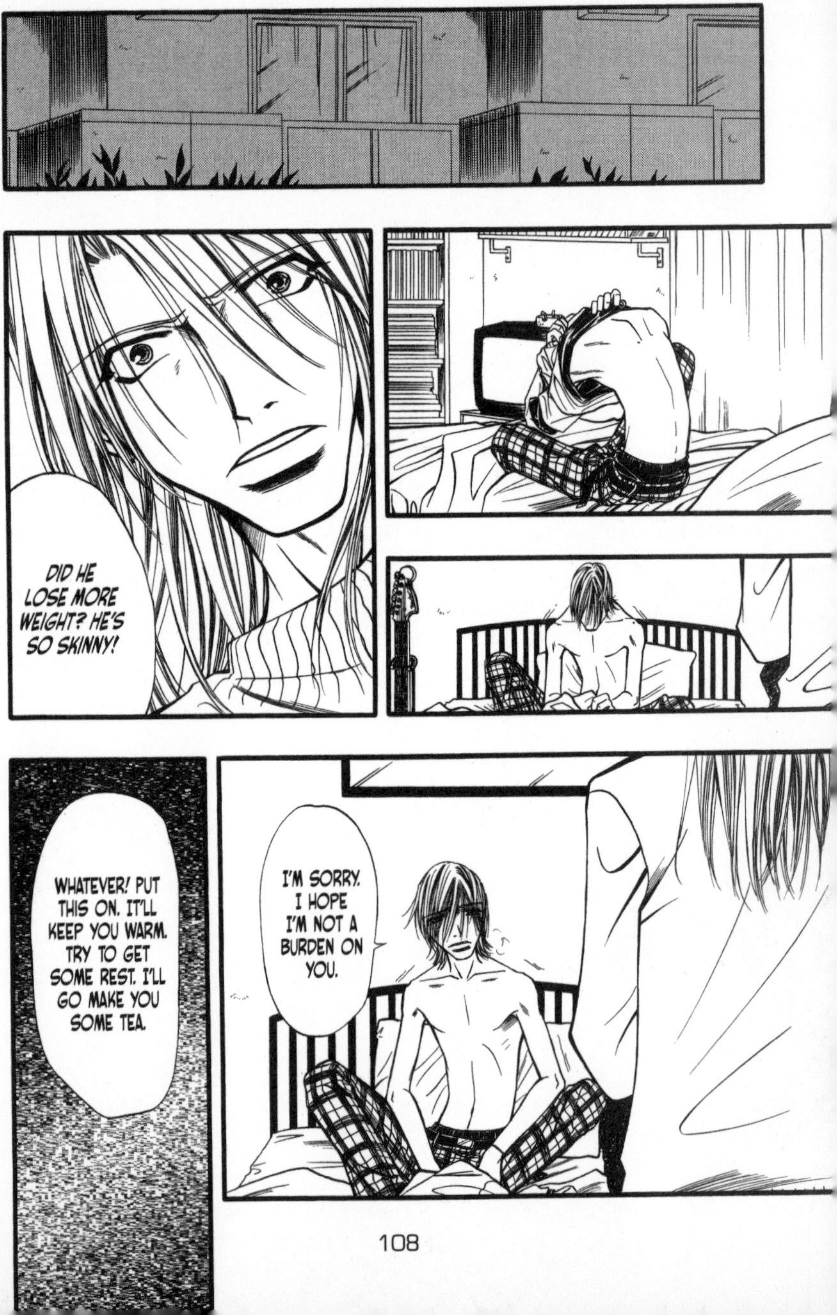
DID HE LOSE MORE WEIGHT? HE'S SO SKINNY!
I'M SORRY. I HOPE I'M NOT A BURDEN ON YOU.
WHATEVER! PUT THIS ON. IT'LL KEEP YOU WARM. TRY TO GET SOME REST. I'LL GO MAKE YOU SOME TEA.

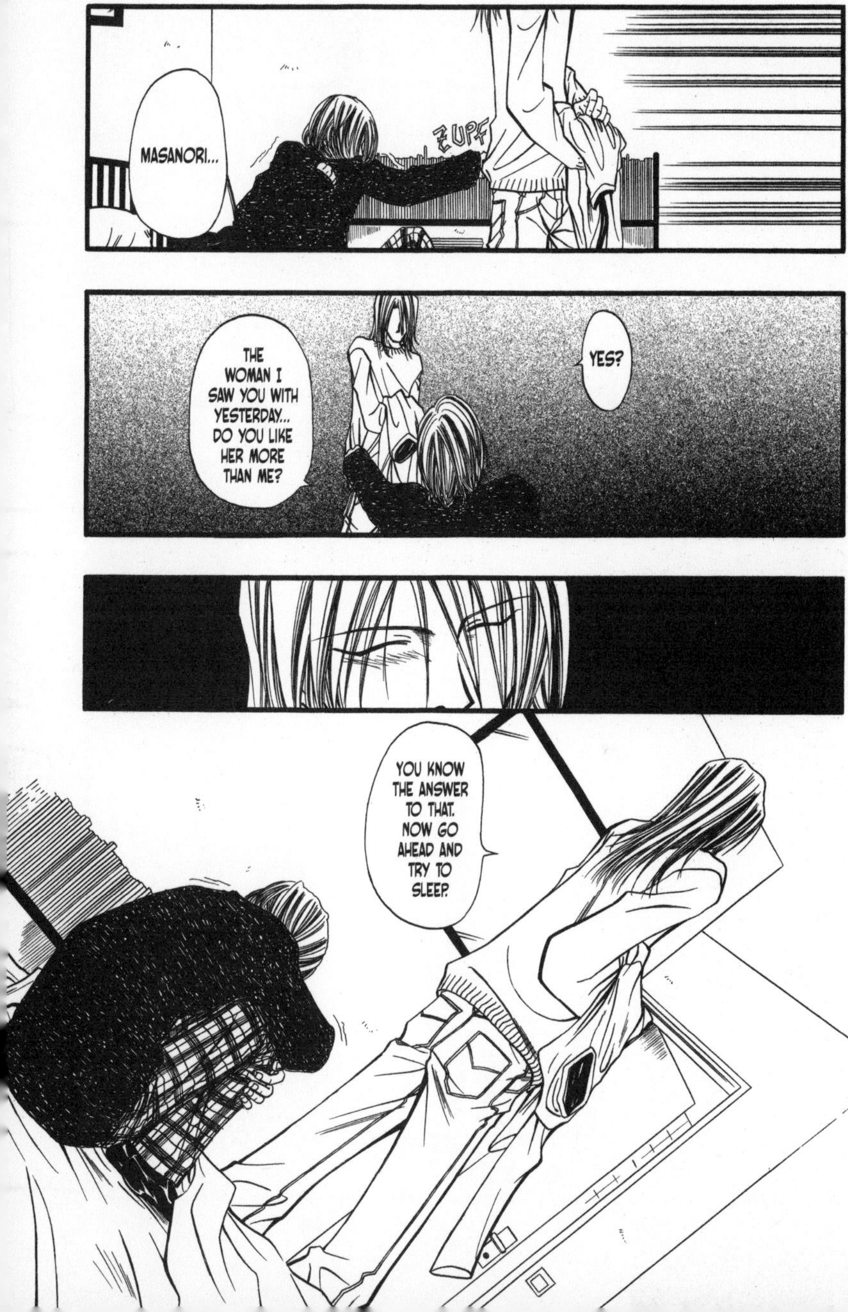
ZUPF
MASANORI...
YES?
THE WOMAN I SAW YOU WITH YESTERDAY... DO YOU LIKE HER MORE THAN ME?
YOU KNOW THE ANSWER TO THAT. NOW GO AHEAD AND TRY TO SLEEP.

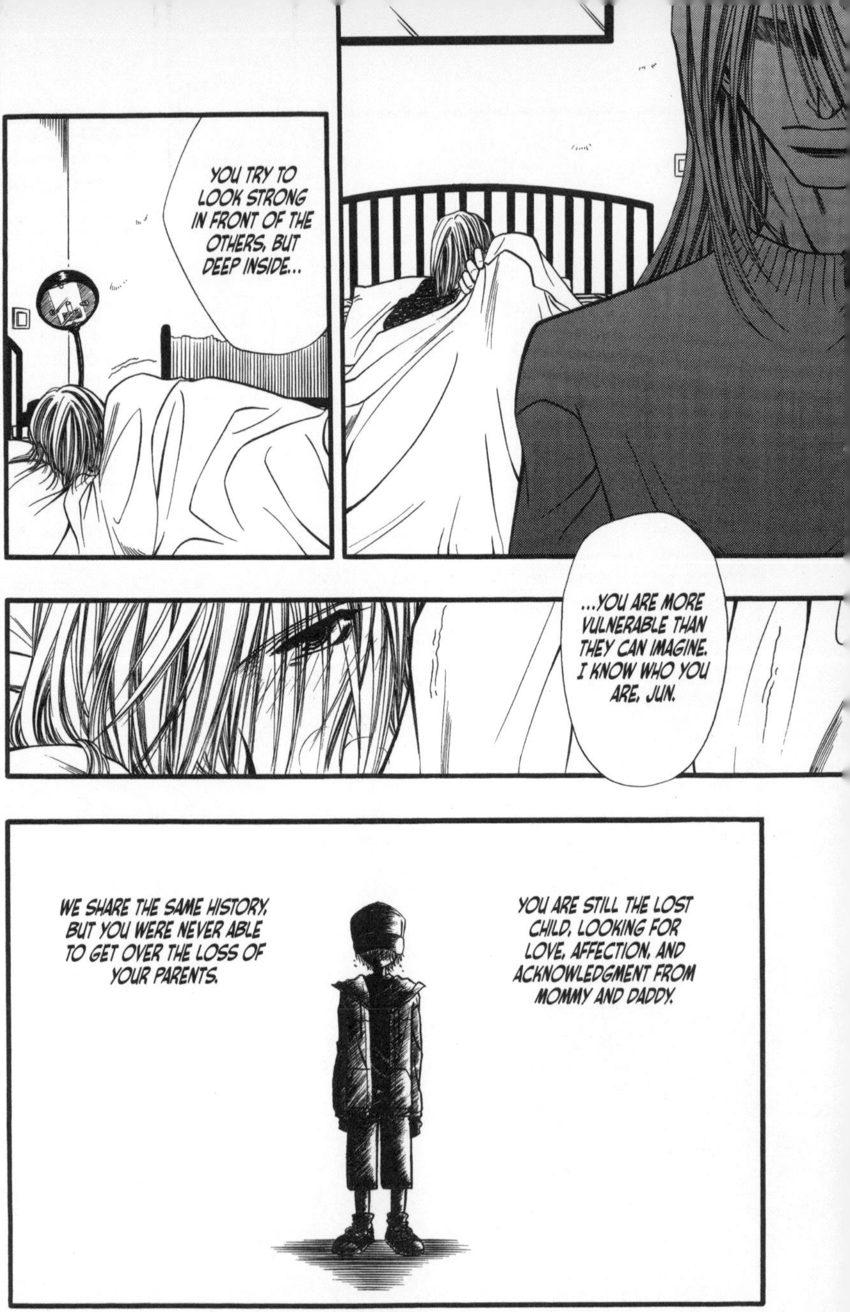
YOU TRY TO LOOK STRONG IN FRONT OF THE OTHERS, BUT DEEP INSIDE...
...YOU ARE MORE VULNERABLE THAN THEY CAN IMAGINE. I KNOW WHO YOU ARE, JUN.
YOU ARE STILL THE LOST CHILD, LOOKING FOR LOVE, AFFECTION, AND ACKNOWLEDGMENT FROM MOMMY AND DADDY.
WE SHARE THE SAME HISTORY, BUT YOU WERE NEVER ABLE TO GET OVER THE LOSS OF YOUR PARENTS.

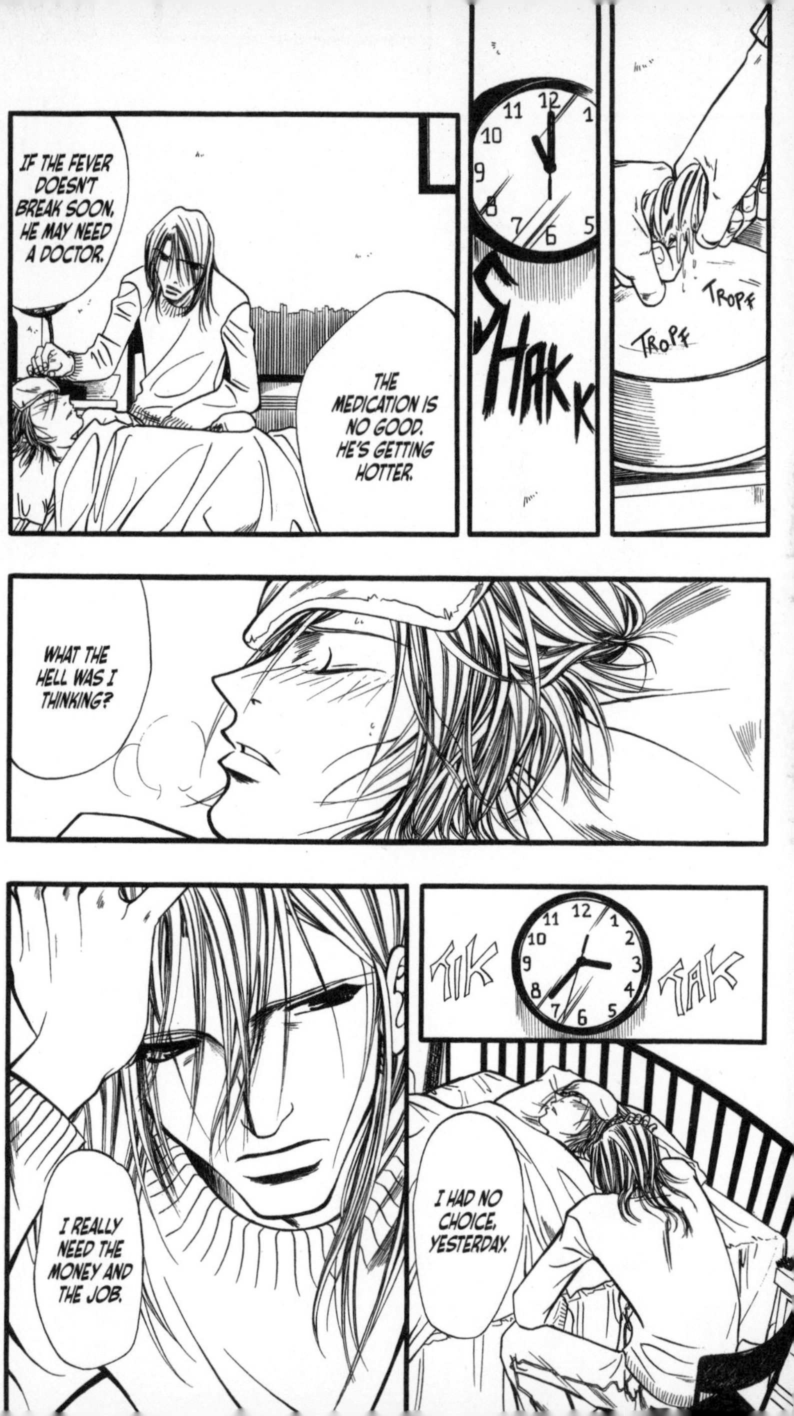
TROPF
TROPF
SHAKK
THE MEDICATION IS NO GOOD. HE'S GETTING HOTTER.
IF THE FEVER DOESN'T BREAK SOON, HE MAY NEED A DOCTOR.
WHAT THE HELL WAS I THINKING?
TIK
TAK
I HAD NO CHOICE, YESTERDAY.
I REALLY NEED THE MONEY AND THE JOB.

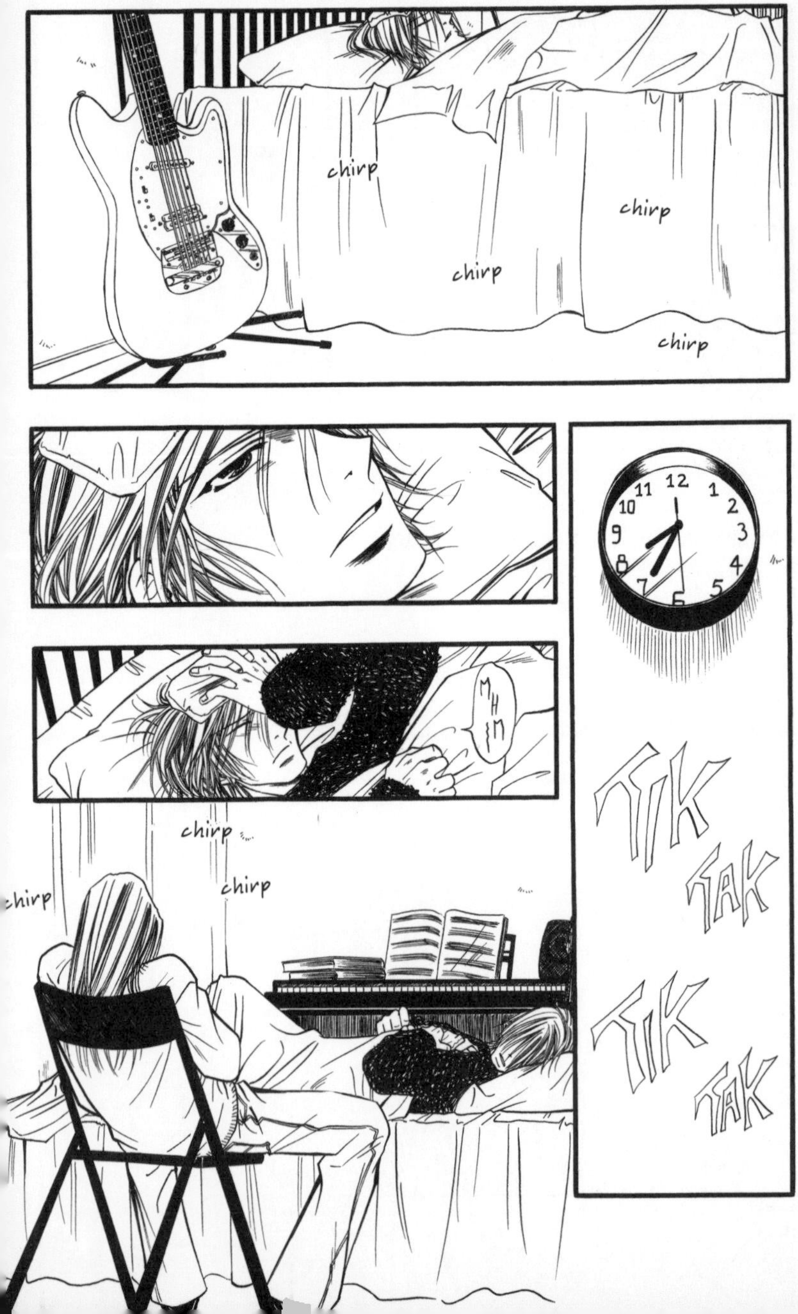
chirp
chirp
chirp
chirp
TIK
TAK
TIK
TAK
MHM
chirp
chirp
chirp

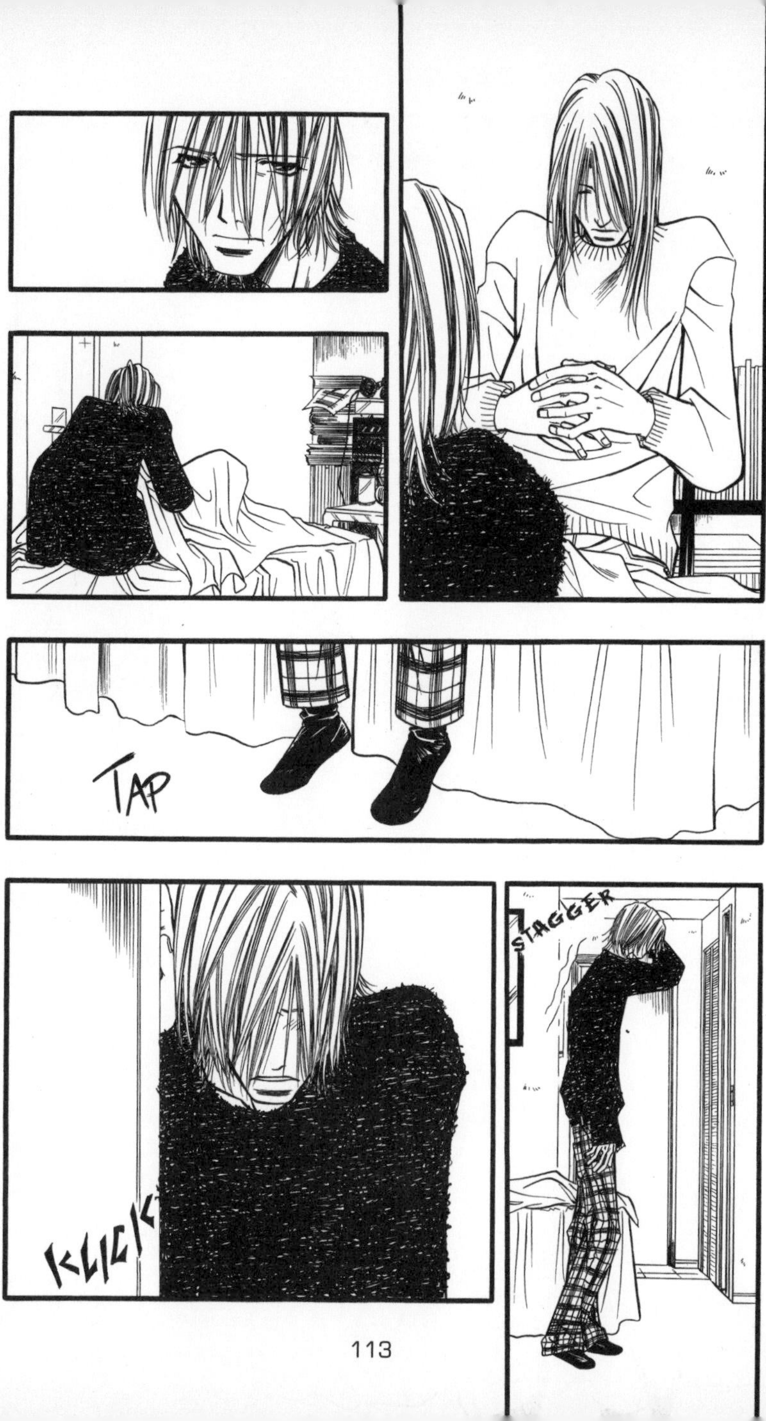
TAP
STAGGER
KLICK

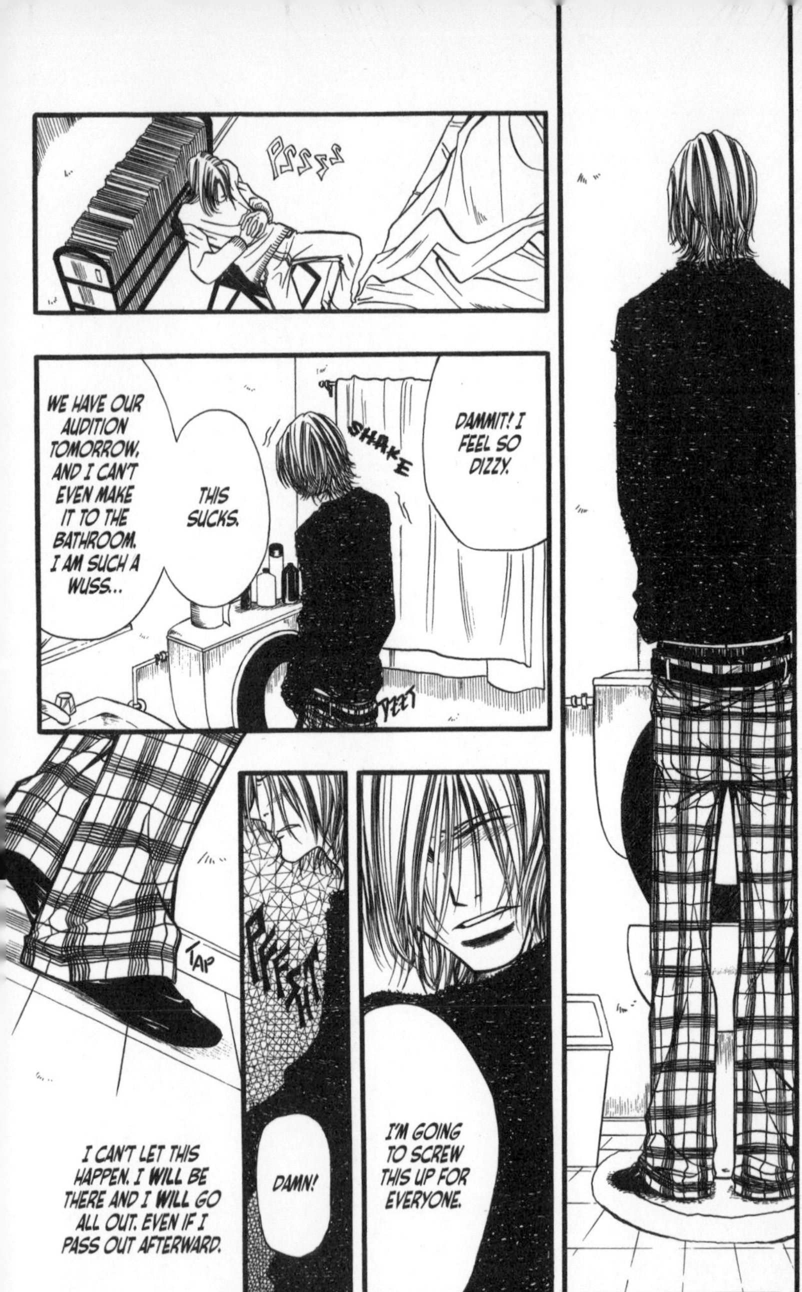
DAMMIT! I FEEL SO DIZZY.
SHAKE
THIS SUCKS.
WE HAVE OUR AUDITION TOMORROW. AND I CAN'T EVEN MAKE IT TO THE BATHROOM. I AM SUCH A WUSS...
I'M GOING TO SCREW THIS UP FOR EVERYONE.
DAMN!
TAP
I CAN'T LET THIS HAPPEN. I WILL BE THERE AND I WILL GO ALL OUT. EVEN IF I PASS OUT AFTERWARD.

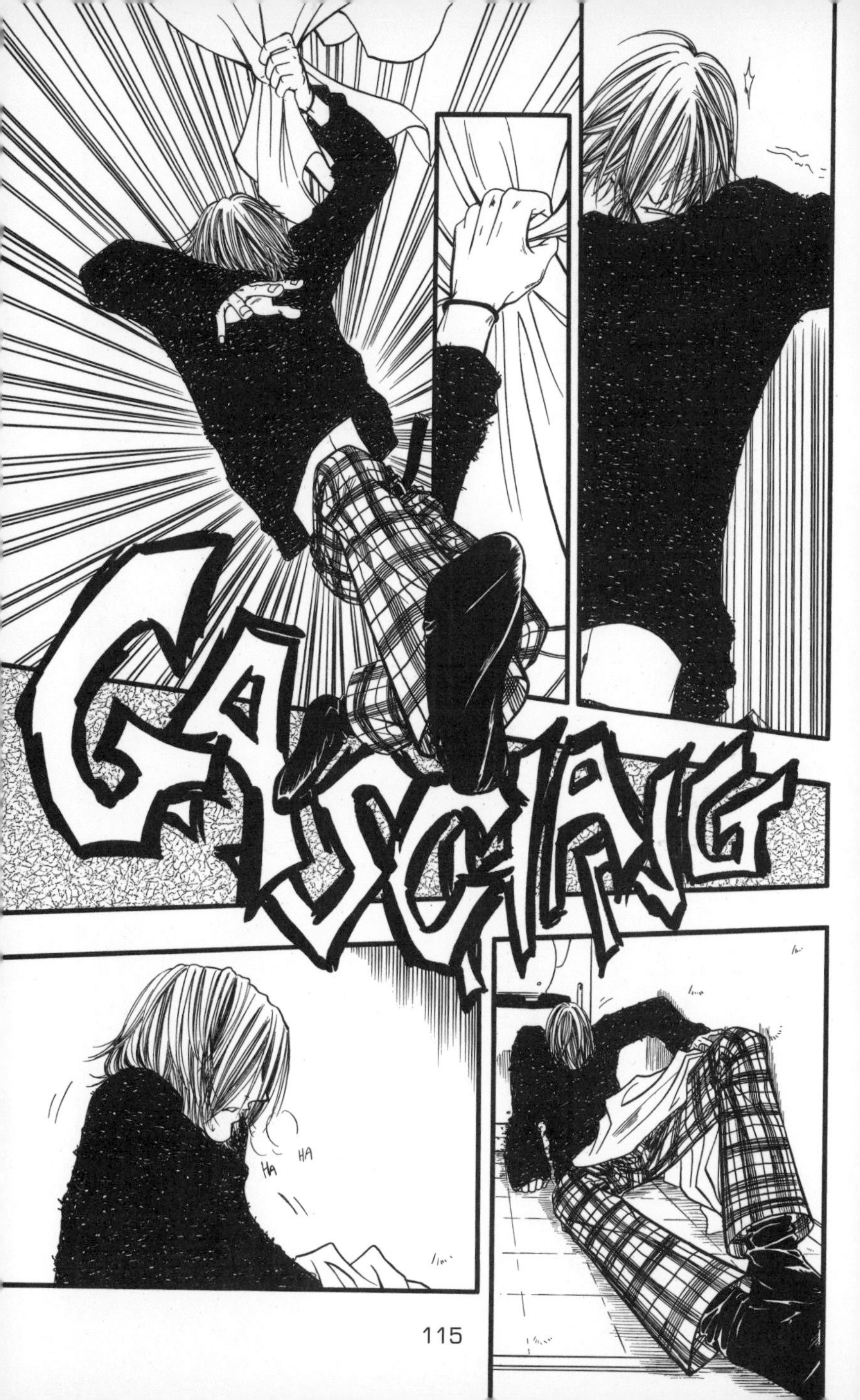
HA
HA

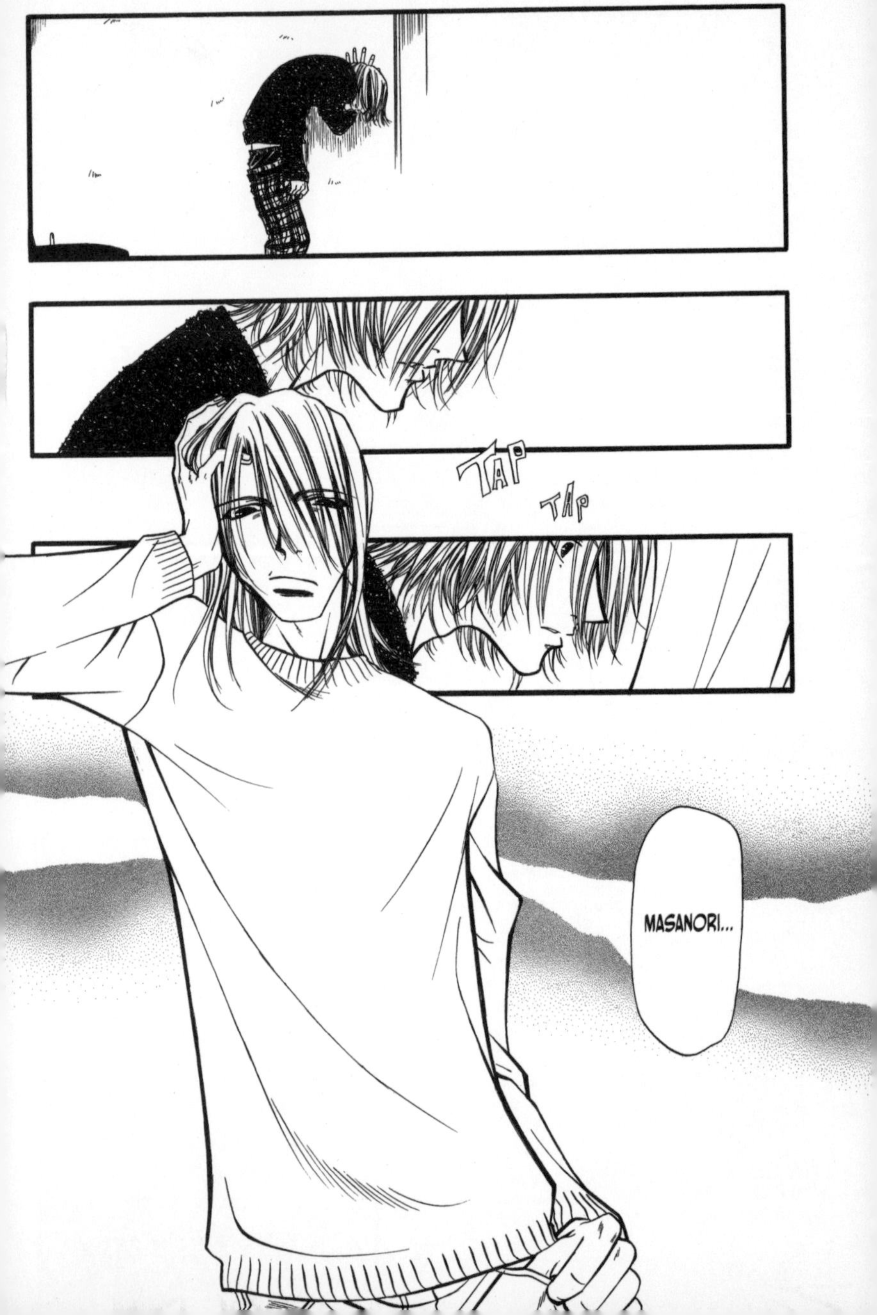
TAP
TAP
MASANORI...

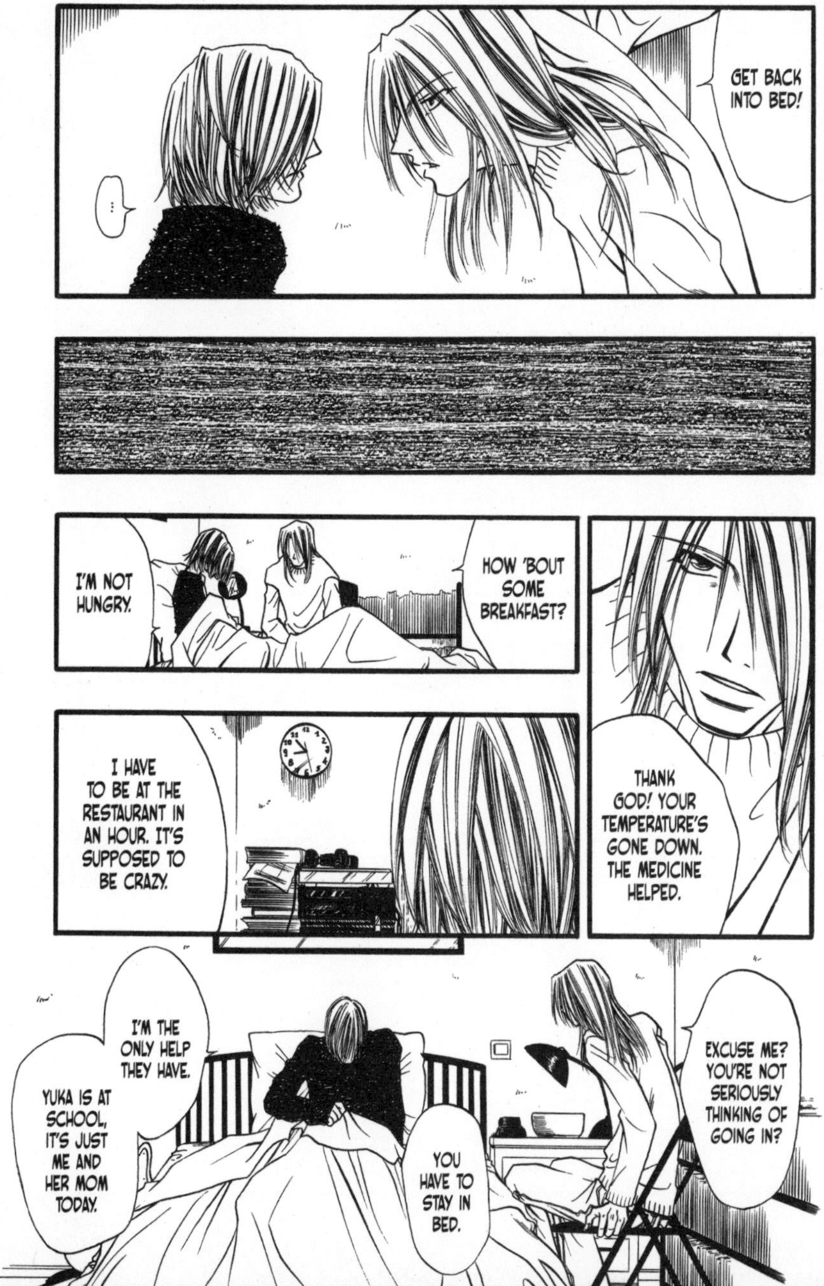
GET BACK INTO BED!
...
THANK GOD! YOUR TEMPERATURE'S GONE DOWN. THE MEDICINE HELPED.
HOW 'BOUT SOME BREAKFAST?
I'M NOT HUNGRY.
I HAVE TO BE AT THE RESTAURANT IN AN HOUR. IT'S SUPPOSED TO BE CRAZY.
EXCUSE ME? YOU'RE NOT SERIOUSLY THINKING OF GOING IN?
YOU HAVE TO STAY IN BED.
I'M THE ONLY HELP THEY HAVE.
YUKA IS AT SCHOOL, IT'S JUST ME AND HER MOM TODAY.

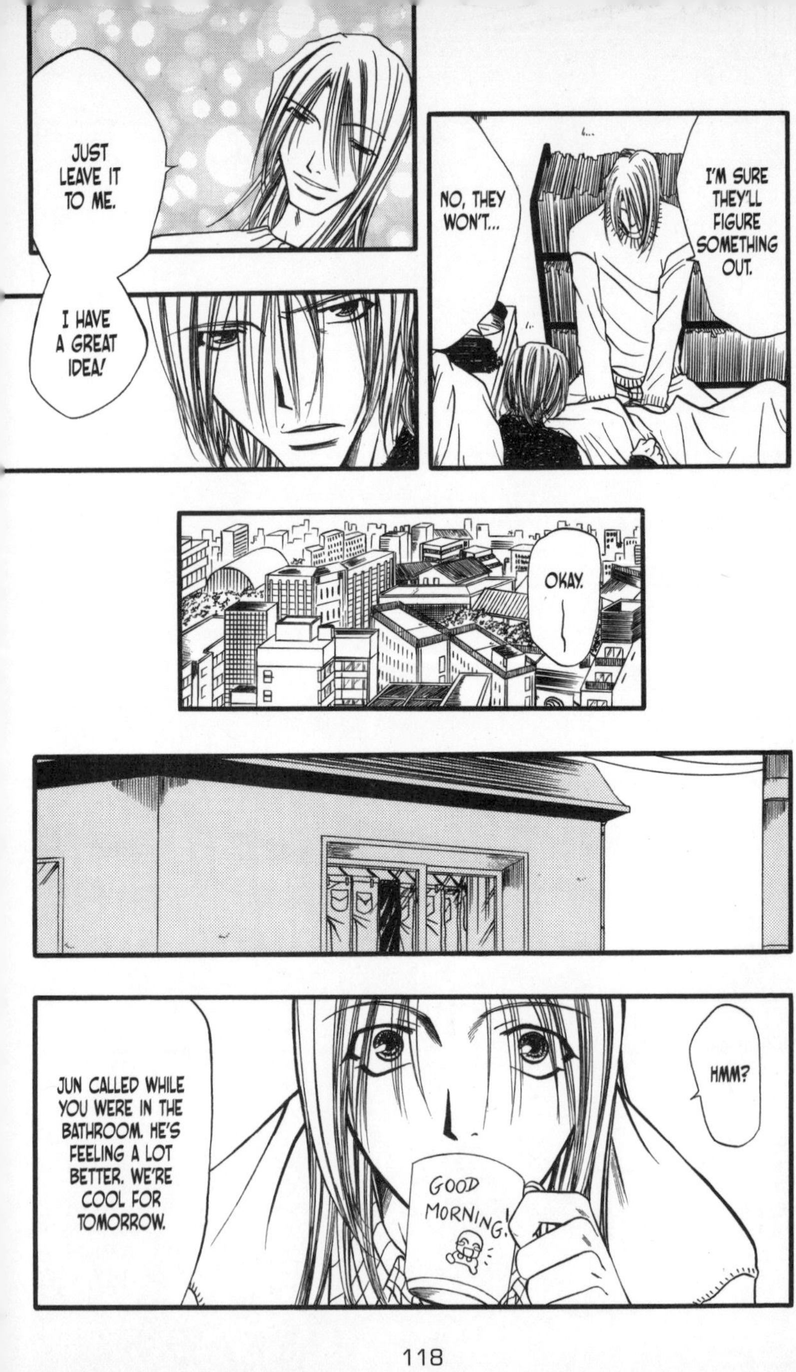

I'M SURE THEY'LL FIGURE SOMETHING OUT.
NO, THEY WON'T...
JUST LEAVE IT TO ME.
I HAVE A GREAT IDEA!
OKAY.
HMM?
JUN CALLED WHILE YOU WERE IN THE BATHROOM. HE'S FEELING A LOT BETTER. WE'RE COOL FOR TOMORROW.
GOOD MORNING!

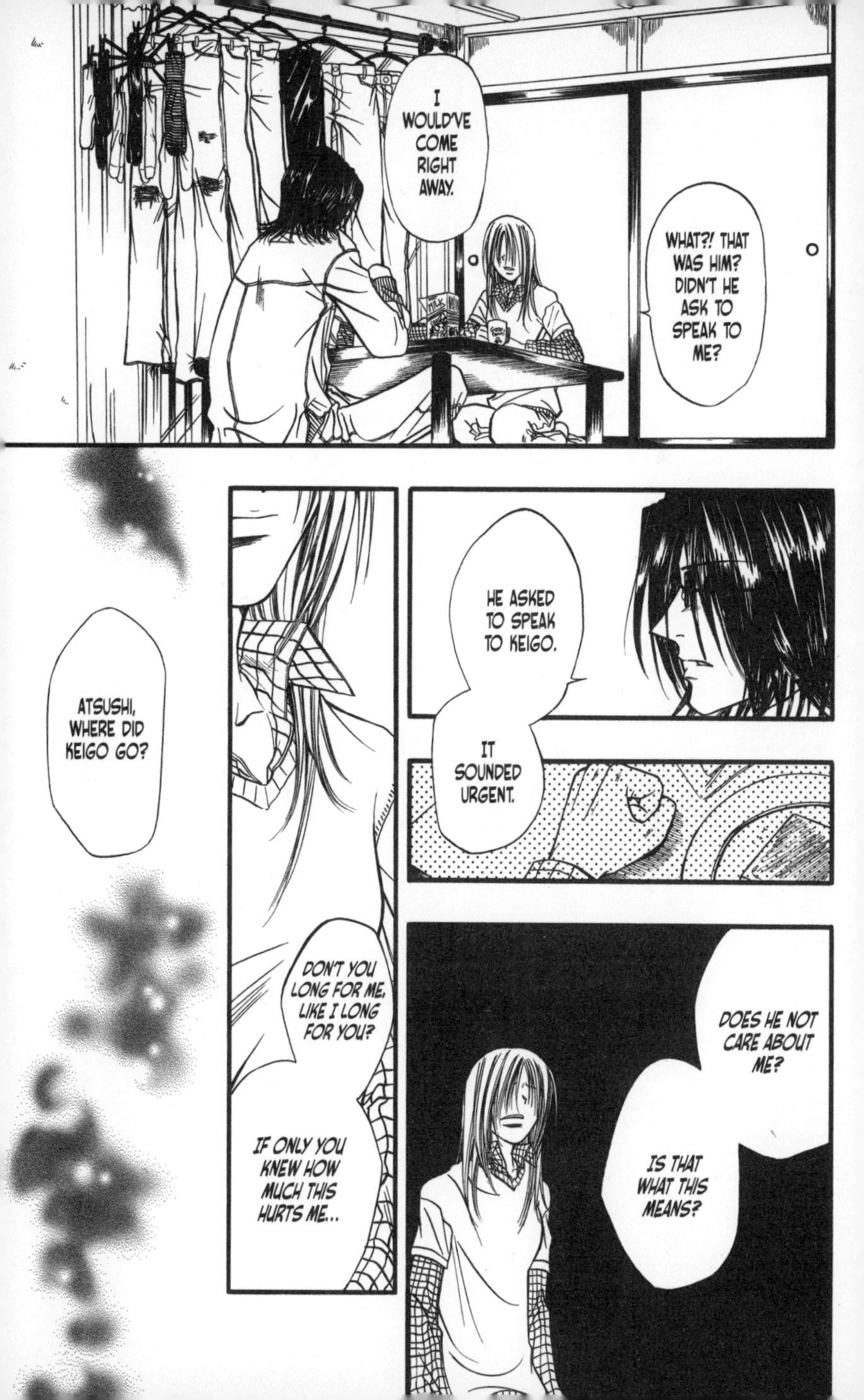
WHAT?! THAT WAS HIM? DIDN'T HE ASK TO SPEAK TO ME?
I WOULD'VE COME RIGHT AWAY.
HE ASKED TO SPEAK TO KEIGO.
IT SOUNDED URGENT.
DOES HE NOT CARE ABOUT ME?
IS THAT WHAT THIS MEANS?
DON'T YOU LONG FOR ME, LIKE I LONG FOR YOU?
IF ONLY YOU KNEW HOW MUCH THIS HURTS ME...
ATSUSHI, WHERE DID KEIGO GO?

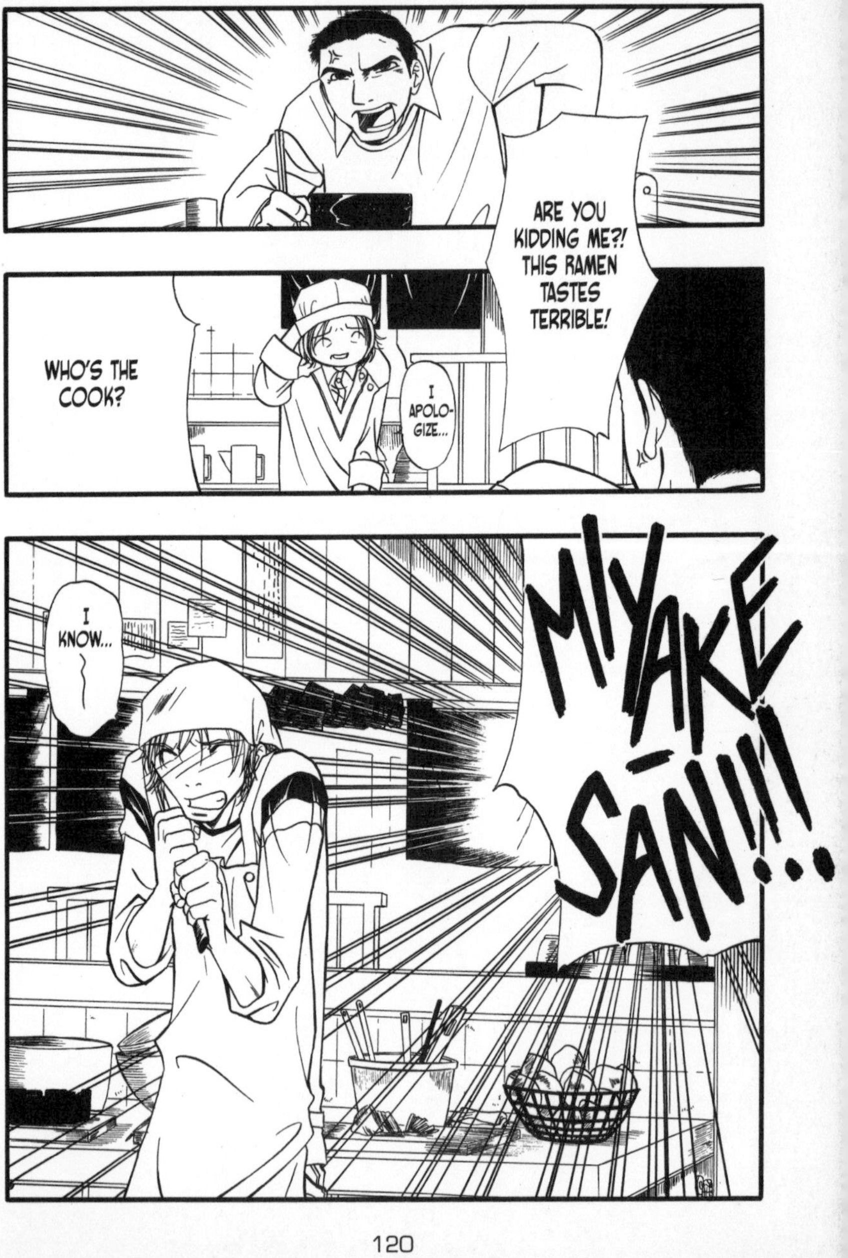
ARE YOU KIDDING ME?! THIS RAMEN TASTES TERRIBLE!
I APOLOGIZE...
WHO'S THE COOK?
MIYAKE-SAN!!!...
I KNOW...

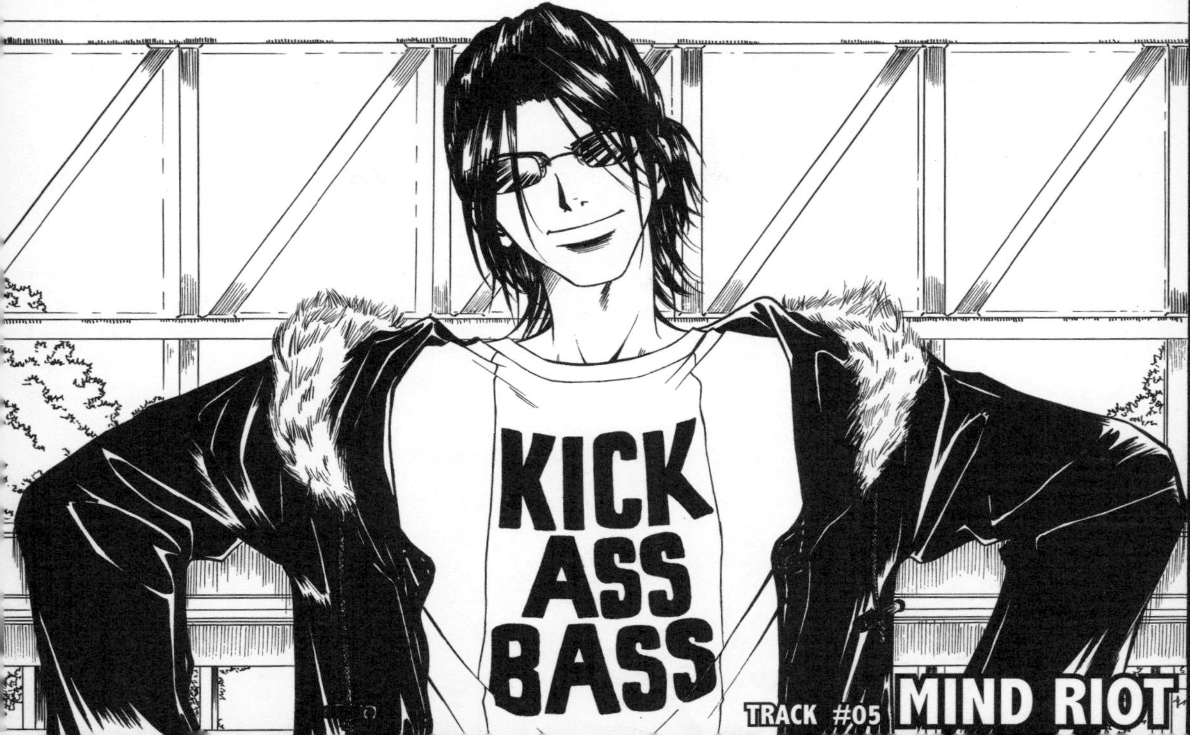
KICK
ASS
BASS

TRACK #05 MIND RIOT

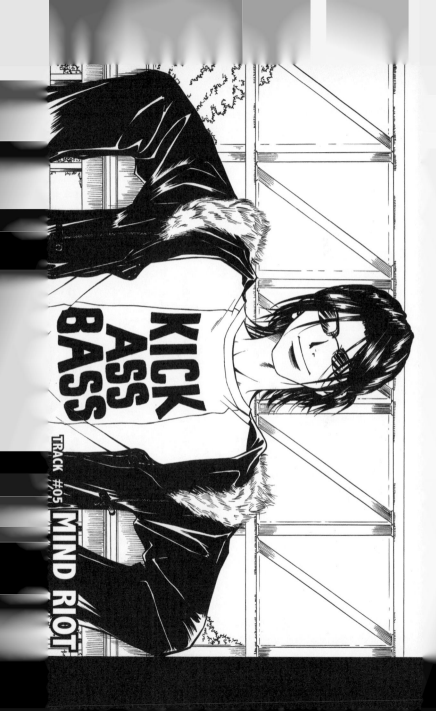

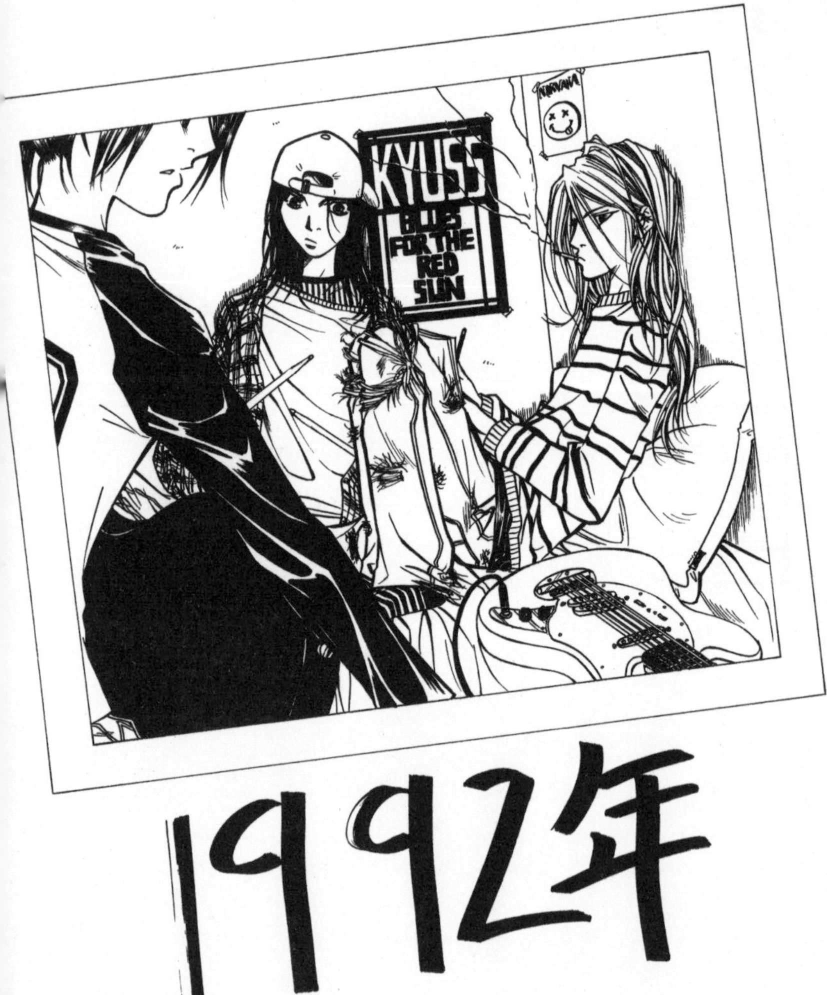
NIRVANA
KYUSS
BLUES FOR THE RED SUN

1992年

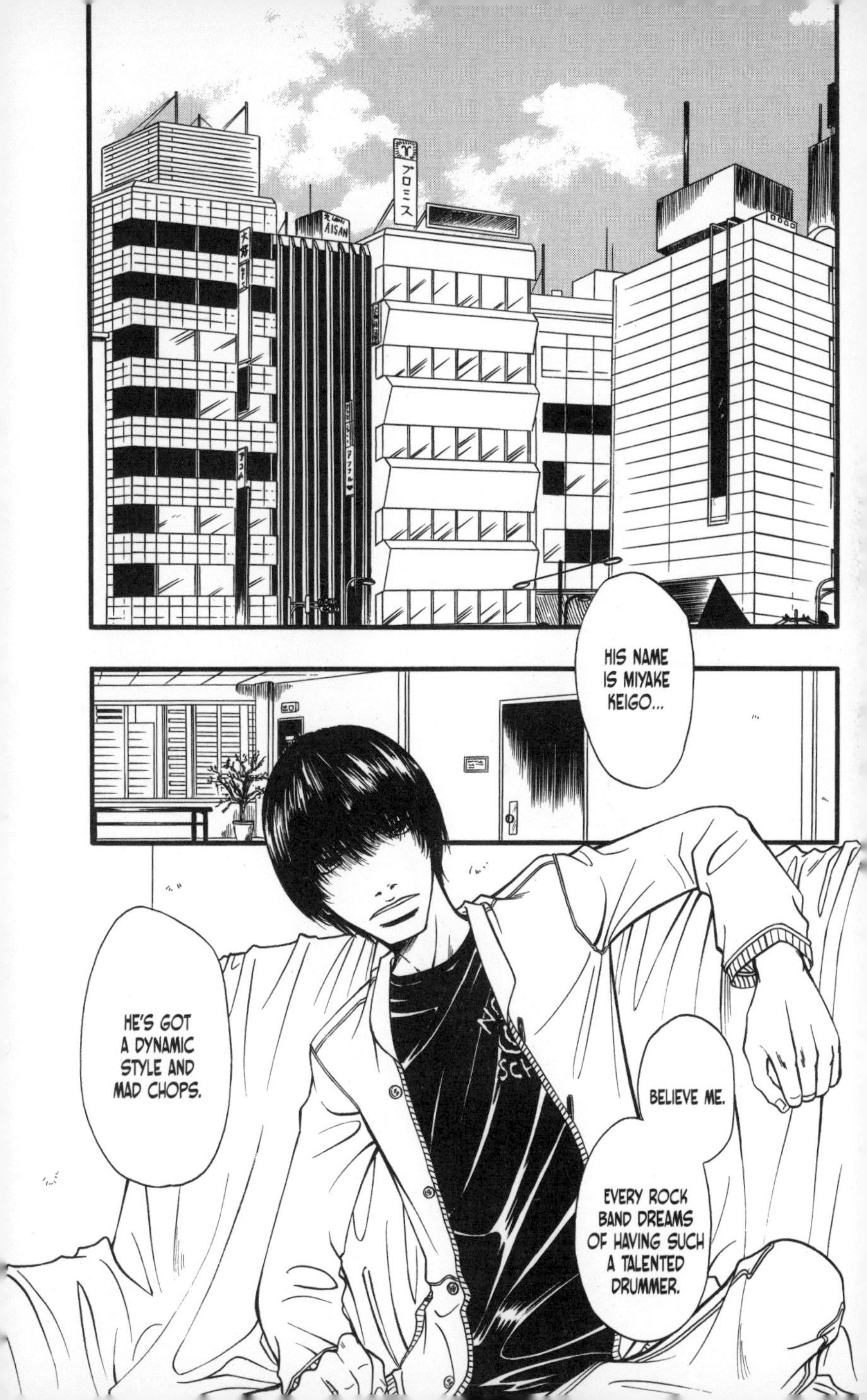
プロミス
AISAN
HIS NAME IS MIYAKE KEIGO...
BELIEVE ME.
EVERY ROCK BAND DREAMS OF HAVING SUCH A TALENTED DRUMMER.
HE'S GOT A DYNAMIC STYLE AND MAD CHOPS.

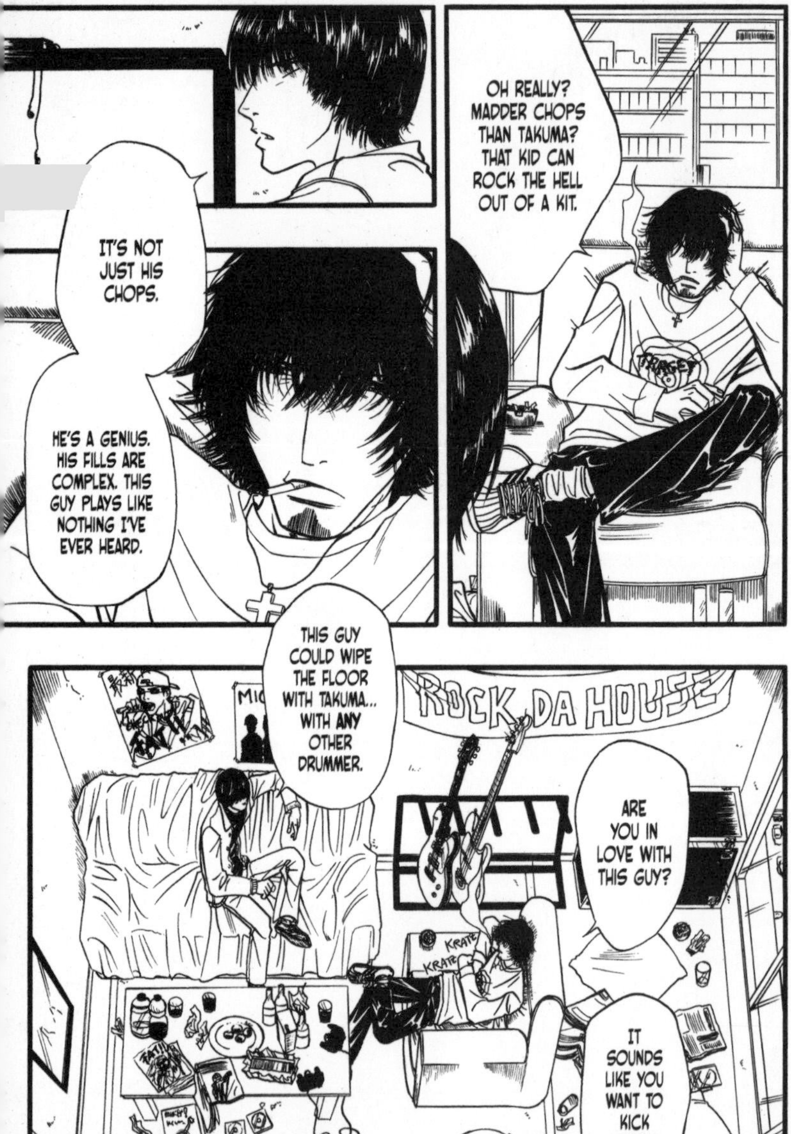

OH REALLY? MADDER CHOPS THAN TAKUMA? THAT KID CAN ROCK THE HELL OUT OF A KIT.
IT'S NOT JUST HIS CHOPS.
HE'S A GENIUS. HIS FILLS ARE COMPLEX. THIS GUY PLAYS LIKE NOTHING I'VE EVER HEARD.
THIS GUY COULD WIPE THE FLOOR WITH TAKUMA... WITH ANY OTHER DRUMMER.
ROCK DA HOUSE
ARE YOU IN LOVE WITH THIS GUY?
IT SOUNDS LIKE YOU WANT TO KICK TAKUMA OUT.

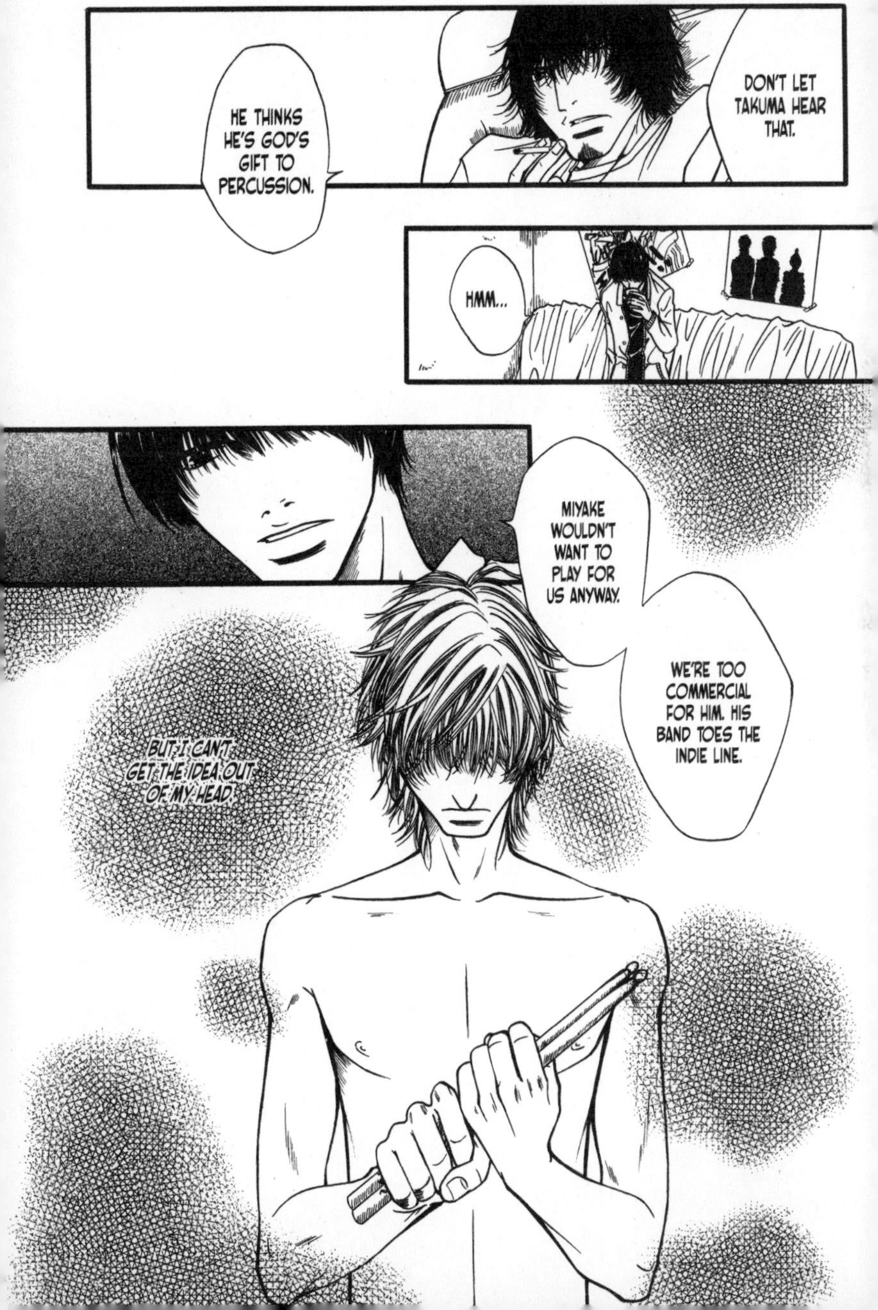
DON'T LET TAKUMA HEAR THAT.
HE THINKS HE'S GOD'S GIFT TO PERCUSSION.
HMM...
MIYAKE WOULDN'T WANT TO PLAY FOR US ANYWAY.
WE'RE TOO COMMERCIAL FOR HIM. HIS BAND TOES THE INDIE LINE.
BUT I CAN'T GET THE IDEA OUT OF MY HEAD.

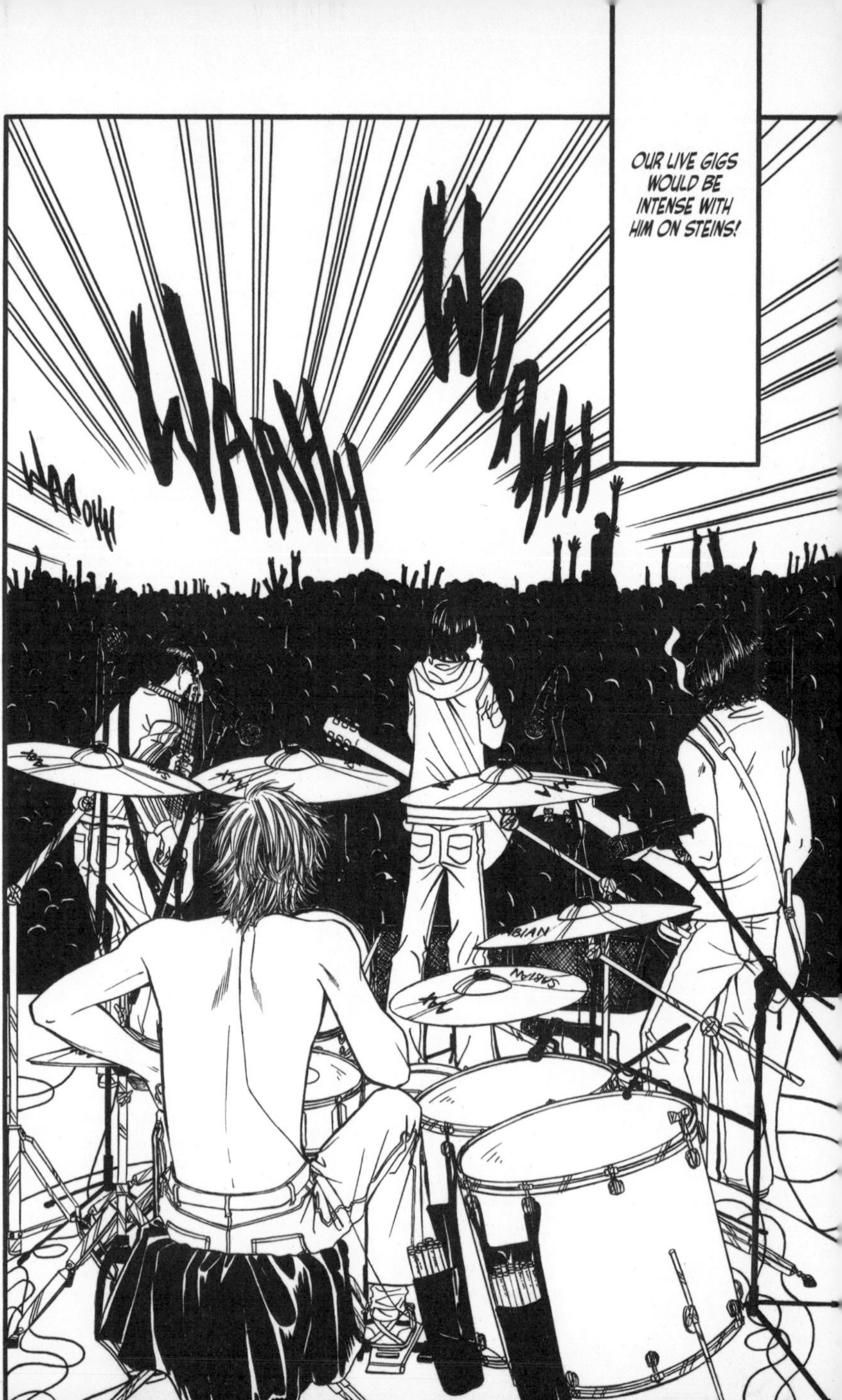
OUR LIVE GIGS WOULD BE INTENSE WITH HIM ON STEINS!
SABIAN

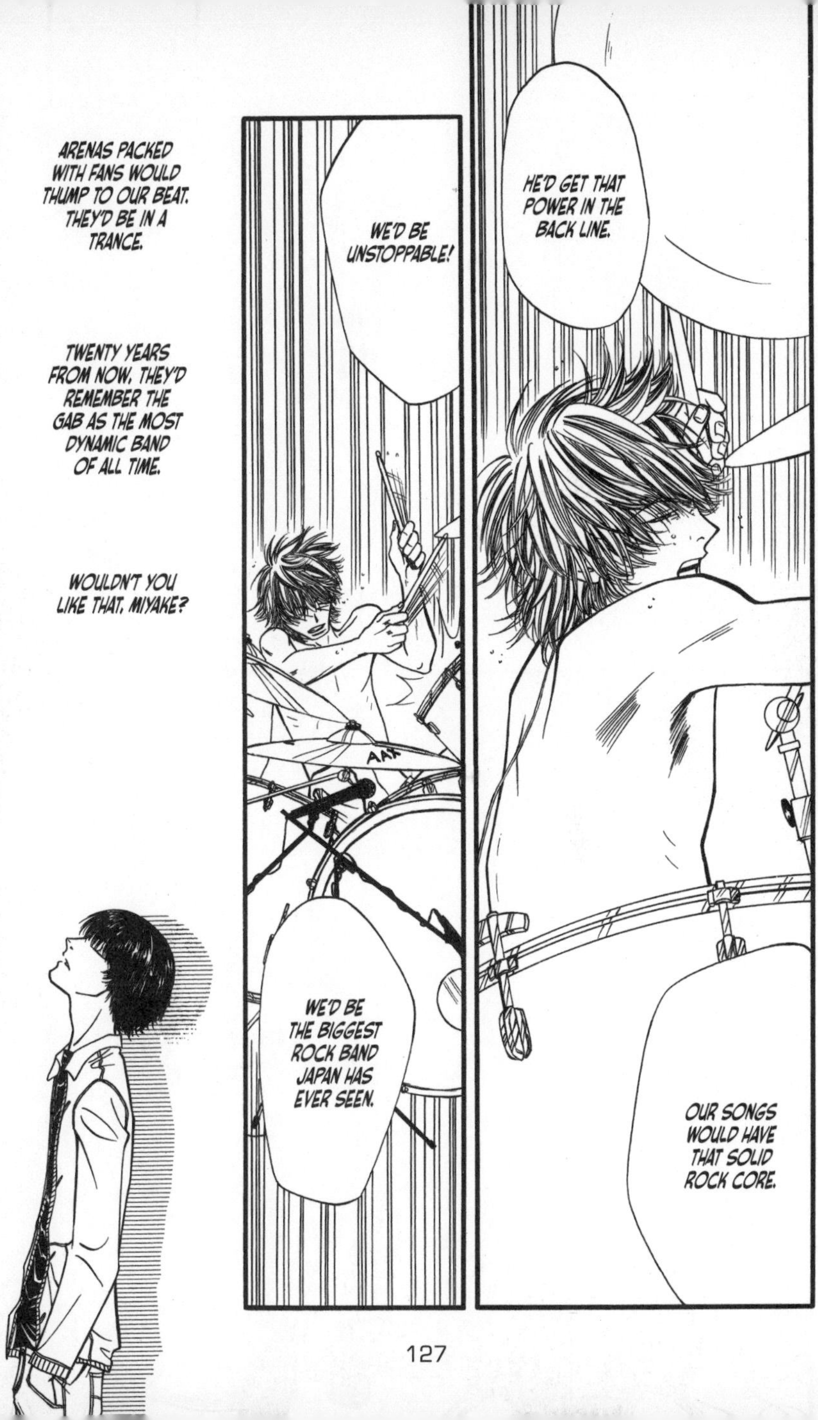
HE'D GET THAT POWER IN THE BACK LINE.
OUR SONGS WOULD HAVE THAT SOLID ROCK CORE.
WE'D BE UNSTOPPABLE!
WE'D BE THE BIGGEST ROCK BAND JAPAN HAS EVER SEEN.
ARENAS PACKED WITH FANS WOULD THUMP TO OUR BEAT. THEY'D BE IN A TRANCE.
TWENTY YEARS FROM NOW, THEY'D REMEMBER THE GAB AS THE MOST DYNAMIC BAND OF ALL TIME.
WOULDN'T YOU LIKE THAT, MIYAKE?

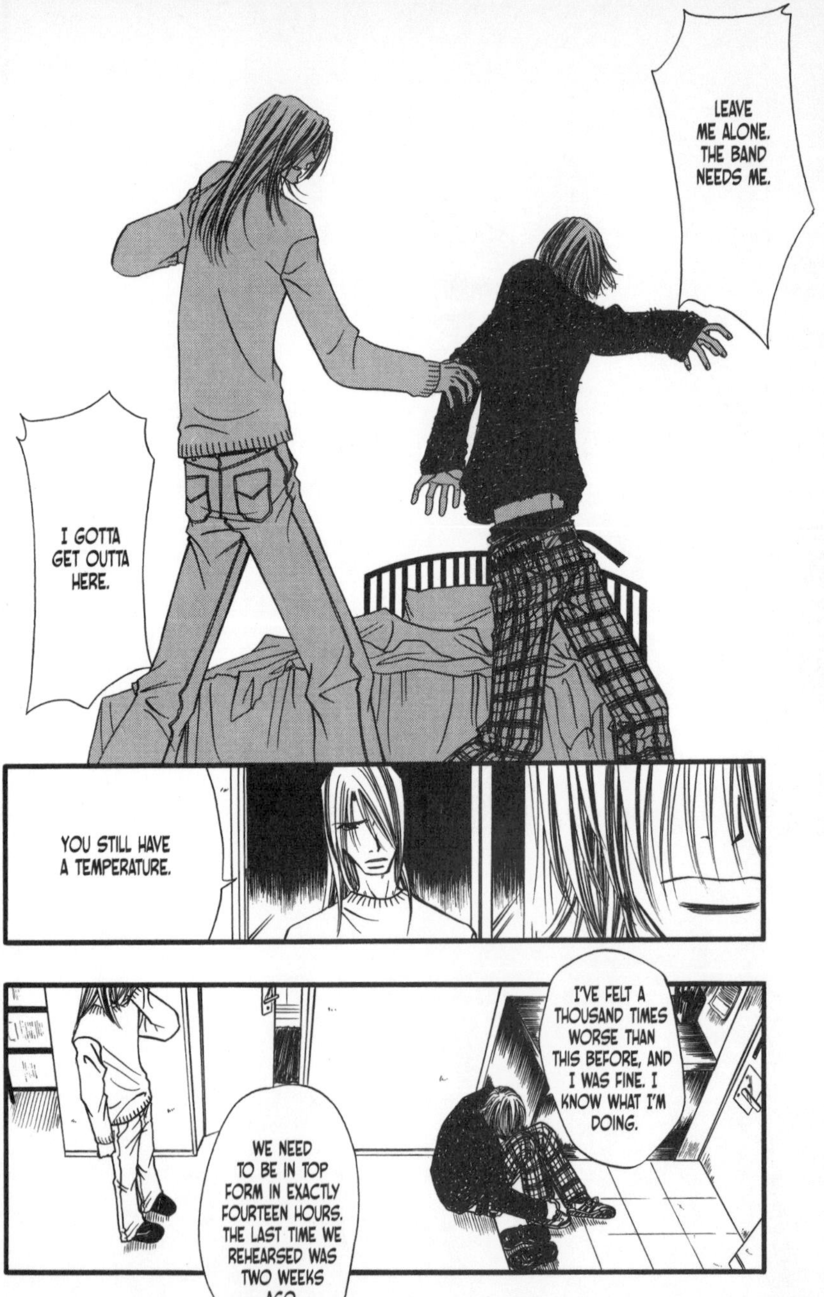
LEAVE ME ALONE. THE BAND NEEDS ME.
I GOTTA GET OUTTA HERE.
YOU STILL HAVE A TEMPERATURE.
I'VE FELT A THOUSAND TIMES WORSE THAN THIS BEFORE, AND I WAS FINE. I KNOW WHAT I'M DOING.
WE NEED TO BE IN TOP FORM IN EXACTLY FOURTEEN HOURS. THE LAST TIME WE REHEARSED WAS TWO WEEKS AGO.

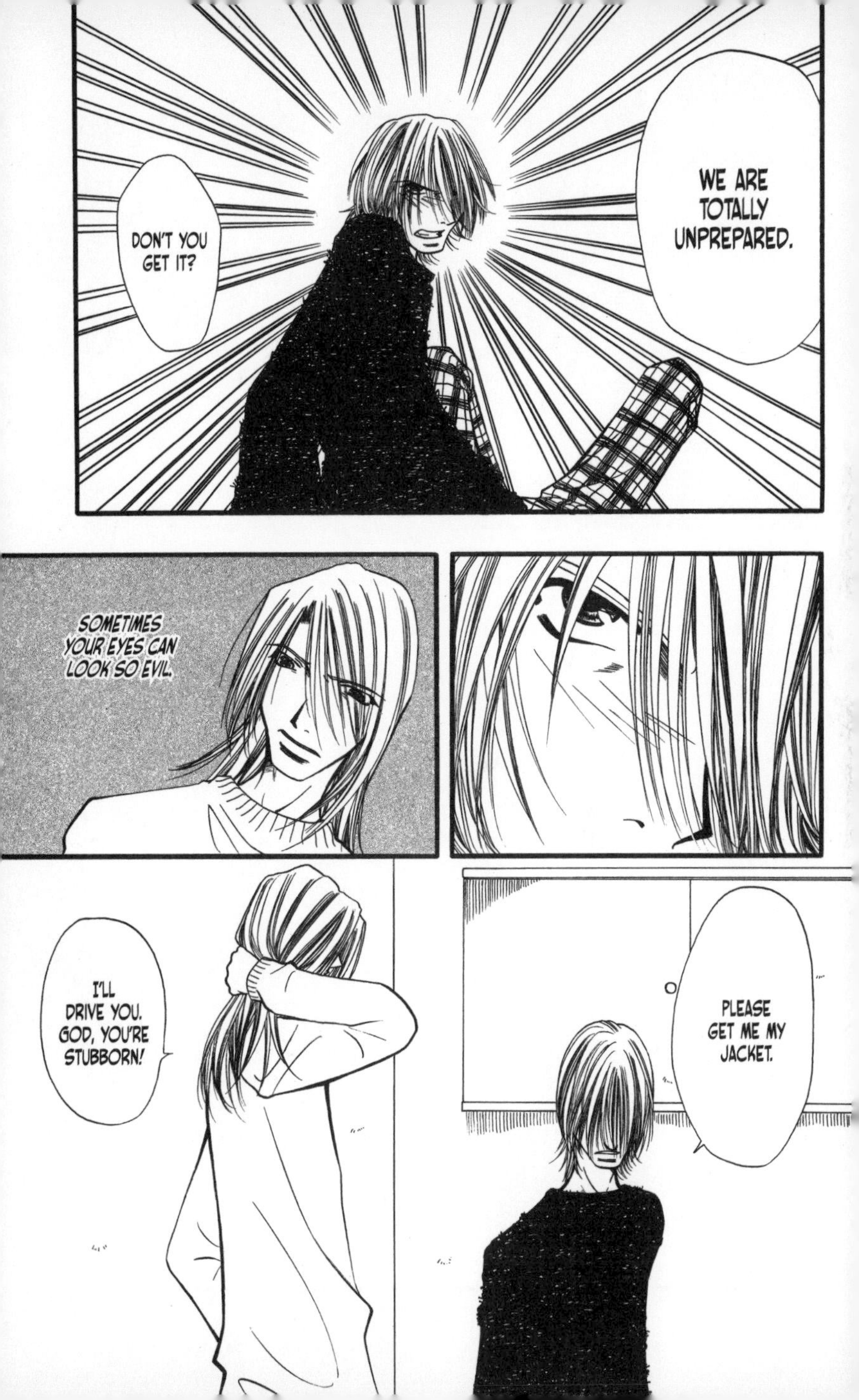
WE ARE TOTALLY UNPREPARED.
DON'T YOU GET IT?
SOMETIMES YOUR EYES CAN LOOK SO EVIL.
PLEASE GET ME MY JACKET.
I'LL DRIVE YOU. GOD, YOU'RE STUBBORN!

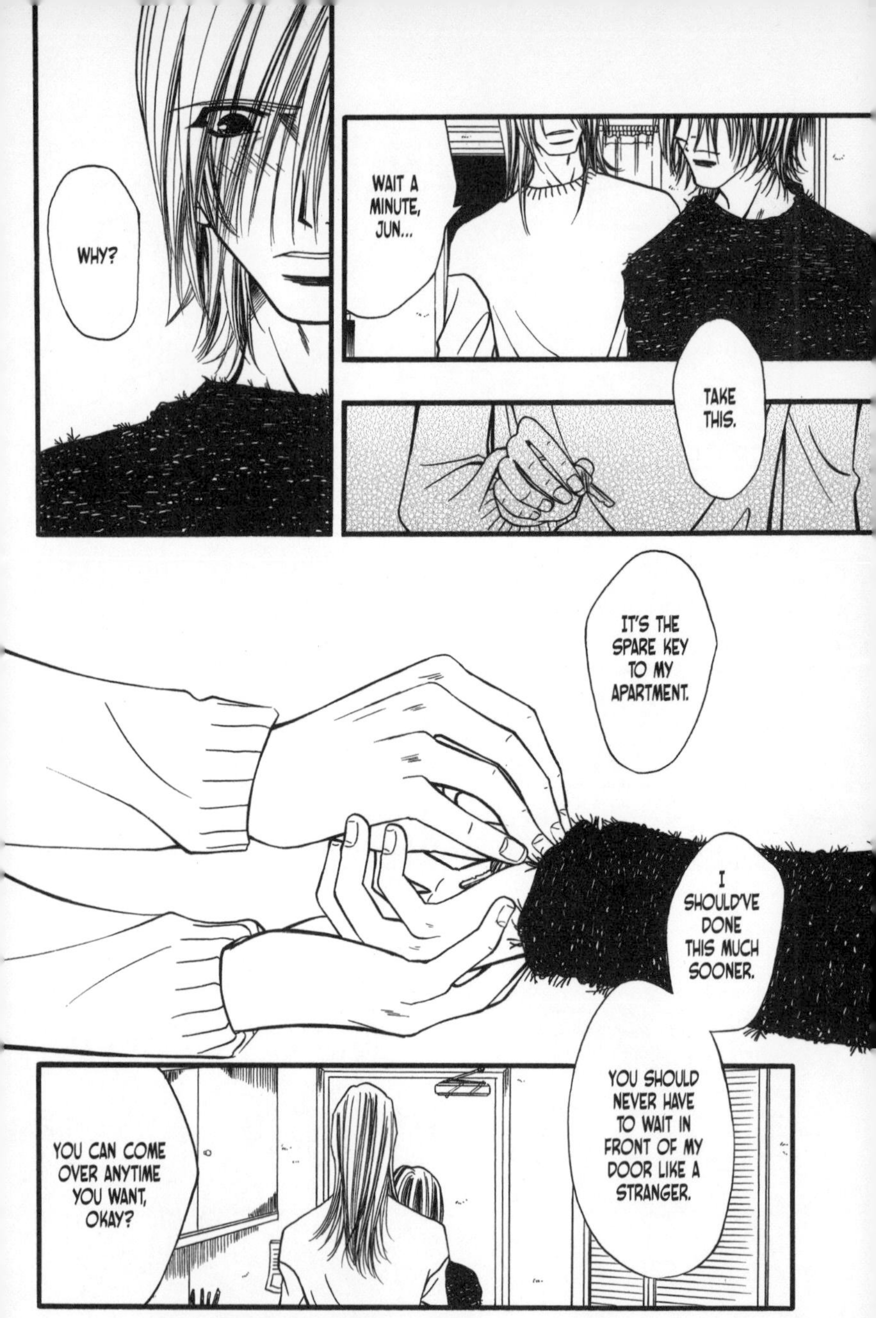
WAIT A MINUTE, JUN...
TAKE THIS.
WHY?
IT'S THE SPARE KEY TO MY APARTMENT.
I SHOULD'VE DONE THIS MUCH SOONER.
YOU SHOULD NEVER HAVE TO WAIT IN FRONT OF MY DOOR LIKE A STRANGER.
YOU CAN COME OVER ANYTIME YOU WANT, OKAY?

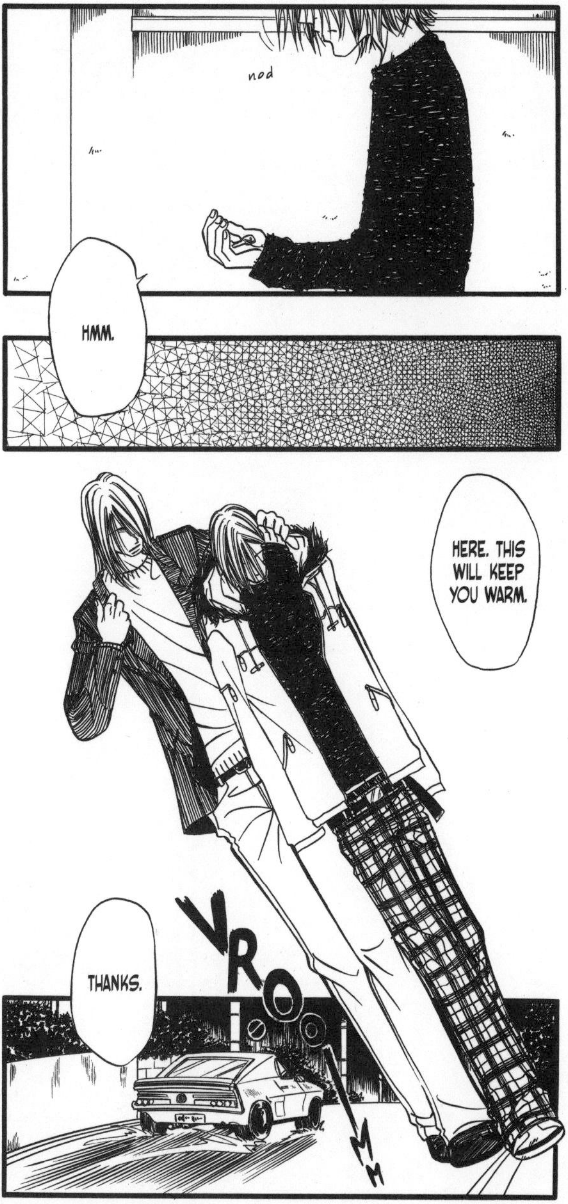
nod
HMM.
HERE. THIS WILL KEEP YOU WARM.
THANKS.
VROOOMMM

In case you ever want to get an idea of how Keigo plays the drums, I recommend the following audio-visual examples...

First, listen to the special drum solo in "Stalked Actors" by Taylor Hawkins on the latest Foo Fighters DVD. Also, check out track number 4, "A Song for the Dead," on the Queens of the Stone Age album. "Songs for the Deaf" by Dave Grohl is also amazing.

Speaking of Dave Grohl...

I think that he's one of the best drummers ever. He's possibly even one of the most talented musicians on the planet.

As a bonus, I can highly recommend the cover song "D-7" by Nirvana (originally by The Wipers) on their album *Hormoaning*.

I dare say that this song would be only half as good without Dave's powerful drumming. Well, whatever--the song is great. The first time I listened to this song, I jumped around like a six-year-old girl--no kidding. So go ahead and check it out!

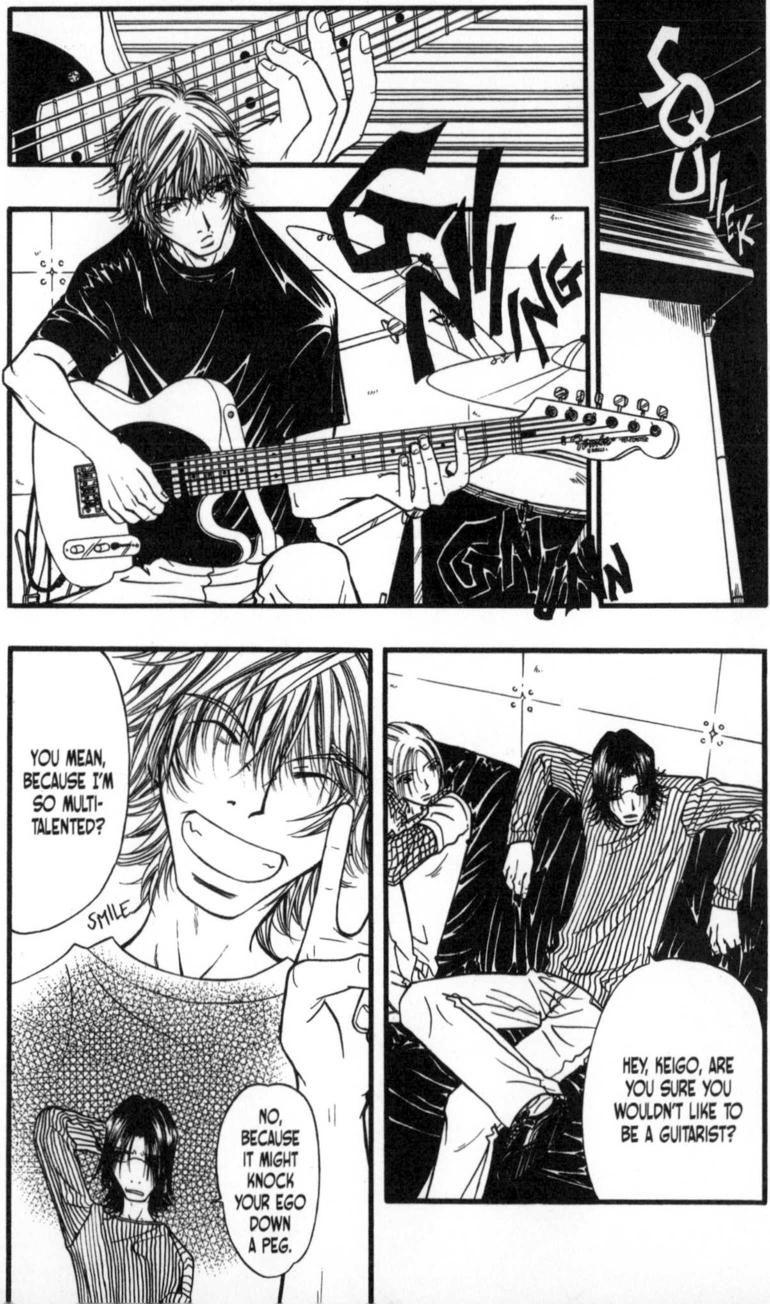
SQUIIEK
GYIING
HEY, KEIGO, ARE YOU SURE YOU WOULDN'T LIKE TO BE A GUITARIST?
YOU MEAN, BECAUSE I'M SO MULTI-TALENTED?
SMILE
NO, BECAUSE IT MIGHT KNOCK YOUR EGO DOWN A PEG.

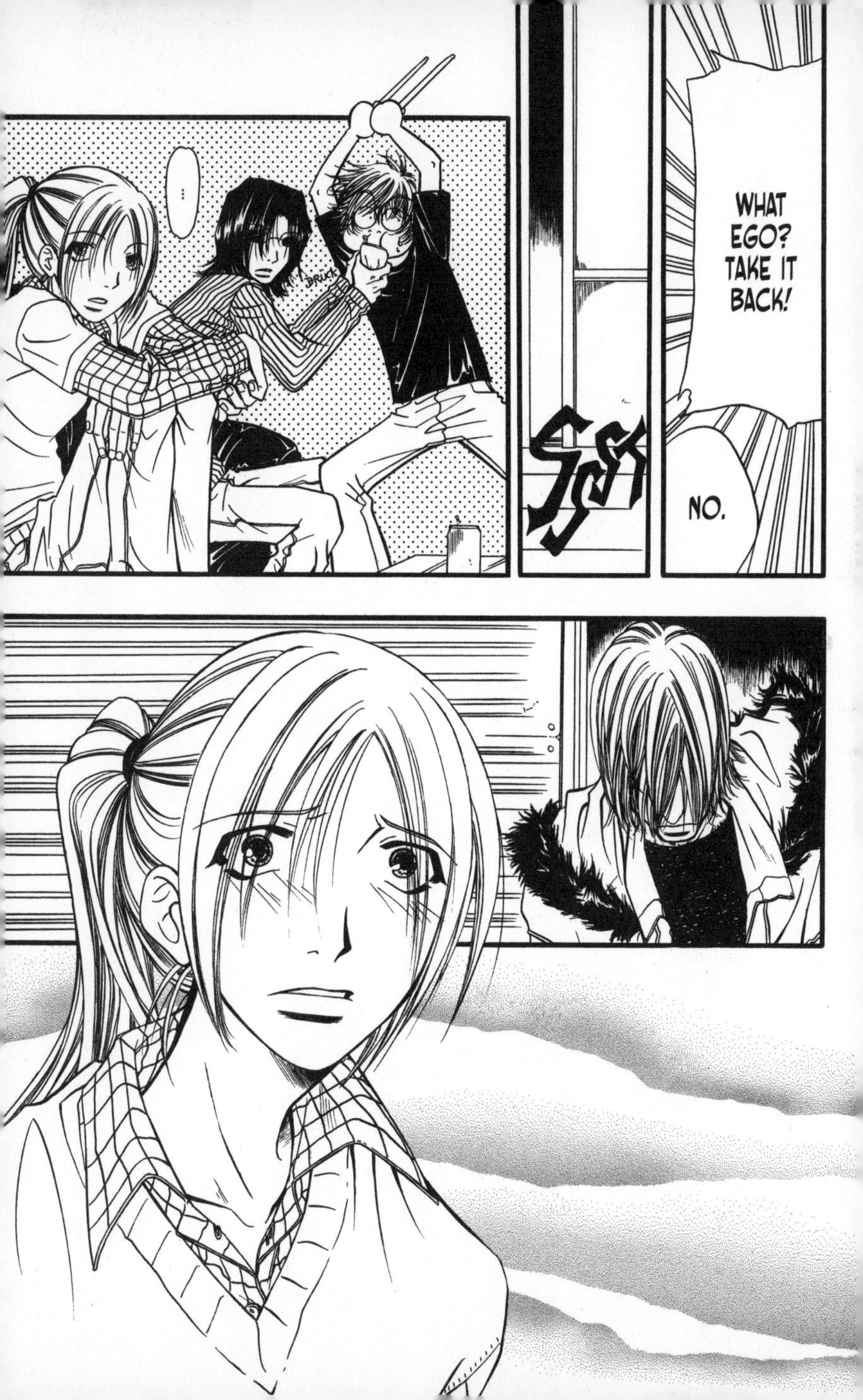
WHAT EGO? TAKE IT BACK!
NO.
SCK
...
DRÜCK

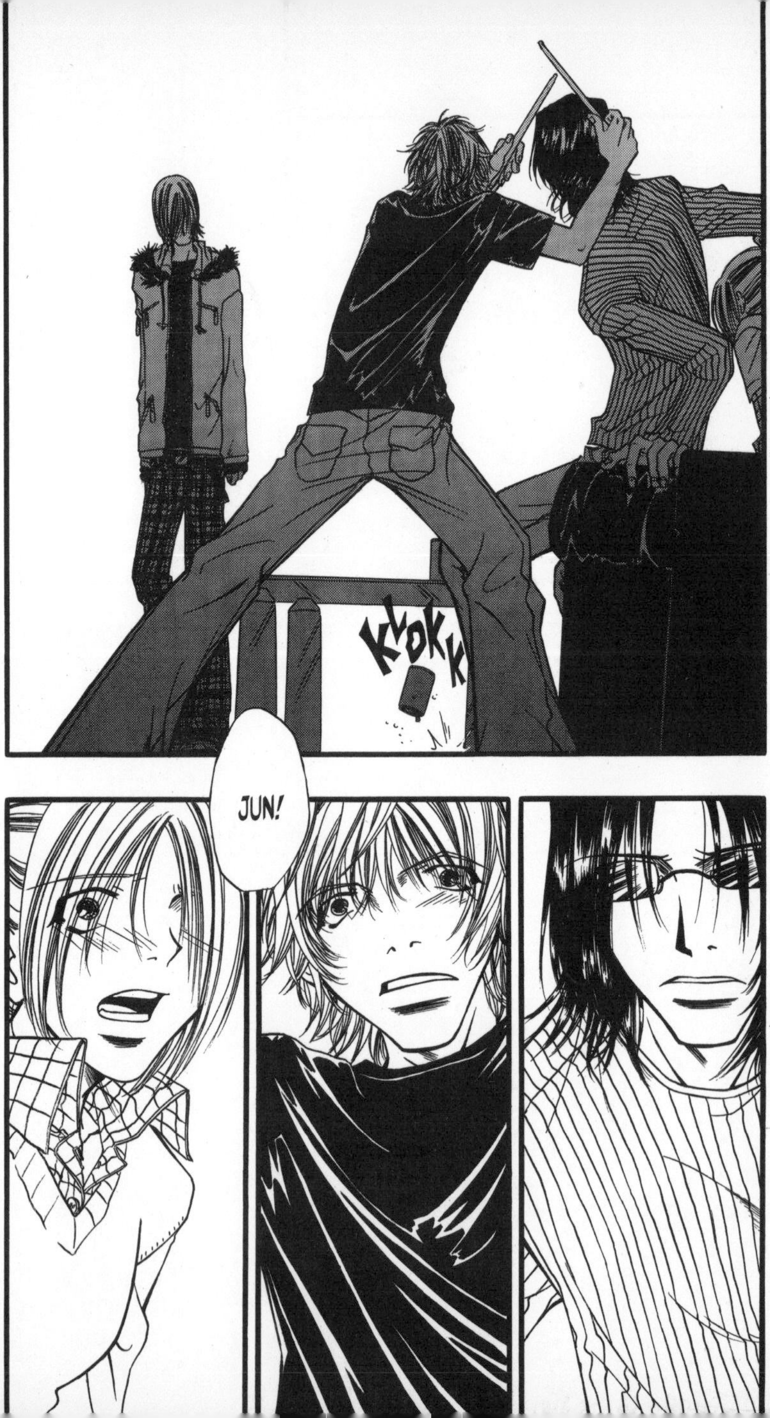
KLOKK
JUN!

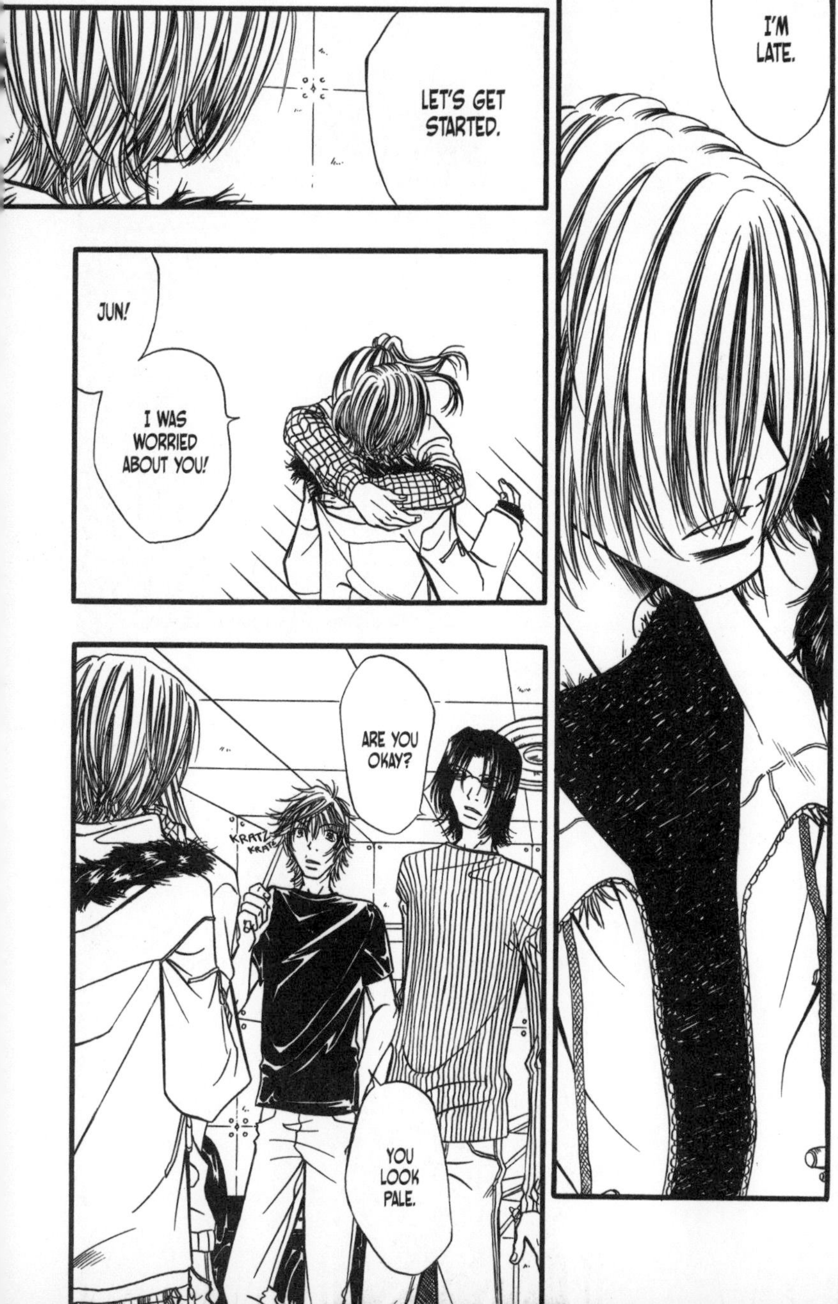
I'M LATE.
LET'S GET STARTED.
JUN!
I WAS WORRIED ABOUT YOU!
ARE YOU OKAY?
KRATZ KRATZ
YOU LOOK PALE.

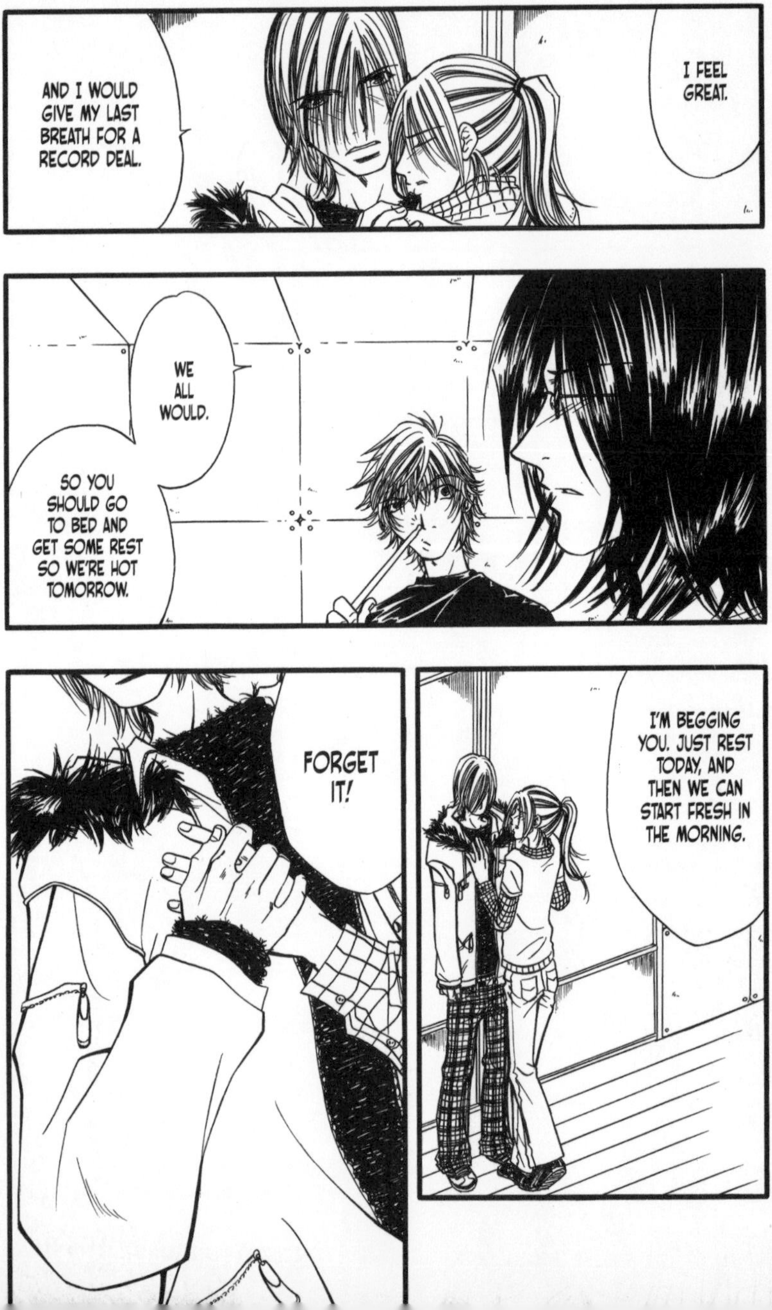
I FEEL GREAT.
AND I WOULD GIVE MY LAST BREATH FOR A RECORD DEAL.
WE ALL WOULD.
SO YOU SHOULD GO TO BED AND GET SOME REST SO WE'RE HOT TOMORROW.
I'M BEGGING YOU. JUST REST TODAY, AND THEN WE CAN START FRESH IN THE MORNING.
FORGET IT!

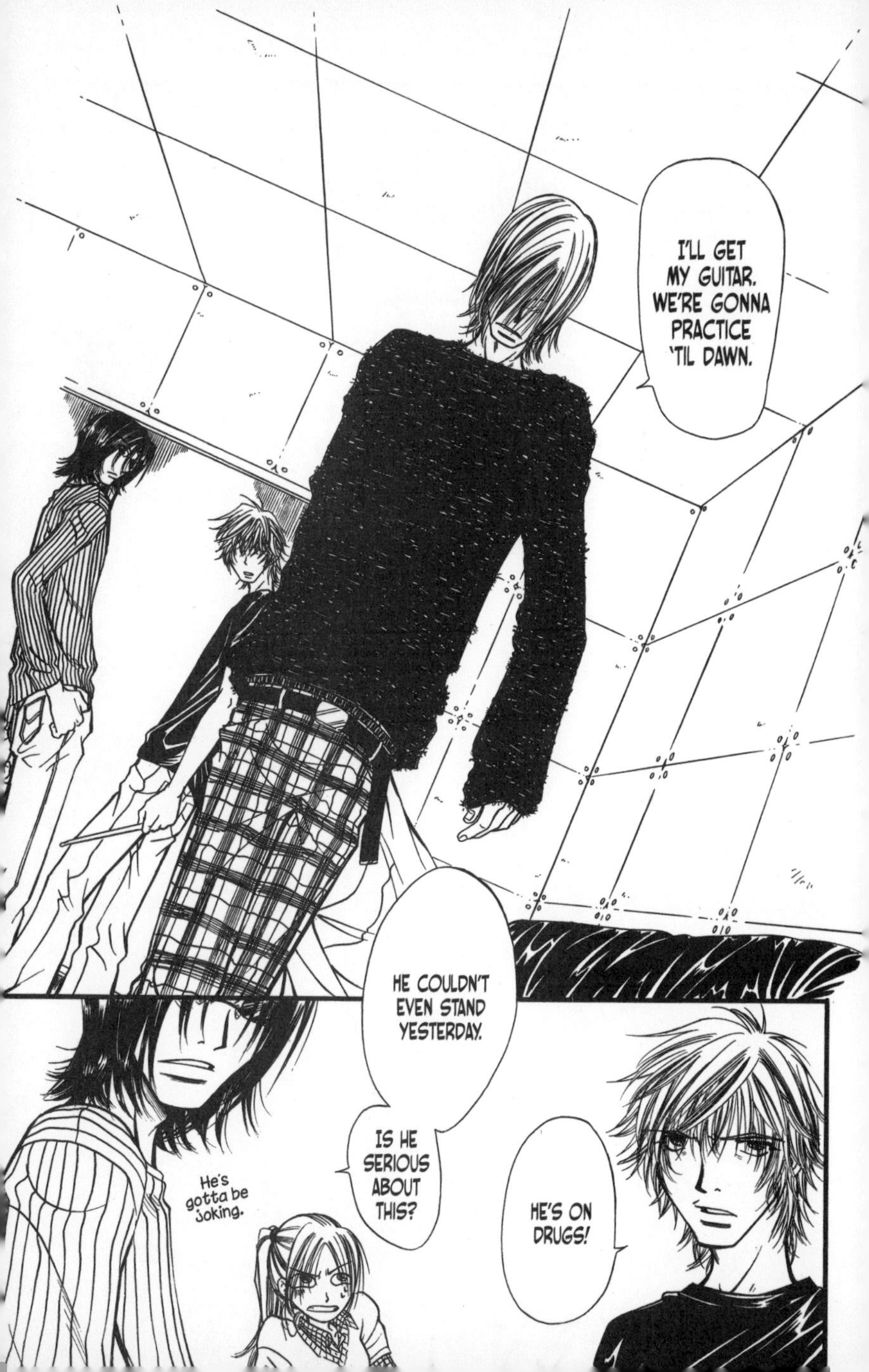
I'LL GET MY GUITAR. WE'RE GONNA PRACTICE 'TIL DAWN.
HE COULDN'T EVEN STAND YESTERDAY.
HE'S ON DRUGS!
IS HE SERIOUS ABOUT THIS?
He's gotta be joking.

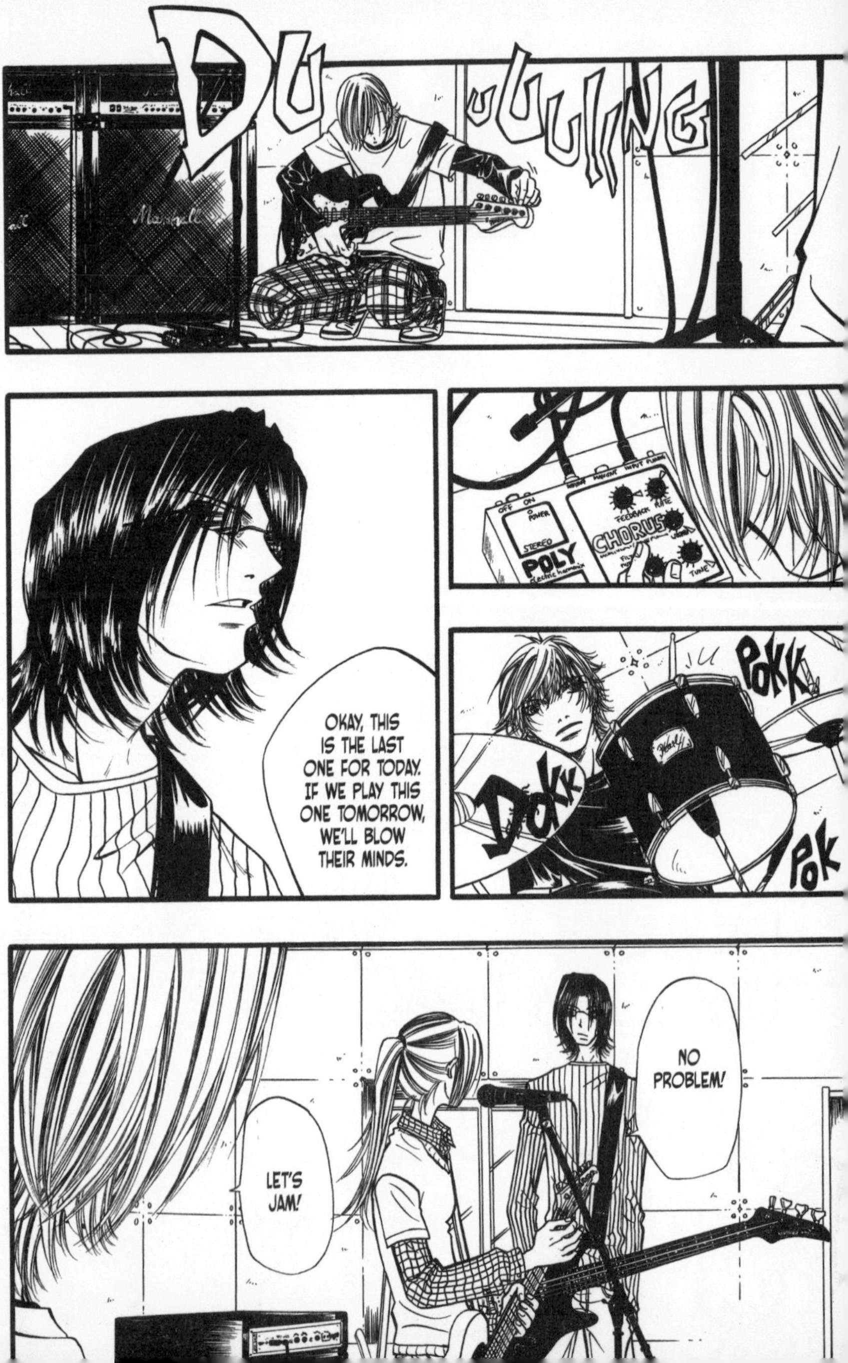
DUUUUING
OFF ON
POWER
STEREO
POLY
FEEDBACK
RATE
CHORUS
TUNE
POKK
DOKK
POK
OKAY, THIS IS THE LAST ONE FOR TODAY. IF WE PLAY THIS ONE TOMORROW, WE'LL BLOW THEIR MINDS.
NO PROBLEM!
LET'S JAM!

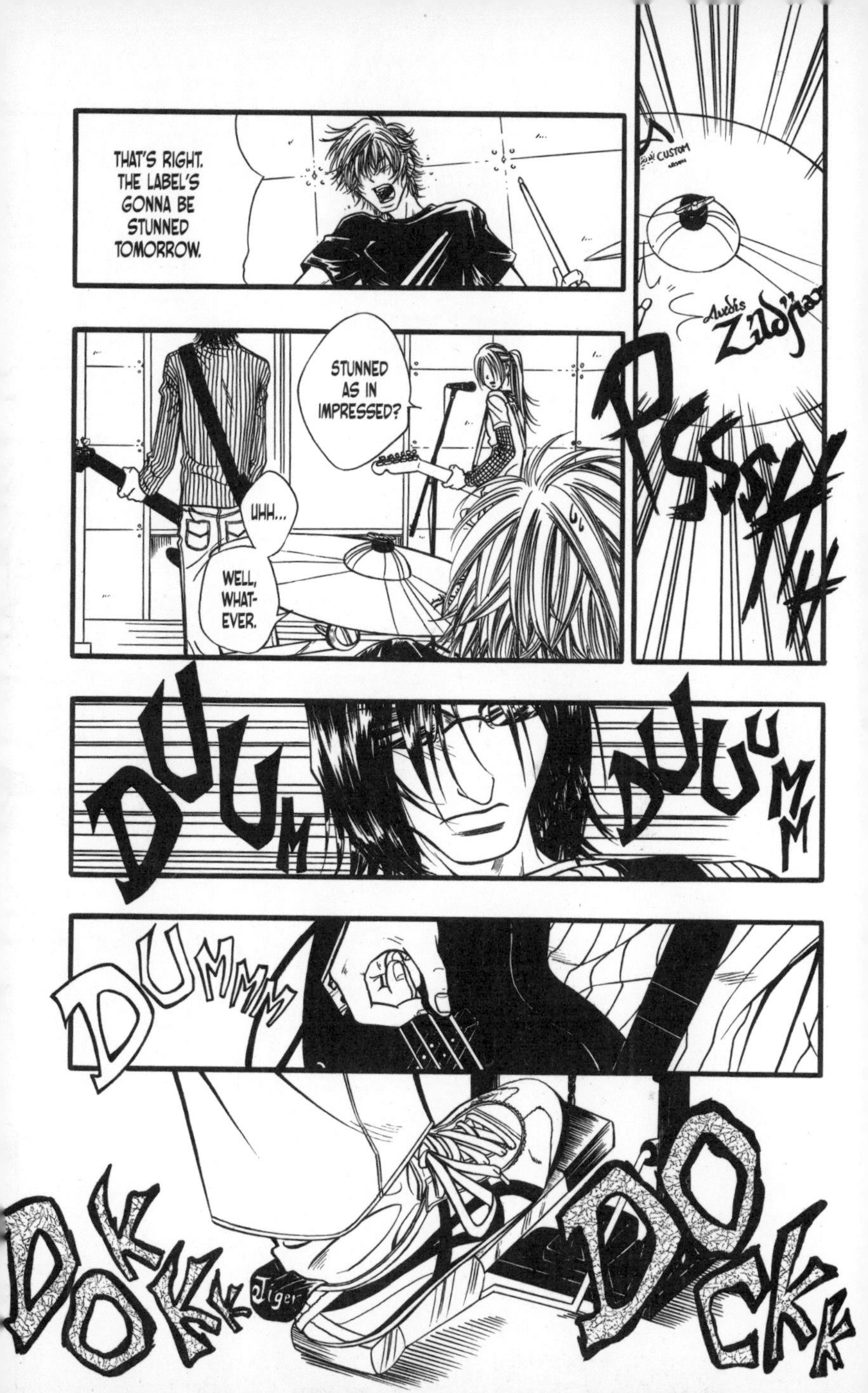
CUSTOM
Avedis Zildjian
PSSSH
THAT'S RIGHT. THE LABEL'S GONNA BE STUNNED TOMORROW.
STUNNED AS IN IMPRESSED?
UHH...
WELL, WHATEVER.
DUUUMMM
DUUM
DUMMM
DOCKK
DOKKK

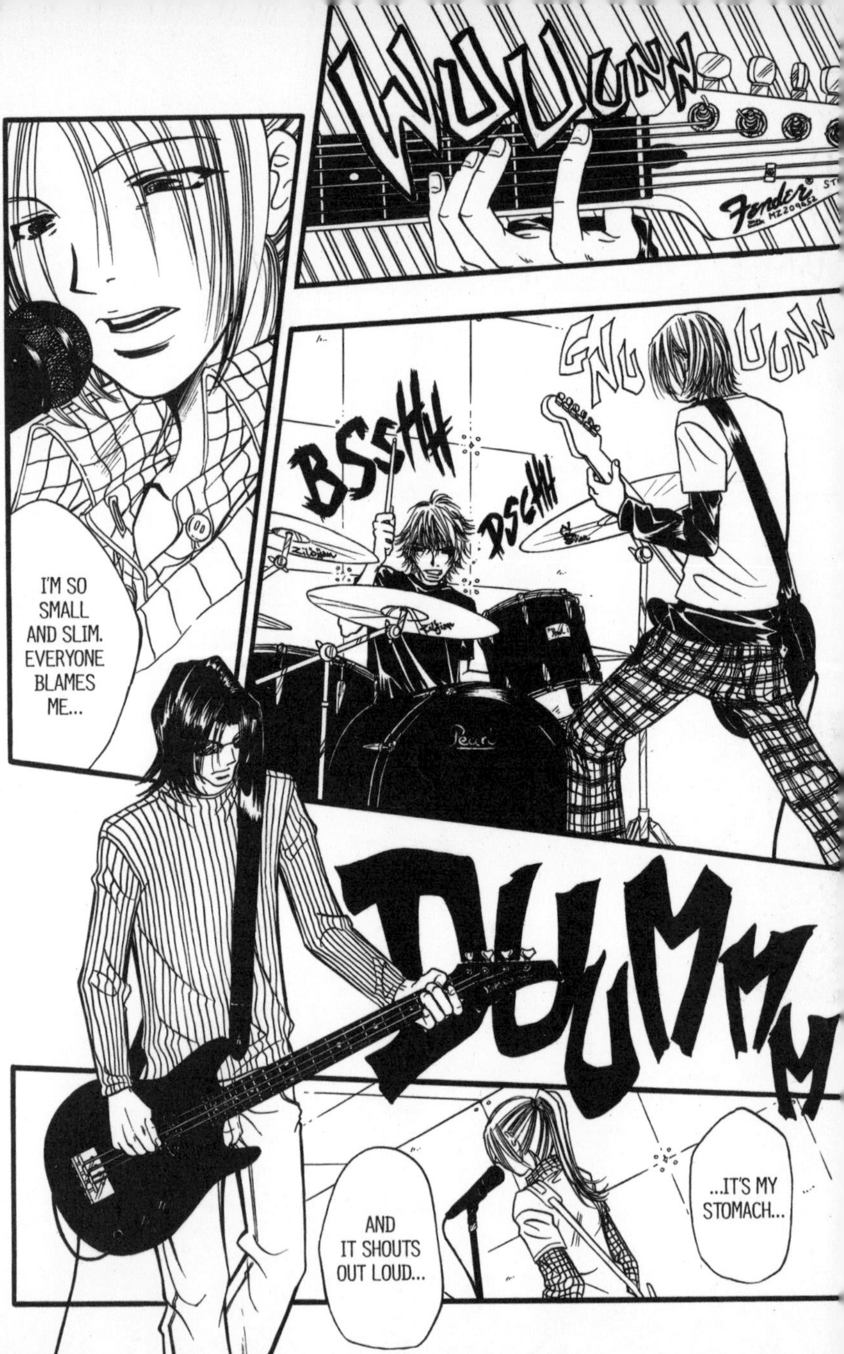
WUUUNN
Fender
GNUUUNN
BSSHH
DSCHH
I'M SO SMALL AND SLIM. EVERYONE BLAMES ME...
DUMMMM
...IT'S MY STOMACH...
AND IT SHOUTS OUT LOUD...

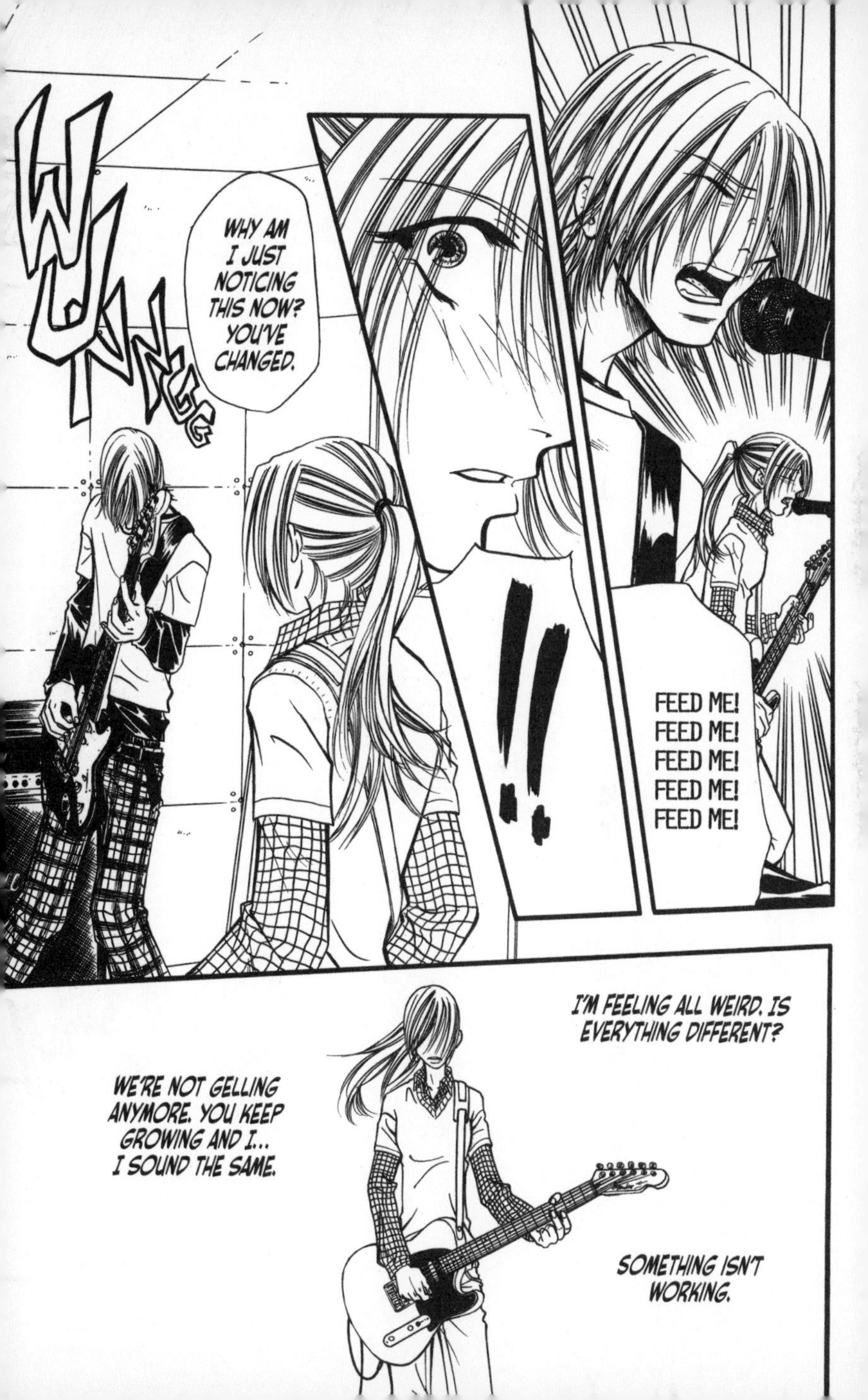
FEED ME! FEED ME! FEED ME! FEED ME! FEED ME!
!!
WHY AM I JUST NOTICING THIS NOW? YOU'VE CHANGED.
WUNNGG
I'M FEELING ALL WEIRD. IS EVERYTHING DIFFERENT?
WE'RE NOT GELLING ANYMORE. YOU KEEP GROWING AND I... I SOUND THE SAME.
SOMETHING ISN'T WORKING.

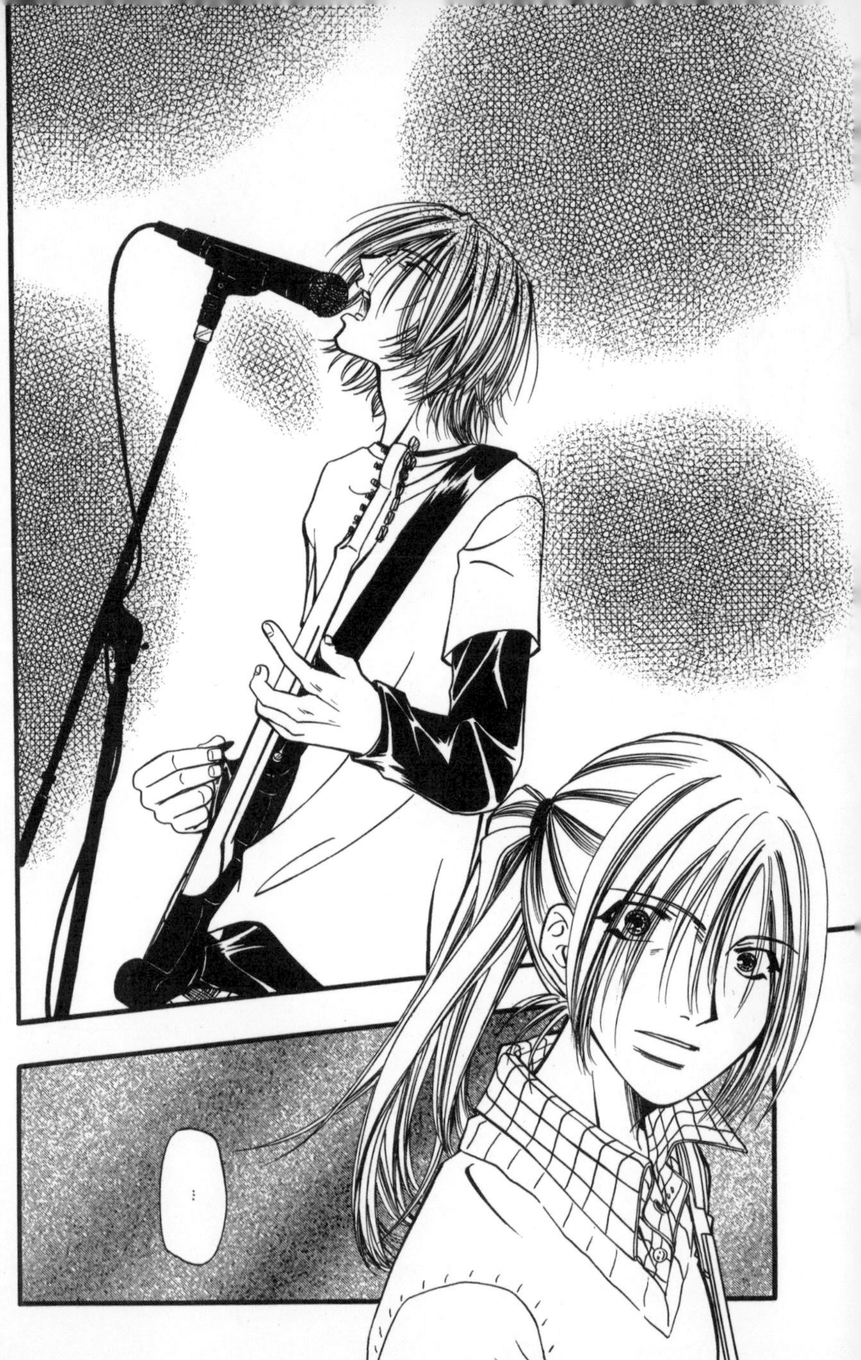
…

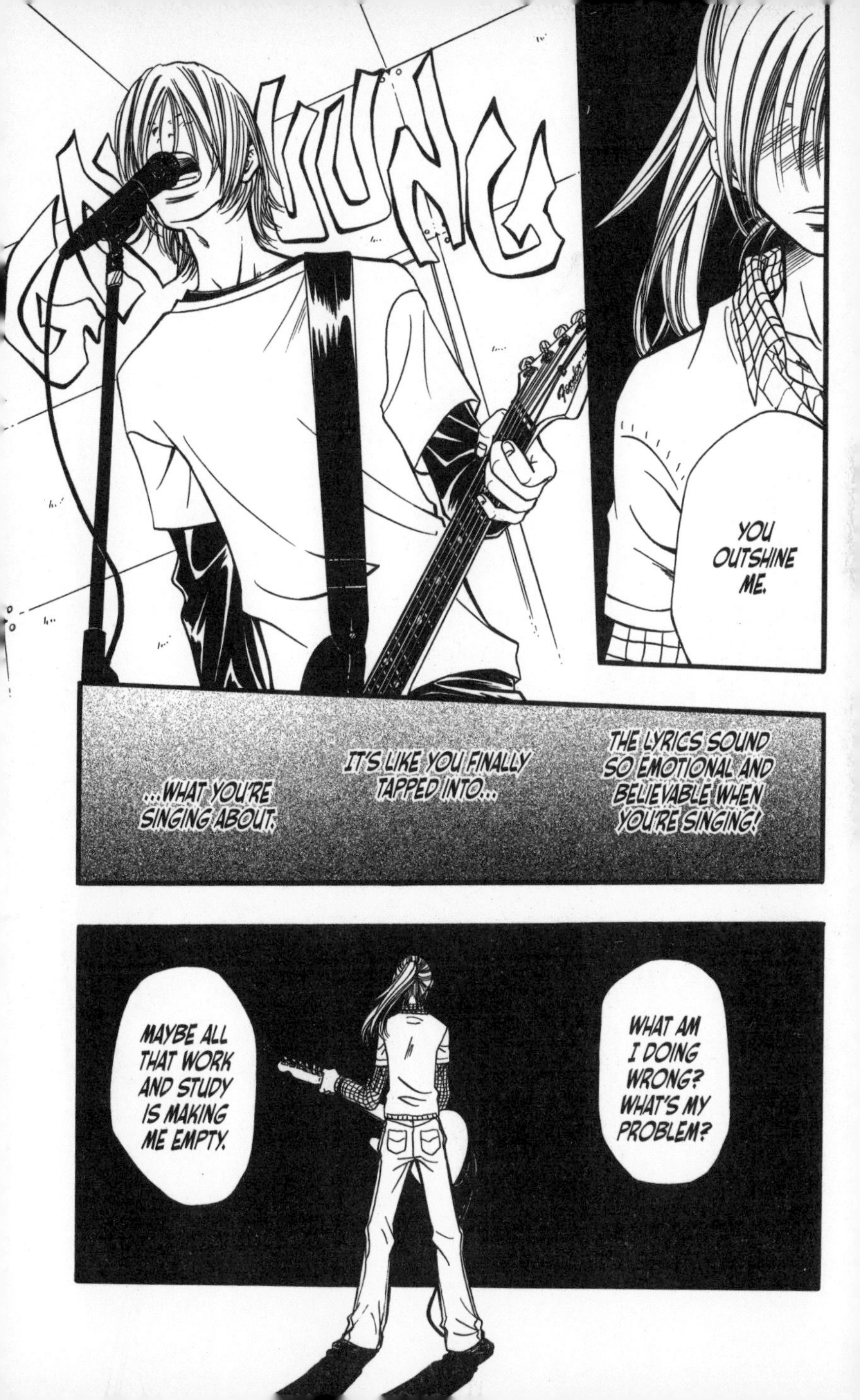
YOU OUTSHINE ME.
THE LYRICS SOUND SO EMOTIONAL AND BELIEVABLE WHEN YOU'RE SINGING!
IT'S LIKE YOU FINALLY TAPPED INTO...
...WHAT YOU'RE SINGING ABOUT.
WHAT AM I DOING WRONG? WHAT'S MY PROBLEM?
MAYBE ALL THAT WORK AND STUDY IS MAKING ME EMPTY.

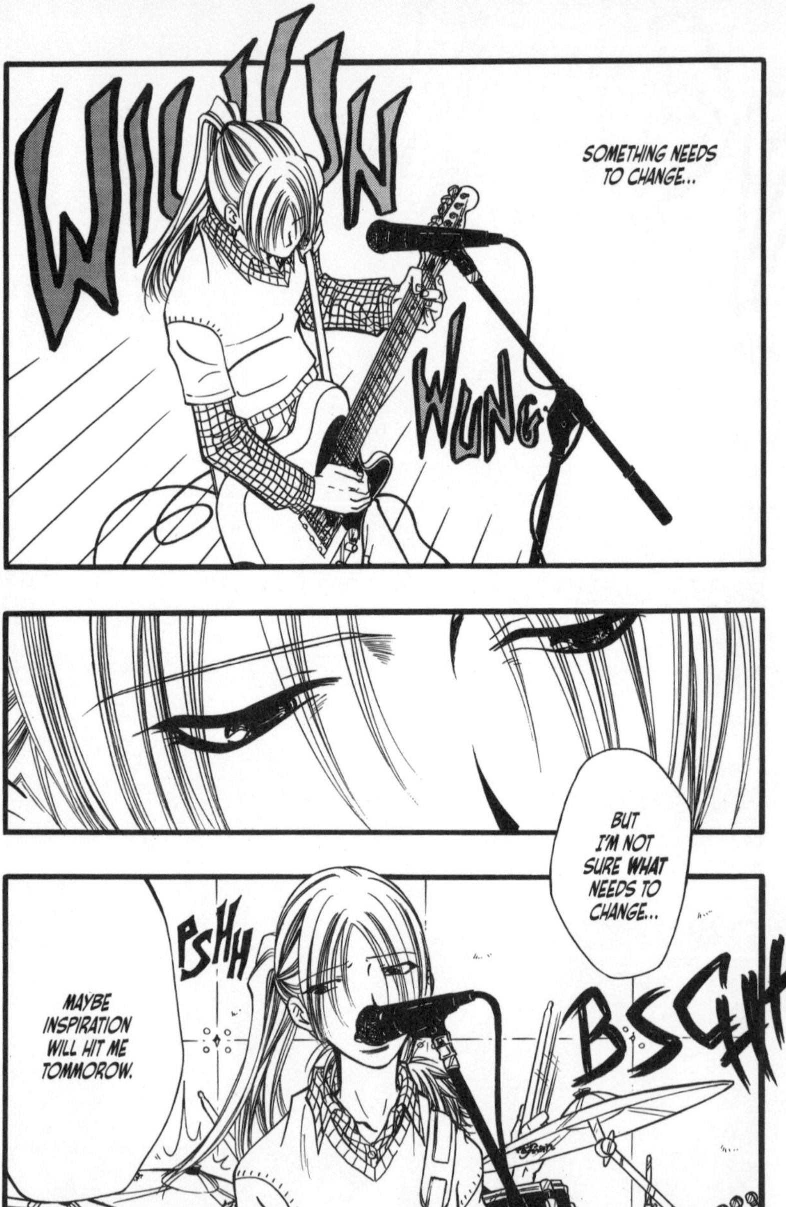
SOMETHING NEEDS TO CHANGE...
WUNG
BUT I'M NOT SURE WHAT NEEDS TO CHANGE...
PSHH
MAYBE INSPIRATION WILL HIT ME TOMMOROW.

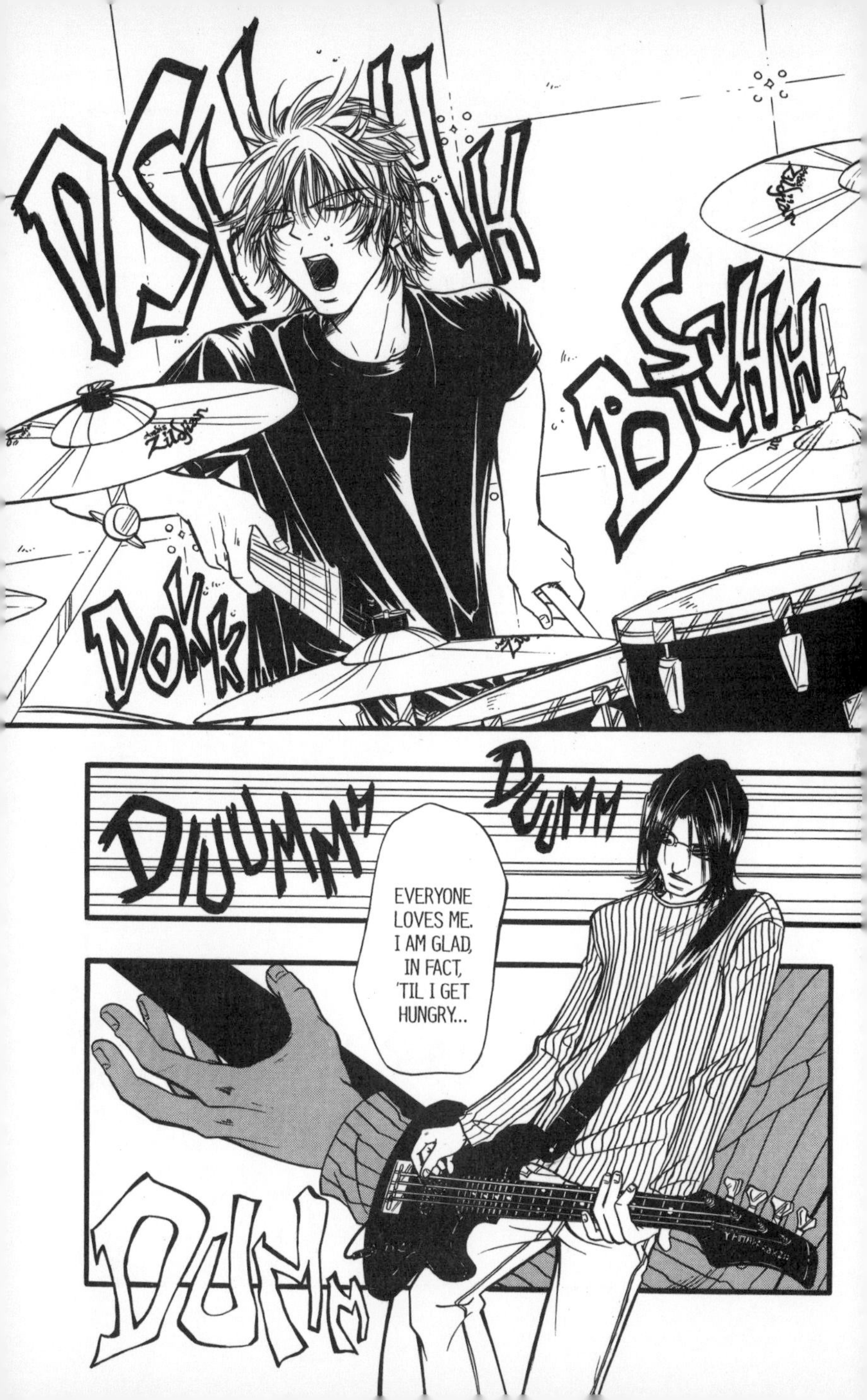
DSCHH
DSCHHK
DONK
DUUMM
DIUUMM
EVERYONE LOVES ME. I AM GLAD, IN FACT, 'TIL I GET HUNGRY...
DUMM

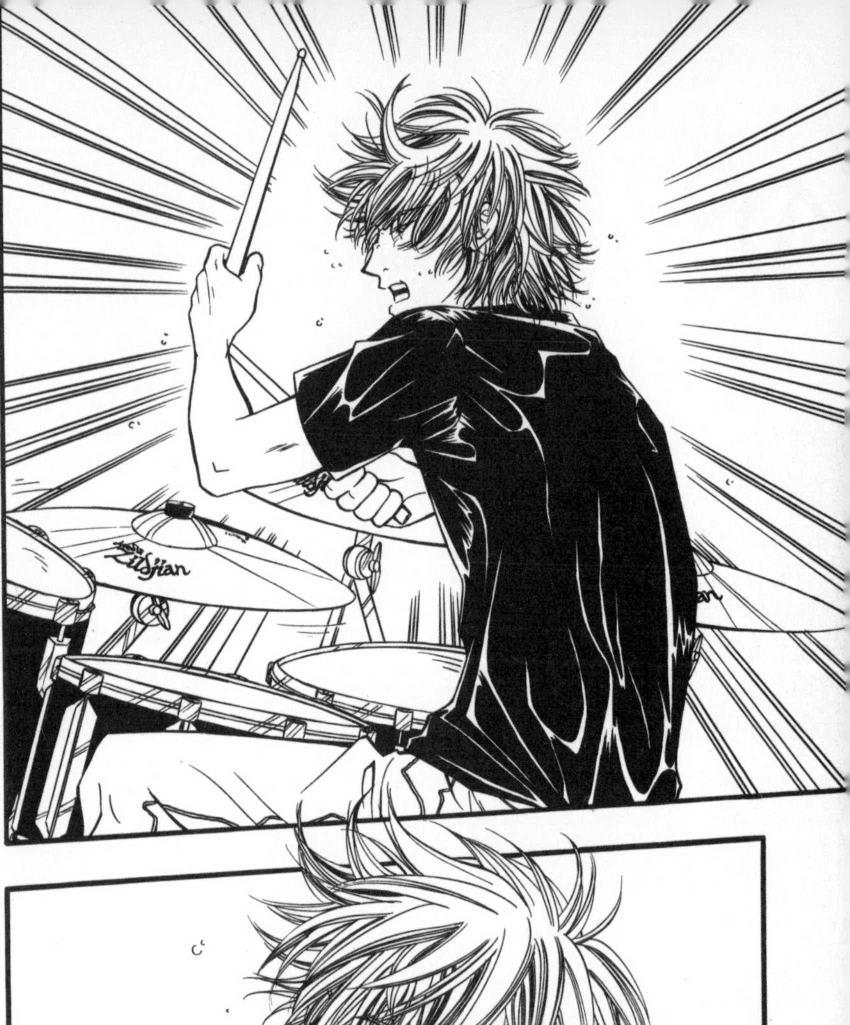
Zildjian

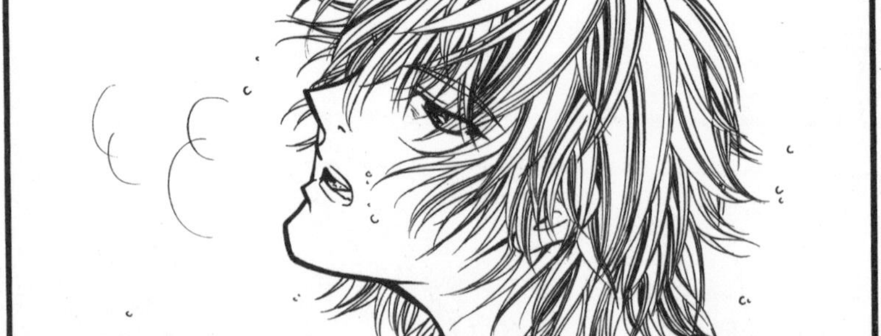

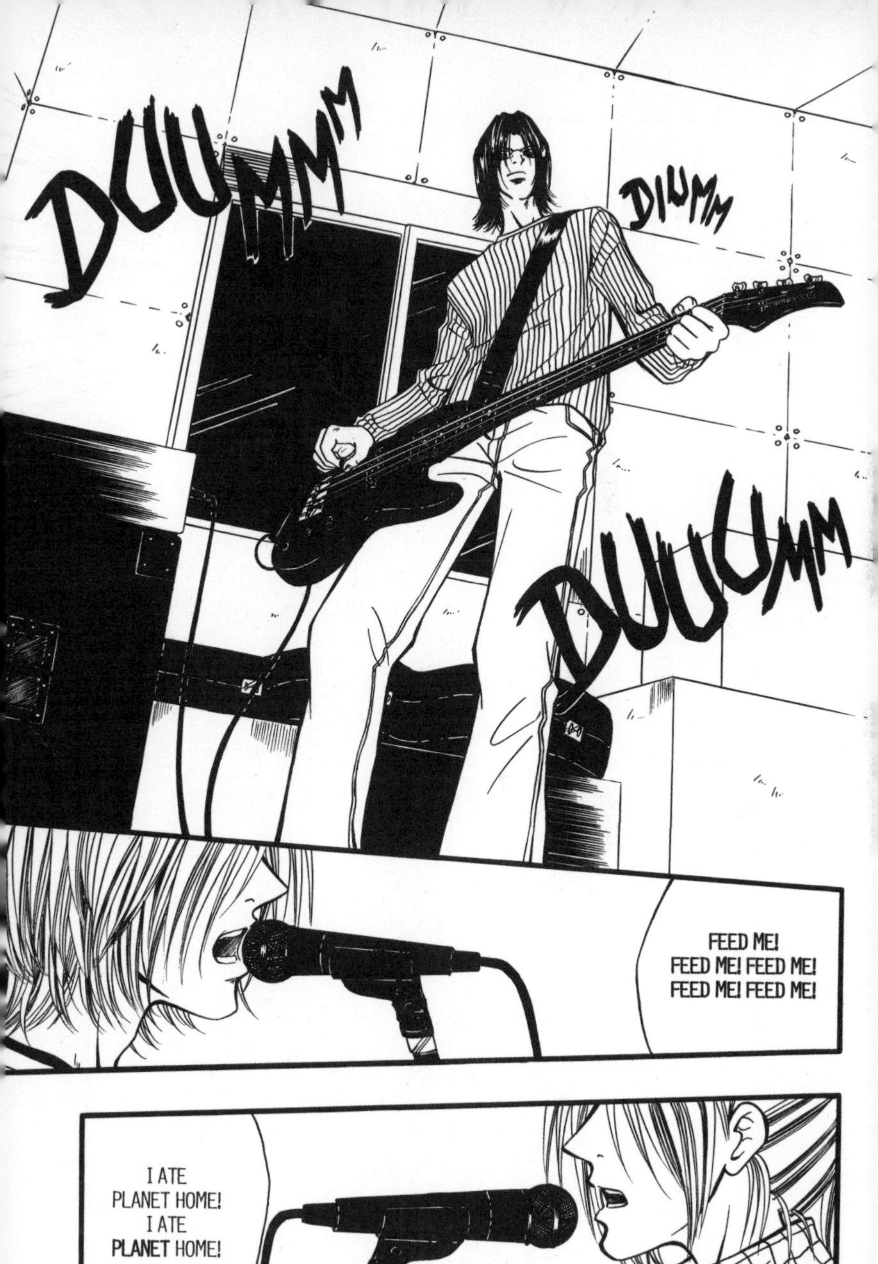
DIUMM
DUUMMM
DUUUMM
FEED ME! FEED ME! FEED ME! FEED ME! FEED ME!
I ATE PLANET HOME! I ATE PLANET HOME!

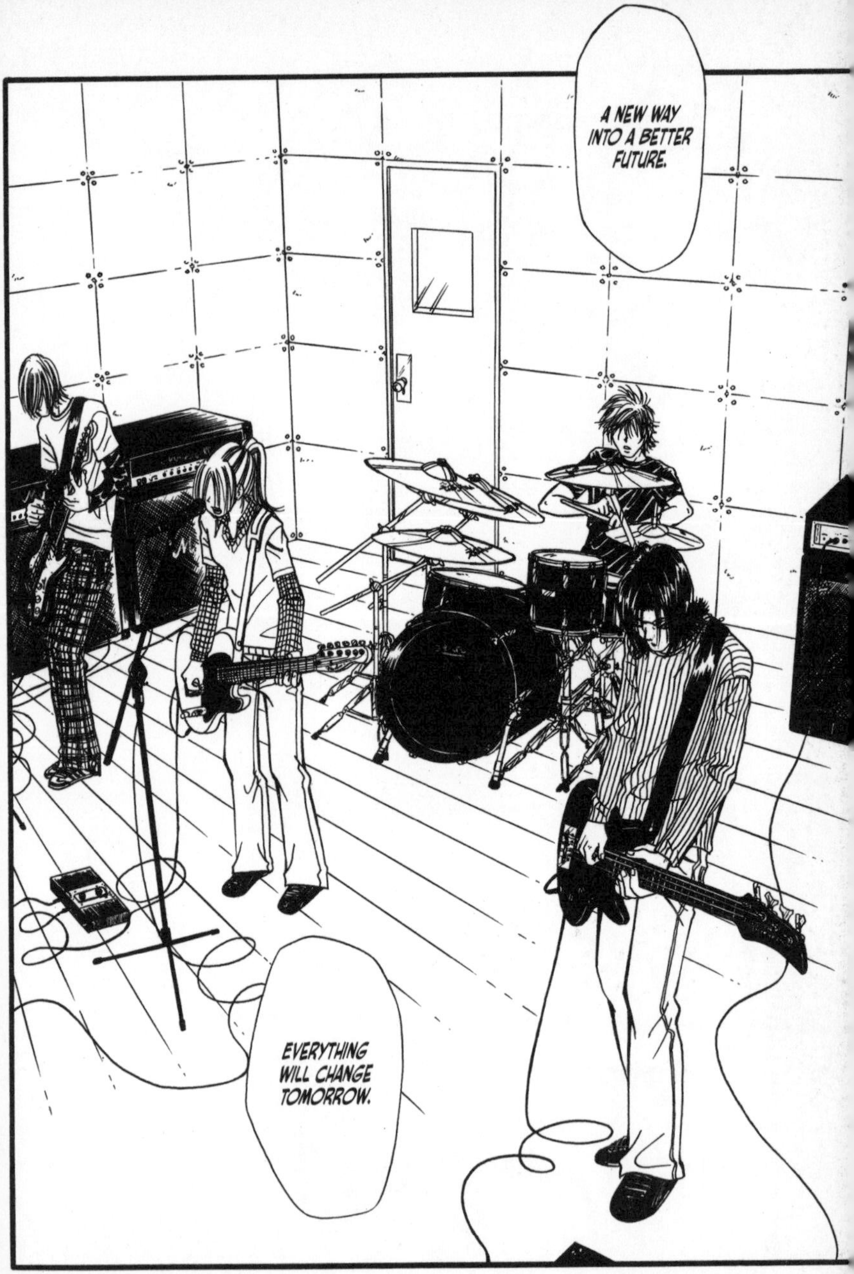
A NEW WAY INTO A BETTER FUTURE.
EVERYTHING WILL CHANGE TOMORROW.

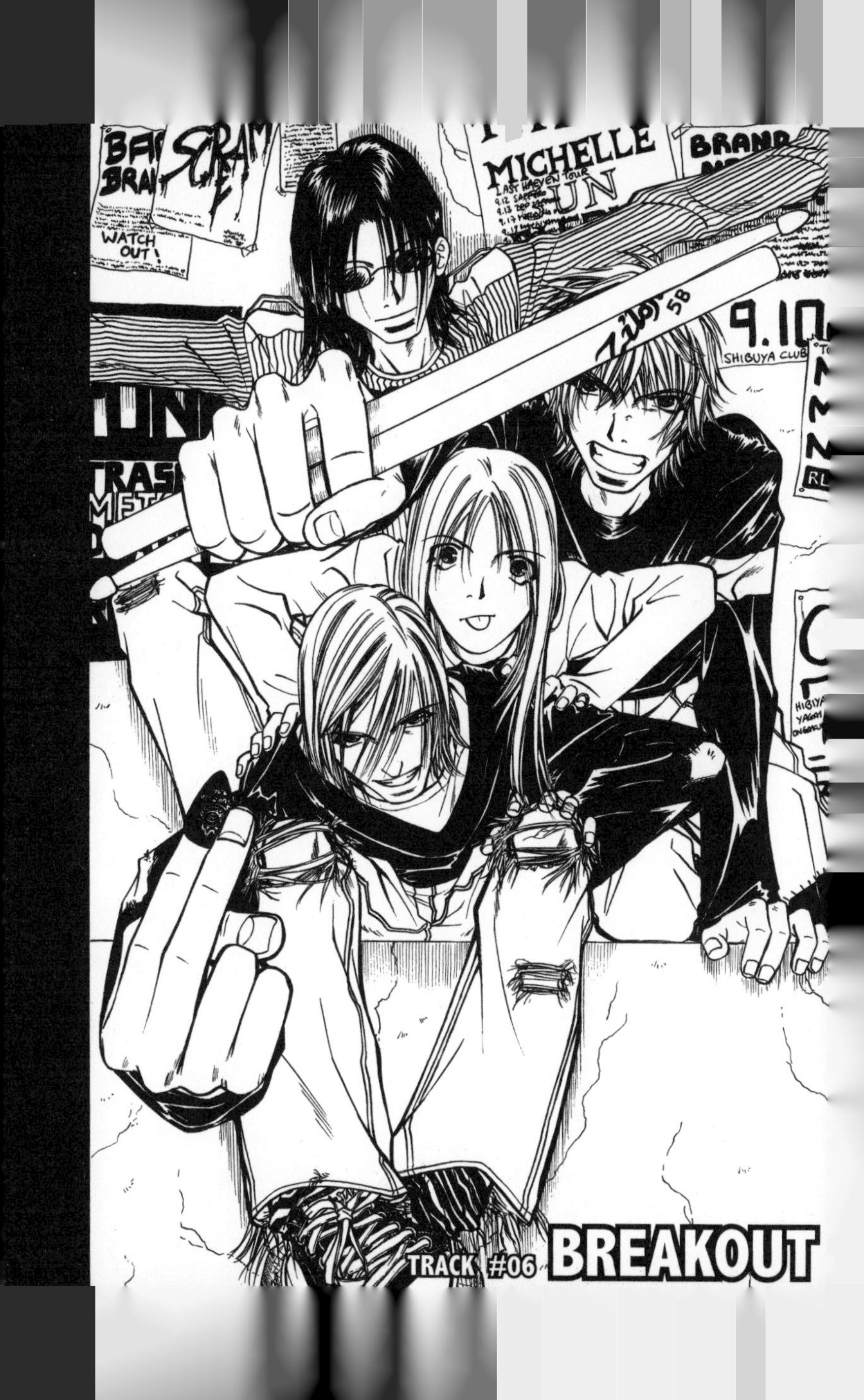
WATCH OUT!
MICHELLE
LAST HAEVEN TOUR
9.10
SHIBUYA CLUB

TRACK #06 BREAKOUT

THE MAN WHO HAD NEVER HAD ENOUGH

I'm so small and slim
Everyone blames me
I can't stand the pain
Till I get hungry
It's my stomach
And it shouts out loud

Feed me! Feed me! Feed me!
Feed me! Feed me!

I'm so weak and pale
Noone really likes me
I'm locked in your jail
Till I get hungry
It's my stomach
And it yells out loud

Feed me! Feed me! Feed me!
Feed me! Feed me!—
It's so easy! Uh!

I'm so tall and fat
Everyone loves me
I am glad in fact
Till I get hungry
It's my stomach
And it cries out loud

Feed me! Feed me! Feed me!
Feed me! Feed me!—
It's so easy! Uginn —

I ate planet home (8x)
What's next...?
Ha ha ——

Lyrics - IMAI Jun

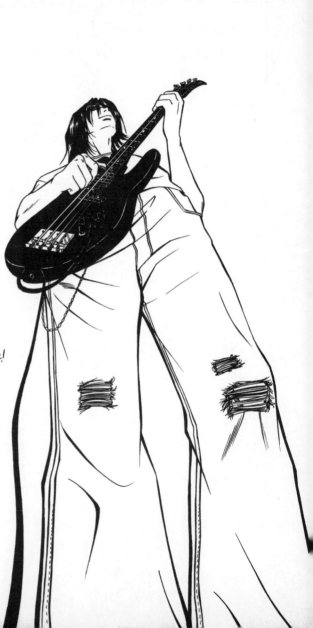

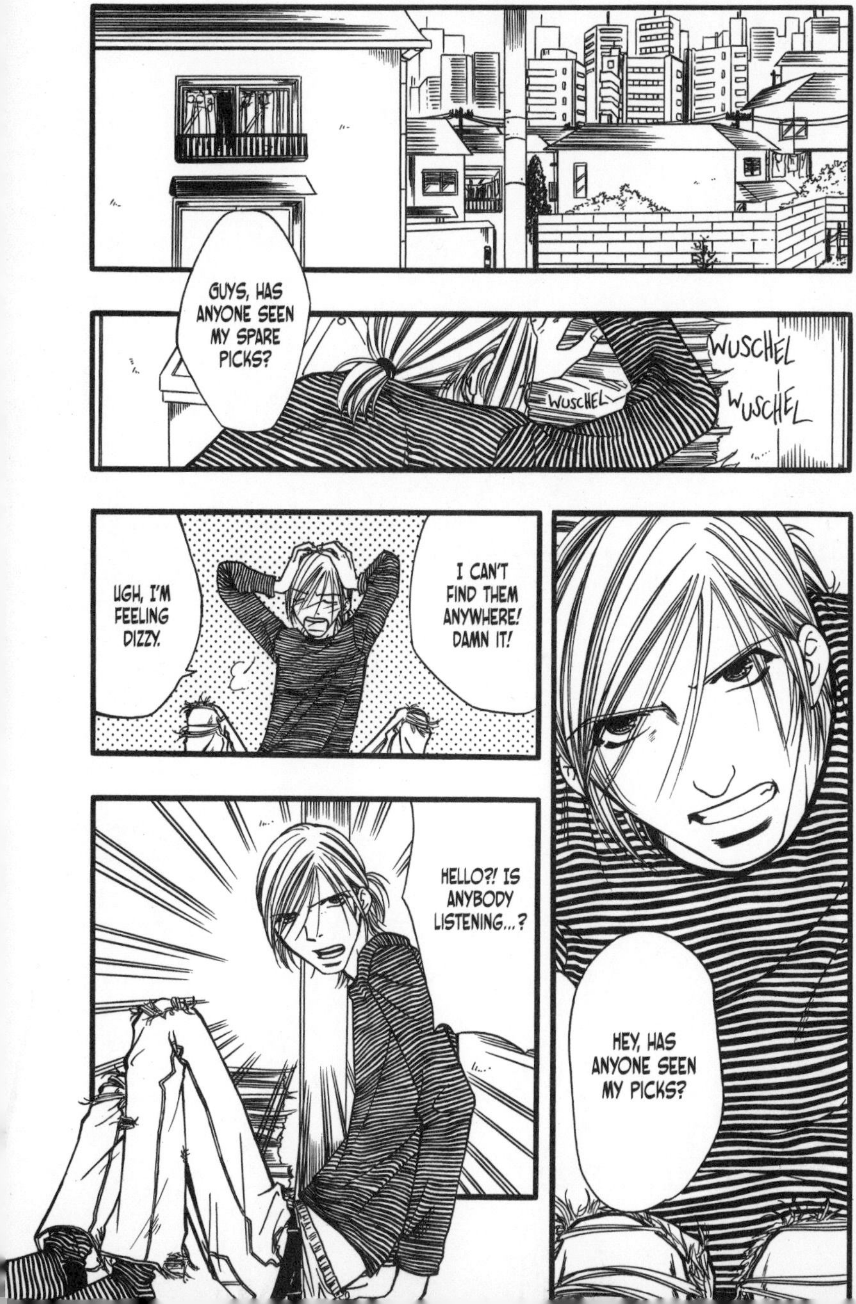
GUYS, HAS ANYONE SEEN MY SPARE PICKS?
WUSCHEL WUSCHEL
WUSCHEL
HEY, HAS ANYONE SEEN MY PICKS?
I CAN'T FIND THEM ANYWHERE! DAMN IT!
UGH, I'M FEELING DIZZY.
HELLO?! IS ANYBODY LISTENING...?

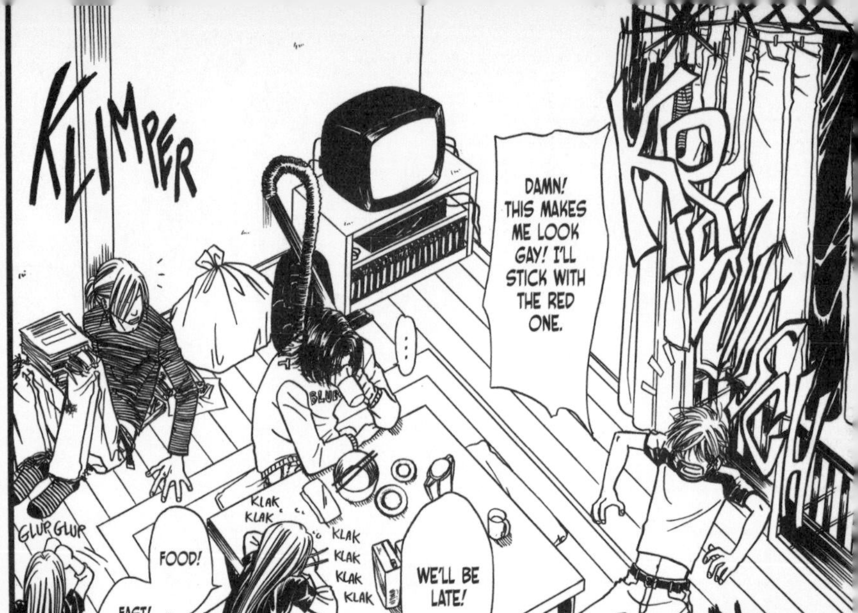
DAMN! THIS MAKES ME LOOK GAY! I'LL STICK WITH THE RED ONE.
...
KLIMPER
WSCHH
BANG
OR MAYBE THE WHITE ONE...?
TAP
TAP
WE'LL BE LATE!
KLAK KLAK KLAK KLAK KLAK KLAK
OH, NO! I NEED TO PEE AGAIN.
FOOD!
FAST! SOME-THING TO DRINK...
GLUP GLUP
WUSHH

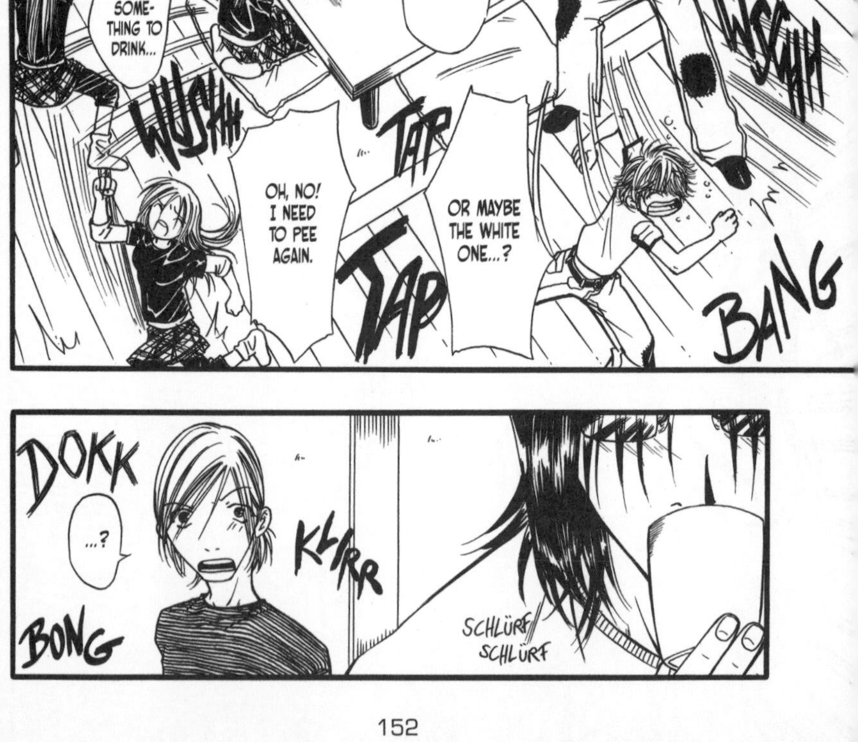
SCHLÜRF SCHLÜRF
KLIRR
DOKK
...?
BONG

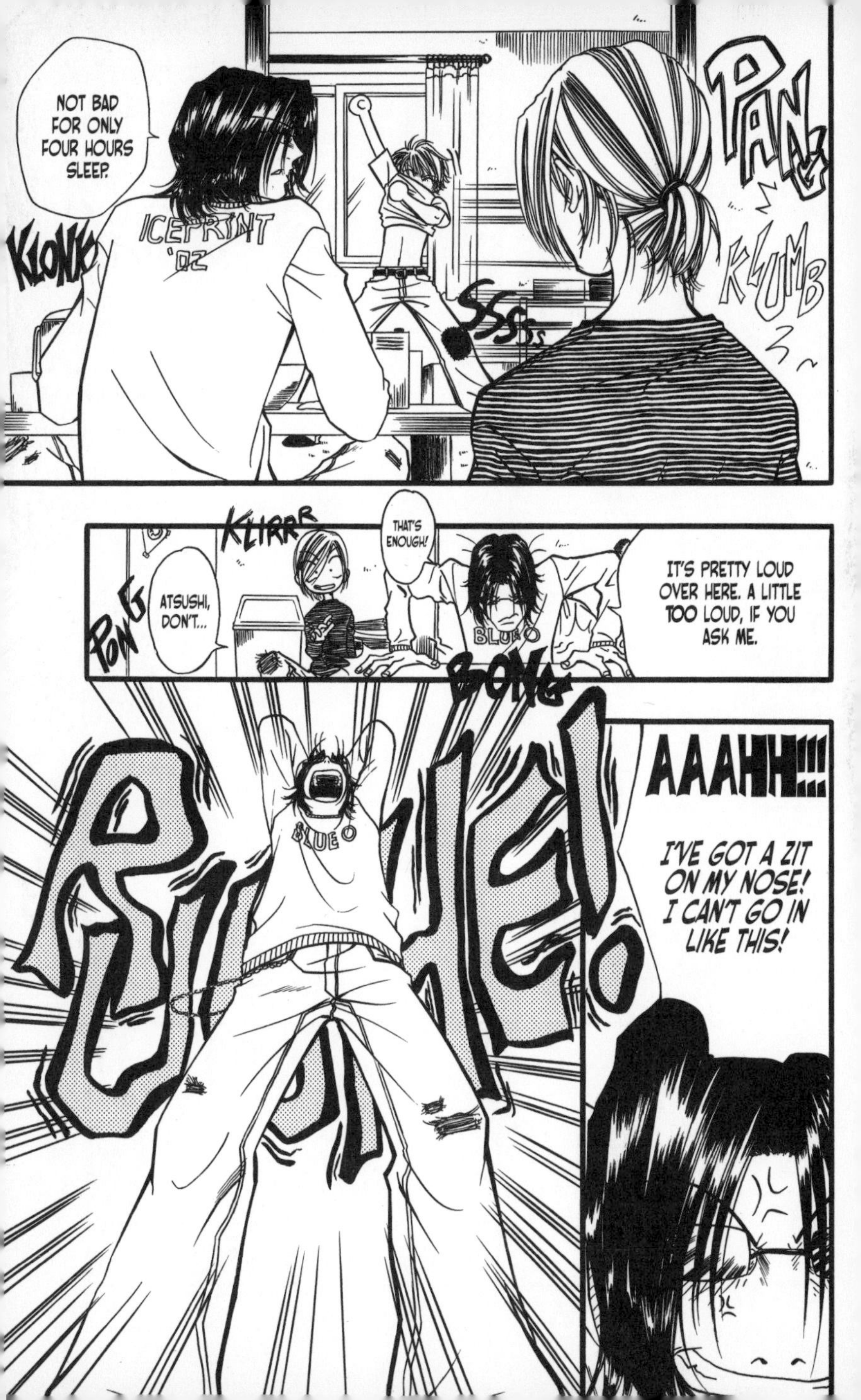
PANG
KLUMB
SSSSs
NOT BAD FOR ONLY FOUR HOURS SLEEP.
ICEPRINT '02
KLONK
IT'S PRETTY LOUD OVER HERE. A LITTLE TOO LOUD, IF YOU ASK ME.
THAT'S ENOUGH!
KLIRRR
ATSUSHI, DON'T...
PONG
BONG
AAAHH!!!
I'VE GOT A ZIT ON MY NOSE! I CAN'T GO IN LIKE THIS!

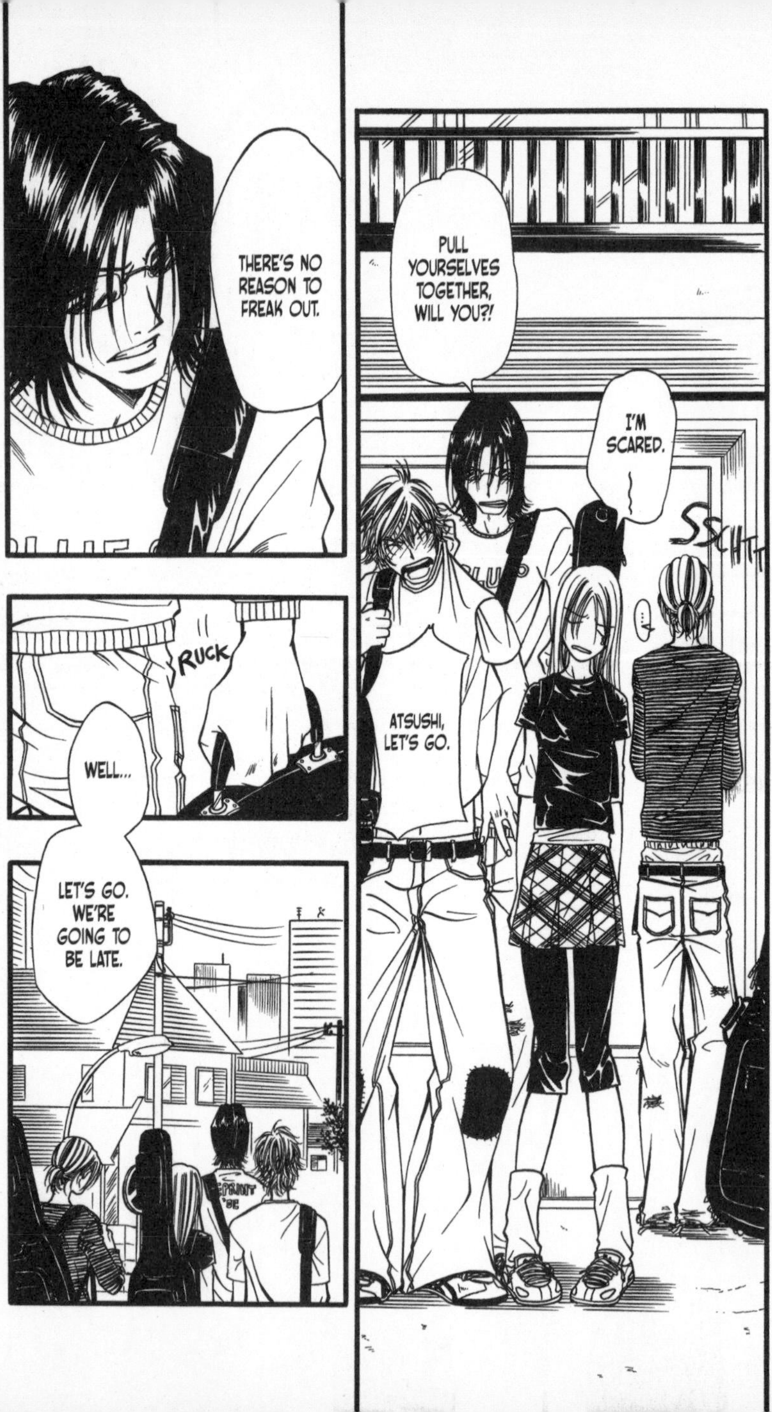
PULL YOURSELVES TOGETHER, WILL YOU?!
I'M SCARED.
SSCHTT
ATSUSHI, LET'S GO.
THERE'S NO REASON TO FREAK OUT.
RUCK
WELL...
LET'S GO. WE'RE GOING TO BE LATE.

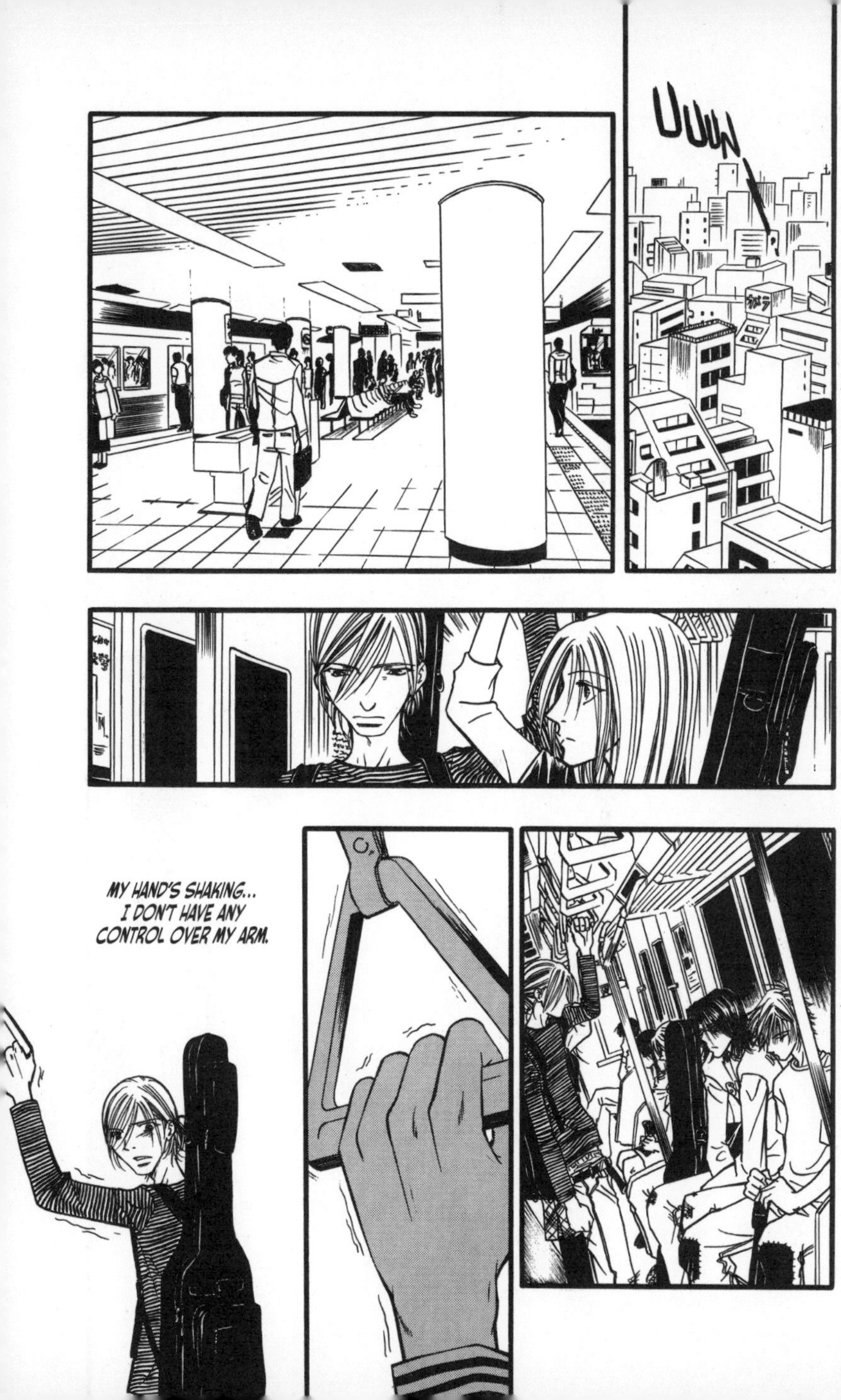
UUUN
MY HAND'S SHAKING... I DON'T HAVE ANY CONTROL OVER MY ARM.

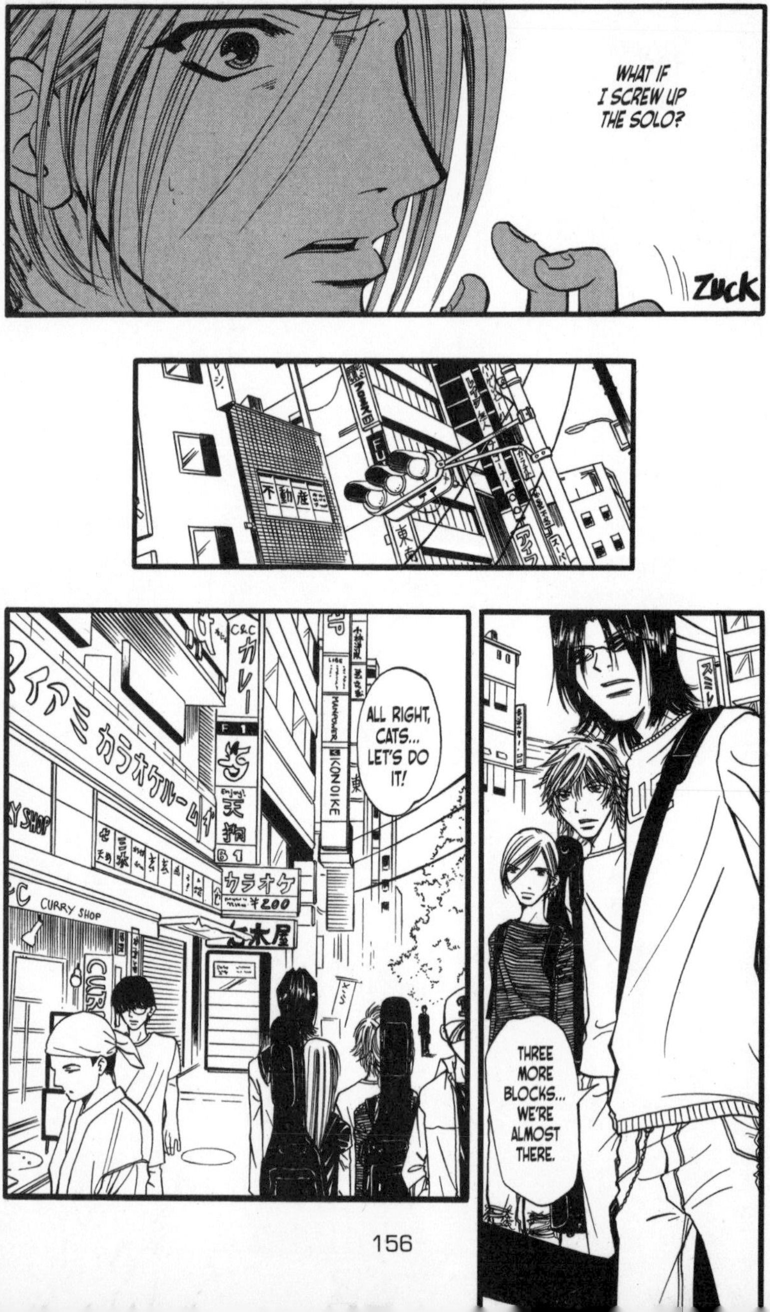
WHAT IF I SCREW UP THE SOLO?
ZUCK
不動産
THREE MORE BLOCKS... WE'RE ALMOST THERE.
ALL RIGHT, CATS... LET'S DO IT!
C&C
カレー
KONOIKE
カラオケ
¥200
CURRY SHOP

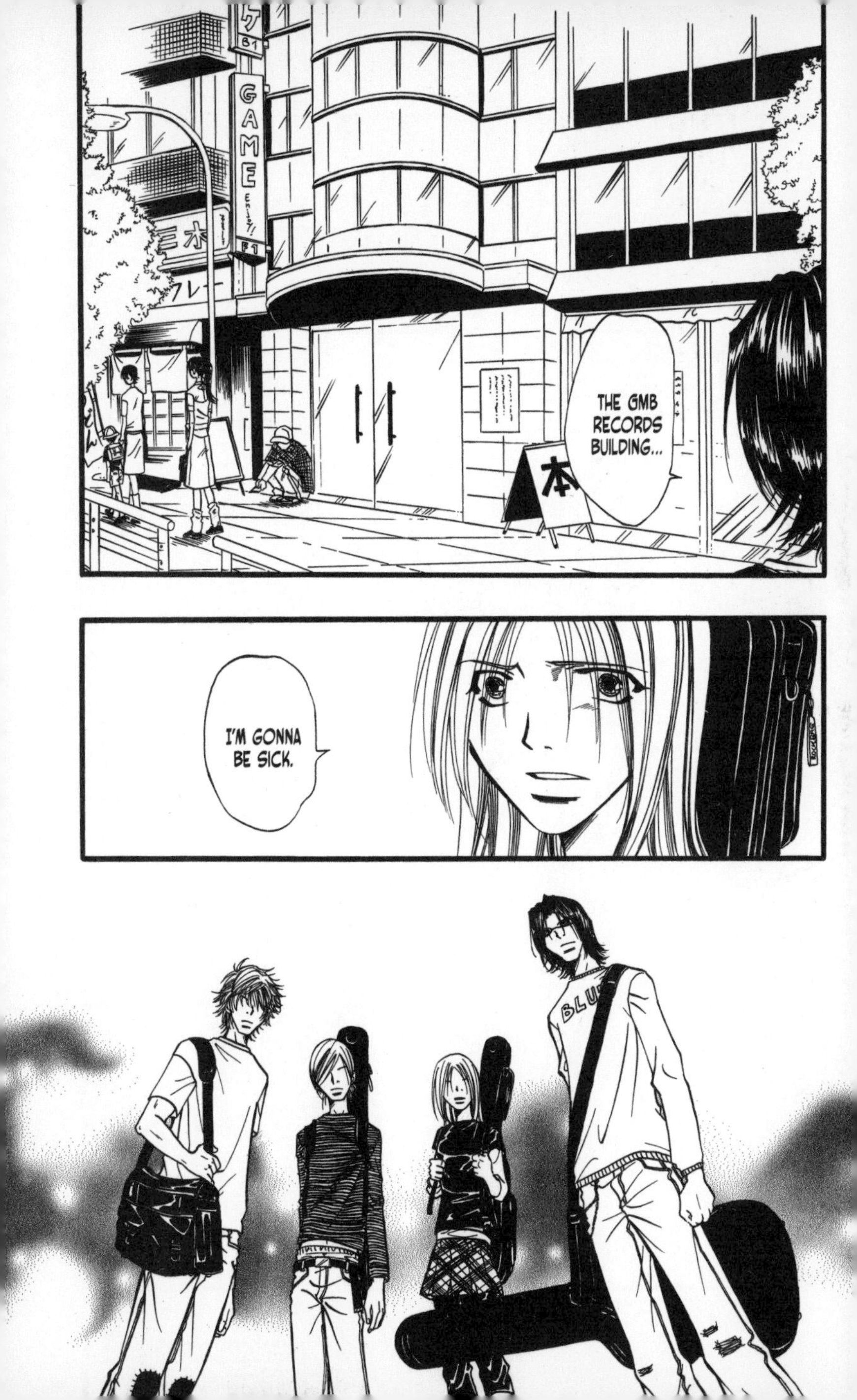
GAME
THE GMB RECORDS BUILDING...
I'M GONNA BE SICK.

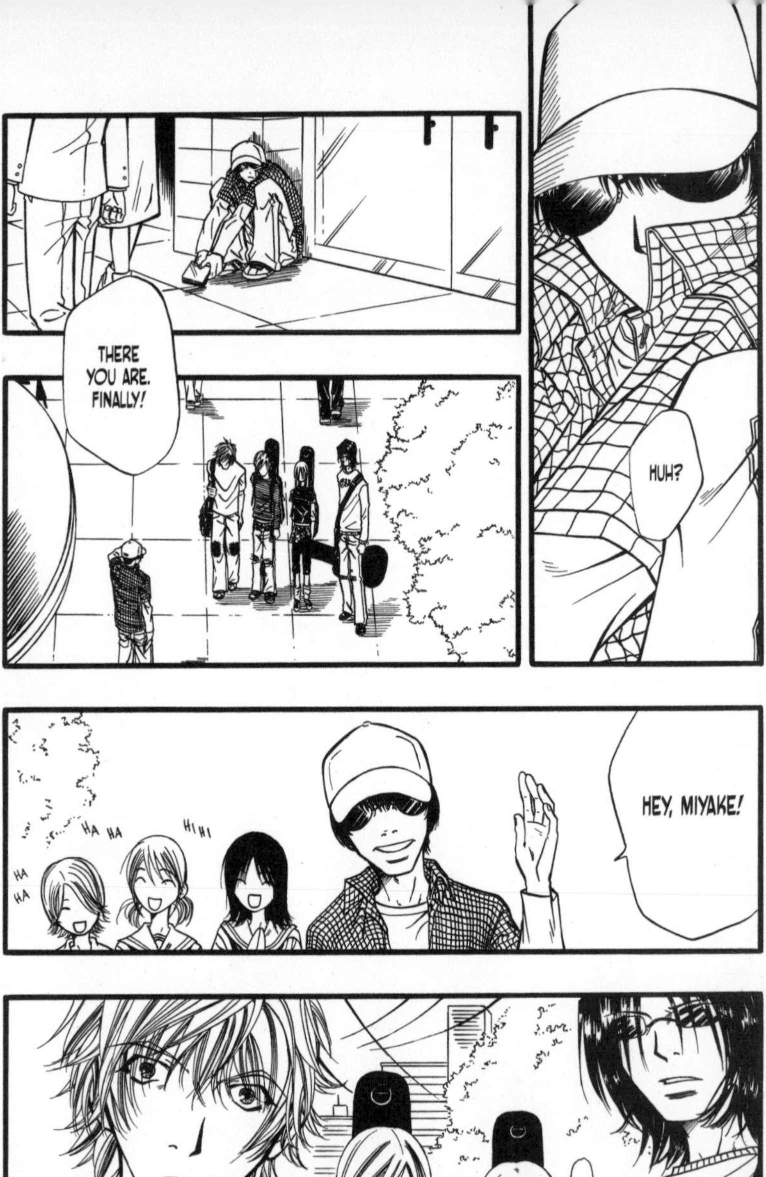
HUH?
THERE YOU ARE. FINALLY!
HEY, MIYAKE!
HI HI
HA HA
HA HA
...
?

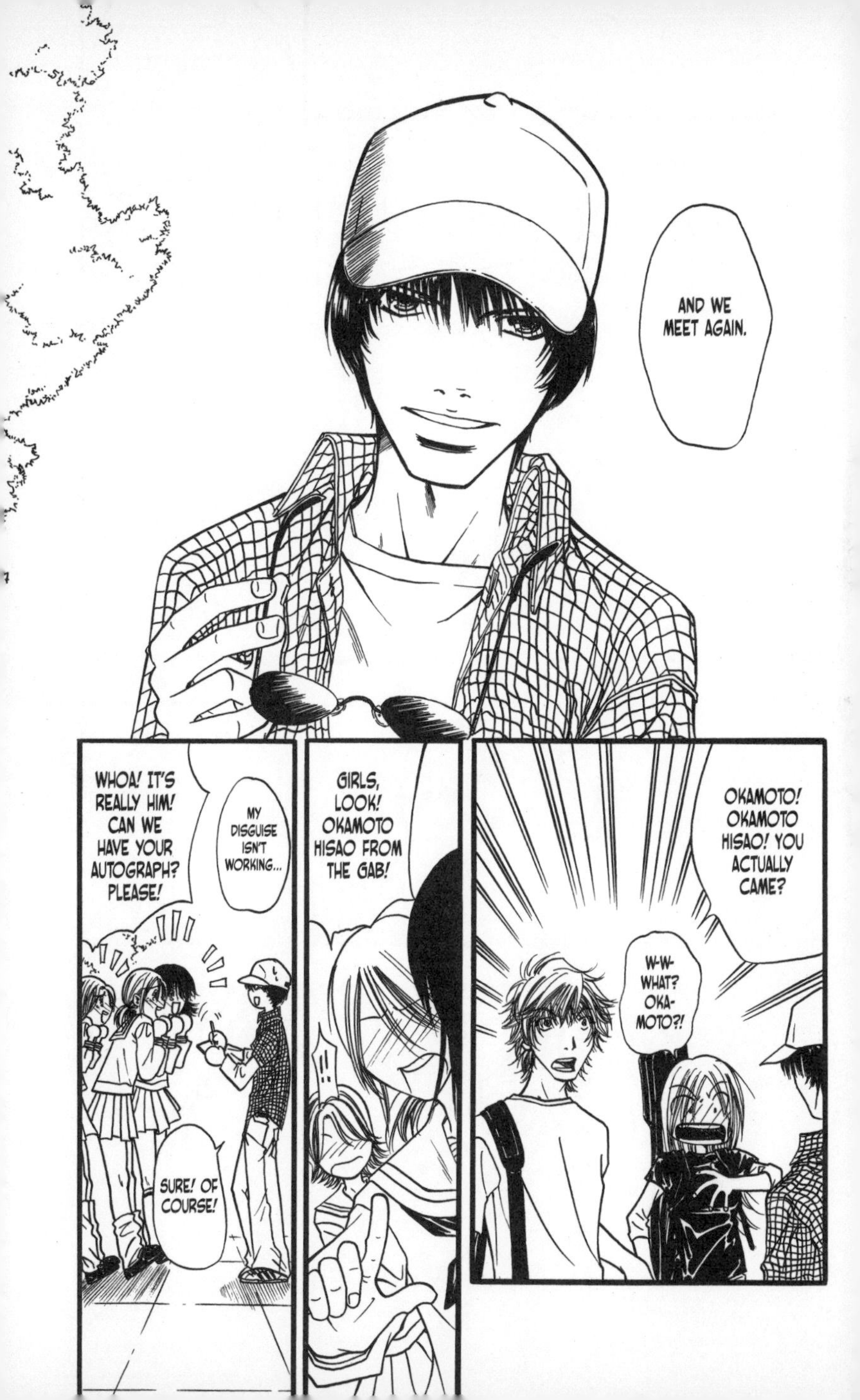
AND WE MEET AGAIN.
OKAMOTO! OKAMOTO HISAO! YOU ACTUALLY CAME?
W-W-WHAT? OKA-MOTO?!
GIRLS, LOOK! OKAMOTO HISAO FROM THE GAB!
MY DISGUISE ISN'T WORKING...
WHOA! IT'S REALLY HIM! CAN WE HAVE YOUR AUTOGRAPH? PLEASE!
SURE! OF COURSE!

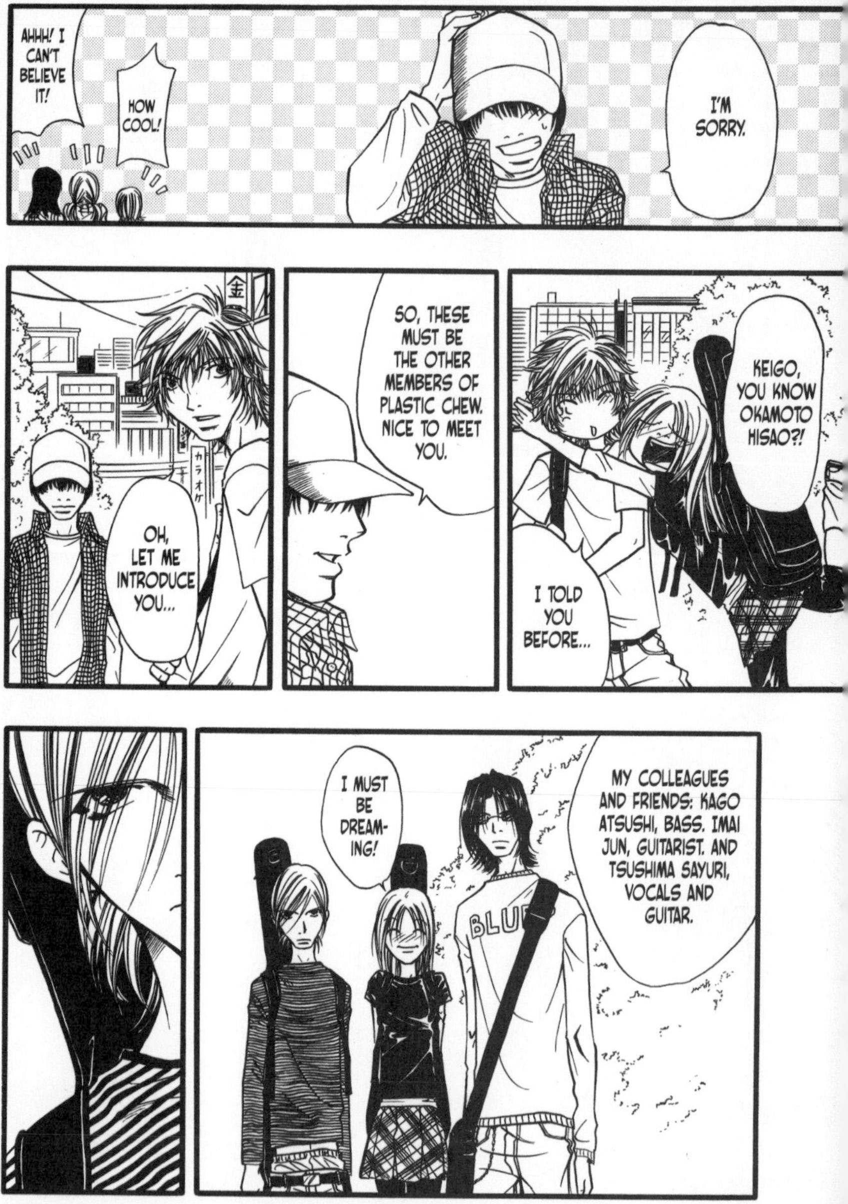
I'M SORRY.
HOW COOL!
AHHH! I CAN'T BELIEVE IT!
KEIGO, YOU KNOW OKAMOTO HISAO?!
I TOLD YOU BEFORE...
SO, THESE MUST BE THE OTHER MEMBERS OF PLASTIC CHEW. NICE TO MEET YOU.
OH, LET ME INTRODUCE YOU...
MY COLLEAGUES AND FRIENDS: KAGO ATSUSHI, BASS. IMAI JUN, GUITARIST. AND TSUSHIMA SAYURI, VOCALS AND GUITAR.
I MUST BE DREAMING!

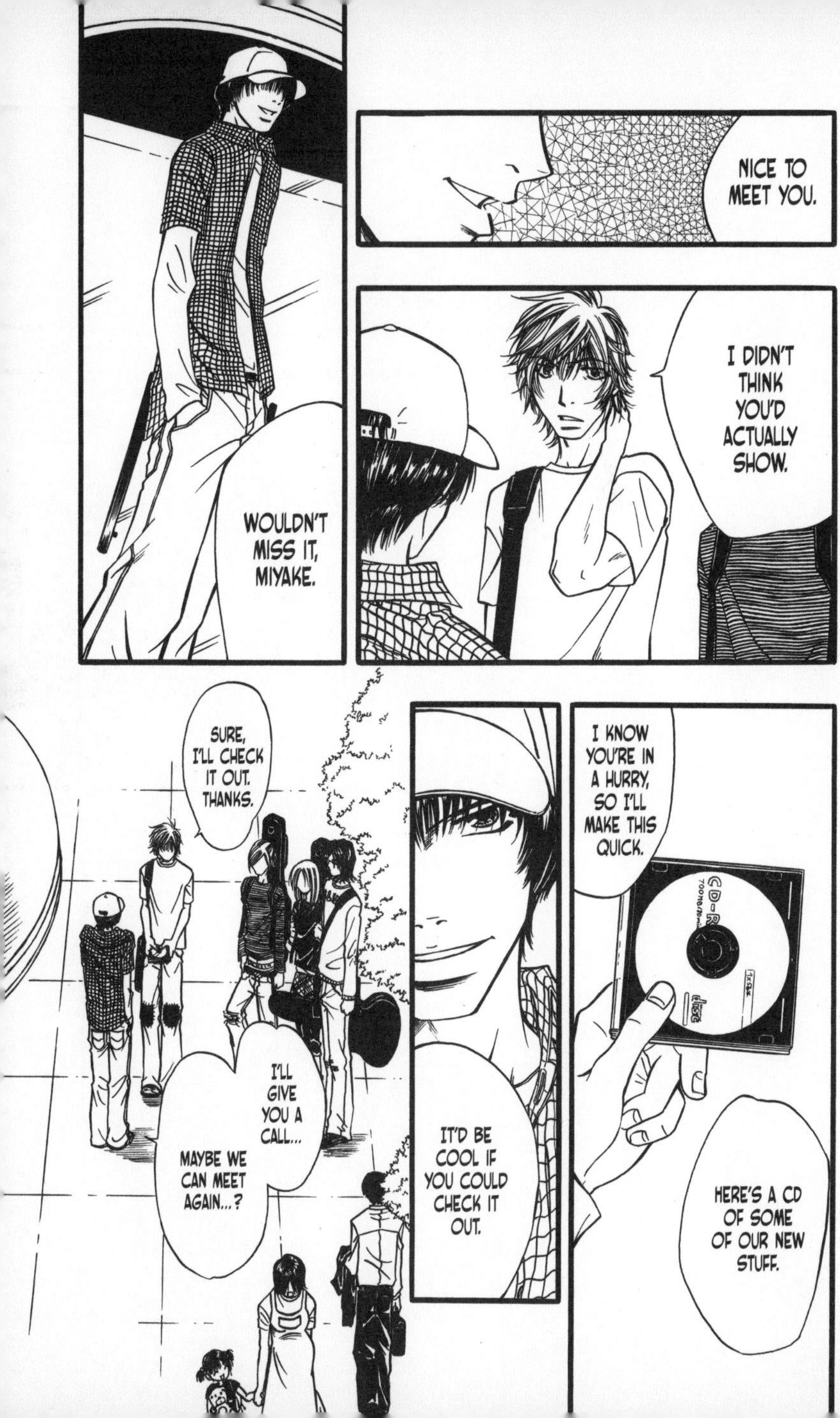
NICE TO MEET YOU.
I DIDN'T THINK YOU'D ACTUALLY SHOW.
WOULDN'T MISS IT, MIYAKE.
I KNOW YOU'RE IN A HURRY, SO I'LL MAKE THIS QUICK.
HERE'S A CD OF SOME OF OUR NEW STUFF.
IT'D BE COOL IF YOU COULD CHECK IT OUT.
SURE, I'LL CHECK IT OUT. THANKS.
I'LL GIVE YOU A CALL...
MAYBE WE CAN MEET AGAIN...?

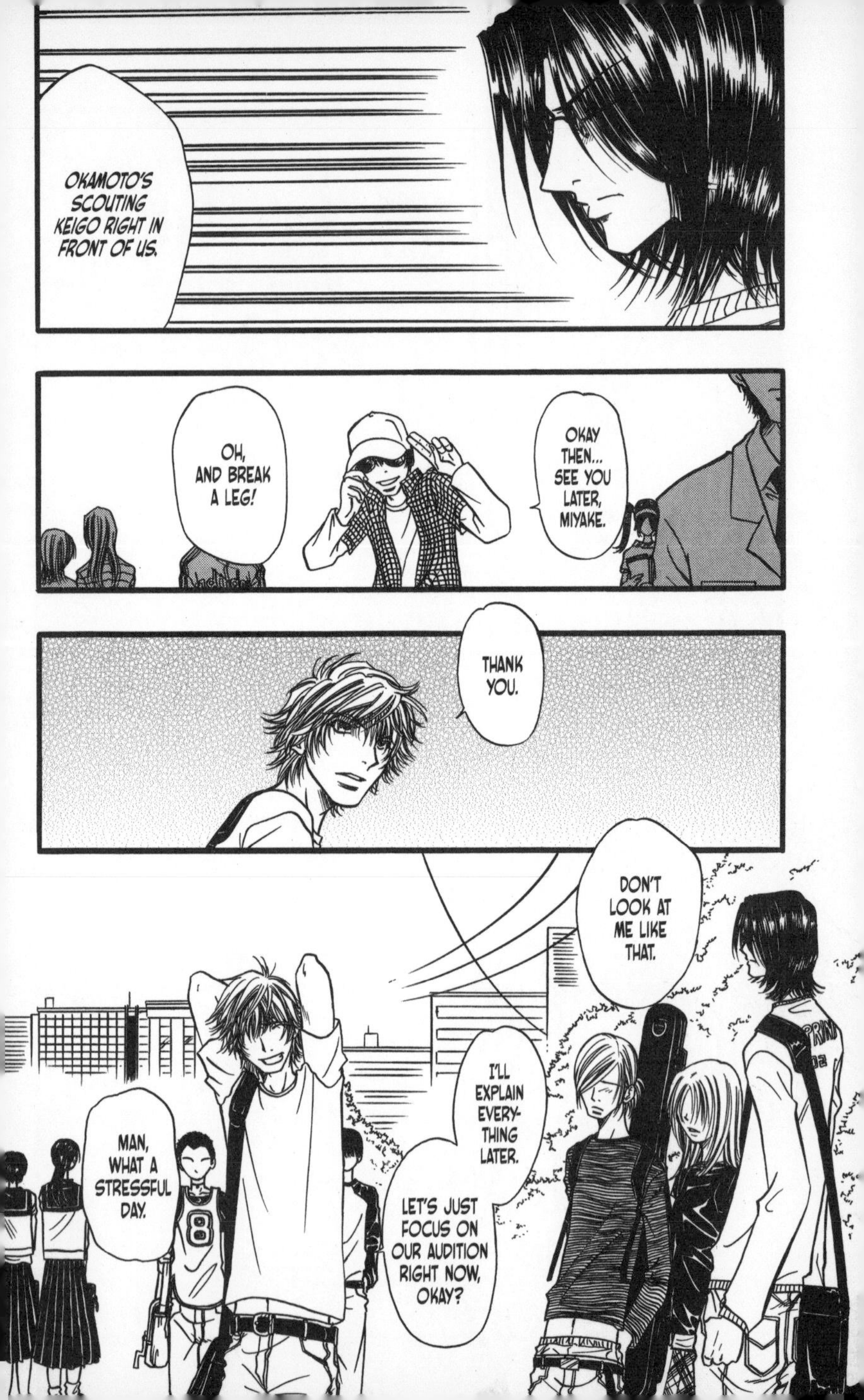
OKAMOTO'S SCOUTING KEIGO RIGHT IN FRONT OF US.
OKAY THEN... SEE YOU LATER, MIYAKE.
OH, AND BREAK A LEG!
THANK YOU.
DON'T LOOK AT ME LIKE THAT.
I'LL EXPLAIN EVERY-THING LATER.
LET'S JUST FOCUS ON OUR AUDITION RIGHT NOW, OKAY?
MAN, WHAT A STRESSFUL DAY.

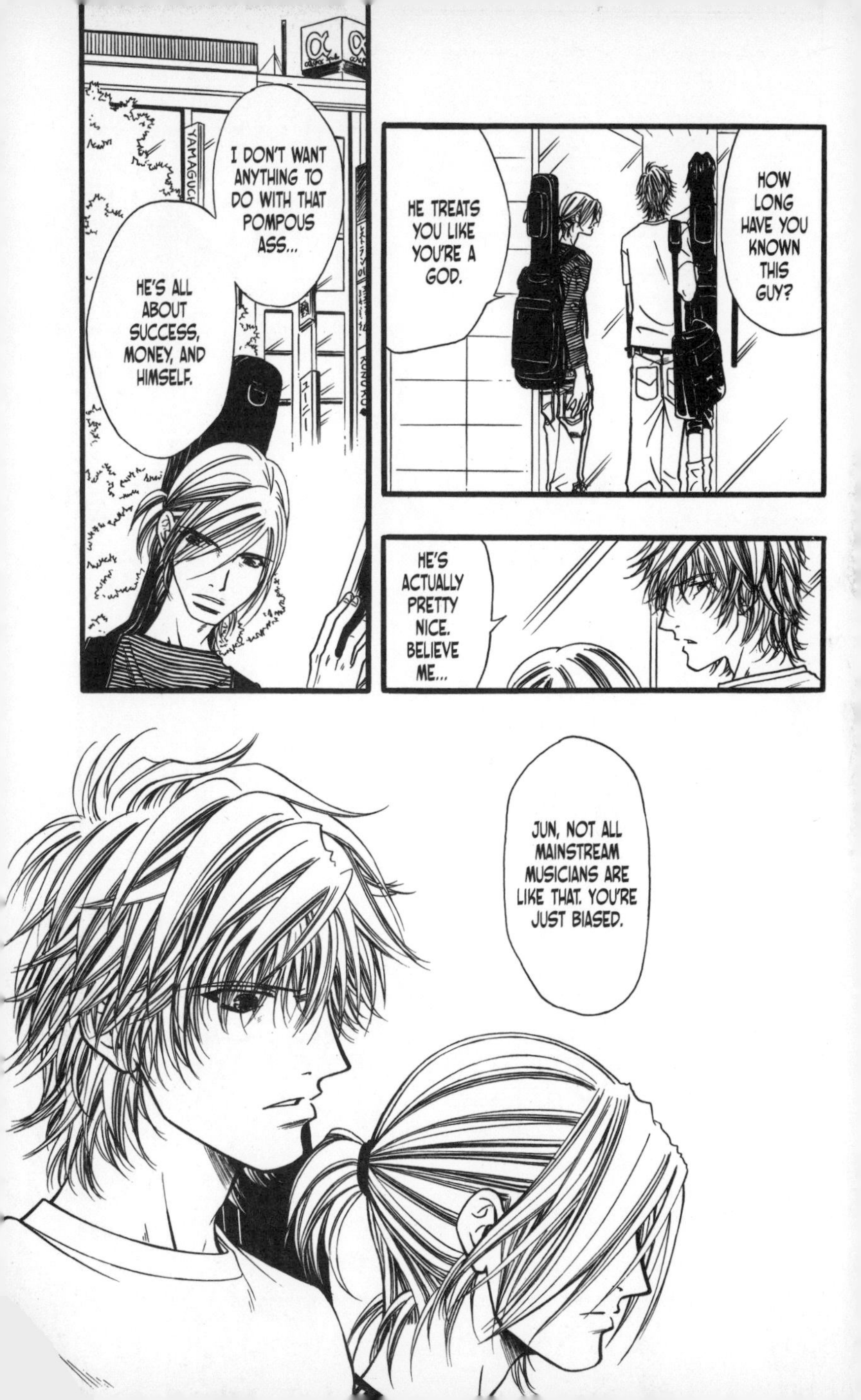
HOW LONG HAVE YOU KNOWN THIS GUY?
HE TREATS YOU LIKE YOU'RE A GOD.
HE'S ACTUALLY PRETTY NICE. BELIEVE ME...
I DON'T WANT ANYTHING TO DO WITH THAT POMPOUS ASS...
HE'S ALL ABOUT SUCCESS, MONEY, AND HIMSELF.
JUN, NOT ALL MAINSTREAM MUSICIANS ARE LIKE THAT. YOU'RE JUST BIASED.

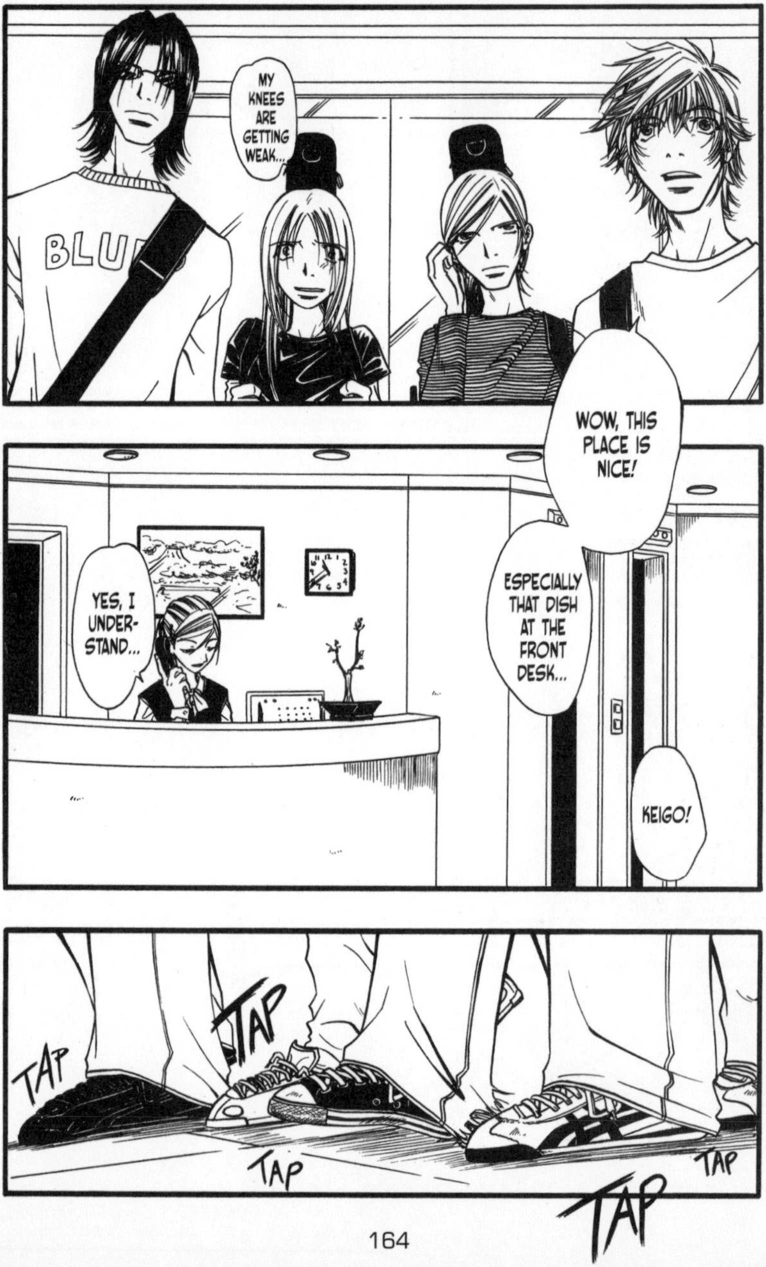
WOW, THIS PLACE IS NICE!
MY KNEES ARE GETTING WEAK...
ESPECIALLY THAT DISH AT THE FRONT DESK...
KEIGO!
YES, I UNDER-STAND...
TAP
TAP
TAP
TAP
TAP
TAP

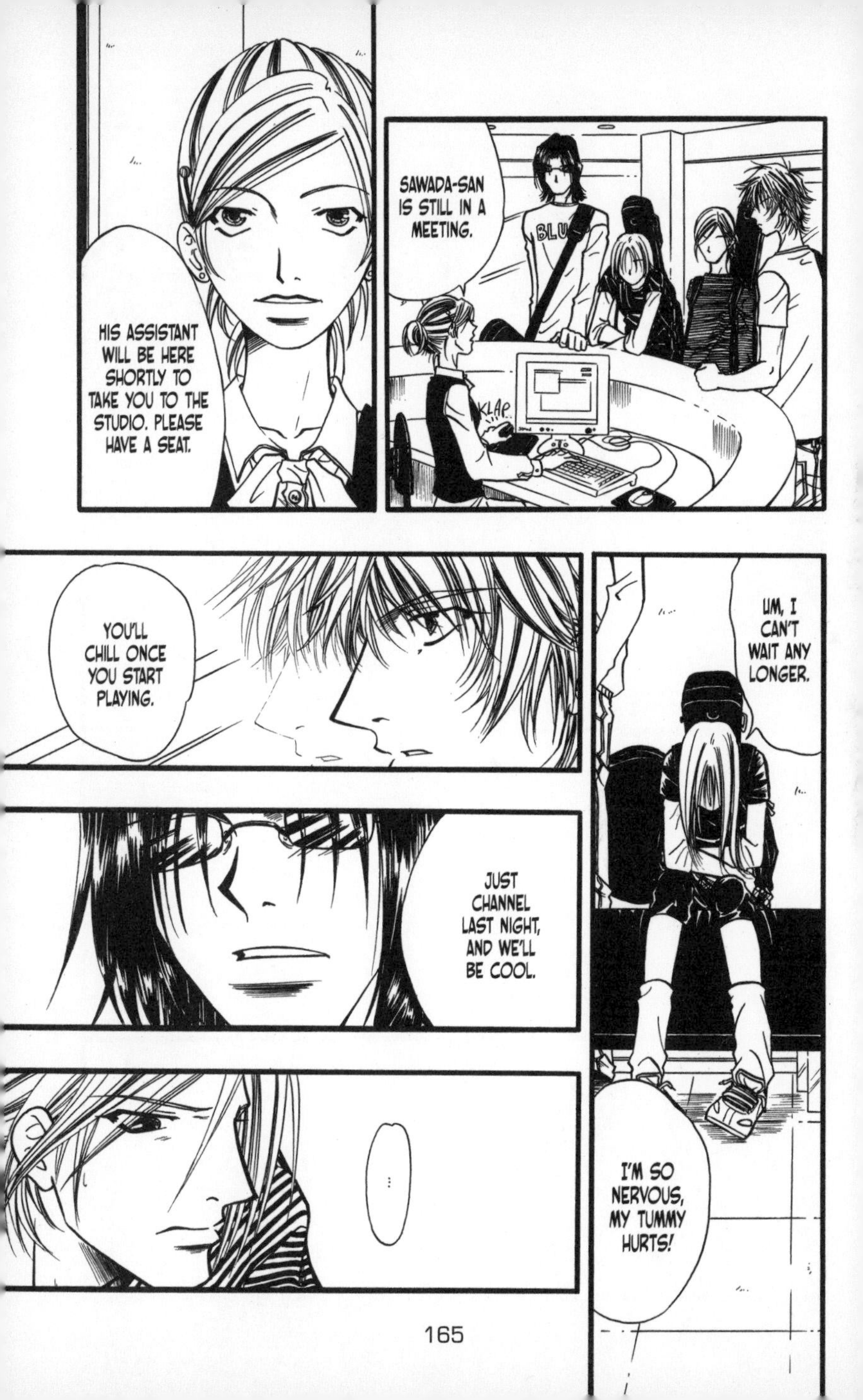
SAWADA-SAN IS STILL IN A MEETING.
KLAP
HIS ASSISTANT WILL BE HERE SHORTLY TO TAKE YOU TO THE STUDIO. PLEASE HAVE A SEAT.
UM, I CAN'T WAIT ANY LONGER.
I'M SO NERVOUS, MY TUMMY HURTS!
YOU'LL CHILL ONCE YOU START PLAYING.
JUST CHANNEL LAST NIGHT, AND WE'LL BE COOL.
...

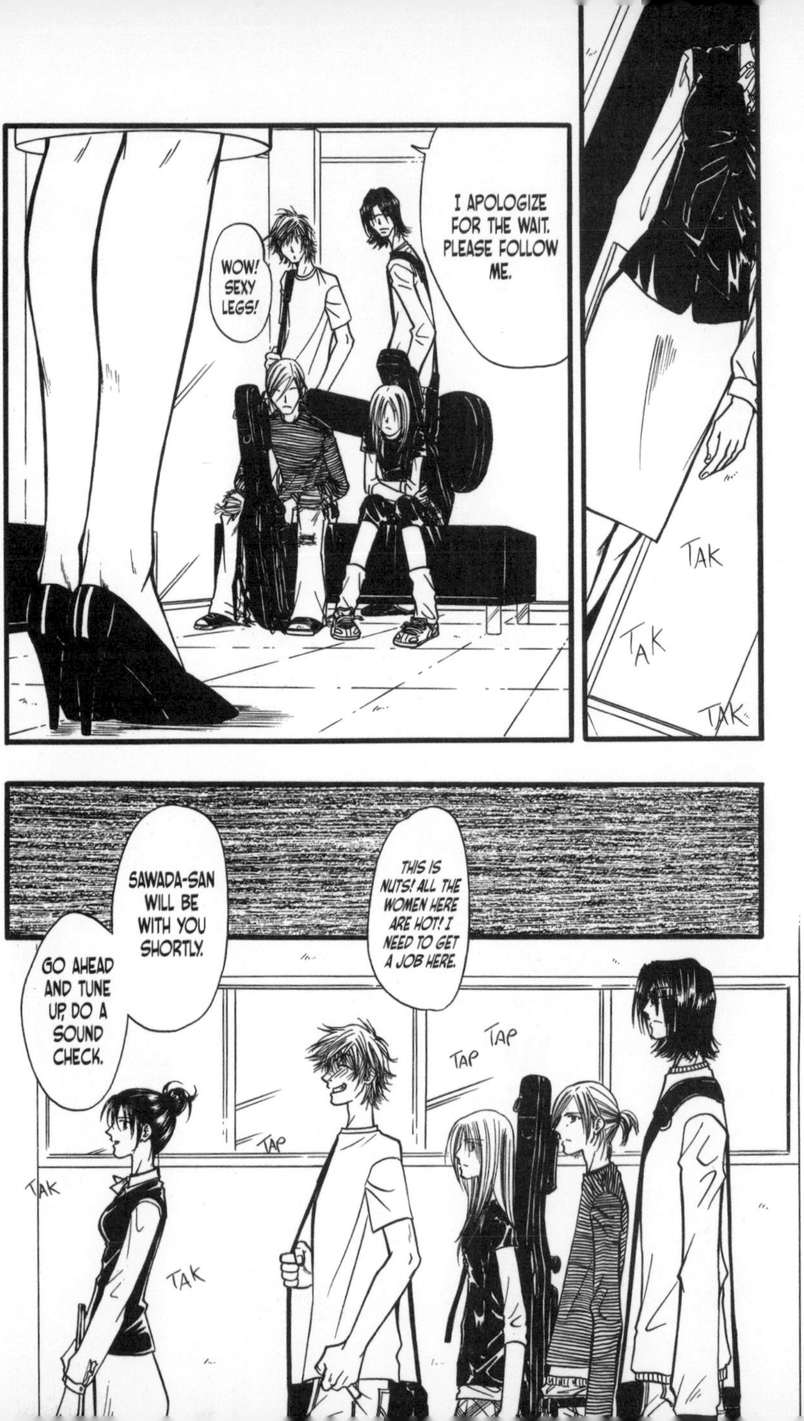
TAK
TAK
TAK
I APOLOGIZE FOR THE WAIT. PLEASE FOLLOW ME.
WOW! SEXY LEGS!
THIS IS NUTS! ALL THE WOMEN HERE ARE HOT! I NEED TO GET A JOB HERE.
SAWADA-SAN WILL BE WITH YOU SHORTLY.
GO AHEAD AND TUNE UP, DO A SOUND CHECK.
TAP TAP
TAP
TAK
TAK

It can happen so quickly. We've almost reached the end of yet another book. What a weird feeling! I'd like to say that the working on this book was a lot of fun. I have a million ideas for the next couple of volumes of Yonen Buzz. Well, I haven't decided yet how many volumes I am going to create.

But I'm hoping to finish the next volume within two years, and also complete my Master's degree. I also want to discover many other ingenious bands, to learn how to play additional songs on the guitar, and stop myself from going crazy.

So, keep your eyes open for Yonen Buzz, volume 2.
See you soon!
-Chris

Personal preferences:
Album:
Q.O.T.S.A.-- Songs for the Deaf
Film: School of Rock
Book: 69 -- Murakami Ryu

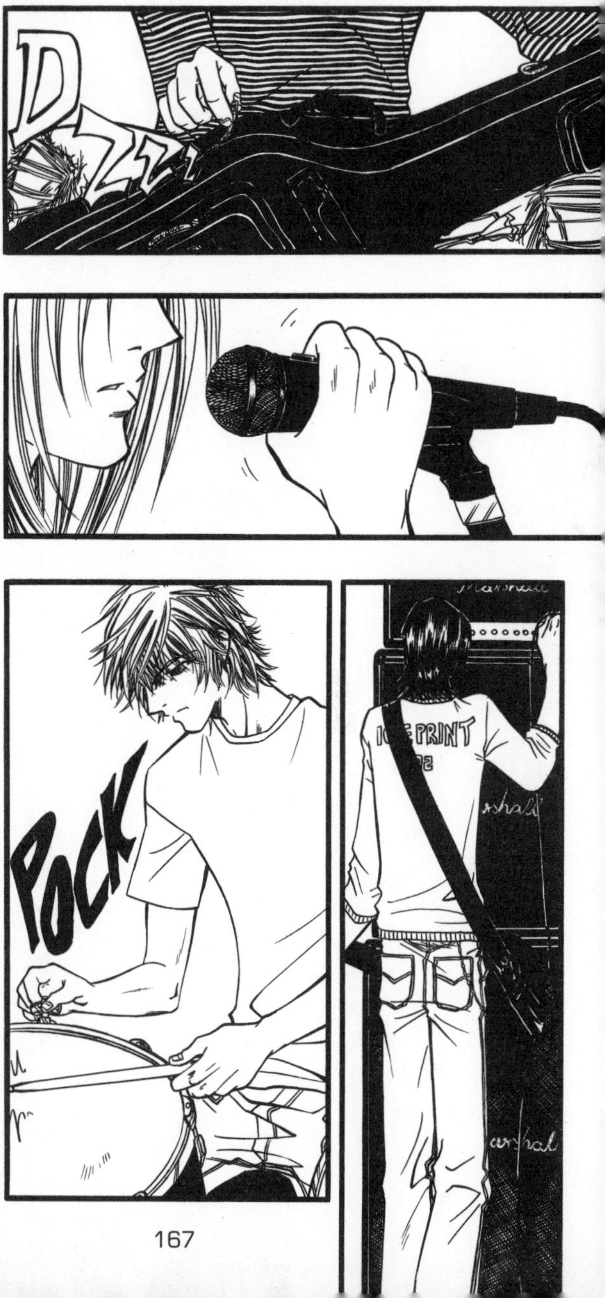
DZZZ
POCK

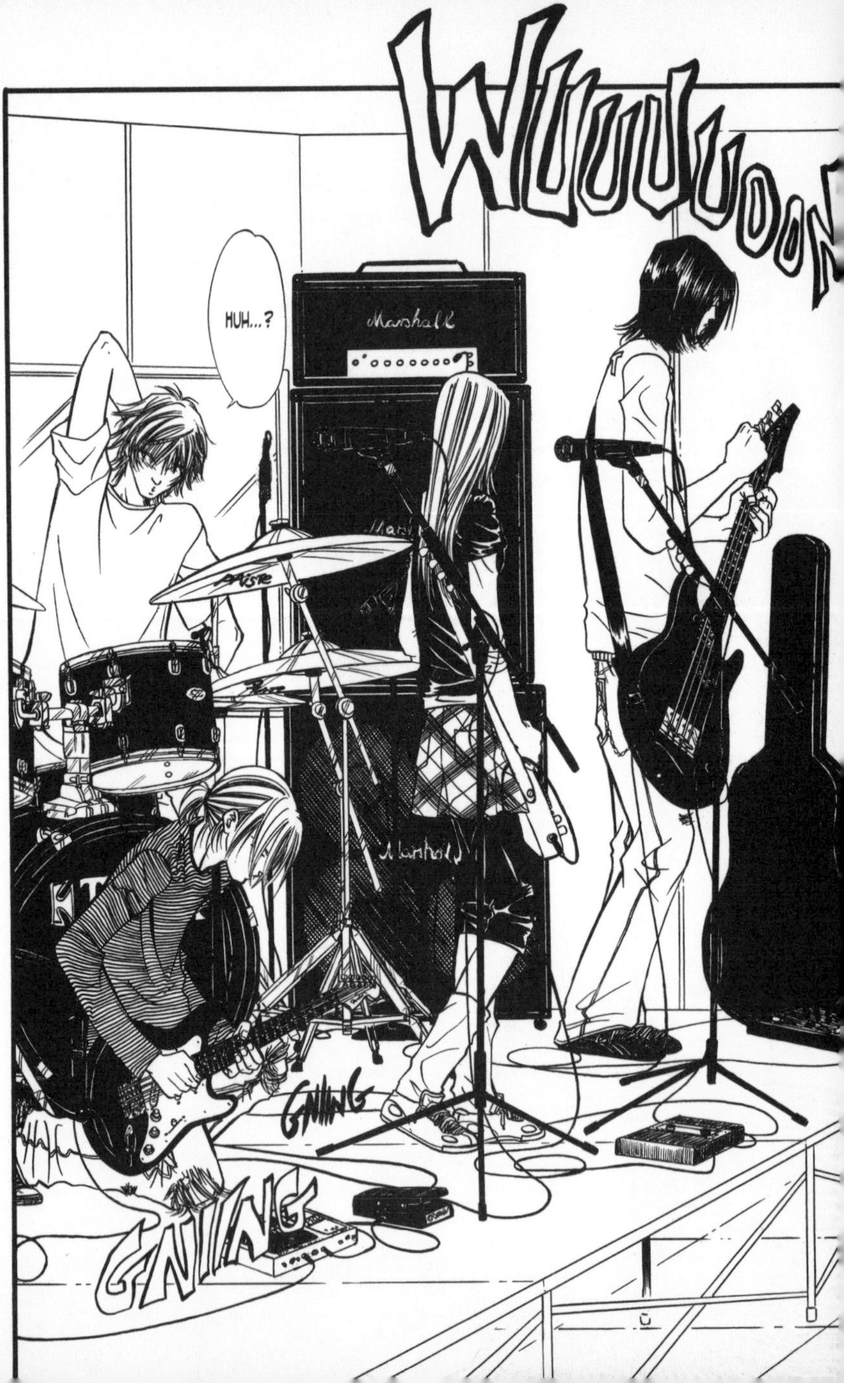
WUUUUOON
HUH...?
GNING
GNING

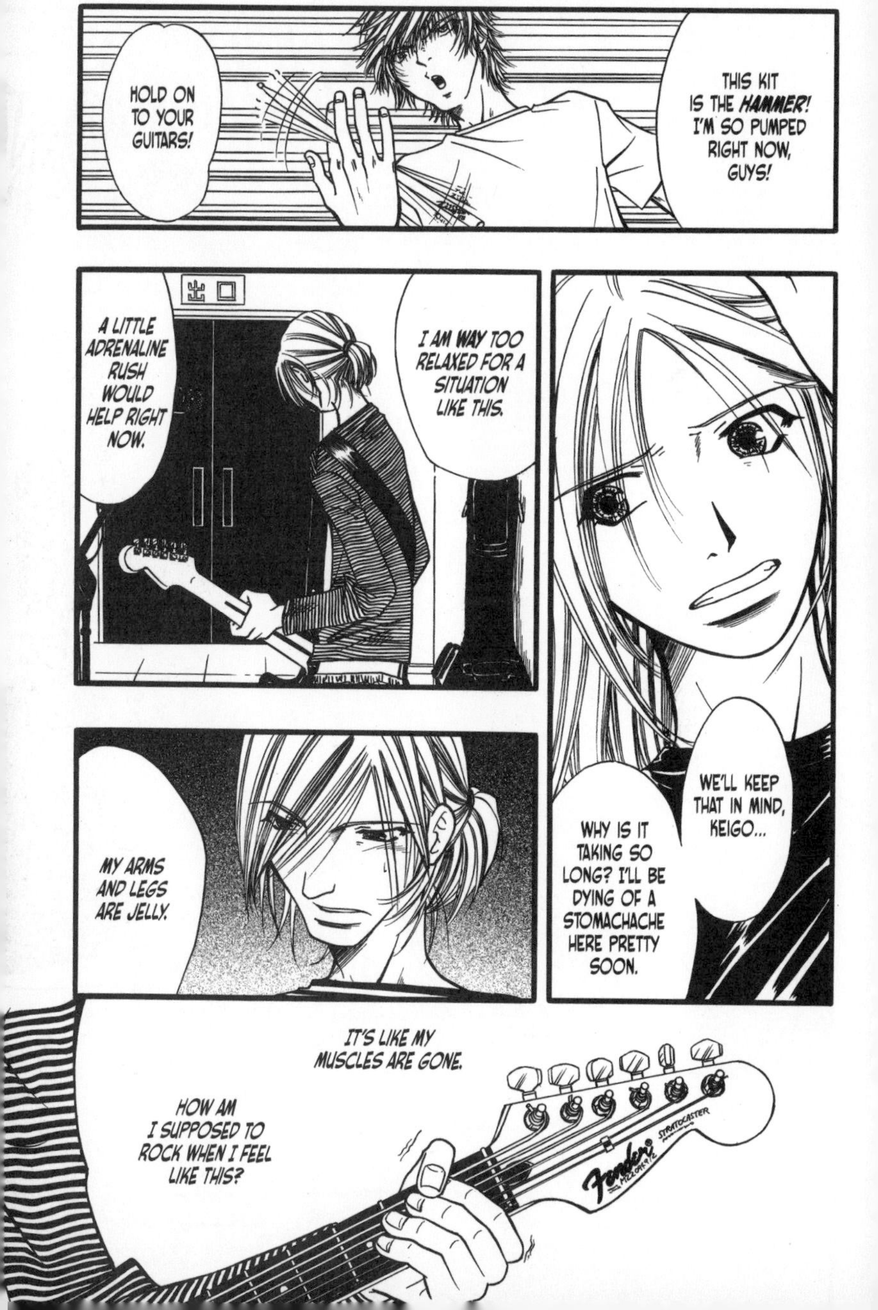
THIS KIT IS THE ***HAMMER!*** I'M SO PUMPED RIGHT NOW, GUYS!
HOLD ON TO YOUR GUITARS!
WE'LL KEEP THAT IN MIND, KEIGO...
WHY IS IT TAKING SO LONG? I'LL BE DYING OF A STOMACHACHE HERE PRETTY SOON.
出口
I AM **WAY** TOO RELAXED FOR A SITUATION LIKE THIS.
A LITTLE ADRENALINE RUSH WOULD HELP RIGHT NOW.
MY ARMS AND LEGS ARE JELLY.
IT'S LIKE MY MUSCLES ARE GONE.
HOW AM I SUPPOSED TO ROCK WHEN I FEEL LIKE THIS?
Fender
STRATOCASTER

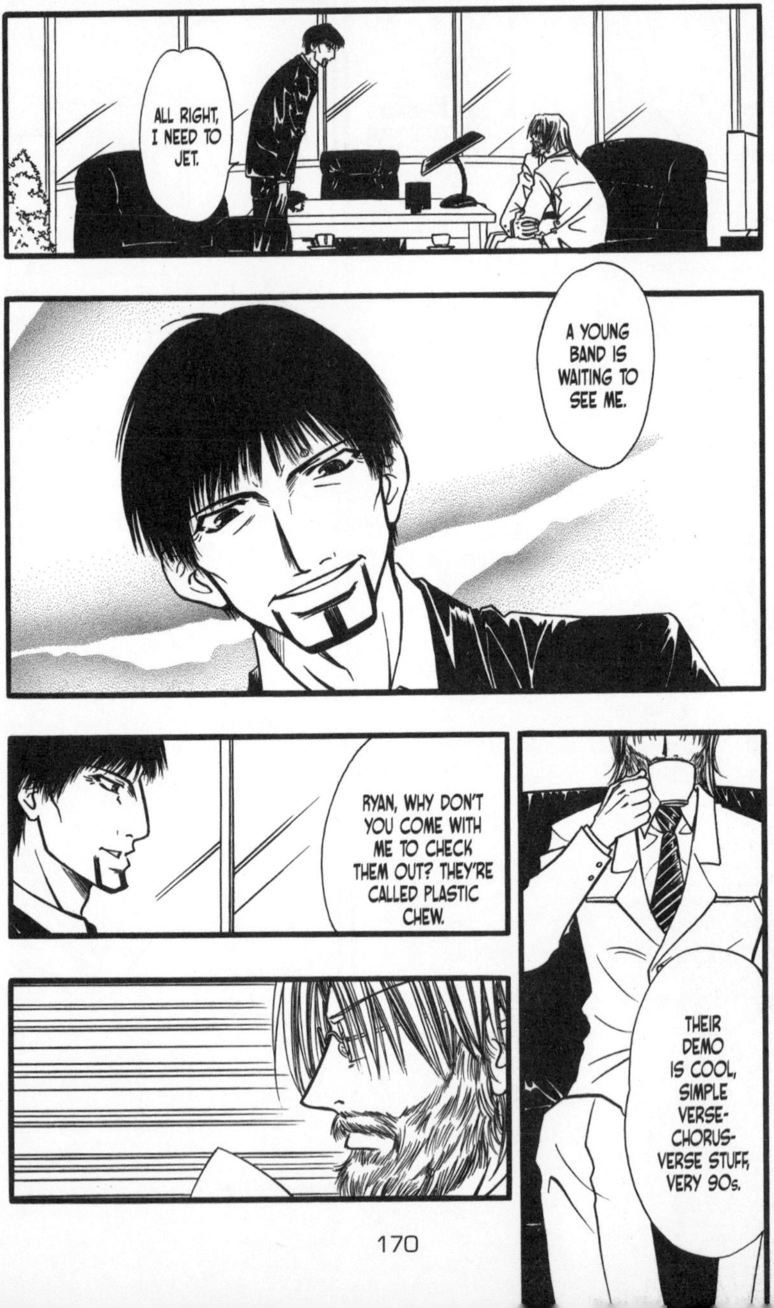
ALL RIGHT, I NEED TO JET.
A YOUNG BAND IS WAITING TO SEE ME.
RYAN, WHY DON'T YOU COME WITH ME TO CHECK THEM OUT? THEY'RE CALLED PLASTIC CHEW.
THEIR DEMO IS COOL, SIMPLE VERSE-CHORUS-VERSE STUFF, VERY 90s.

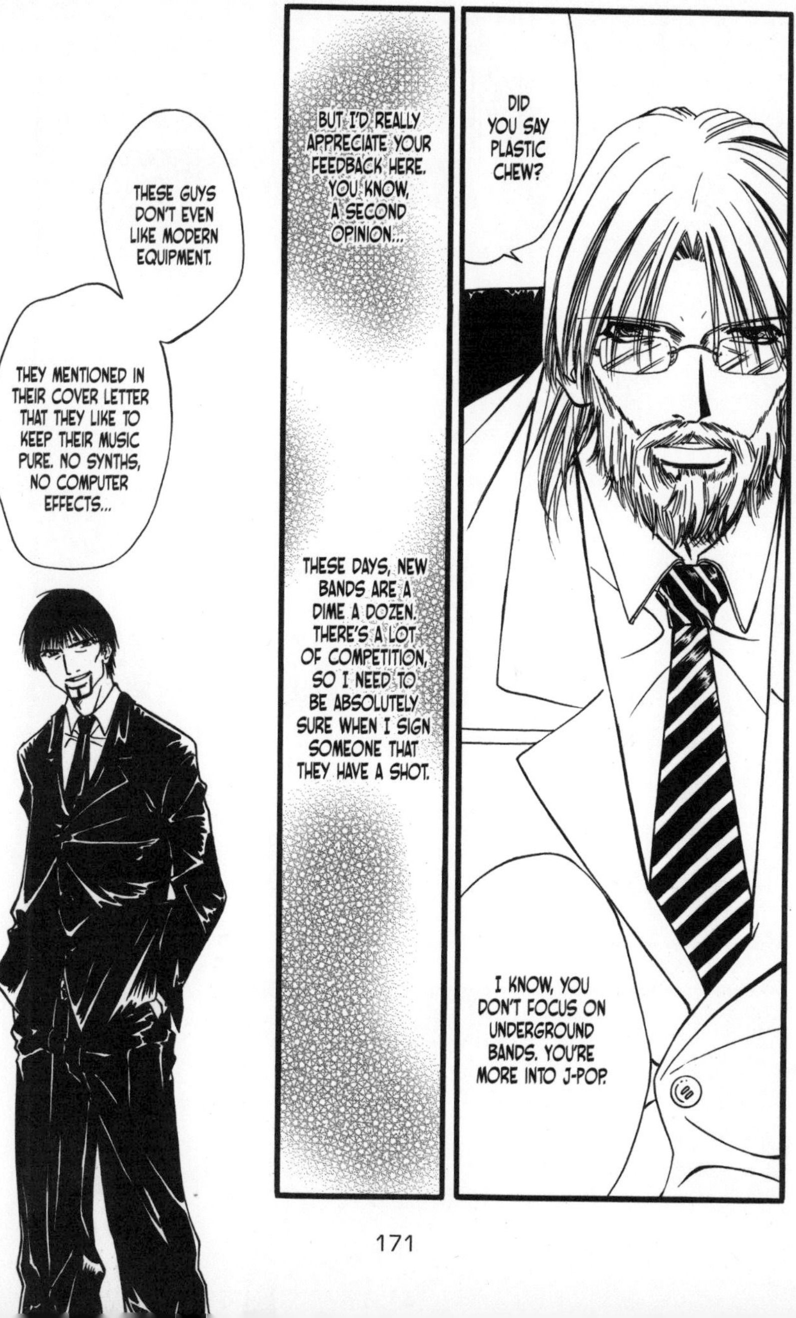
DID YOU SAY PLASTIC CHEW?
I KNOW, YOU DON'T FOCUS ON UNDERGROUND BANDS. YOU'RE MORE INTO J-POP.
BUT I'D REALLY APPRECIATE YOUR FEEDBACK HERE. YOU KNOW, A SECOND OPINION...
THESE DAYS, NEW BANDS ARE A DIME A DOZEN. THERE'S A LOT OF COMPETITION, SO I NEED TO BE ABSOLUTELY SURE WHEN I SIGN SOMEONE THAT THEY HAVE A SHOT.
THESE GUYS DON'T EVEN LIKE MODERN EQUIPMENT.
THEY MENTIONED IN THEIR COVER LETTER THAT THEY LIKE TO KEEP THEIR MUSIC PURE. NO SYNTHS, NO COMPUTER EFFECTS...

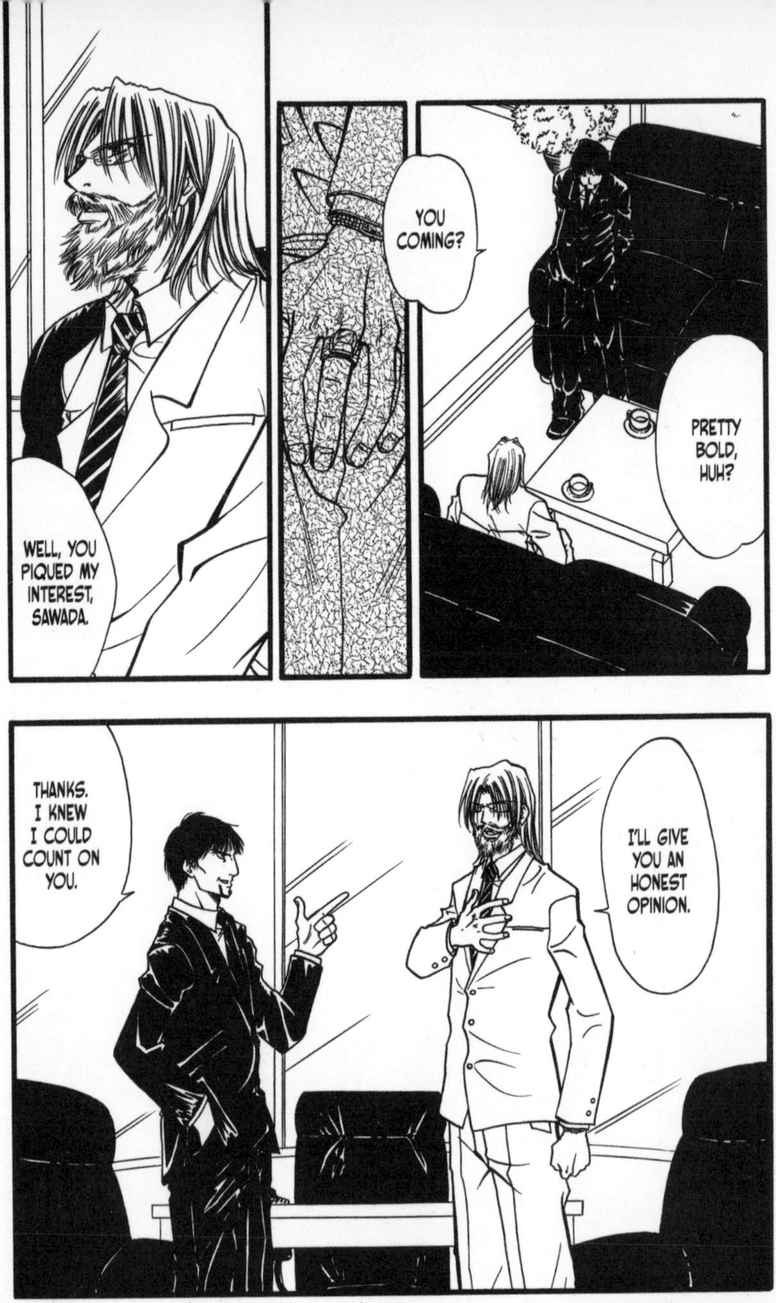
PRETTY BOLD, HUH?
YOU COMING?
WELL, YOU PIQUED MY INTEREST, SAWADA.
I'LL GIVE YOU AN HONEST OPINION.
THANKS. I KNEW I COULD COUNT ON YOU.

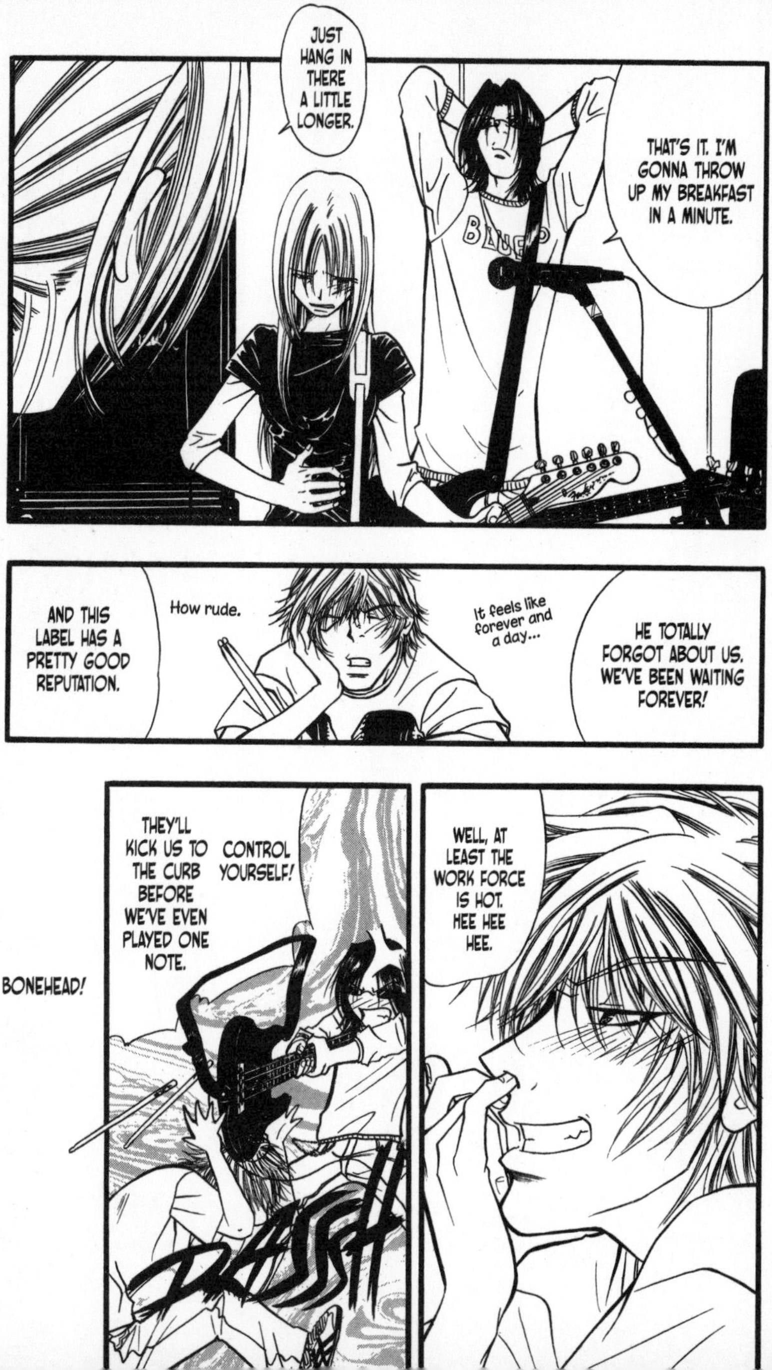
THAT'S IT. I'M GONNA THROW UP MY BREAKFAST IN A MINUTE.
JUST HANG IN THERE A LITTLE LONGER.
HE TOTALLY FORGOT ABOUT US. WE'VE BEEN WAITING FOREVER!
It feels like forever and a day...
How rude.
AND THIS LABEL HAS A PRETTY GOOD REPUTATION.
WELL, AT LEAST THE WORK FORCE IS HOT. HEE HEE HEE.
CONTROL YOURSELF!
THEY'LL KICK US TO THE CURB BEFORE WE'VE EVEN PLAYED ONE NOTE.
BONEHEAD!
DASH

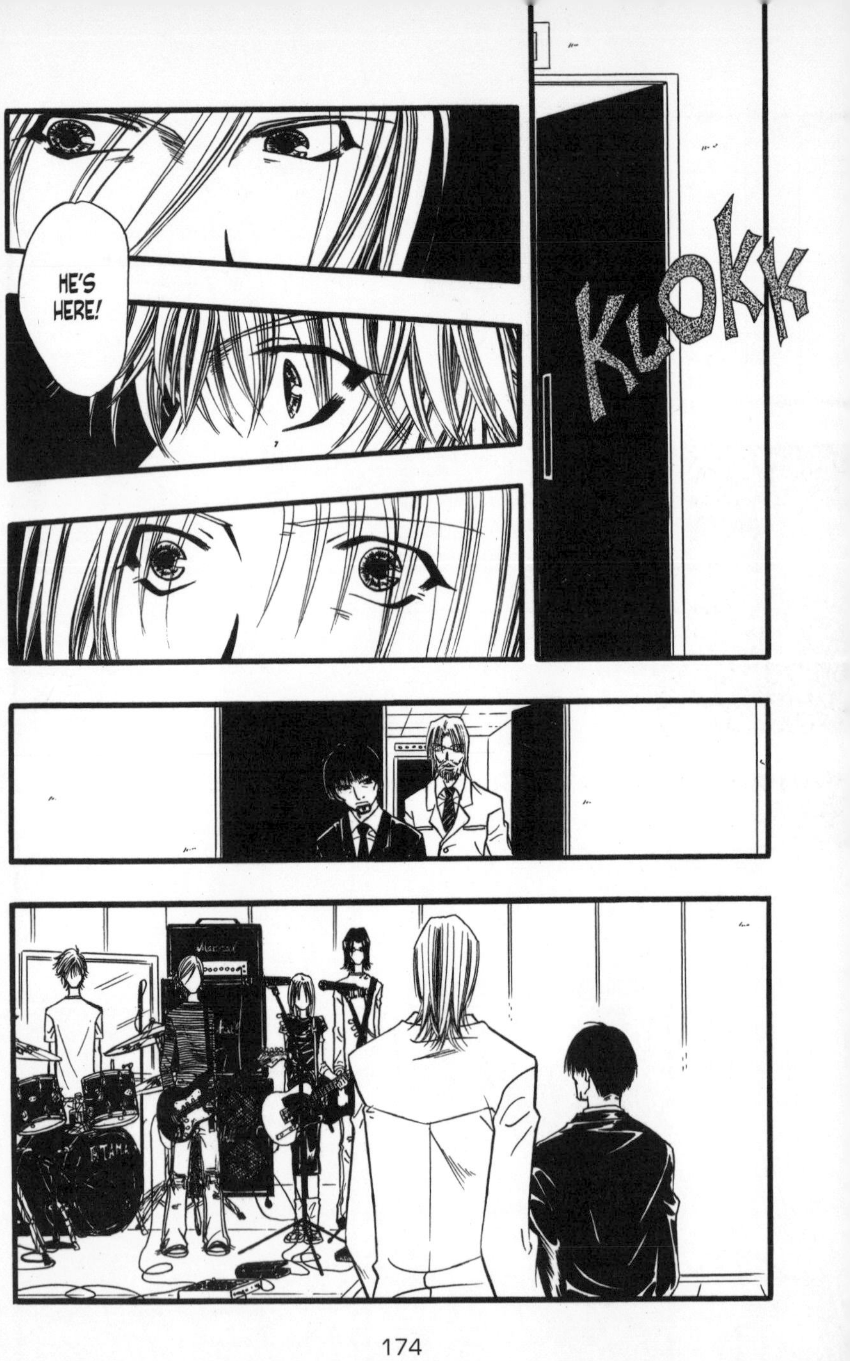
KLOKK
HE'S HERE!

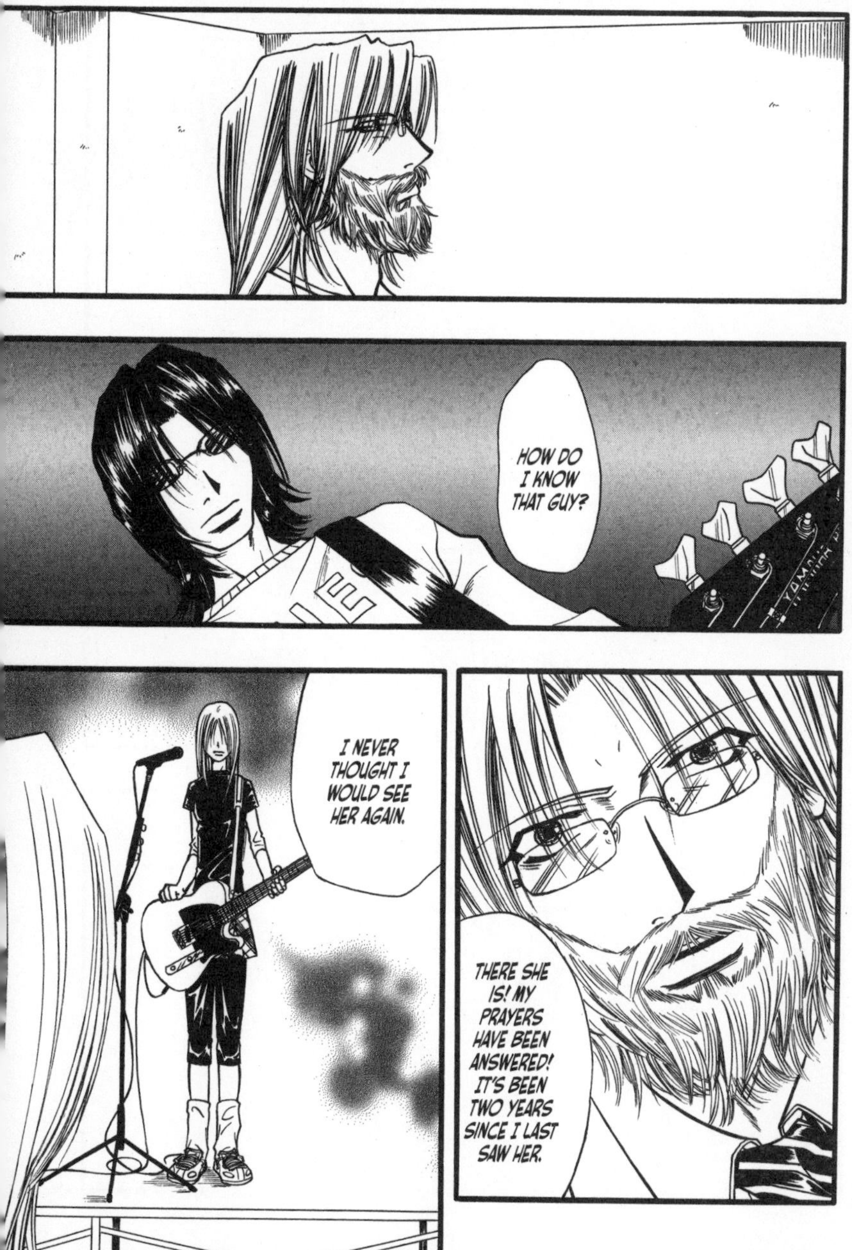
HOW DO I KNOW THAT GUY?
I NEVER THOUGHT I WOULD SEE HER AGAIN.
THERE SHE IS! MY PRAYERS HAVE BEEN ANSWERED! IT'S BEEN TWO YEARS SINCE I LAST SAW HER.

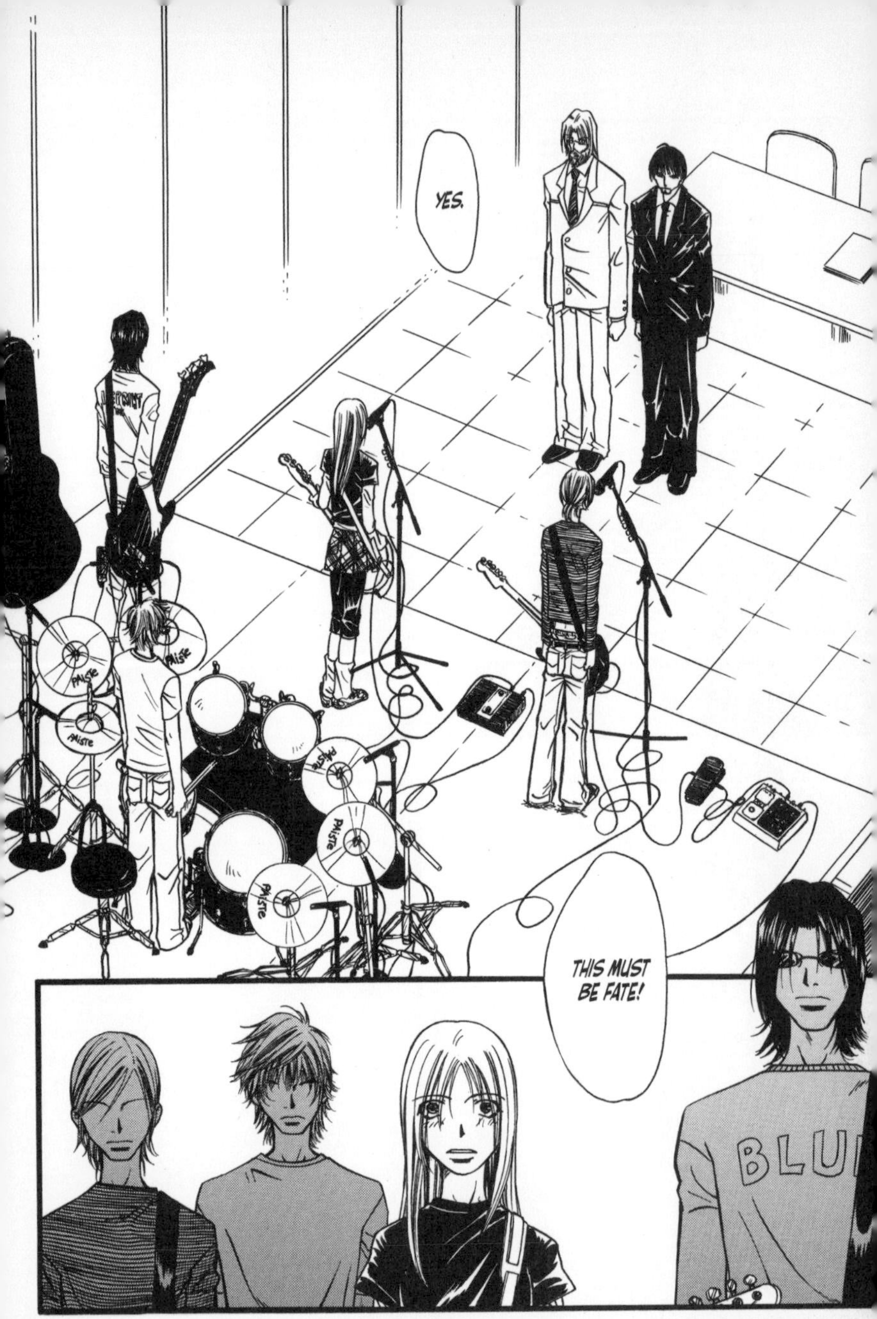
YES.
THIS MUST BE FATE!

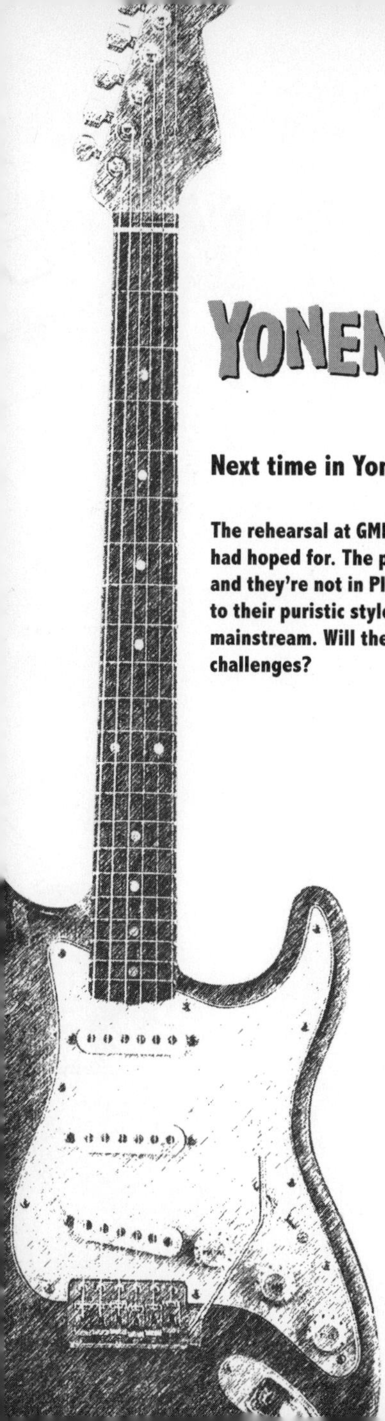

YONEN BUZZ

Next time in Yonen Buzz 2:

The rehearsal at GMB did not exactly produce the results the band had hoped for. The producer, Ryan, seems to have ulterior motives--and they're not in Plastic Chew's favor. While Atsushi and Jun stick to their puristic style, Sayuri and Keigo will be tempted to go more mainstream. Will the group be able to withstand all of these challenges?

Jun Imai

Name: Imai, Jun
(guitar, vocals)

Date of birth: 4/2/83
Blood type: B
Height: 5'6"
Weight: 119 lbs
Instruments: Guitar, bass
Guitar: Fender Stratocaster
Pick: Dunlop USA 1.14 mm
Started to play instruments: age 9 (guitar), age 14 (bass)
Influences: Nirvana, Soundgarden, Sex Pistols, Flipper, Shonen Knife
Current favorites: Q.O.T.S.A., The Vines, The White Stripes, Foo Fighters, Buqy Craxone

Music and Style: Jun loves simple but memorable music. It could be described as a mix of dynamic, skewed, calm, and melodic music. He is highly experimental and he values the freedom of composing.

He is not an exceptional singer, but he is able to outdo himself whenever he releases his emotions. He also likes to make fun of his singing. Jun is very good at playing the guitar. He prefers simple combinations of accords (hooks), which are easy to remember. This also applies to his bass playing.

He mostly writes his lyrics in English, because this gives him a greater sense of freedom. He absolutely loves to perform in front of a small but loyal group of fans.

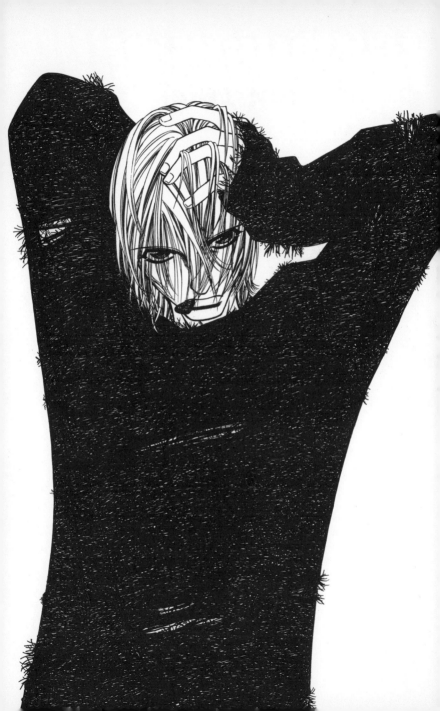

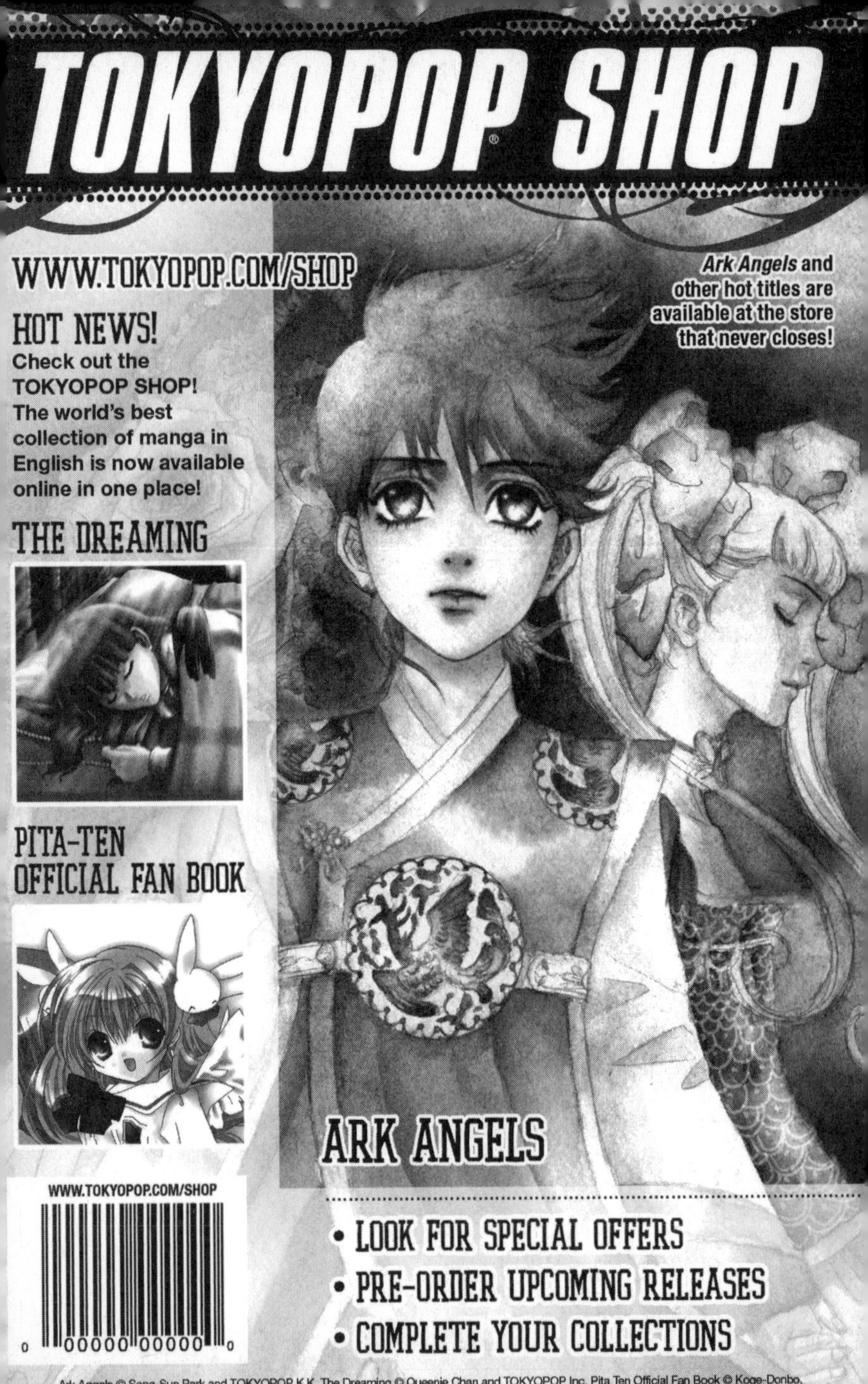
TOKYOPOP® SHOP
WWW.TOKYOPOP.COM/SHOP
HOT NEWS!
Check out the TOKYOPOP SHOP! The world's best collection of manga in English is now available online in one place!
THE DREAMING
PITA-TEN OFFICIAL FAN BOOK
Ark Angels and other hot titles are available at the store that never closes!
ARK ANGELS
WWW.TOKYOPOP.COM/SHOP
0 00000 00000 0
• LOOK FOR SPECIAL OFFERS
• PRE-ORDER UPCOMING RELEASES
• COMPLETE YOUR COLLECTIONS

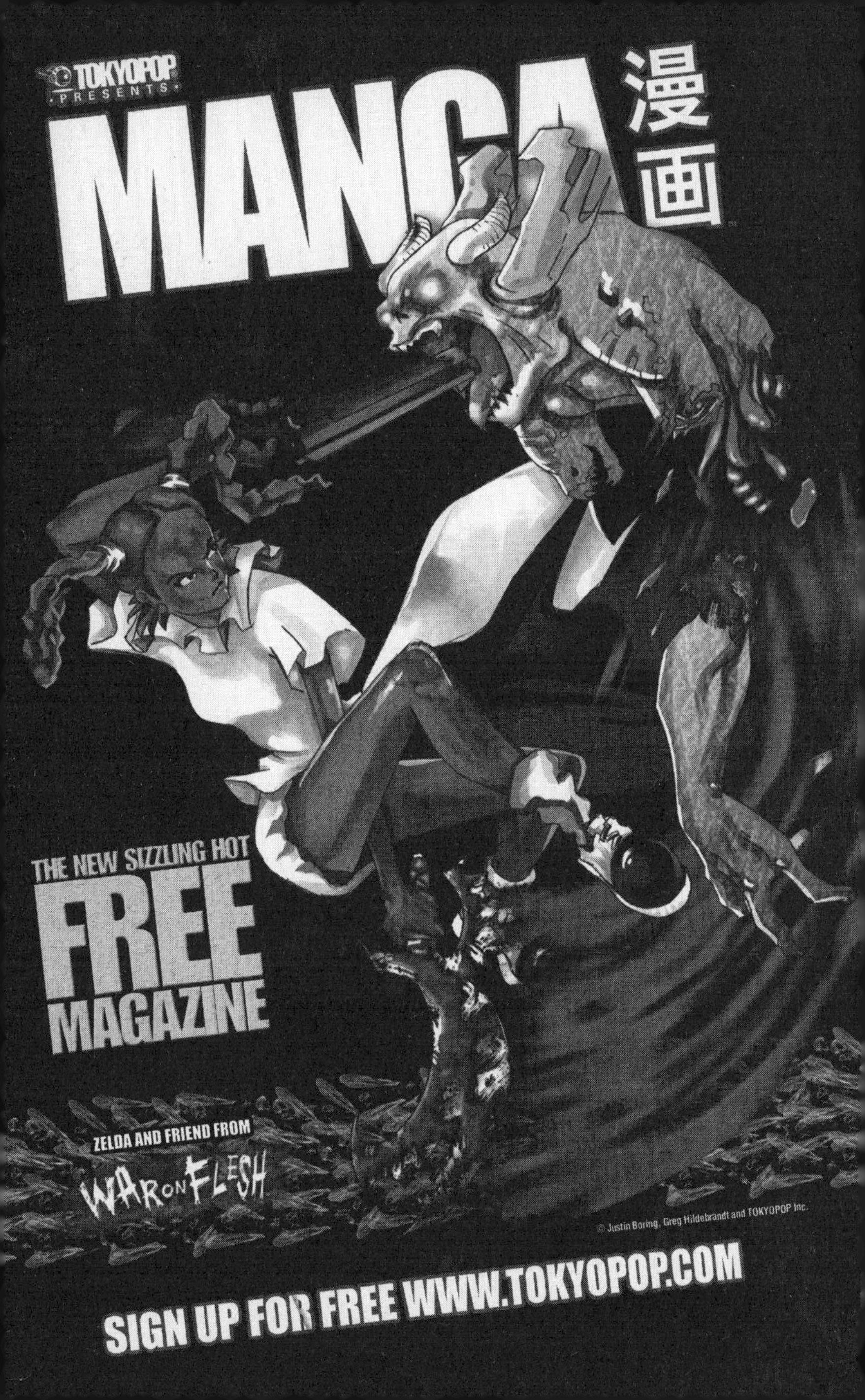
TOKYOPOP PRESENTS
MANGA 漫画
THE NEW SIZZLING HOT
FREE
MAGAZINE
ZELDA AND FRIEND FROM
WAR ON FLESH
© Justin Boring, Greg Hildebrandt and TOKYOPOP Inc.
SIGN UP FOR FREE WWW.TOKYOPOP.COM

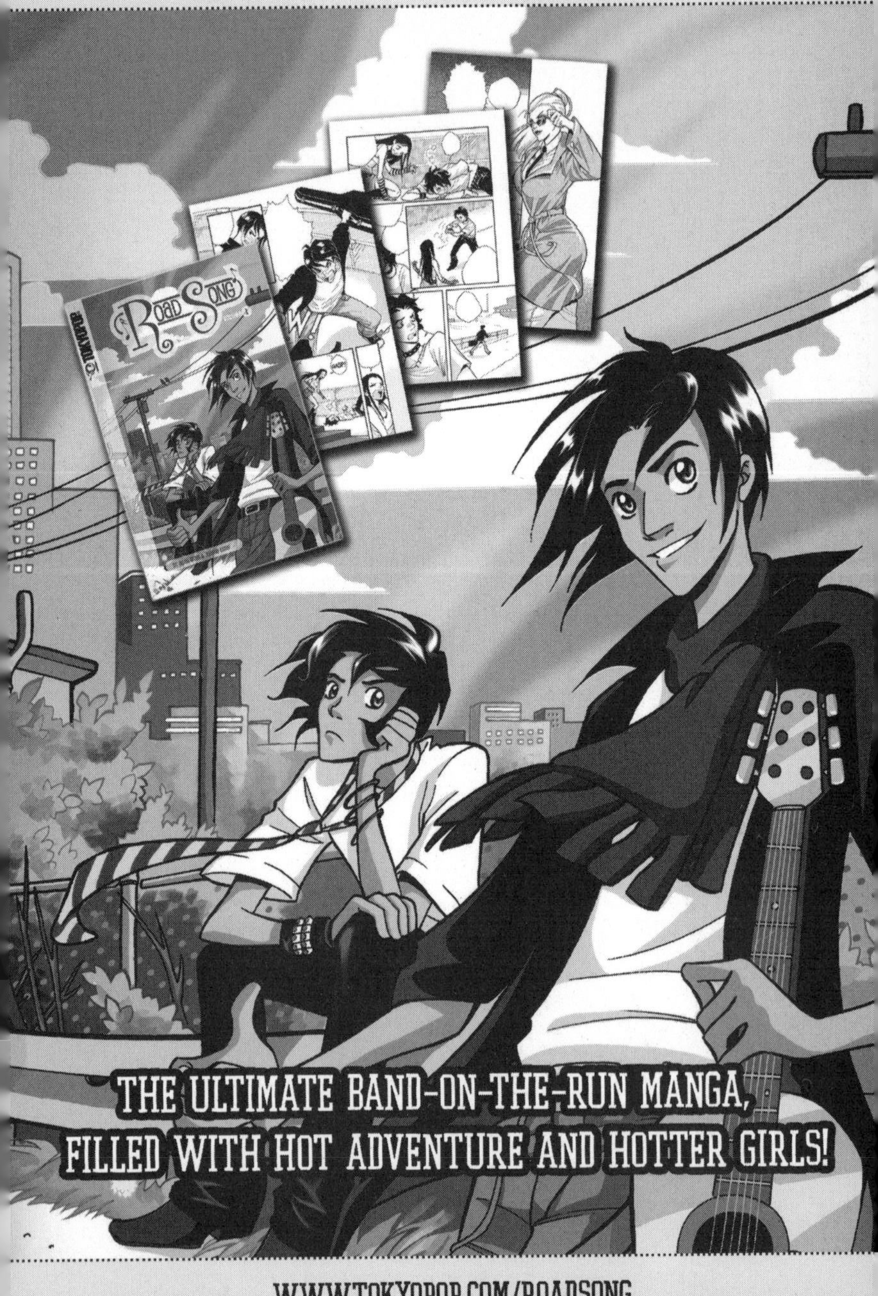

THE ULTIMATE BAND-ON-THE-RUN MANGA,
FILLED WITH HOT ADVENTURE AND HOTTER GIRLS!

ROADSONG

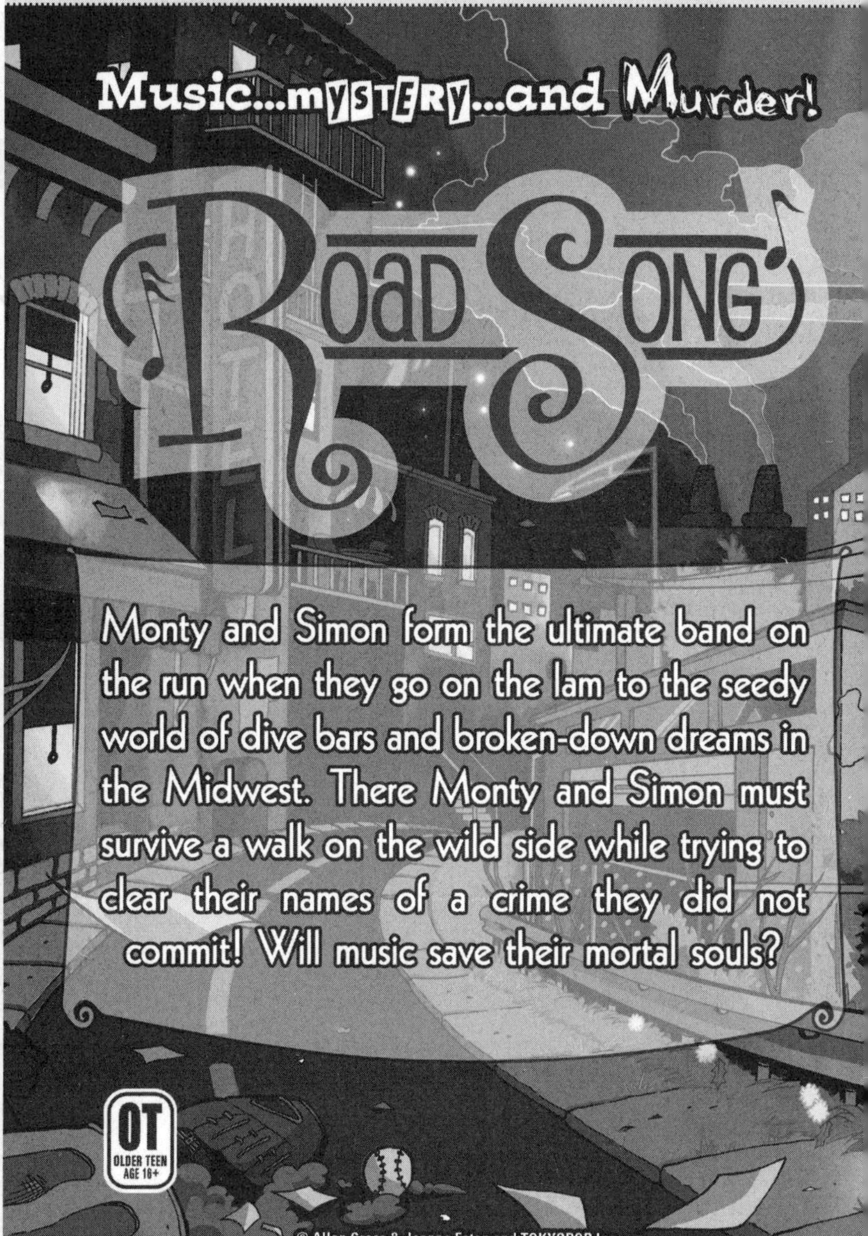
Music...mystery...and Murder!
RoadSong
Monty and Simon form the ultimate band on the run when they go on the lam to the seedy world of dive bars and broken-down dreams in the Midwest. There Monty and Simon must survive a walk on the wild side while trying to clear their names of a crime they did not commit! Will music save their mortal souls?
OT
OLDER TEEN
AGE 16+
© Allan Gross & Joanna Estep and TOKYOPOP Inc.

READ A CHAPTER OF THE MANGA ONLINE FOR FREE:

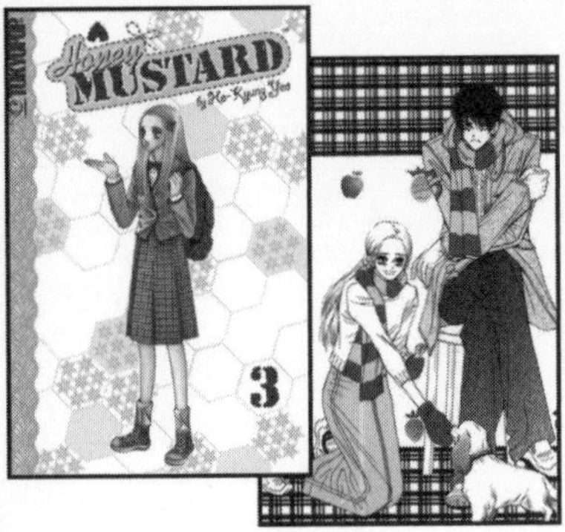
Honey
MUSTARD
by Ho-Kyung Yeo
3

BY HO-KYUNG YEO

HONEY MUSTARD

I'm often asked about the title of *Honey Mustard.* What does a condiment have to do with romance and teen angst? One might ask the same thing about a basket of fruits, but I digress. Honey mustard is sweet with a good dose of bite, and I'd say that sums up this series pretty darn well, too. Ho-Kyung Yeo does a marvelous job of balancing the painful situations of adolescence with plenty of whacked-out humor to keep the mood from getting *too* heavy. It's a good, solid romantic comedy...and come to think of it, it'd go great with that sandwich.

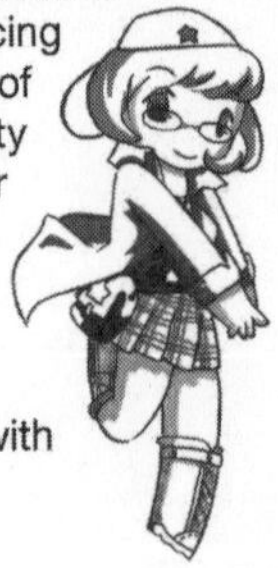

~Carol Fox, Editor

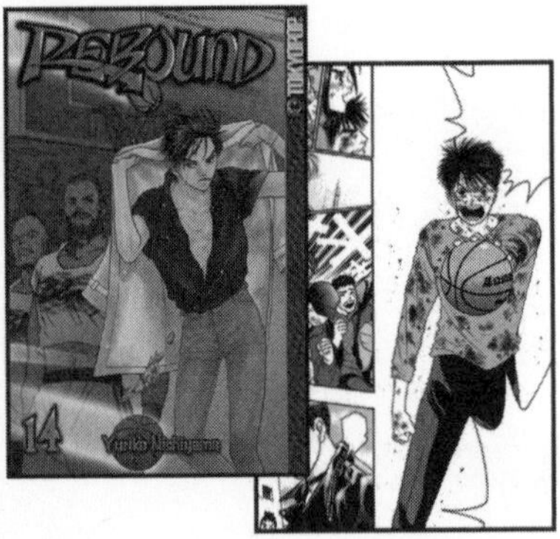
REBOUND
14

BY YURIKO NISHIYAMA

REBOUND

At first glance, *Rebound* may seem like a simple sports manga. But on closer inspection, you'll find that the real drama takes place off the court. While the kids of the Johnan basketball team play and grow as a team, they learn valuable life lessons as well. By fusing the raw energy of basketball with the apple pie earnestness of an afterschool special, Yuriko Nishiyama has created a unique and heartfelt manga that appeals to all readers, male and female.

~Troy Lewter, Editor

© Minari Endoh/ICHIJINSHA

DAZZLE
BY MINARI ENDOH

When a young girl named Rahzel sets out to see the world, she meets Alzeid, a mysterious loner on a mission to find his father's killer. Although the two share similar magical abilities, they don't exactly see eye-to-eye...but they will need each other to survive their journey!

An epic coming-of-age story from an accomplished manga artist!

TEEN
AGE 13+

© CHIHO SAITOU and IKUNI & Be-PaPas

THE WORLD EXISTS FOR ME
BY BE-PAPAS AND CHIHO SAITOU

Once upon a time, the source of the devil R's invincible powers was *The Book of S & M*. But one day, a young man stole the book without knowing what it was, cut it into strips and used it to create a girl doll named "S" and a boy doll named "M." With that act, the unimaginable power that the devil held from the book was unleashed upon the world!

From the creators of the manga classic *Revolutionary Girl Utena*!

TEEN
AGE 13+

© Keitaro Arima

TSUKUYOMI: MOON PHASE
BY KEITARO ARIMA

Cameraman Kouhei Midou is researching Schwarz Quelle Castle. When he steps inside the castle's great walls, he discovers a mysterious little girl, Hazuki, who's been trapped there for years. Utilizing her controlling charm, Hazuki tries to get Kouhei to set her free. But this sweet little girl isn't everything she appears to be...

The manga that launched the popular anime!

TEEN
AGE 13+

STOP!

This is the back of the book.
You wouldn't want to spoil a great ending!

This book is printed "manga-style," in the authentic Japanese right-to-left format. Since none of the artwork has been flipped or altered, readers get to experience the story just as the creator intended. You've been asking for it, so TOKYOPOP® delivered: authentic, hot-off-the-press, and far more fun!

DIRECTIONS

If this is your first time reading manga-style, here's a quick guide to help you understand how it works.

It's easy... just start in the top right panel and follow the numbers. Have fun, and look for more 100% authentic manga from TOKYOPOP®!

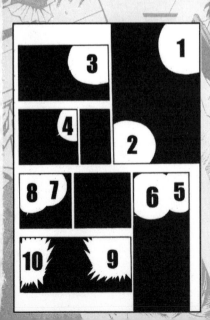